THE ART OF COERCION

ANTONIO GIUSTOZZI

The Art of Coercion

The Primitive Accumulation and
Management of Coercive Power

HURST & COMPANY, LONDON

First published in the United Kingdom in 2011 by
C. Hurst & Co. (Publishers) Ltd.,
41 Great Russell Street, London, WC1B 3PL
© Antonio Giustozzi, 2011
All rights reserved.
Printed in India

The right of Antonio Giustozzi to be identified as the author
of this publication is asserted by him in accordance with the
Copyright, Designs and Patents Act, 1988.

A Cataloguing-in-Publication data record for this book is
available from the British Library.

This book is printed using paper from registered sustainable
and managed sources.

ISBN: 978-1-84904-081-5

www.hurstpub.co.uk

CONTENTS

Preface and Acknowledgements   vii

Introduction   1
1. The Ruthlessness of State Formation   23
2. Maintaining the Monopoly: The Risk of Disloyalty   43
3. Maintaining the Monopoly: When Ruthlessness is Still Needed   75
4. Maintaining the Monopoly: The Role of Political Policing   105
5. Maintaining the Monopoly: The Political Micromanagement
   of Population Control   131
6. External Intervention and the Monopoly: Kicking Away the
   Ladder?   155
7. Beyond the Monopoly: Origins and Development of Policing   199
Conclusion   227

Notes   237
Select Bibliography   261
Index   287

PREFACE AND ACKNOWLEDGEMENTS

The *Art of Coercion* is the result of six years of debates and theoretical elaboration during my time at the Crisis States Research Centre (LSE). As we went on discussing factors of state weakness and resilience, my task within the team rapidly emerged as looking specifically at the security dimension of statebuilding. That was the start of a process which was to eventually produce the present book. The choice of title is deliberately (self-)ironic: it paraphrases Machiavelli's *Arte della Guerra* (*The Art of War*), knowing that Machiavelli was notoriously treading on dangerous ground when discussing military issues. One of his main warnings in *The Art of War* was that firearms had no future and therefore deserved no big investment. Matteo Bandello in one of his sixteenth century novels makes fun of Machiavelli when he shows him proudly taking over command of a company from *condottiero* Giovanni dalle Bande Nere during a parade, in order to demonstrate his ideas on how to manoeuvre troops in battle. Giovanni, presumably irritated like other professional mercenaries by Machiavelli's boasting of military theories, was deliberately tricking Machiavelli into exposing his lack of basic understanding of soldiering. In the novel, Machiavelli indeed makes a mess of the parade. I do not know whether the novel is based on any real episode in the life of Machiavelli, but in any case I take it as a reminder of the need to be cautious when recommending solutions without having any direct work experience in the field. At the same time, I shall not forget that Machiavelli was infinitely closer to predicting the fate of the states of Renaissance Italy than people like Giovanni dalle Bande Nere and other practitioners of war could even imagine.

The title hints at what I think is an obvious as much as disregarded truth, that there is coercion and coercion. In other words, my intent is to demonstrate that in the real world the opposition is not between Hobbes and Kant, that is between political realism and idealism, but between Hobbes and Machiavelli, that is between different types of political realism. Contemporary international idealism is incarnated (in truth in a spurious way) by liberal interventionism; in this book I try to show its obvious limitations and how in practice it tends to degenerate in a disguised form of political realism, typically more pernicious and ineffective than the original political realism that it was supposed to refute.

Apart from drawing from the debates at the Crisis States Research Centre, this book is based on extensive reading of a huge literature on the subject and related matters. It is also informed by the author's actual research experience in the field in related matters. The literature on the issue of security tends not to be very academically oriented; the contrary is also true, that academics tend not to be inclined to discuss matters of security and state coercion in detail, except in order to criticise policy makers. By contrast, I felt that this short-circuit had to be broken and that the issue of the role of coercion in state formation and state building had to be addressed from a perspective wider than a merely technical or amateurish one. I hope that this book will be a significant contribution in that direction.

Although this book owes much to discussions with colleagues within and without the Centre, I am of course solely responsible for its content and for any mistake that I may have made. I wish to thank those who participated in the debates at the Crisis States Research Centre and stimulated the thinking behind this book, in particular Francisco Gutierrez and James Putzel, who also deserves to be thanked for having employed me and therefore having made this book possible. Special thanks also to those who commented and offered advice on the manuscript: Zoltan Barany, Jim Boyce and Chris Cramer. Many thanks to Wendy Foulds for her administrative support and also to Michael Dwyer, who edited the book, and to the whole team at Hurst.

INTRODUCTION

'There has never been a document of culture which is not simultaneously one of barbarism.'

Walter Benjamin (trans. Dennis Redmond)

The UN involvement in settling the Cambodian conflict was one of the most ambitious attempts to usher in a new era of peace-building since the end of the Cold War. As Michael W. Doyle puts it:

Not since the colonial era and the post-World War II Allied occupations of Germany and Japan had a foreign presence held so much formal administrative jurisdiction over the civilian functions of an independent country.[1]

The idea was that only a degree of UN control could guarantee the emergence of a neutral political environment before the elections. Paris points out that:

Not only did the peace accords explicitly prescribe the remoulding of the Cambodian state into a liberal democracy, but they also empowered international civil servants, working under the auspices of the United Nations, to oversee and expedite these reforms by occupying positions within the Cambodian government ministries themselves.[2]

The assumption was that a liberal market democracy offers the most propitious conditions for a stable and lasting peace. The plan rapidly revealed 'some major weaknesses', such as the lack of 'a coherent logistical estimate of the situation on the ground', the failure to 'take sufficient account of the political and practical difficulties inherent in trying to assume a quasi-administrative role with existing government structures still in place' and an 'extremely compressed timetable for elections'. In particular, 'UNTAC's attempts to control the administration with any effect were wholly unsuccessful.'[3]

1

However, by 1993 the mission was being hailed as an at least relative success:

To its credit, the UN had prevailed politically up to a point in refusing to reconsider the election results in spite of threats from the [ruling CPP party]. The post-election interim solution then became a working political compromise.[4]

By 1998 the perceptions of the achievements of international intervention in Cambodia had changed. The clash between the leading figures in the royalist party (FUNCIPEC) and in the pro-Vietnamese CPP highlighted the precariousness of the settlement. Paris argues that:

the process of political liberalization had also served to exacerbate tensions among the Cambodian parties in the period leading up to the elections—tensions which, according to many observers at the time, had threatened to destroy the fragile truce between [parties]. [...] Anticipation of new elections scheduled for 1998 soon led to a deterioration in relations between Cambodia's two co-prime ministers. Ranariddh was determined to bolster the military forces loyal to FUNCINPEC before the 1998 elections in order to deter CPP-sponsored violence and intimidation, which he and his supporters had faced during the 1993 campaign. Hun Sen was similarly determined to weaken FUNCINPEC before the 1998 elections in order to avoid another embarrassing loss at the polls.[5]

President Hun Sen's strategy of intimidation succeeded in forcing the other parties to collaborate in his own terms, despite having received fewer votes.

By the end of the decade, Cambodia had only the 'veneer' of democracy, and Hun Sen ruled 'by virtue of a monopoly of muscle, the readiness of thuggish subordinates to use it and a tight grip on the machinery and resources of the state'. Indeed, one could argue that Cambodia's relative stability after 1997 was due primarily to Hun Sen's largely successful but patently illiberal maneuverings to re-establish his de facto hegemonic control of Cambodian politics. In other words, it is unclear to what degree Cambodia's relative stability can be attributed to the internationally sponsored democratization process, or instead to Hun Sen's efforts to suppress political opposition in the country. [...] The country became *more* stable in the late 1990s as Hun Sen increasingly backed away from his earlier democratic commitments.[6]

This story tells us something about the ambition to export a particular model of state-making from the West towards 'late developers' and hints that the role of coercion cannot be neglected. The UN mission in Cambodia had in principle the teeth needed to enforce its role, but could not use them effectively:

For the first time in UN peacekeeping history, UN civil police forces were given powers of arrest. This provision marked a potentially significant departure from the principle of non-enforcement. The efficacy of the Prosecutor's Office turned out to be very limited, however. In the first place, the directive was strongly opposed by other UNTAC components, most prominently by the civil administration, which argued that it went beyond UNTAC's mandate. Similarly, UNTAC's military component was unwilling to use force when making arrests.[7]

Hun Sen succeeded where the UN could only fail, that is in asserting his monopoly of violence.

The Fatal Attraction of State-Building

In the early years of the post-Cold War era, the expansion of peace-building into state-building was mostly welcomed as addressing key weaknesses of the earlier 'quick-fix' approach. Paris wrote that:

The assumption that political and economic liberalization could be achieved in the absence of functioning, legitimate institutions—an assumption that implicitly underpinned the design and conduct of peacebuilding in its early years—was deeply flawed.[8]

State-building was at this point largely understood as institution-building, even if scholars were stressing the importance of state-society relations as well.[9] More recently, state-building efforts in the Balkans, Iraq, Afghanistan, East Timor and elsewhere have raised doubts over the understanding of state-building that predominates in the West. Paris recognised that things turned out differently from what was hoped:

As the mandates and time-frames of postconflict missions expanded, however, the problematic aspects of externally-assisted state-building became more apparent.[10]

Paris and Sisk identify several contradictions in state-building fostered by outside intervention:

- Outside intervention is used to foster self-government;
- International control is required to establish local ownership;
- Universal values are promoted as a remedy for local problems;
- State-building requires both a clean break with the past and a reaffirmation of history;
- Short-term imperatives often conflict with longer-term objectives.[11]

A sub-sector of state-building which turned out to be particularly problematic is security sector reform (SSR). In the words of the *OECD Handbook*:

The traditional concept of security is being redefined to include not only state stability and the security of nations but also the safety and wellbeing of their people. The recognition that development and security are inextricably linked is enabling security in partner countries to be viewed as a public policy and governance issue inviting greater public scrutiny of security policy. A democratically run, accountable and efficient security system helps reduce the risk of conflict, thus creating an enabling environment for development.[12]

This turned out to be a much more ambitious agenda than was initially understood. Some of the potential pitfalls are now recognised:

The challenge for donors remains how to ensure that they: support reform processes that are sustainable; underpin poverty reduction through enhanced service delivery; and help develop effective and accountable systems of security and justice in partner countries.[13]

A DCAF study accepted that:

In cases where an inter-state war such as a foreign military intervention aimed at regime change and resulting in a transitional occupation preceded postconflict reconstruction efforts, the security environment may simply be too adverse to implement a comprehensive and effective SSR programme as evidenced in Afghanistan [...] and particularly so in Iraq, where armed resistance means that SSR is taking place under combat conditions. [...] Even without armed resistance against the intervention troops, irrespectively if their presence is legitimised by a UN mandate or not, postconflict contexts pose the most formidable challenges to SSR.[14]

In this volume, concepts like 'good governance' and 'SSR' are treated like ideologies of north-south (and east-west) relations. They reveal more about the way Western powers try to present themselves than about how they operate on the ground, not to mention actual state-building processes per se, to which (as will be argued) they bear little relationship. Because *The Art of Coercion* is not a study of ideology, rather than dealing with good governance and SSR as grand concepts we shall split them up into their constitutive elements, such as police reform, DDR (Disarmament, Demobilisation and Reintegration), etc., in order to test their impact on the ground. Although the debate on good governance and SSR is the point of departure, our discussion of state-building goes much farther than that.

The identification of several problems in the practice of state-building, highlighted above, has yet to yield dividends in the field, certainly not in Afghanistan or Iraq, thereby deepening the crisis of confidence among practitioners and scholars alike. Mutual accusations of incompetence in implementing state-building are one consequence, as experienced widely by practitioners from different agencies. Perhaps Western states do not have the capability to do state-building, or have lost it. Others have argued that the West is unique and that its model of state-building cannot be exported, at least not as quickly as Western policy-makers seem to assume.[15] The truth may lie in either interpretation, or even in both of them. In *The Art of Coercion* we consider the possibility that perhaps developed Western states are no longer really interested in fostering state-building after all.

In Western democracies, the predominant understanding of 'virtuous' state-building is that there is little role for coercion as a key ingredient of the process. Although some scholars have already challenged this assumption, Western politicians and policy-makers cling stubbornly to a bottom-up evolution of a coalition of communities, interacting with a ruler until a 'social contract' is successfully formulated. The social contract is of course deeply rooted in Western political philosophy; Kant's view of it is the most prevalent today, not least because of John Rawls' writing on the concept in the 1970s. Violence is considered the realm of extremist groups and terrorists, or of rogue and dysfunctional states or politicians. Liberal states, based on a 'social contract' with their citizens, do not sully themselves with coercion. Most authors therefore prefer to stress the importance of legitimacy, dispute-settling and/or the provision of public goods and political order as the key ingredients of state formation.

While this might be an attractive *ideological* presentation (as already suggested by Hume in *Of Civil Liberty*), it seems quite at odds with the results of historical research. As our discussion of the contending opinions shows, such research unequivocally suggests a much more complex interaction of various factors, among which coercion is of great importance. Understating the role of coercion in state-building has to be dealt with if we are to move beyond the ideological self-regard of elites, states and international relations. There is in fact a rich literature, scholarly and otherwise, on specific aspects of state coercion, but its evaluation has struggled to find a legitimate place in academia and has been too often left to the attention of non-specialists and amateurs, particularly as far as the more technical aspects of it are concerned. Although the accumulated body of literature cannot answer all the questions and fill all the gaps in our understanding of state-building, it certainly represents a point of departure for developing a new interpretation.

The Art of Coercion was developed out of a large research project, aimed at understanding the role of coercion in state-building, and draws only indirectly on fieldwork carried out by the author and his colleagues. Nor does the volume present major case studies, which will instead be treated in detail in follow-up publications. Rather, it seeks to identify recurring patterns of action in the use, transformation and adaptation of coercion in state-building, based on the available literature. Since there are thousands of books in many languages dealing in one way or another with state coercion, the author had to be selective in his choice of sources. This therefore does not pretend to be an exhaustive review of a huge field of enquiry, and the examples selected in the chapters that follow constitute only what the author considers sufficient evidence for the purposes of testing the book's principal arguments. For example, countries like Afghanistan and Colombia, among others, do not figure as prominently as they could have, because they were selected early on as case studies and the author opted to privilege other examples.

1. Institution-Building Strategies

As hinted already, this book is not the first to make the case for giving coercion its due place in state-building. While Max Weber's statement about the importance of the monopoly of violence in the rise of the state is rarely challenged these days, the exact role of this monopoly is still debated. Azar Gat for example argues that:

...armed force was a major, and sometimes the major, factor, side by side and together with co-optation and all other—economic and religious—means of power accumulation. [...] Without the underpinning of superior, covert or overt, coercive force, political power accumulation, with all the benefits that it entails, cannot be achieved in the teeth of opposition from others who stand to lose from it...[16]

Although few would dispute that a degree of coercion is necessary in establishing and maintaining a state, the implicitly violent character of coercion is rarely acknowledged in all its importance. In reality, as this book will show, Kalyvas' remarks that 'violence is primarily a resource rather than the final product; it is intended to shape the behavior of a targeted audience by altering the expected value of particular actions,'[17] could be applied to almost any state in history, perhaps all. In other words, it is analytically more productive to view internal coercion as a tool, which may or may not be used to achieve certain aims depending on the circumstances, rather than as the exclusive attribute of specific ('rogue') actors.

There is of course violence and violence. The 'taming' of violence, that is the growing sophistication of coercion and the significance of this process for state-building, is one of the key concerns of this study. A recent contribution by North et al. has received much praise for its treatment of how states have dealt in different ways with reducing and controlling violence. North and his co-authors distinguish between 'natural states' (or 'limited access orders') and 'open access orders', which mostly tend to coincide with liberal democracies. They explain state-building in limited access orders as follows:

> The natural state reduces the problem of endemic violence through the formation of a dominant coalition whose members possess special privileges. The logic of the natural state follows from how it solves the problem of violence. Elites—members of the dominant coalition—agree to respect each other's privileges, including property rights and access to resources and activities. By limiting access to these privileges to members of the dominant coalition, elites create credible incentives to cooperate rather than fight among themselves. Because elites know that violence will reduce their own rents, they have incentives not to fight.[18]

How can a transition out of the limited access orders towards open access orders occur?

> In order for elite groups and organizations to concede control of military assets to a single organization, they must believe that they can collectively discipline the military organization.[19]

Only the growth and consolidation of formal institutions can allow this: '… External control of the military involves the coevolution of perpetually lived organizations in the state and in the private sector'.[20]

The success of North et al. might in part be due to the fact that they manage to reconcile a recognition of the role of violence in state-building, while pointing towards an historical pattern and a strategy (the Western democracies, institution-building), which essentially ends up expunging violence from the picture. *The Art of Coercion*, too, recognises the role of formal institutions, hence the first hypothesis to be tested is that institution-building is a key aspect of any process of taming violence.

2. The Political Dimensions of the Monopoly

The concept of the monopoly of violence is subject to many misunderstandings. As some authors have pointed out, a complete monopoly of violence by the state occurred relatively rarely in history; for example it never featured in North America.[21] This imprecision in defining the monopoly has led to some confusion in the debate, for example concerning the current trend towards private policing, which is one of the reasons why some authors prefer to speak of a 'monopoly of *large-scale violence*'.[22] I too adopt this distinction, as it is very useful in understanding patterns of monopolisation of violence in the context of state formation. The capability for large-scale violence should be understood as the ability to conduct war (internal or external), that is the ability to mobilise and organise large numbers of men (at least hundreds) in a coordinated fashion to achieve specific military and political aims. A monopoly of such capability implies that no internal force is able to challenge the ruler[23] and constitute a military threat to him.

It is important to point out that a challenge to the monopoly of large-scale violence does not arise merely from the existence of large numbers of armed men independent of the ruler or even opposed to him somewhere within his country;[24] there has to be a capacity to mobilise and organise them for collective action. Even when large scale mobilisation occurs, there are issues of leadership (charisma and management), logistics (the ability to supply and feed such men), organisation/coordination and politics/diplomacy (coalition-building) that might prevent a substantial challenge from materialising. Hence it is not strictly necessary for a ruler to completely eliminate or co-opt all armed men (small groups or individuals) existing within his territory; he can achieve a monopoly of large-scale violence by preventing the coming together of such groups and individuals, so that they cannot achieve the critical mass required to challenge him.

This could be achieved by eliminating any figure capable of exercising the leadership required, or by disrupting the political organisation(s) which could potentially bring together these same groups. Alternatively the ruler could establish relations with non-state groups and manipulate them to prevent their coalescence into a coherent force ('divide and rule'). Finally, he could prevent the establishment of the financial and economic bases for a large scale challenge to be logistically viable, either by practising a 'scorched earth policy' or by targeting individuals and groups who hold the necessary resources, that is centralising patronage.

In the words of Gerald of Wales (1194):

The prince who would wish to subdue this nation and govern it peaceably, must use this method... Let him divide their strength and by bribes and promises endeavour to stir up one against the other. [...] In the autumn let not only the marshes, but also the interior part of the country be strongly fortified with castles, provisions and confidential families. In the meantime the purchase of corn, cloth, and salt, with which they are usually supplied from England, should be strictly interdicted; and well-manned ships placed as a guard on the coast, to prevent their importation of these articles from Ireland or the Severn sea, and to facilitate the supply of his own army. Afterwards, when the severity of winter approaches, when the trees are void of leaves, and the mountains no longer afford pasturage—when they are deprived of any hopes of plunder, and harassed on every side by the repeated attacks of the enemy—let a body of light-armed infantry penetrate into their woody and mountainous retreats, and let these troops be supported and relieved by others; and thus by frequent changes, and replacing the men who are either fatigued or slain in battle, this nation may be ultimately subdued.[25]

The other possible path, usually taken in combination with the previous one, is co-opting potential rivals. In North's words, '…natural states are always governed by coalition of powerful individuals; only in exceptional circumstances will one faction of group in the dominant coalition have an effective monopoly on violence'.[26] Raymond Aron pointed out that warfare is foremost a question of maintaining the capacity to use organised force and of disrupting an opponent's capacity to do the same.[27]

As a result, the monopoly of large-scale violence is not merely a matter of military strength; there is a crucial political dimension to it too. This is the second hypothesis advanced in this volume: pre-empting hostile collective action through co-option, alliances, manipulation and intimidation is as important as the mere accumulation of means of coercion, and entire agencies of the state have been developed historically to implement this task. We do not refer here to legitimacy: this is about elite bargaining,[28] divide and rule, political communication, intelligence, political policing (chapter 4) and political micro-management of the population (chapter 5). Coercion practised by the political police only seems to differ from its large-scale equivalent if we consider it as a series of single actions. In fact it consists of a multitude of coordinated small acts of violence, linked to each other by political design and by the aim of securing the monopoly of violence, hence it can be considered as large-scale violence for the purposes of this book. Indeed it can be argued that the key distinction between the secret police (a term combining intelligence and political policing) and ordinary police forces is exactly that the former deal primarily, albeit indirectly, with the monopoly of large-scale violence, while the latter primarily deal with small-scale violence. Linked to the same aspect of the monopolisation of violence as the secret police is the activity of local government (sub-national administrations), to which I specifically dedicate chapter 5. In a sense it could be described as the other (non-secret) side of the coin of political policing.

Another important distinction is between gendarmerie and police. In a sense, the police as defined in this volume (see Box 1) represents a greater degree of 'taming of violence' than the gendarmerie, which is a militarised force meant to suppress political disorder. In Europe it is often debated whether gendarmeries are now redundant and should be disbanded or 'civilianised', but historically, gendarmeries played an important role in securing control over territory and population, particularly in rural areas and against organised opposition.

Cheaper than armies and more disciplined than police, gendarmeries acted both to address initial threats to the monopoly of large-scale violence and to deal with small-scale violence, even if lacking the sophistication and specialisation which characterises, in principle, the police.

3. The Ruthlessness of State Formation

Another basic distinction at the core of this book is between establishing a monopoly of large-scale violence and maintaining or consolidating that same monopoly. Within the complex process of state-building, two main phases can be distinguished. State formation is exactly the process of establishing such a monopoly; state consolidation follows from it. Completely different 'rules of the game' apply to each process; in fact it could be argued that in state formation there are no rules of the game at all. Neither process is necessarily carried out consciously by political actors; indeed early cases of either were almost certainly unconscious. Chapter 1 below focuses on the establishment of the monopoly, a process more often than not brutal and merciless, which usually includes:

- a phase of early accumulation of armed force, with a local monopolisation of violence;
- the expansion of such armed force to become predominant throughout the territory of a given state, through conquest, co-option and coalition-making; in the long run this implies a process of centralisation of patronage in order to enable co-option and coalition-making;
- the creation of a large (that is capable of dealing with perceived internal threats), standing, centrally controlled army; this also implies securing financial support for it and the development of mobilisation and organisational techniques more advanced than kinship and personal charisma or patronage;
- the subsequent or parallel elimination of major private or contracted armed forces.

The third hypothesis of *The Art of Coercion* is that what can be defined as the 'primitive accumulation of coercive power',[29] tends to be ruthlessly violent. 'Ruthless' here is used in opposition to 'tame'; as will be explained later, this distinction is not the same as that between 'selective' and 'indiscriminate' violence.

As North et al. point out, 'groups in the coalition are satisfied and comfortable with not having access to military resources' only in exceptional circumstances.[30] Convincing them to lay down their weapons and agree to a political settlement in a context of ongoing conflict is inevitably extremely difficult, which is why, short of external intervention, civil wars tend to end in one side's victory rather than in compromise and peace agreement. This does not mean that even in state formation, coalition-building is irrelevant; what it does make more unlikely is an inclusive deal. For the latter, a good many rivals will have to be physically eliminated or coerced into subservience, which is at odds with inclusiveness. The establishment of the monopoly of violence is the topic of chapter 1 of this book.

It is worth noting that the establishment of the monopoly may occur repeatedly in the history of a country; as explained below, monopolies may be destroyed or may decay for a variety of reasons. In such cases, a process similar to that just described (of state formation) once again becomes necessary. Moreover such processes are controversial and difficult to conclude successfully in any case; we could, for example, view the various phases of a civil war as a series of unsuccessful attempts to establish a monopoly. Using that criterion as a basis for our estimates, we would find that only a small proportion of all attempts at state-making are successful.

4. The Crucial Importance of Selective Violence

Some authors have recently drawn attention to the importance of the distinction between indiscriminate and selective violence, foremost among them Kalyvas. Although the recent debate focused on violence within the context of civil wars and insurgency/counter-insurgency, its conclusions seem fully applicable to the more general context of state formation and most of all state consolidation. Kalyvas argues that indiscriminate violence is ineffective or even counter-productive because 'compliance guarantees no security [...], joining the opponent can actually increase the probability of individual survival'. By contrast, 'if people are targeted on the basis of their actions, then refraining from such actions guarantees safety'.[31] There are cases in which indiscriminate violence might succeed, but they are limited, for example against a:

- 'small population in a relatively confined space', because otherwise 'there is little chance that the incumbent will be able to exert effective control, and the logical choice is to defect to the other side';
- or when the opposing side is 'unable to offer a credible alternative to the government that disaffected civilians can join.'[32]

It is opportune to specify that targeted violence is not necessarily small scale; mass violence can be targeted at specific sections of the population, such as, for example, all the communities that cooperate actively or passively with opposition to the ruling elite. Large-scale violence also serves a purpose of general intimidation when the ruling elite lacks the capability to direct violence against individuals, or when the targets are not legitimate enemies. (An example of the latter is the case of power struggles within a ruling elite or a coalition.) Nor should the symbolic value of extreme violence as a form of political communication be dismissed, as discussed in chapter 4. If narrowly targeted, coercion and terror are 'useful' tools to push 'an undecided group into support it would otherwise not give'.[33]

Kalyvas shows how often in internal conflicts, violence is employed according to a logic and is therefore only seemingly indiscriminate, while it is undeniably ruthless. But sophisticated military-political actors clearly understand what kind of violence is counter-productive; this is the fourth hypothesis of *The Art of Coercion*. 'Sophisticated' in this context means that at least a significant proportion of military-political actors has this understanding; the less sophisticated may not. Once the monopoly of large-scale violence has been established, the ability to target carefully increases. At the same time the incentives to deploy indiscriminate violence weaken, since there is no longer an open challenge to the existing monopoly.

Given Kalyvas' argument, would not targeted violence be useful even in a context of state formation? Kalyvas made the point that selective or targeted violence is expensive as it requires detailed information-gathering and, one could add, sophisticated organisational arrangements effectively to process and manage that information.[34] This is why in state formation conflicting parties usually cannot afford to invest much in the business of carefully targeting violence. Also, in state formation the problem is in part the *destruction* of one's adversaries; without demonstrating brute force, it is difficult for any aspiring leader to convince any rival to cooperate. With these preliminary qualifications, indiscriminate violence is arguably counter-productive in state formation too.

5. Policing as a Strategy of Consolidation of the Monopoly

Once achieved, the monopoly of large-scale violence has to be maintained. Changing internal and external conditions means that a monopoly of large-scale violence may always be subjected to challenges: for example, because a ruler's control over the agents of violence might not be entirely reliable, among other reasons. The management of coercive power has substantially different characteristics from the original establishment of the monopoly:

- it benefits from the 'taming of violence',[35] that is a process to bring under full control military forces and discipline and 'civilise' them;
- as the original charismatic leadership which engaged in the primitive accumulation inevitably wanes, the ruler is exposed to the risk of disloyalty of his own agents of coercion and secure and has to protect himself against them (this aspect is discussed in detail in chapter 2);
- as the state machinery expands and becomes more complex, management problems arise and the ruler is increasingly unable to rely purely on his direct, patrimonial control;
- the funding of the machinery of coercion tends to be subject to different rules once a monopoly of large-scale violence has been successfully established; as long-term financial accumulation is enabled by the newly formed state, new prospects also emerge that allow it to tap into such accumulation in a less predatory and disruptive way.[36]

The management of coercive power is therefore fraught with difficulties and contradictions. Another one that is worth mentioning is that the interest of the elite at the centre might not coincide with the interest of the peripheral elites or subordinated actors within the state. Taming the violence might make sense in the capital, but much less so in the provinces, where junior members of the ruling power block might feel, for example, the need to increase their leverage and contractual power *vis-à-vis* their senior colleagues. This might explain the seemingly erratic behaviour of some polities with regard to taming violence: ruling elites and allies in a coalition might be divided with regard to it.

Over time, several specialised functions of the state have emerged to deal with all these aspects of the monopolisation of violence. While the desire of any ruling elite to protect itself against direct internal and external threats is easy to explain, the factors driving the taming of violence and the problems related to the management of the security apparatus are more complex to untangle. As noted by Janowitz:

one is struck by the efforts of military regimes and their political leaders to search for and experiment with acceptable forms of civilian involvement.[37]

The 'taming' takes multiple shapes and includes processes such as the establishment of a complex system of procedural justice, of a police system, of a political intelligence system and of a sub-national governance system. Coercion never disappears as one of the key ingredients of the state; it only becomes more 'civilised' and recedes from the public eye. As Rejali shows, Western democracies developed 'clean torture' techniques that leave no traces on the body; they certainly did not abandon torture altogether.[38] The army loses parts of its importance and mainly dedicates itself to protecting the regime against other states, but remains the ultimate repository of the monopoly and as such itself represents a threat because of its potential disloyalty. As a whole, these multiple processes of specialisation and taming of violence have at their core the attempt to make coercion (hence violence) more carefully targeted and selective, as opposed to the untamed, indiscriminate violence which tends to characterise the initial establishment of the monopoly of violence.

It follows from what was argued above in 'the fatal attraction of state-building' that although a total monopoly of violence might best guarantee the durability of a particular regime, it is not a prerequisite for the establishment of a political order. Indeed almost always the history of states has been characterised by the co-existence of non-state armed groups which were not politically motivated; these could include bandits, communities, local leaders, landlords, even party, sectarian or factional militias, if they are aiming to fight each other rather than the state. The lack of a state monopoly over small-scale violence in the United States is a well-known fact, but even in Europe the 'monopoly' enjoyed by the police was mostly symbolic, as forms of effective non-state policing were quite widespread, at least well into the nineteenth century.[39] Such co-existence does not mean that rulers could largely ignore the management of small-scale violence; the fifth hypothesis of this book is that policing is a specific strategy of consolidating the monopoly of violence. Every state had, for several reasons, to develop a strategy towards small violent actors, even if they did not represent a direct threat to the regime. The first and most obvious one is that such actors have to be monitored and kept in check, lest they develop the capacity or willingness to challenge the core of the state. The second reason is that perpetrators of small-scale violence may disrupt specific interests that the state might introduce at some point, such as taxation and the mobilisation of human resources. In a sense, small violent actors compete with the state for the resources of the territory which it claims to control or to 'own'; a ruling elite might see an interest in eradicating rival 'bandits' simply in order to raise additional revenue or expand its control over human resources. However, it is important to consider that claiming a 'monopoly over theft' might be very expensive, depending on such factors as geography, the capacities of the state and its agencies, etc. and therefore a strategy of monopolisation of theft might well be economically unsound. Furthermore, a policy of further centralisation of the means of coercion may also run the risk of non-state armed groups coalescing by giving them a shared enemy to fight against, namely the state itself. The long-term advantages deriving from strengthening the monopoly of violence to near absoluteness can be offset by the short-term risk of wrecking the relatively fragile structures of the existing state. This helps to explain why rulers often have chosen to ignore this option.

A third reason for not overlooking non-political small violent actors has to do with the consolidation of the state's legitimacy. The ruling elite might see some advantage in improving the conditions of internal order for the population in general. In other words, it could offer policing as a service provided by the state to its subjects in order to win their gratitude, and more importantly to make them more dependent on the state. The provision of state policing often went hand in hand with the at least partial and gradual disarmament of the population and/or the disbandment of non-state armed groups, which in turn resulted in the inability of local communities to police themselves. What we could describe as the 'deepening' of the monopoly of violence is functional to the desire of some states to mobilise more fully their populations and acquire a fuller control over them.

A fourth and final reason is the commitment of the state, or of influential lobbies around it, to specific aims of economic and social development. In this case the state would have to develop policing as a response to growing social differentiation or to regiment the population.

The fact that in developed countries armies have eschewed the management of internal coercion does not mean that they have lost their role as ultimate repositories of the monopoly of violence. Nor does it mean that their role in less developed countries must *ipso facto* be similarly 'modest'. Although analysts might often get confused about the priorities of state-building, practitioners (politicians) have very clear ideas in this regard. It says something that the army, the repository of the monopoly, has always been considered politically more important than the police. Officers interested in a political career would typically opt for the army over the police.[40] The monopoly of large-scale violence is the ultimate claim to power; in the rare cases where the police dared confront the army, it always lost. Even tiny armies, such as Togo's 200-strong one in the immediate post-colonial era, were capable of political interventions.[41] This predominance of the army should not be construed to mean that in a context of civil war, that is of an open contest for the monopoly of violence, the police have no role. The role of police and army in counter-insurgency has been widely discussed; in reality much depends on the size and maturity of the insurgency, as the following chapters will show. Chapter 7 deals with policing in detail; it also briefly discusses the role of the judiciary in the management of coercion and violence.

6. The Monopoly Undermined by Reform

Efforts to maintain the monopoly of violence do not always succeed. Civil wars occur when the monopoly is challenged; an external military defeat can also result in the disintegration of the state, or in a loss of the monopoly. There is a relatively abundant literature on revolutions and civil wars. The debate on the causes of such traumatic historical events continues. One of the latest elaborations on the subject is Pincus' acclaimed work on England's Glorious Revolution:

> In contrast to both the classical modernizing and class struggle perspectives, I suggest that revolutions occur only when states have embarked on ambitious state modernization programs. Revolutions do not pit modernizers against defenders of an old regime. Instead revolutions happen when the political nation is convinced of the need for political modernization but there are profound disagreements on the proper course of state innovation. For all the emphasis that the approaches of Huntington and Skocpol place on 'political and institutional factors', I suggest, they have missed this crucial point. State modernization, as political aim and as political process, is a necessary *prerequisite* for revolution.[42]

Particularly relevant for the perspective adopted by this book is the following passage:

> [...] Revolutions are more likely in situations in which the modernizing regime is not clearly perceived to have a monopoly of the forces of violence. This may happen when the modernization program has been so rapid as to create the perception of administrative weakness, as in the case of late-eighteenth-century France or late-seventeenth-century England. Or it may happen when the regime has proven unable to repress fledgling opposition movements, as in Cuba and China. When the modernizing state quickly demonstrates its control of resources and disarms the opposition, as in seventeenth-century Denmark and Sweden or late-nineteenth-century Japan, revolutions do not occur.[43]

While this book does not directly look at civil wars and revolutions per se, it deals with decaying or weakening monopolies of large-scale violence and at the factors underpinning such processes. One problem with Pincus' statement is that the concept of modernisation is slippery: what is modernisation as opposed to change and adaptation? It presupposes a direction of movement, that in some cases might have been clear to those implementing change, but in others might not. In *The Art of Coercion*, therefore, we shall not talk of modernisation, but of adaptation and change. The sixth hypothesis of this book is that the renegotiation of the terms of the political settlement, which may include changes in the command and control structure within the coercive apparatus, may weaken the ability of the ruling elite to operate in a coordinated fashion and endanger the monopoly of violence. Chapter 3 discusses the challenges to the monopoly of violence as well as factors causing its decline.

7. The Counter-Productivity of Intervention

In the context of the early twenty-first century, processes of primitive accumulation of coercive power and its later management cannot be understood without taking into full account the role of the international system. The presence of a large number of sophisticated and wealthy states, able to project their influence well beyond their borders if not across the globe, inevitably impacts on state formation and state-building among the latecomers. Such impact takes several shapes:

- Direct interference: neighbouring states and regional or world powers might object to a particular process of state formation or a particular strategy of state-building, either because of rival international alignments, or because of vested interest in the particular country undergoing such process. This was, of course, particularly common during the Cold War, but pre-dated it and continued after its end. It can take multiple forms, such as military occupation or intervention, pro-insurgency and covert operations, foreign military aid, etc.

- Influence: successful states (real or perceived) may affect processes of state formation even without interfering directly, for example, by providing advice or offering 'special relationships' which *de facto* limit the strategic choices available to new state elites. Arguably some international organisations, such as the World Bank or the IMF, may be viewed as a tool of such influence, particularly to the extent that they are largely dominated by a limited number of member states.

- Contagion: ideas, organisational models and technologies do not necessarily spread on the basis of rational considerations, but also as fashions, riding on the wave of perceived success and ease of implementation. The very concept of modernisation, for example, spread rapidly in the 1960s on the basis of the misplaced perception that it indicated the universal path to the future. The same could be said to some extent of 'socialism'.

- Imitation: models of state formation and state consolidation can be adopted by ruling elites which are just embarking on the process. Although the Cold War once again provides many examples of this, in reality imitation has been occurring since the appearance of the first states.[44]

- Trade and travel: these by-products of the emergence of wealthy states facilitate the spread of ideas and information, as well as of technology; they might also create new sources of funding for state-building enterprises.[45]
- The formation of an international society: a genuinely new development of the twentieth century, this embryonic attempt to establish international rules and standards has had some impact on state formation and state consolidation. The constraints imposed on state formation can to a large extent be circumvented. However, the 'international community' can withhold from new states at least international recognition, one key dimension of the legitimacy of the state.[46]

Interference, influence and imitation have occurred since the establishment of the first states thousands of years ago, but arguably they have intensified as a result of the Industrial Revolution and of the consequent growth in the ability of developed states to project power and influence at great distances from home.

The impact of changes in the international system is fully recognised by this author, and indeed *The Art of Coercion* is concerned with analysing not just historical experiences and trends in coercion and state formation/state-building, but also the contemporary context and how that has changed compared to the historical period. Although the importance of the international environment surfaces at different points in the book, the chapter 6 is dedicated specifically to discussing international intervention, respectively in the case of armies and of police forces and intelligence agencies. Chapter 1 deals with the issue of imitation. The seventh and final hypothesis of this book is that external intervention, even in its milder form of advice and support, is more likely to be counter-productive in achieving and maintaining the monopoly of violence.

It is essential for the purposes of this book to provide some clear, functional and analytical definitions of the different components of the state which specialise in coercion (the 'security sector'), without being misled by their self-definitions. Many self-proclaimed armies are in fact mere gendarmeries, several 'police' forces are in fact gendarmeries, others resemble more an irregular militia, etc. In this book I will therefore adopt the following definitions:

Army:
- an organisation capable of large-scale violence, with the necessary logistical capabilities, equipment and organisation;

- the command structure is monolithic and strongly hierarchical;
- supervision is very bureaucratised, but not very strong as stress is on delivery heavy blows to the enemy, not on maintaining balance and avoiding excesses;
- the operational structure runs parallel to its internal command structure, potentially making of the army a single unit able to operate as an entity;
- it is expensive as it costs money to create the required logistics and complex bureaucratic structures;
- it has limited investigative capabilities, usually limited to its military intelligence and military policing branches;
- it has long-range mobility through territory, but for limited amounts of time; for logistical and cost reasons tends to be stationed in permanent bases most of the time.

Civilian police:

- in charge of enforcing law and order;
- it operates in small and very small units, often individuals and pairs; it does not have the capability to operate in a coordinated fashion in units larger than tens of men;
- it has no heavy weaponry and little logistical capacity, sometimes even makes limited use of light weapons;
- in principle use of force has to be authorised externally, by the judiciary or the executive;
- it has well developed investigative capabilities;
- its command structure might be monolithic or decentralised, but individual units are generally assigned to specific areas and do not rotate;
- it has limited or no long-range mobility;
- supervision is in principle strong and multi-layered and is both internal and external.

Gendarmerie:

- it has some capability for large-scale violence, although not for sustaining long battles;
- it can operate in units of hundreds, but not much larger than that;
- it has a hierarchical structure and is based on military discipline;
- it deals primarily not with ordinary crime, but with internal threats to state security;
- it has little or no investigative capabilities;

- it is cheaper to maintain than an army, although it is more expensive than the police;
- it is permanently based in localities, so it can develop local knowledge;
- its operational command and logistical structure exist at the local level mainly, although a central reserve force may also exist, and it cannot usually operate in a coordinated fashion beyond the local level;
- supervision is bureaucratised and stronger than in the army, but not as strong as in the police as stress is on eliminating direct threats to regimes and quality control is not as important;
- because of their military background and organisation gendarmes may be useful in tasks such as crowd management, where discipline and hierarchy have to take over once disorder has broken out.

Intelligence/security service:
- its prime task is undercover information gathering and political manipulation/repression;
- it often has some capacity for violence but usually not on a very large scale;
- it is often divided into separate services (counter-intelligence, civilian/military, external/internal); branch of police and army also have intelligence functions;
- it has advanced investigative capabilities;
- supervision tends to be handled directly by politicians, with only limited bureaucratisation.

Irregulars (militias):
- these are semi-trained forces (sometimes untrained), with limited organisation and capability for large-scale violence;
- their equipment is usually limited too;
- most importantly, they have little or no logistical ability to deploy far from home.
- they are cheap to maintain;
- they do not have a monolithic command structure, nor a bureaucratised system of supervision;
- their loyalty to the authorities is often based on personal relations, even if protocols and signed agreements might well exist.

Local government:
- it more or less openly gathers information and manipulates politically potential sources of opposition to the government;

- it advises the security forces about the local political context;
- the level of supervision to which it is subjected can vary widely, but it is usually relatively loose and it is mostly handled by politicians;
- it has usually some investigative capability.

1

THE RUTHLESSNESS OF STATE FORMATION

'If thou findest a man whose adherents are many... and he is... a talker—remove him, kill him, wipe out his name, destroy his faction, banish the memory of him and of his adherents who love him. [...] [Apart from rebels] do not slaughter; it is not of advantage to thee. But thou shouldst punish with beatings and arrests; this land will be firmly grounded thereby'.

'Instructions to King Merikare', in J. B. Pritchard, *Ancient Near Eastern Texts*, Princeton: Princeton University Press, 1955, p. 415

The Arab writer, Ibn Khaldun, proposed in his *Muqaddimah* an interpretation of how states rise and decline. It all starts with charismatic leaders and their retinue of followers:

Royal authority... (is) attained only through a group and *'asabiyya* ['group feeling']. This is because aggressive and defensive strength is obtained only through group feeling which means (mutual) affection and willingness to fight and die for each other.

'Asabiyya 'gives protection and makes possible mutual defence...' and is centred around an individual who has 'superiority over the others in the matter of group feeling' and can 'act as a restraining influence and mediator [...]' in order to keep its members from (fighting) with each other'. The *'asabiyya* rises at the margins of civilisation, the 'desert life' which makes the Bedouins 'more disposed to courage'. 'The hamlets of the Bedouins are defended against outside enemies by a tribal militia [...]' whose 'defence and protection are successful only if they are a closely knit group of common descent' or clients and allies

23

who because of close contact with the master develop a strong relationship. When urban civilisation becomes weak and unable to dominate the 'Bedouins', an *'asabiyya* can emerge to threaten the city, particularly if religion helps its members to mobilise for collective action.[1] In Ibn Khaldun's words, 'when people [who have a religious colouring] come to have the (right) insight into their affairs, nothing can withstand them, because their outlook is one and their object one of common accord. They are willing to die for (their objectives)'.[2]

Ibn Khaldun continues describing the dynamics which follow the establishment of the new polity:

glory was the common (property) of the group, and all members of the group made an identical effort (to obtain glory), their aspirations to gain the upper hand over others and to defend their own possessions were expressed in exemplary unruliness and lack of restraint. [...] In this stage, the ruler serves as model to his people by the manner in which he acquires glory, collects taxes, defends property, and provides military protection. He does not claim anything exclusively for himself to the exclusion of (his people), because (such an attitude) is what is required by *'asabiyya*, (and it was group feeling) that gave superiority (to the dynasty).[3]

Some time after having conquered power:

(the rulers) will not need much *'asabiyya* to maintain their power' and [...] 'maintain their hold over the government and their own dynasty with the help, then, either of clients and followers who grew up in the shadow and power of the *'asabiyya*, or (with that) of tribal groups of a different descent who have become their clients.

Moreover, '(royal authority), by its very nature, must claim all glory for itself'. Once the power of the ruler is consolidated, he:

claims all glory for himself, he treats the others severely and holds them in check. Further, he excludes them from possessing property and appropriates it for himself. People, thus, become too lazy to care for fame. They become dispirited and come to love humbleness and servitude. [...] When the dynasty continues in power and their rulers follow each other in succession, they become sophisticated.

'Luxury will at first give additional strength to a dynasty', as 'a greater number of clients and followers is acquired'. However, the result is the fragmentation of the original solidarity group and the over-taxation and over-exploitation of the subjects, which may have disintegrative effects if not met by effective counter-measures.[4]

Ibn Khaldun describes a historical pattern of state formation in the Arab context. Why does it matter? How relevant is this example today? These are among the questions that this chapter tries to answer.

THE RUTHLESSNESS OF STATE FORMATION

Early Accumulation, Expansion and Consolidation of Armed Force

Big Men and Their Retinues

Historically the establishment of a monopoly over large-scale violence has followed several different patterns. A common one in Western Europe (but not only there) was not so different from that described by Ibn Khaldun. It saw the shift to an increasingly intensive agriculture allowing for the emergence of chiefs and big men and their retinues from within 'egalitarian' tribal societies. The latter, despite the presence of a strong 'warrior spirit':

lacked a coercive central authority that would mobilize and organize the tribal manpower for mass organised warfare'. [...] 'Even though [the big men and their retinues] were relatively small, because they were the only organised forces within society could be checked only by other such forces. In consequence, their dominance tended to grow in a snowball process, making society increasingly more stratified.[5]

The 'progressively subservient population' could not resist this process because of its inability to act collectively, scattered at it was through the countryside and mostly unable to communicate and cooperate. It started with the formation of solidarity groups, characterised by strong personal relationships between the leaders and the members, like Ibn Khaldun's *'asabiyya*. This is one of the two 'trajectories' of early state formation identified by Ronald Cohen; the other one sees 'a nonstate group of sedentary agriculturalists' reacting to incursions from a neighbouring power by developing an effective defensive reaction, which then leads to statehood as leaders emerge and become stronger while taking an increasingly important role of dispute management and decision-making.[6] The 'Bedouins' therefore play a role in any case, either as a charisma-driven solidarity group which conquers other communities and forges them into a state structure, or by eliciting the reaction of the same communities and forcing them to adopt a more hierarchical structure, eventually leading to state formation.

A Military Class Emerges

The consolidation of the solidarity groups into a military class is the second stage of this process of state formation. This could be defined in Gallant's terms as 'a category of men who take up arms and who wield violence or the threat of violence as their stock in trade',[7] but I shall add as part of the definition that they must have acquired self-awareness of their specific role in society . In this regard an important stage of accumulation of coercive power is the replacement of kinship with clientage as the base of political organisation. In particular, the recruitment of uprooted social elements ('broken men') or migrant minority groups as soldiers or militiamen appears historically to have been a frequent occurrence. The result would have been to insulate the ruler from society and allow him a greater degree of arbitrary power:[8] 'A troop of armed men under the command of a leader can be turned to many purposes other than those for which they were first recruited'.[9]

The fact that local leaders and their 'henchmen' managed to bring under their control a much larger population, even if males were usually armed, reflected the advantage of having a small retinue of loyal followers ready to obey orders without question.[10] What this discussion highlights is the role of charismatic leaders able to gather armed men around themselves for collective action, as opposed to the mere control and ownership of weapons. From among the military class some emerged as particularly successful in war-making:

Successful war leadership, probably even more than most leadership, requires various talents. These talents are always found in complex combinations, as in other leadership, but in any case the leader must be a successful manager of human relations as well as a tactician, a person of at least moderate bravery. He may or may not have a 'drive for power', or a deep sense of responsibility for his fellows [...].[11]

These 'warlords' often started their career as *primus inter pares* and established their hegemony as service providers for the military class. The warlord rises above the mass of military leaders to provide services such as coordination, planning, management, logistics, foreign relations as well as skilled military leadership (of a more strategic type). He can also use a portion of war booty to reward his followers and strengthen their loyalty:

He uses these resources to set up transactions requiring reciprocal returns, to attract clients, to act as a protector for those in need, as well as to increase the mystery of his officer or increase the social distance between himself and others.[12]

By providing services and rewards to otherwise autonomous members of the military class, the warlord improves the chances of survival and success of each of them. To the specialists of violence, winning battles means more opportunity for looting, for example, or for the expansion of territorial control and hence a greater tax base.[13] The ability of generals and warlords to gather the support of the wider military class can be described as 'military charisma', while their ability to win battles confers to them a 'military legitimacy',[14] recognised well beyond the military class itself. In a Hobbesian environment, individuals and communities might well prize the protection afforded by the monopolist of large-scale violence against external threats, particularly if it is perceived that such threats also affect civilians. Thus military leadership might be recognised by the wider population too as a useful quality and earn the warlord wider support, although usually not full political legitimacy. Where violence (using Ernest Gellner's formula) is 'pervasive, mandatory and normative', military leaders like warlords may represent an element of order, as opposed to the Hobbesian chaos where hundreds or even thousands of small military leaders all fight their own wars. If it is true that agrarian societies are characterised by the logic of the elimination of rival 'specialists in coercion', warlords may represent a stage in this process. Examples of this type of warlords are relatively common in late antiquity and the early Middle Ages in Europe.[15]

Although detailed information concerning the earlier historical period is scant, the role of warrior bands in the power accumulation process leading to statehood is well established at least as far as northern Europe is concerned. The typical structure which emerged in Scandinavia featured a mercenary/ paid force of a few thousand, then the king's retinue, finally a local militia, subject to call-up in times of emergency and to more selective recruitment in lesser cases. In the context of non-bureaucratic polities, the control exercised by the military class over armed men and territory (military patrimonialism) may have been irreplaceable at least in the early stages of state formation. Once these warrior bands and local military leaders started coalescing under a warlord, arguably the process of state formation was underway. In principle, the rationale for the establishment of the state seems compelling. Bates argues that since non-state provision of security is 'fragile and unforgiving', leading to 'cycles of retaliation', and because the provision of private security is costly, the political and economic elites gradually merged in the rural areas. 'Households which were rich also becoming the households that dominated militarily'.[16]

Economic growth, violence and the rise of feudal political organisation went together: growth elicits violence by creating wealth; and it was landowning elites who had the incentive privately to organize for the defense of property. In the course of this violence, some kin groups did better than others and formed ruling lineages and provided kings.[17]

Among the Franks, King Clovis (V-VI CE) 'started out with a retinue that is estimated at no more than 400–500 warriors' and then brutally eliminated all of the other Frankish 'petty kings', 'incorporating the defeated rulers' retinues as he went'. A similar process occurred in England.[18] The process started gaining speed quickly:

Man to man, tribal warriors were more than a match for state conscripts, and many tribal lands [...] could potentially produce a large number of fighting men. Still, tribal societies were of small scale, were divided among themselves, and possessed little coercive power over their members. Although emergencies and desperate situations such as enemy invasion or tribal migration could force a general participation in warfare, such concerted efforts were hard to sustain for long, and in other circumstances self-interest and self-preservation encouraged 'defection' from the common effort. Among other things, states greatly reduced 'cheating' and worked to eliminate 'free riders' by coercing their members into co-operation...[19]

The Virtuous Cycle of State Formation

The turning point in processes of primitive accumulation of coercive power was often the 'conquest' of urban centres. In a sense, the birth of the state has historically often been the result of the union of cities and 'territorial monarchs', even if the kind of cooperation which emerged in medieval Europe was of 'a very particular kind' and 'culminated in the rise of nation-states'.[20] Elsewhere the 'cooperation' might often have looked more like a 'forced marriage' or even a 'concubinate'. In this regard too the model proposed by Ibn Khaldun may be useful. It focuses on the attraction exercised on the tribes by the city, but in my view it can be adapted to explain the relationship between cities and warlords. Not only is the city at the centre of a 'vortex' that leads to the creation of surplus-extracting structures from the surrounding tribes or communities, but it draws tribal leaders and warlords into the city, or towards the formation of coalitions trying to establish control over it. The leaders/warlords sometimes capture the city, sometimes just move in, but are always attracted by the city because of its importance as a transport hub, as a financial and services centre and because of its prestige. The control of the city may prove a major competitive advantage against the leader's rivals, but over time in the Ibn-Khaldunian cycle the leader or his descendants distance themselves from the solidarity group ('asabiyya) which was their original power base, to the extent that they remain isolated and are easily overthrown.[21] This is why unsophisticated warlord polities are eminently unstable. With the help of the resources of the city, warlord polities might potentially break the cycle by starting processes of legitimisation, institutionalisation and bureaucratisation. The city holds the keys to the specialisation and professionalism necessary for state consolidation.

The emergence of relatively large warlord armies, able to capture or co-opt cities, also enables economic accumulation on a relatively large scale. But conflict among warrior bands may easily lead to unregulated predation due to the difficulty of exercising control over agents, in turn compromising the long-term economic bases of accumulation and starving the war factions of resources. Moreover, the ability to mobilise for fighting erodes once accumulation starts benefiting members and leaders in disproportionate ways.[22] As constant strife and the uncertainty of outcome become problematic, a virtuous cycle of state formation can then emerge. The formation of economic interests around the leaders represents an incentive to seek some form of stabilisation and consolidation, offsetting the interest of other actors in persisting with war, namely those who have not yet succeeded in accumulating sufficiently large fortunes or who are not motivated by financial gain. The new rich become potential targets of enemies, as well as of friends not endowed with such riches, and develop an interest in the stability and rule of law that peace could bring about. Those military leaders who have benefited economically from the war, gradually lose interest in fighting and taking personal risks on the battlefield. Moreover, the accumulation of capital through war is likely to stabilise after an initial rapid increase, as war is unlikely to generate a virtuous economic cycle capable of sustaining ever greater returns. In fact, the contrary is likely, and diminishing returns from an increasingly devastated economy are to be expected. Peace (or at least 'a certain kind of peace') therefore becomes a more attractive option, if a charismatic leader is available to drive the process.

Access to outside ideas or models (neighbouring states) might facilitate the task of organising for collective action.[23] For example, German mercenaries recruited into the Roman army brought 'civilisation' back to their 'barbarian' tribes and launched the development of more sophisticated (and dangerous) polities.[24] A particularly common and successful way of pacifying the military class of a given region and of incorporating it into a polity, has historically been exporting war to the neighbours, that is mobilising it for external conquest. But even an economy of conquest will eventually run out of territory to expand towards.

In sum, it is clear that once state formation takes off, implementing and strengthening command and control from the centre becomes one of the key problems characterising the primitive accumulation of coercive power. The feudal model is interesting in this regard, given its recognised military origins and its later consolidation into a system endowed with a specific mode of production and source of legitimisation.[25] The Carolingians controlled the fragmentation of their polity, using monetary payment for services, which had the effect of curtailing the decentralised tendencies implicit in feudalism. Local military leaders were forced to rotate residencies every few years. The king would travel throughout his territory to exercise on-site control; sometimes he would use paid administrators to do the same.[26] Scholars of feudalism have been trying to explain one of the main trends of feudal systems, towards fragmenting into many smaller and increasingly autonomous polities that differ widely in the way they are ruled. Because each vassal granted parts of his fief to a number of lower vassals (vavassors), there was no direct relationship between the lord and the vavassors. The incoherence of the system made control difficult. Moreover, the lord was trying to reassure his vassals by gradually conceding hereditariness to the fiefs, with the result that in the medium and long term the power of the lord was diminished.[27]

The Role of Brinkmanship

Given the weaknesses of feudalism in particular and in general of decentralised systems, it is not surprising that the centralisation of patronage was widely adopted to achieve polity consolidation. It implied the ruler trying to establish exclusive control over as many sources of wealth as possible, which could then be redistributed to create political support.[28] The real problem with the centralisation of patronage is how to achieve it. Apart from the radical option of an all-out war, always a risky choice because of its uncertain outcome, a more frequent option has been brinkmanship, a tactic that political leaders often used to force partners and adversaries to concede as much as possible. The success of brinkmanship was very much dependent on the personal skills of the leader; the idea that politics is a form of art derives in part from this. The risk associated with it is of course the undoing of coalitions and alliances and the consequent internal collapse, a common occurrence throughout history. The example of the Kuomintang, whose leaders precipitated a new series of civil wars in 1930 when they tried to enforce a disbandment of the warlords' armies, should be borne in mind. In chapter 2 I will discuss how the inherent instability of polities based on charismatic leadership has been dealt with.

The Impact of the World System

The development of 'world systems' inevitably affected this process; although we know relatively little of the exact impact of world systems in earlier times, one would think that the impact was particularly strong since the nineteenth century, given the increased ability of the leading states to project power and influence away from their borders. A similar process of state formation to the ones described above can be discerned in nineteenth- and early twentieth-century Central America. Here, some caudillos who were able to capture control of the centre tried to concentrate coercive power in their hands, gradually undermining regional caudillos. The speed and strength of the process varied greatly from one country to the other, depending on the charisma and abilities of individual leaders, but the trend was clear. They eventually started borrowing ideas and tools for the monopolisation of violence from more developed countries, such as military academies, military equipment, organisational techniques, etc. In most cases political and practical support from the United States played a decisive role, most obviously so in 1920s Nicaragua.[29]

A particularly fitting example of conscious imitation of state-making techniques by emerging ruling elites is that of a number of 'revolutionary' groups importing organisational models, ideology and tools relevant to the monopolisation of violence. The spread of Maoism from the original Chinese experience to much of Asia and even some parts of Africa and Latin America is well documented; the fact that Mao took care to set down his blueprint for building a new state from the bottom up favoured the spread of the model.

Pragmatically speaking, the Maoist approach offers the most highly developed construct available for 'making a revolution'. Hence there is little need for would-be revolutionaries to look elsewhere for a template. [...][Mao's] approach has been used by insurgents of all persuasions [...]. Maoist insurgency is a technique for purposive (i.e., deliberate) action. It is a means to an end, political power [...] to be seized for the purpose of overthrowing the existing order.[30]

The appeal went well beyond leftists: the adoption of Maoist techniques by the Afghan Islamists in the 1980s is attested, for example.[31] Nowhere have the patterns of imitation proven stronger than in the fields of ideology and organisation.

The Role of Ideology

In the context of the twentieth century, the role of warrior leaders and their retinues was played by what are now called 'non-state armed groups', which in principle include both ideological and ideological organisations. In fact a tendency in that direction already emerged in the late eighteenth century with the American Revolution. In recent years there has been a tendency to assert that, after the end of the Cold War, ideological movements have been replaced by non-ideological ones based on coercion or instrumental inducements; similarly in the 1970s and 1980s it was common to stress the difference between the then contemporary ideological movements and previous examples of 'traditional', non-ideological anti-government movements.[32] In reality already Ibn Khaldun in the fourteenth century was discussing the role of (religious) ideology in terms of mobilisation and motivation of a fighting force, as mentioned at the beginning of the chapter.

Rather than appearing from nowhere to disappear in the dark once again, ideologies have been subject to cycles. The end of the Cold War and the so-called 'collapse of ideologies' might well have contributed to the displacement of a particular brand of ideological guerrillas, who lost the support of international powers.[33] However, external support does not appear to be as crucial a factor as the strength of ideological mobilisation itself. A cycle of ideological build-up started with the Russian and Chinese civil wars of 1917 onwards, when weakly resourced ideological movements defeated externally supported rivals. There is clearly a strong imitation factor in explaining how a particular ideology picks up in popularity and spreads; as imitation becomes more and more common, 'antidotes' are developed by rivals, and at the same time the ideology gets applied to increasingly unlikely contexts. Sooner or later, the ideology gets discredited by a series of failures and by the increasingly low quality of the 'recruits'. The exhaustion of a particular ideological cycle (communism) does not mean however that others cannot follow, such as 'national liberation' in the 1950s-1970s or the current wave of Islamist movements. It is in the gap between ideological cycles that non-ideological armed groups found a ground free from strong competition and appear to prosper. Otherwise, non-ideological violent actors have usually been operating in the shadow of ideological actors.[34]

A census of state-formation efforts in the twentieth century would likely highlight the disproportionate role played by ideological organisations. Various authors have pointed out the role of ideology in fields such as legitimisation, the development of loyalty and cohesion among 'the agents of coercion'[35] and more generally for management of collective action. In Geertz's words, ideologies are 'matrices for the creation of collective conscience'.[36] Ideology provides 'the motivation to seek [...] technical skill and knowledge, the emotional resilience to support the necessary patience and resolution, and the moral strength to self-sacrifice and incorruptibility...'[37] It is possible to carry out a mobilisation, exercise hegemony and obtain legitimisation within a relatively weak organisational/bureaucratic framework (for example, through the clergy and local notables). But as a tool of legitimisation and of sophisticated long-term management of collective action, ideology needs a specialised carrier, a political organisation.[38] This fact alone tends to confer an advantage to ideological organisations in state formation and state consolidation, as it prepares them for the future task of running the state. There are important factors militating against ideology too. We must bear in mind that ideology represents a constraint to the arbitrary action of the leader, and as such it will always be seen with suspicion by the patrimonial ruler. Ideologisation is at odds with the patrimonial character of a state, and the ruler is likely to have sooner or later to rein it in, or accept the risk of being sidelined at some point. A clash is likely in any case, with potentially disastrous consequences.[39] For all the American efforts to sponsor a 'nationalist' government in South Vietnam, they failed because nationalism cannot be developed successfully in a patrimonial environment. This is one anecdote from FitzGerald:

When Halberstam, interviewing enemy defectors, asked a North Vietnamese major what he could do if given command of an ARVN battalion, the major replied, 'I could command a division in North Vietnam. I have the ability to do that. But a platoon here, even a squad, I could not do that. What can you do? They have no purpose.'[40]

Patrimonial leaders are not very likely to penetrate through international opposition to the formation of new states as it arose during the latter half of the twentieth century. Here we can identify a factor which differentiates the twentieth and twenty-first centuries from earlier periods: the creation of international organisations after the Second World War and the rise of an 'international community' (as expressed in the formation of international organisations such as the United Nations), which has the ambition to prevent state collapse and the formation of new states (except for former colonies). Particularly once such attitudes became widely shared by existing states after the end of the collapse of the Soviet Union in 1991, they were inevitably going to interfere with and even prevent the state-making process, as described in the previous paragraph, from reproducing itself in the time-honoured fashion. In fact, the historical process of state formation had already been interrupted by the colonial era, except in some of the most remote corners of the world or in peculiar circumstances. I mentioned above the impact of the shaping world system on state-building in Central America. It took the ideological waves of communism and nationalism to give a new chance to the formation of new states. Because only strongly motivated ideological movements will take the risk to confront the 'international community' head on, other types of insurgent movements and non-state armed groups have now a low success rate in state formation. The demands of the international community can still be sneakily eluded even today by non-ideological actors, but the outcome is unlikely to be state formation.[41] If patrimonial polities can develop façades of bureaucratic processes in order to interact with the 'modern' world,[42] why should warlords and the like not adopt similar tricks to develop their polities into states?

The Wonders and Worries of Organisation

Ideology is relatively easy to imitate because it does not require large investments to reproduce. Organisational imitation is a somewhat more complex matter, but still within the reach of non-state groups. One factor genuinely differentiating movements engaged in the primitive accumulation of coercive power during the twentieth century from their predecessors might have been organisational development, although often we know little of the way the predecessors operated. Non-state armed groups experienced substantial organisational innovation in the twentieth century, with some of them developing effective tools of political and military command and control in combination with the old-fashioned coercion. This was probably the consequence of some fall-out from developments such as spread of education as well as of the reliance on ideology for mobilisation and collective action. The first example dates back to the very early years of that century. The IMRO anti-Turkish guerrillas in Macedonia were the first to attempt to build a counter-state and had a very advanced organisation.[43] Mexican rebel leader Zapata in Morelos also had a comparatively advanced organisation, even developing a structure to take care of the civilian population.[44] The new 'political technology' of command and control reached maturation in the 1930s and 1940s, in Yugoslavia and China. Drawing on some of the organisational principles pioneered by the Bolsheviks (see below), the local communists refined the institution of the political commissar and associated it to an administration dedicated to the welfare and well-being of the troops. As Mao wrote:

In all armies, obedience of the subordinates to their superiors must be enacted... but [...] a discipline of coercion in ineffective, discipline must be self-imposed, because only when it is, is the soldier able to understand completely why he fights and how he must obey.[45]

Mao 'was very clear that any armed force divorced from central control could never be an effective revolutionary body'.[46]

Galula pointed out that 'once the insurgent has succeeded in acquiring stable geographical bases, [...] he becomes *ipso facto* a strong promoter of order within his own area, in order to demonstrate the effectiveness of his own rule and the inadequacy of the opponent's'.[47] The transition towards the formation of a regular armed force, as dictated by the Maoist stages theory, is often interpreted exclusively in terms of mounting the final and direct threat to state power. However, there is more to it. Irregular and guerrilla warfare is very demanding on the civilian population and if protracted it can alienate the villagers:[48] the insurgents have a limited amount of time to develop a counter-state in order to win and a regular army, effectively monopolising violence, is one key aspect of it. Moreover, the management of centralised insurgent organisations required a safe haven, which might not be safe forever.[49] Clearly this represents a risky enterprise as it implies a fine strategic judgement of whether forming a regular army can succeed or not. If a misjudgement occurs, the insurgents can be crushed in a confrontation against superior forces. Callwell pointed out that 'the more nearly the enemy approximates in system to the European model, the less marked is the strategical advantage he enjoys.'[50] However, at the same time the insurgents cannot indulge forever in guerrilla tactics.

History records several clamorous failures, like that of the Greek communists in the second half of the 1940s, who in their struggle against the right-wing government decided to form their guerrilla units into battalions and regiments and accept battle against a vastly better equipped enemy and were crushed.[51] The Greek communists might have been inspired by the contemporary Chinese success, but failed to consider the local situation carefully enough. Other political-military leaderships were more careful in matching ambition and reality. There is little doubt that the Viet Minh firmly believed in the need to defeat the French in a direct engagement, but managed to do it at a time and place of its choice. As late as 1953 the French forces in Indochina found a study made by the Viet Minh command, which determined that in Viet Minh territory there was no area and no fixed installation worth defending.[52]

Another consideration against the premature formation of a regular army is its cost, particularly if this has to be deployed in battle. Even if an insurgent army would likely still cost a fraction of its counter-insurgent enemy, the resources available to insurgents are also always vastly inferior. The Algerian FLN in the 1960s was estimated to have a yearly budget equivalent to what the French were spending in two weeks to fight it, but even these $30–40 million were only available because of relatively generous external support from other Arab countries (mainly Egypt).[53]

While the risks of centralisation might seem discouraging, the failure to centralise has other dangers in addition to the above-mentioned risk of alienating villagers. A classic example of what could be described 'insurgent warlordism' is Chad, where Frolinat, which started itself in 1965 as a merger of different groups opposed to the first post-colonial government, disintegrated into multiple factions.[54] Warlordism often arises as a problem of command and control of military organisations and derives from the autonomisation of military commanders, who separate themselves from the political leadership.

An additional plus of a strong organisation is that it allows insurgents to know how they stand in relation to each other and to have confidence in the stability of their relationships.[55] Here organisation links up with ideology. Inevitably, insurgents' attempts to build large organisations have regularly been threatened by free riders, and as organisations grew in size the problem worsened. In the end the solutions developed to strengthen management and control did not differ very much from those adopted from armies, and can be reduced to two:

- create an environment in which members can expect that their comrades and commanders share the same long-term goals for the movement, by building shared identities and beliefs (hence the role of ideology pointed out earlier);
- develop an internal set of relationships organised around short-term rewards, such as for example access to looting, when shared identities and beliefs are weak or non-existent.[56]

Clearly, the latter of the two sounds less appealing for a movement with long-term ambitions. Once a revolutionary movement has succeeded in monopolising large-scale violence by defeating the opposing state, a consolidation phase usually follows. The problems faced are similar to those faced by any new government which has to rebuild an army from scratch. As mentioned above, revolutionary movements often relied on ideology as a tool of motivation and control, but its impact would be limited in the absence of supporting organisational structures. Cromwell's New Model Army has often been touted as the first ideological army in history, but on a closer look such characterisation seems inadequate. In reality it might have been not very different from the Royalists' armies. As it relied on conscription with a large percentage of criminals in the ranks, it was badly behaved and strict discipline was necessary with corporal punishment and death penalty. Radical preachers played a role to encourage and motivate the troops, but few of them were in a position to play anything even remotely resembling the role of a sort of political commissar *ante litteram*.[57] The main advantage of the New Model Army might have been that its men had stayed together long enough for both officers and men to acquire experience in working together.

As already mentioned, during the twentieth century revolutionary movements developed organisational tools which helped ideology to play a more effective role in exercising control and motivation functions. The figure of the 'political commissar' was introduced by the Bolsheviks and later became a standard feature of armies inspired by the Soviet example or forced to copy from it. I discuss it in greater detail in the next chapter. Here, suffice it to say that the system experienced quite a few problems in its early years. For example, Bolshevik party cadres had a tendency to interfere in the conduct of military operations, and the political leadership had to issue a decree in 1919 ordering them not to do so and limit their work to raise political consciousness among the ranks.[58] Once fine-tuned, the system resolved the problem experienced by the French revolutionaries (always the object of keen study by the Bolsheviks), who had to choose between loyal but incompetent officers, who proved unable to defend the revolution on the battlefield, and able ones whom they could not control (epitomised by Bonaparte). The Soviet political commissars system still tended to weaken the initiative and creativity of the commanding officers, but the price was deemed worth paying. Nazi Germany, too, toyed with the idea of something like the political commissars and experimented with some milder versions of it, but Hitler feared that the chain of command of the army would be disrupted and opted not to go that far, establishing instead political officers in charge of propaganda and ideological leadership, without control over the commanders. By the time they came into place in 1943, the war was already being lost and in any case the military never took the new category of officers seriously.[59]

The Role of Technology I

A particular case of imitation is the import of technology. Clearly, it plays a role as waves of technological innovation can confer an unprecedented advantage to any competitor which enjoys greater financial resources or privileged access to the new technology; this is usually the case of governments, particularly through networks of international alliances that often result in the cheap or even free provision of relatively advanced military technologies. Hence it could be expected that the gradual development of trade and the formation of world superpowers, able easily to supply client regimes with plentiful military equipment, would play against insurgent movements. The introduction of rapid-firing firearms in the second half of the nineteenth century certainly gave at least a temporary edge to whoever could afford them, as in contrast to older types of firearm they were expensive to produce and not easily manufactured by artisans. In Latin America, repeating rifles like the Mausers, Remingtons and Winchesters were credited with contributing to the end of regional caudillismo and securing borders.[60]

However, it was not long before competition among internal powers and war allowed bolt-action and lever rifles, and machine guns to spread around the globe and reach non-state armed groups. They were extensively used by the Boers at the turn of the century already, and then by the Berber insurgents in the Rif war of the 1920s, who also extensively used captured machine guns and some artillery.[61] During the 1920s and 1930s, some European powers were already planning to supply insurgent groups with these or similar weapons.[62] The practice then became standard during the Second World War. Because of their small size, limited maintenance and ease of use, these weapons did not confer any particular advantage to states over insurgents; the introduction of a new generation of infantry weapons during and after the Second World War made it even easier for non-state armed groups to handle firearms. After the chaotic and muddy experience of infantry fighting in that war, weapons started being designed with ease of maintenance and ruggedness in mind. The best known achievement of this new tendency was the AK-47 and its derivatives, whose ruggedness became legendary as it increasingly became available to insurgents.[63]

In order to identify a role for technologies in facilitating the establishment of the monopoly over large-scale violence, we have to look at weapon systems which are not easily manageable by non-state armed groups and particularly insurgents. As I discuss later in the book (chapter 6), not all advanced military technologies are equally suitable for achieving or strengthening monopolies of large-scale violence. The most extreme example of limited impact of technology is that of nuclear weapons, as demonstrated from 2004 onwards in Pakistan, a state which successfully developed these weapons and almost immediately thereafter was faced with the most serious series of insurgencies in its history. Armoured vehicles and aircraft are more plausible candidates for a role in the primitive accumulation of coercive power. In Afghanistan, for example, the introduction of tanks and jet aircraft in the 1950s effectively put an end to large-scale tribal revolts. The employment of aircraft by the Royal Air Force was essential in putting down the 1920 Iraqi revolt, the Dervish revolt in Somaliland in 1920 and the 1919 tribal uprising in support of the attacking Afghan forces in the Pashtun tribal areas of present-day Pakistan.[64] In his 1971 study, Gann expressed the belief that if the Turks had had armoured cars and aircrafts like the British had in 1919–20, they would easily have defeated the

British-sponsored Arab revolt during the First World War, which effectively brought down the Ottoman Empire.[65]

However, when dealing with sophisticated organisations staffed by educated cadres, technological escalation might not be so effective. It should always be borne in mind that the spread of technology is more difficult to control than it might appear. Insurgents are not going to build tanks for sure, but might have access to anti-tank technology either from supportive countries or through technological 'percolation', that is the tendency of technological knowledge to spread wider and wider once it enters the industrial production stage. For example, the introduction of armoured forces in many 'new countries' in the 1950s and 1960s seemed to be leading towards a nearly unchallengeable strengthening of the monopoly of large-scale violence, until the spread of cheap and easy to use anti-tank rocket launchers (mainly RPG-2 and RPG-7) took place from the 1960s onwards.[66] Later the introduction of armoured vehicles on a larger and larger scale and the outclassing of the RPGs with more advanced armour led to the development of an underground cottage industry of mines and roadside bombs.[67]

Finding technological responses to air power proved somewhat more problematic for insurgent movements, particularly once guided bombing was introduced and armoured aircraft appeared. Although there has been a spread of portable anti-aircraft missiles in the hands of non-state armed groups since the 1970s,[68] they were rarely used efficiently or to great effect in the absence of direct and continuing foreign assistance. The only cases of insurgencies using anti-aircraft missiles on a scale that would affect the military balance in a conflict have been the Afghan mujahidin, the Nicaraguan contras and the Angolan UNITA.[69] However, it is also evident that the introduction of air support first and of helicopters on a large scale afterwards has not prevented the proliferation of armed insurgencies from the 1940s onwards, suggesting that organisational innovation in insurgent movements more than offset the advantages accruing to state monopolies of large-scale violence from such technological innovations. Indeed it could be argued that some of the most successful military counter-insurgency efforts benefited from the limited availability of helicopters, which forced the troops to learn to fight in small units and interact with the local population.[70]

In sum, technology might facilitate in the short term the monopolisation of violence, but not because it reduces the necessity of coercion. Moreover, a degree of fluidity and uncertainty always remains implicit in it.

Utopia and State-Making: Coercion Despite All

Although the heightened role of ideology and organisation impacted on state-building processes, this has not reduced the role of coercion. The best way to demonstrate this is to look at the experiences of insurgent movements arguing in favour of decentralisation or even utopian new orders and show how the way coercion is carried out may have changed, but certainly not disappeared. Fragmented and decentralised insurgent movements which did not use coercion internally have occurred often in history; in fact until the post-World War II period, insurgent movements had largely belonged to this category. When faced with a central state, in most cases such movements failed unless they received external help,[71] even when their potential for disruption was immense, as in the case of the Villistas in Mexico in the early twentieth century.[72]

As Mao compellingly argued, without developing a centrally controlled military force it would not be possible ultimately to defeat the state. The Sepoy mutiny of 1857 offers an interesting proof of this: despite having been trained by the British and having fought effectively in many battles under the orders of the Empire, once the command structure was removed the Sepoys became unable to fight effectively as they lost discipline. Their elected representatives lacked coercive authority and were easily defeated by the numerically inferior but better organised British.[73] In a number of cases, decentralised insurgent movements succeeded in forcing foreign armies out or indigenous governments down through tactics baptised as 'war of the flea' by Robert Taber.[74] One example is Makhno's guerrillas in Ukraine, which expelled the Germans (by 1918 in fact weakly motivated), but ultimately failed against the more determined Bolsheviks.[75] Decentralised movements did not need a high degree of coercion, except when they had recruitment problems and tried to coerce fighters to stay in the ranks or forcefully recruited them.[76]

Whenever the leadership tries to centralise control and resources in order to capture (and maintain control of) central state power, coercion became essential. The efforts of the American revolutionaries against the British crown, for example, were characterised by Washington's distrust of independent and decentralised guerrillas, whom he thought would have turned out to be politically dangerous once victory was achieved. Faced with the parochialism of the rank and file, he advocated the creation of a strong class of military officers with higher salaries and privileges and rejected any prospect of adoption of a radical socio-political programme.[77] Washington was not alone in his feelings. Benjamin Thompson lamented:

the existence of that very spirit which induced the common people to take up arms and resist the authority of Great Britain ... [because it induces] them to resist the authority of their own officers, and by that means effectively prevents them ever making good soldiers.[78]

Alexander Hamilton from his part commented:

Let officers be men of sense and sentiment, and the nearer the soldiers approach to machines, perhaps the better.[79]

An even more extreme case of a gap between the revolutionary leadership and indifferent rank and file was that of the Bolivarian armies fighting against the Spanish in Latin America.[80]

When the reliance on voluntarism and democratic principles to run a revolutionary army was tried, the results were not positive. In France during the 1790s not only conscription soon became unpopular, but existing military forces did not respect officers and often insulted and mistreated them. Soldiers' councils were formed in defiance to officers and soon within the revolutionary leadership itself warnings started to rise about the risk of government degenerating into a 'military democracy'. Soldiers often refused to learn the drill and the lack of discipline started obviously compromising military efficiency. The revolutionary troops also had the tendency to loot. Political control was exercised through the appointment of politically reliable officers, at the expense of professional competence. Indeed several good officers were removed or executed as the result of distrust in Paris. The situation proved untenable and councils were soon forbidden and the revolutionary militias started being gradually turned into regular army.[81]

In times closer to the present, both Lenin and Trotsky radically opposed peasant irregular warfare, considering it as a threat to the emergence of a 'proletarian' state organisation, and rejected the demand by the left wing of their own party to form 'a decentralised army based on volunteers and elective principles'. Lenin and Trotsky argued instead that armed peasants would be impossible to control and that the army cannot be socialist in its structure, as military affairs are governed by their own law; indeed they proceeded to incorporate former Tsarist officers and to adopt the command techniques and traditions from ancient regime. To quote Trotsky:

The command will always be obliged to place the soldiers between the possible death in the front and the inevitable one in the rear. [...] The lack of revolvers creates an impossible state of affairs at the front. There is no hope of maintaining discipline without having revolvers.[82]

They planned to retain political control through the party, the political commissars and the Cheka political police.[83]

Examples abound even for later periods. After having propagated the principle of egalitarianism in the ranks during the insurgency and civil war periods, the Chinese Maoists set out in 1949 to modernise and professionalise their system. By 1955 this resulted in the introduction of new 'Regulations' which centralised command and control, and established titles and honours for the officers, as well as meritocratic criteria for career advancement.[84] In 1966 (during the 'Cultural Revolution') the Chinese army flirted with the abolition of military ranks to 'bring back the tradition of equality among soldiers and commanders', but the experiment was short-lived.[85] Again in the 1980s Jerry Rawlings, the progressive officer who led the Ghanian army to take power, initially indulged in experiments of control of the armed forces from below, but then quickly moved to restore the chain of command and de-link the armed forces from the popular movement, re-establishing control from the government.[86]

In sum, it seems unquestionable that state-making is not possible in the absence of extreme coercion and violence. This does not just concern coercion and violence against enemies, but also coercion within the very coalition which emerges to lead the new state. Changes in technology, the development of new organisational skills, a succession of ideologies of varying utopian content: none of this has altered the basic fact. In this sense, the third hypothesis of this book is fully confirmed: *the 'primitive accumulation of coercive power'[87] tends to be ruthlessly violent.* Even at the stage of state formation, however, it is possible to discern features and qualities which are more likely to lead to successful state-making. However unpleasant ideology and tight organisation might sound to the average Western academic, the evidence suggests that more than ever if new states have to come into being they are likely to be characterised by a mix of the two.

This sombre statement about state formation should not be misunderstood to align this author with right-wing extremism. Although ruling elites remain motivated by self-interest, once a new state consolidates, new dynamics start playing off and new incentives appear to influence the behaviour of a ruling elite. If the liberal paradigm seems irrelevant to state-making, it is more relevant to state consolidation, because the problems faced in maintaining and consolidating the monopoly are essentially different, as the next chapters are going to explain.

2

MAINTAINING THE MONOPOLY

THE RISK OF DISLOYALTY

'The soldan of Egypt, or the emperor of Rome, might drive his harmless subjects, like brute beasts, against their sentiments and inclination: But he must, at least, have led his *mamalukes*, or *prætorian bands*, like men, by their opinion'.

David Hume, *Of the first principles of government*

Although Paul Bremer has often been accused of disbanding the Iraqi army in 2003 as soon as he took over control of the occupation authorities, he defended himself with some plausibility that the army had already self-disbanded following defeat. There was some exaggeration in this claim, as the conscripts had largely left, but officers and specialists were still there. Although 'not a single Iraqi unit remained intact', the option of retaining the professional cadre and reorganising the army was seriously discussed. The decision to disband the army was in part motivated by the conviction that the majority of Iraqis did not want a return of the Baathist army or would even oppose it actively. The argument that keeping at least part of the officers in service would help co-opt them into supporting the new system that the Americans were planning to establish was considered, but dropped because it was judged unfeasible given that the army had been 400,000 strong, suffered from a huge rank inflation (11,000 generals) and therefore only a small portion could satisfactorily kept on board. While much of this makes sense, American plans to start forming a new Iraqi army were naive: the idea was to recruit officers and NCOs selectively from the old army, as well as from the Kurdish and Shiite militias, and to deploy one division within a year and two more within the following year.[1]

The pace of development was relatively slow (given the availability of many trained recruits) because it was uncertain whether the new army would get involved in internal security and stabilisation; with the US army in place, external threats did not appear an immediate concern. Moreover, the insurgency had barely started in those days and nobody expected it to turn into a serious threat. It is also likely that the Americans might have been reluctant to field an Iraqi army before 're-educating' it to some extent. It would not be long before the occupation authorities had to reconsider. By 2006 the Iraqi security establishment was not far from the levels of personnel strength of early 2003, before Saddam Hussein's overthrow.[2]

Bremer's perception of what the Iraqi wanted with regard to the Baathist army is contested. Allawi argues that:

only in Kurdistan was the decision to dissolve the armed forces uniformly popular. The Shi'a had a more ambivalent attitude. A minority supported the dissolution of the army, but not along the lines that the Order implied. The Order basically postulated a tabula rasa upon which a new army, structured along modern, professional lines, would be built. It was implicit that the CPA, and by inference the Coalition, would model it along the lines that they saw fit. The new Iraqi army, which the Order said would be a self-defence force, was one that would be shorn of most of the offensive capabilities of a modern army. This was not the army that most of the Shi'a, especially the Islamists, wanted. The Shi'a aimed to remove the biases against themselves in the military institutions of the state, but not to diminish or eliminate the army's fighting capabilities. While the CPA (and presumably Washington) wanted a military force that would not pose a serious threat to its neighbours, and that would be kept small and dependent, Shi'a Islamists wanted a strong army, but only in the context of a state in which they would predominate. The Bremer Order therefore came as a shock to most Iraqis in terms of its sweep and implications.[3]

By disbanding the army, the provincial occupation authorities also raised questions over the future of Iraq as a unified country, particularly because:

General McKiernan, the top American military commander in Iraq, issued a disarmament order in May, which seemed to cover all groups and parties. But he pointedly exempted the Kurdish pesh merga forces from this order. The pesh merga had, in addition to their light weaponry, a sizeable arsenal of tanks and artillery. To the angry officers of the old Iraqi army, this seemed a deliberate attempt to create an imbalance in military capabilities between the centre in Baghdad and the Kurdish regions. Some talked darkly about the disarmament order being the harbinger of the dismemberment of the country.[4]

The Iraqi example illustrates how thinking of dealing with the status of the army in any country is never going to be a technical issue, but instead a deeply political one. As the repository of the monopoly of violence, the army is at the centre of the state and of the political settlement underpinning it. Eliminating it inevitably undermines the state itself. But if the army cannot be eliminated from the equation, how can it be dealt with? This is the topic of this chapter.

The Underlying Dilemmas

Effectiveness vs. Loyalty

The more threatening the security environment of a country is, the more likely it is that a regime will be keen to maintain efficient and capable armed forces. Practices like nepotism, to mention but one, imply high costs in terms of morale and commitment among the troops, and this is well understood within the military and by and large among politicians too. However, direct observation shows that even in the presence of a direct threat, the effectiveness of the armed forces is often not the primary concern of the ruler. Even in the presence of major conflicts, political leaders can be resilient against accepting meritocracy and professionalism as the only criteria for selecting the officer corps. Quite the contrary, the repository of the monopoly of violence (the army) is likely to continue being seen as an at least implicit source of threat. One often forgotten aspect of the famous Tillyan argument about the role of warfare in the development of unusually efficient states in Europe has to do with guaranteeing the loyalty of these armies to their rulers.

Examples of this abound. During the English Revolution, the House of Lords resisted the attempts by Fairfax to appoint officers on meritocratic grounds, on the ground that they were not Presbyterians.[5] During the French Revolution and specifically during its Jacobin phase the pressure to ensure the loyalty of the army at all costs led to massive purges: during 1792–9, 994 generals out of 1,378 were tried by the tribunals.[6] Maintaining control was a problem that even sophisticated bureaucratic systems have long been facing. In China, for example, the predominant attitude towards army commanders was 'divide and rule'. The system was geared towards preventing an internal threat and offering disincentives to the generals for rebelling.[7] Stalin's distrust of the Red Army's officer corps famously led to the bloodiest of all purges in the 1930s, which eliminated 15–30,000 officers out of 75–82,000.[8]

The Limits of Coalition-Making

The control over armed force, therefore, is not easily achieved even in the presence of relative political sophistication and coalition-making. The latter can be described as the formation of alliances among equal partners based on free will; this does not exclude the possibility of 'incentives' being offered to facilitate coalition-making. Over time, political leaders developed the expertise and experience to distribute rents and access to resources in such a way that elites would:

have little incentive to:

- mobilise or create promises of future rewards to factions of the military to instigate rebellion;
- mobilise and make promises of future rewards to groups within the population to take up arms against the state; or
- to make alliances with neighbouring states or insurgent movements to mount an armed challenge to the state.[9]

The problem is that coalition-making does not necessarily represent an effective answer to the concerns of rulers over the loyalty of their specialists in coercion. Even when based on a distribution of rents and resources, coalitions have an implicitly temporary character.

Historical experience clearly shows that simply relying on political alliances, even within the officer corps, is not sufficient to secure a regime. The Iraqi ruler, Qasim, allied himself to the Iraqi communists and the nationalists in the 1950s, in order to offset the strong influence of the pan-Arabists within the army (such as Nasserists and Baathists). However, he never created a sustainable network in the officer corps, based on patronage or on ideological, tribal, clan or regional belonging; for some time his divide and rule tactics managed to keep him in power, but eventually the Baathists unseated him.[10] Coalitions tend to be precarious because the perception of what is a fair deal might change over time, as are going to change the individuals and groups which are partners to the coalition. Divergences over the character of the coalition are bound to resurface periodically, with potentially disrupting and even explosive consequences. Moreover, the stress on coalition-making may still come at the expense of the effectiveness of the army, for example because of the need to satisfy allies by appointing cronies in positions of power, status and influence.

In sum, the combination of the political loyalty of their armed forces with a sufficient degree of military effectiveness has been a major headache for rulers throughout the ages. In order to examine the issue in greater depth, we have to identify with greater precision the points of friction between military effectiveness and political loyalty. Attempting to define military effectiveness, an author identified a number of causes and sources:[11]

- culture;
- social structure (cleavages, etc.);
- political and economic institutions;
- international factors;
- strategic assessment and coordination processes (among top political and military leaders);
- weapons and equipment procurement process;
- strategic command and control;
- intelligence and internal monitoring;
- officer selection, rotation and promotion procedures;
- tactical command and control;
- training and military education.

From this superficial listing it emerges already how some of these sources of military effectiveness (strategic command and control, officer selection, rotation and promotion, intelligence and internal monitoring) tend to be particularly at odds with the demands of coalition-making. This is true regardless of whether coalitions are inclusive or not. In contexts where the military commands high social status and a large portion of the resources of the state, thereby having successfully been incorporated in the political order, the incentive for the civilian wing of the ruling elite to contain or reduce the weight of the military grows inevitably; who can tell how much is enough in the division of the spoils? It is highly significant that when effectiveness appeared unachievable anyway, or was considered to be unnecessary due to favourable security conditions, rulers opted to prioritise political loyalty without hesitation.[12]

Solutions?

Making Concessions to the Ruled

Regimes which experienced constant military threats over extended periods of time could go as far as shaping society and the political system to meet their security needs, making major concessions to the ruled. Typically however this would not take so much the shape of coalition-building, but of unilateral decisions taken at the top, even if it usually implied social major concessions by the ruler. According to Gat, there is evidence to suggest that effective military systems bear some relationship with the social and political order of a society. Effective infantrymen regularly proved to be the winning factor in war, but to be effective they had to be motivated: free men fight better.

Subjugated and desolate peasants, who had no stake in social and political affairs and little interest in the fruits of fighting, universally made poor warriors.[13]

This view might be somewhat overblown, as freedom is not necessarily the only motivating factor for armies, but there is truth in it. A good example of the ineffectiveness of military systems based on infantry but decoupled from an inclusive political system is the Italian state of Etruria (VI-V century BCE): it used the same phalanx system as the Romans, but from a social standpoint the Etruscans were still a force of aristocratic warrior retinues. The Romans prospered while the Etruscans, who had likely once conquered Rome, declined.[14] Of course, the supreme form of political concession to the ruled are electoral, property and welfare entitlements (see below), but the range of historical solutions is huge. Sometimes there is actual evidence that creation of a class of freeholders was the deliberate result of a state policy and was linked to the desire for an effective military force. During the warring states period (c. 450–221 BC), the Ch'in state freed the peasants from their subservience to the aristocracy and granted private possession of their land. As a result, feudalism was crushed and huge state armies were created. Although Ch'in was extremely ruthless and despotic, it took special care to safeguard the class of small peasants, which they regarded as the economic and military backbone of the state. Although the later Han were the first to introduce conscription and a reserve system, during their rule land accumulation in large estates brought about a decline of the small peasantry, which in turn contributed to the decline of militia armies. Moreover, conscription was ill suited to control large territories, as troops would not be familiarised with their area of service and were likely to have low motivation. The trend was soon towards military professionals.[15]

These few examples notwithstanding, clearly surrendering entitlements to the ruled has never been the preferred option of rulers. Since antiquity, rulers have been trying hard to build armies that were not dependent on strong links to society to function. Aristocratic regimes in Europe proved reluctant to recruit infantry forces from among the lower classes, for fear that they would challenge their dominance, particularly after the Swiss had risen to eliminate their own aristocrats (in the fourteenth century). The initial solution to the dilemma was the hiring of mercenaries, but they proved expensive and not very effective after all.[16] In a sense, mercenaries, archers, chariots or horsemen were all surrogates employed with varying effectiveness by rulers who could not afford or did not want to allow a degree of freedom to their subjects.[17] These alternatives however were ultimately less effective than a motivated infantry. When autocratic and authoritarian regimes did draft large peasant armies, they had to make sure that these were under solid control.

These concerns were highlighted in the debate over non-conventional tactics. During the Napoleonic age, military professionals often discussed the use of guerrilla tactics, stimulated by the Spanish guerrilla war against the French. The Prussians were the keenest to learn some lessons and established a popular militia (*Landsturm*), which in the mind of some reformers should have used popular warfare tactics. However, the worry to avoid any potential disturbance of the status quo soon undermined the idea: the 'popular' struggle was to be strictly managed from above. The Russian army used it to a certain extent when harassing the French communication lines deep inside Russia in 1814, but typically they conceived guerrilla war merely as a tactic, to be used by regular army. There were serious concerns about what armed peasants would do after the expulsion of the French and isolated attempts by Russian officers to mobilise peasants were rejected. Almost 130 years later Stalin proved only moderately more inclined to mobilise 'partisans' against the invading German army: the Soviet partisan movement was mostly mobilised from above and subjected to the control of the NKVD.[18]

A particular option, which in some cases can seem at least in appearance to bypass the dilemma of effectiveness vs. loyalty, is perhaps conceptually the simplest: reliance on foreign military presence (French deployments in the former French colonies,[19] Afghanistan, Vietnam, etc.) or strong external support.[20] As I will elaborate later, there are important drawbacks associated with this option too (see chapter 6).

Military Professionalism

Professionalism is about the adoption of a code of conduct and of meritocratic criteria in the selection and promotion of personnel. Quinlivan argues that professionalisation can represent a defence against military coups, because more professionally skilled officers will understand better the risks involved in a coup, particularly in the presence of parallel military forces (see below). 'The very dependence of technically skilled officers on the creation of detailed plans and their coordination opens the conspirators to active measures by the security forces'.[21] This thesis might have some value, but ignores the constraints and pressures that the wider political environment can place on professional officers.

While it could be argued that in general highly professional military systems are more effective, they do not always respect civilian rulers. Huntington and others' argument, that professionalism prevents the involvement of the army in politics, is also contradicted by such notorious cases as Pakistan's and Turkey's multiple coups: both armies have a reputation of being highly professional. Indeed it has been argued that 'the promotion of a corporate spirit and professionalism might encourage a sense of self-importance among senior officers that inflates regime vulnerability to a coup'.[22] In Africa, some of the more professional armies like Senegal's and Botswana's are considered to be loyal, or at least have been so far.[23] However Ghana's, which is also considered one of the most professional African armies, twice carried out coups in the past.

The Ethiopian army was also considered a professional force when it conducted its 'revolution' in 1974–5. Indeed, in line with the examples of Portugal and Chad discussed above, it was exactly its professionalisation that placed it at odds with the patrimonial regime of Haile Selassie and his use of 'personal surveillance networks' to assure loyalty.

There was a growing gap between the military elite, who could secure personal advancement from the court, and the bulk of the lower-ranking officers and men in their ranks, who were increasingly frustrated by poor pay, inadequate barracks, promotion barriers and, above all, the unresponsiveness of their seniors and of the government to their grievances. The first major manifestation of military discontent was the failed coup attempt of 1960. This was organised by well-connected reformers in the elite Imperial Guard and the civilian bureaucracy, and aimed to reform rather than replace the imperial system. [...] The 1974 coup started with a series of barracks revolts by NCOs and junior officers in regional garrisons during January and February 1974.[24]

Even after the suppression of the 1960 coup, loyalist army units used the leverage they had gained to force the Emperor to concede repeated pay increases. The forced conscription of an important part of the officer corps from the ranks of the intelligentsia to bring in the needed highly educated human resources facilitated the spread of subversive ideas to the army. The sense of inadequacy of the imperial government extended to senior officers with aristocratic connections. It might be true that the more threatening military mutinies in Addis Ababa in 1974 were instigated by aristocratic elements, in an attempt to dislodge a prime minister whom they did not like. However, it rapidly emerged that the regime was powerless when faced with military dissent.[25]

This was also the case of the Iraqi monarchy, under which many officers started drifting towards Arab nationalist movements,[26] or of the Afghan one, where the frustrated officers gradually radicalised and allied with left-wing groups.[27] This aspect of professionalism derives or is strengthened by the fact that 'in the developing world, the military establishment has an enunciated commitment to managed and contrived socio-political change, in contrast with the conservative essence of western military institutions'. Since 'at the root of military ideology is the acceptance of collective public enterprise as a basis for achieving social, political and economic change', leftist ideas could often sound attractive. The new professional armies were already attracting 'the ambitious and the visionary', who believed that 'in the long run it would supply the opportunity for liberating and modernising their homeland'.[28] The extent to which political patronage and loyalty-building can constrain the military effectiveness of an army is illustrated by the performance of the Ottoman army in the First World War, which greatly surprised its enemies; Enver Pasha moved swiftly in early 1914 to replace many ineffective senior officers with younger and tested ones.[29]

Not all patrimonial regimes have been wiped out by the wave of professionalisation of their armed forces, much depending on the skills and abilities of the rulers. The Kingdom of Jordan represents such an exception, as the monarchy managed to build an effective and professional army, which by all accounts has remained stubbornly loyal to the King. There are different accounts of how this loyalty was maintained throughout Jordan's struggles. Most authors stress the predominant Bedouin character of the army, but few have been able to analyse what impact the introduction of conscription in 1976 might have had in the long run, as the army gradually came to represent society more closely at the various levels of its hierarchy. By the 1980s, the Bedouins were still largely dominant among the higher ranks and among the officers leading the combat units, with Palestinians having mainly made inroads in logistics and other support and technical services. Lawrence Tal believes that such loyalty can be explained simply by the army's defence of its vested interests: good pay, excellent benefits, prestigious position in society.

Another factor, highlighted by Haim Gerber, relates to the heavy and long influence of British trainers, which by promoting a more egalitarian, non-class based force which would have prevented the army from being affected by the same destructive class struggle which characterised the armies of its Arab neighbours.[30] Finally King Abdullah served in the army when he was a prince and is widely seen as a 'real soldier', a fact that strengthened his legitimacy within the officer corps.[31] In any case there was significant turmoil within the Jordanian army, mainly having to do with the rivalries of tribal networks, but also with the influence of Arab nationalism. The King succeeded in navigating these rivalries and in using them to stay afloat, at the same time also playing external actors off against each other.[32] The personal skills of the Jordanian kings do not mean, however, that the monarchy did not come under serious stress in the 1950s and 1960s.

A key aspect of why professional armies can end up representing a political liability to rulers is that they behave like other institutions do: they are not loyal to an individual or group thereof but to abstract principles and rules. If they become disloyal, they are generally motivated by a perceived betrayal of the ruler: see the already mentioned examples of Jerry Rawlings in Ghana, the Ethiopian army, the Portuguese army, etc. The Syrian army experienced serious friction during Damascus' intervention in Lebanon against the PLO in the mid-1970s, because many officers saw that as a betrayal of the Baath's proclaimed Arab nationalism.[33] This type of friction usually starts within the army itself, taking often the character of generational conflict, pitting the elite of experienced but poorly educated high rank officers against the emerging new generation of inexperienced, but professionally prepared junior officers. A deficient system of promotion and career development can also contribute to the frustration of part of the officer corps and to the creation of politicised factions.[34]

Moreover, the transition towards professionalisation from a patrimonial or in any case non-meritocratic system can, per se, be problematic. In Nigeria already in the 1950s the British started to accept growing numbers of indigenous officers mainly from the educated urban classes, but this intensified ethnic rivalry between Ibo officers from the south and soldiers from the north.[35] Access to education and alternative professional avenues is rarely going to be evenly distributed across the territory of a country, and trying to mobilise the educated class into the army can result in regional, sectarian or ethnic imbalances.

In sum, military professionalism is not suitable to all types of political regimes. Discussing US-led attempts to reform the Liberian military, one author remarked that President Doe did not want it to succeed because of the threat that it would have posed to him. 'He supported military training programs for the opportunity and leverage they gave him with the United States', but he 'was leery of the results'.

Just as Doe was afraid of education because of the inherent threat an informed citizenry posed to his reign, so too he was afraid of an effective and competent military. [...] In his view, once competence was achieved, the military leaders (or students) would be a threat to his power.[36]

Rarely have rulers embraced military professionalism enthusiastically, and the attempt to limit its impact has often backfired badly. Finally, professionalism is extremely costly, as it implies the absorption of large numbers of educated and skilled personnel. Even in the absence of full bureaucratisation, professional recruitment requires the development of a sophisticated structure to manage it. Hence, even when in principle inclined to favour professionalisation, rulers might not be able to achieve it, at least not in the medium and short term. Indeed, in Finer's terms the cost of building an armed force could be placed on a par with effectiveness and loyalty as one of the dilemmas of army-building.[37] The example mentioned above about Selassie of Ethiopia was not isolated. As repositories of the monopoly of force, professional armies were regularly able to impose higher salaries, creating spiralling costs and kicking off the decline of imperial polities.[38]

Tying Army to Society: The Virtuous Version

Governments have tried a whole range of solutions to keep their militaries under control, of which tying military to society or structuring the political system accordingly have been argued to be the most effective ways, as we have seen.[39] It must be considered that there are virtuous and not-so-virtuous ways of tying army and society; the virtuous one is to facilitate interaction between army and society as a whole, recruit beyond a narrow group of families with a military tradition, expose the army to the influence of civilians, facilitate army involvement in civilian politics, as well as in livelihood and public works. The not-so-virtuous one is described below. Often the solution recommended by the scholars is 'professionalism'. There are methodological problems with the approach of many scholars, as professionalisation is often defined as including political neutrality. Since loyalty to the rulers is built into the definition, the hypothesis of professionalisation leading to loyalty is self-demonstrating. If we (more reasonably) define professionalism simply as the adoption of a code of conduct and of meritocratic criteria in the selection and promotion of personnel, the picture is more confused. It is worth pointing out that professionalisation does not coincide with the wider process of bureaucratisation (see below); in particular, the element of supervision is notably absent. I shall return to this point later.

A more substantive concern is that tying the army to civil society can only work when regimes themselves have popular support; otherwise exposing armies to society can be very dangerous and have the opposite effect of compromising the loyalty of the army. Subversive ideas can spread very rapidly in coercive environments like an army, particularly in the presence of frustration within the ranks. This point highlights the naivety of some SSR efforts, where autocratic regimes are expected willingly to undergo reform. As a result some rulers might actually not want to tie their armies to society, because their own relationship with the ruled is far from smooth. Janowitz himself pointed out that 'the military establishment cannot be controlled and still remain effective by civilianising it' because 'despite the growth of the logistical dimension of warfare, the professional soldier remains a military commander'. Particularly in relatively unsophisticated and low-technology armies, tying to civil society is problematic because what Janowitz called 'heroic leaders' remain predominant and their importance has not been reduced by the strengthening of the roles of 'military managers' and 'military technologists'.[40]

An alternative strategy which eliminates the risk of excessive fraternisation between army and society involves increasing non-military support for the ruler by cultivating social, economic and religious groups, keeping the army aside. This is for example the case of Asad of Syria's controlled liberalisation after 1970, but it could only work because Asad had significant support within the army itself.[41]

Institutionalisation

Although professionalisation does not coincide with institutionalisation, the two processes are related as enforcing meritocratic criteria requires a strong institutional environment. Institutionalisation therefore either has to precede professionalisation or proceed in parallel to it. This is easier said than done. While there seem, to be an assumption in much policy debate that institutionalisation is, per se, positive and therefore desirable by everybody, in reality rulers might get caught in what Joel Migdal described as the 'dilemma of state-building': domestic and international dangers can be met through building agencies of the state, but this holds its own perils for state leaders. Agencies of the state such as the army may themselves pose threats to state leaders who still have only limited ability to marshal widespread public support, hence agency manipulation and even recourse to weakening the same state agencies. In particular, leaders of new states in the post-colonial age quickly learned their lessons and often started viewing the state bureaucracies they were creating or developing as 'Frankensteins' which ought to be weakened.[42]

The existence of external threats (real or perceived) could force rulers to promote the professionalism of their own army, but not without trying to counter-balance it with patrimonial strategies of containment. In practice, what we observe on the ground is a variety of attempts to combine political tactics of loyalty-building and a degree of meritocracy in the policy of appointments. In Sandinista Nicaragua the Minister of Defence, Humberto Ortega, was deeply irritated by the demands of his own brother, Daniel Ortega, and other dignitaries of the regime who were trying to protect their own sons from serving in dangerous areas. Humberto himself would use sinecures and personal favours to cultivate the loyalty of his officers, making clear that any career advancement they achieved was due to him, although keeping capabilities into account too.[43] Ortega managed to combine the two aspects of his activity quite well and always maintained a solid control over the army and a solid relationship with the rest of the Sandinista political leadership. However, it is clear that the combination of patrimonial or class-based appointment systems with elements of professionalism is a potentially explosive mix, which can easily lead to the professional officers rapidly developing the sense of being trapped by a glass ceiling and of not being able to obtain the career advancements that they deserve. From there to developing distaste for their privileged but less educated and skilled colleagues and the regime that protects them, the way is short.[44]

Such strategies did not always work. Portuguese dictator Salazar managed to turn his army into an effective counter-insurgency tool, but his efforts to restrain the political influence of the professional officers eventually backfired.[45] The Portuguese army under Salazar had been very inefficient and badly organised in the early years of the conflict; its 'successes' against its Angolan and Mozambican opponents were the result of the enemy's weakness rather than of its own strength. In Guinea, where the rebels were better led, the Portuguese were rapidly cornered. Here a capable commander like Brigadier Spinola managed to recover ground from the late 1960s onwards, adopting new military, intelligence and political tactics. But the unwillingness of the regime to follow Spinola's inclination to negotiate a settlement from a position of relative strength not only led to a new deterioration in Guinea, but also to the radicalisation of opposition to Salazar's rule in the army.[46] The army had already been humiliated by Salazar's attempt to scapegoat it for the loss of Goa to India in 1961, and the nationalist feelings of the officers were offended by the economic decline of the country, oppressed by the excessive military commitments in Africa.[47]

On a parallel path in 1970s Chad, the army which the French had revamped, trained and enlarged to confront the threat of the FROLINAT insurgency became the object of President Tombalbaye's fears and worries. His attempt to play divide and rule tactics among the senior officers, promoting some and arresting others, did not suffice to prevent the military coup in 1975.[48]

Bureaucratisation

The consequences of the uncertain relationship between military and political power described at the beginning of this chapter can be summed up as the inefficiencies deriving from 'fear of failure, authoritarian attitudes and political instability, all contribut[ing] to organizational systems in which vast numbers of decisions are routinely bucked up to scant numbers of top leaders'.[49] As it has been said of the contemporary Middle East, when 'political and military leaders compete for control of military affairs', making a strategic assessment is likely to be problematic:

Protective of their access to information, military leaders will share the information only selectively with the political leader. In contrast, when a political leader is firmly in control, these competitive pressures on processes and structures for strategic assessment are dampened. When leaders at the apex are competing with one another, they have strong incentives to ensure that checks and balances are included in the chain of command to allow them influence over military activity. The result is likely to be convoluted structures, which tend to undermine the integrity of command and control,

as well as a greater emphasis on the political reliability of appointments.[50]
Starting from Western Europe, greater loyalty and control were gradually developed through a whole series of 'new' tools:

- the technique of drilling;
- creation of smaller and smaller units in order to foster primary ties among the troops;
- using food in armies as a generator of reciprocation-based dependencies that could be used to elicit a certain degree of desired behaviour;
- decorations, monetary rewards, differential access to spoils and captured women all used to encourage bravery;
- fostering the aura of military life for the peasantry;
- monetary incentives to officers and privileged access to luxury goods, standards of life higher than in civilian administration jobs;[51]
- and most of all the development of a bureaucratic apparatus (after the Thirty Years War, initially using sub-contracting to local dignitaries);[52]
- more recently, development of civilian oversight through the establishment of strong institutions; it should be noted that this 'tool' would not have been compatible with the patrimonial regimes that were characteristic of most of Europe until the twentieth century.[53]

Old tools like coercion still maintained their paramount importance: 'fear their officers more than the perils to which they are exposed' (Frederick the

Great).[54] Wellington's troops were still poorly motivated and desertion rates were high.[55] The lasting importance of coercion is best seen in those armies which suddenly experience the removal of the coercive element, either because of a politically twisted chain of command or because an attempt to replace at least in part coercion with different incentives. The post-Saddam Iraqi army is a case in point: putting it back together proved quite difficult.[56]

In the long run, however, it was the bureaucratisation of armies that made a huge difference. In the specific European context at least, this development was associated with the professionalisation of the officer corps.[57] Exactly as institutions were developed which were meant to stabilise coalitions and political systems, by making transition, succession and change more predictable or in any case more tolerable with regard strictly to the monopoly of large-scale violence, these states developed increasingly sophisticated systems of bureaucratic control and management over their armed forces. Compared to other aspects of the bureaucratisation of the state, armies pose particular problems. Kiser and Baer list them as follows:

1. it is more difficult to measure their 'output';
2. they are more mobile and more distant, often on foreign soil;
3. they have very strong incentives for non-compliance (avoiding death).

As a result:

these factors make monitoring very difficult. The key monitoring problem is in the relationship between the high command and the troops in the field. [...] Local monitoring will be essential because central monitoring will be ineffective. Centralized monitoring is not as important a factor in the military as it is in tax administration. Because of the difficulty and importance of monitoring, it is clear that highly motivated agents are even more essential in the military than in tax administration.[58]

Janowitz's identification of 'heroic leaders' as a key component of the officer corps of developing armies springs to mind again here.[59]

This meant historically that striking a balance between supervision and centralisation on one side and sufficient freedom of initiative on the other was never easy. I should add that although as an ideal type bureaucratisation is opposed to most of the techniques described above (but not to the manipulation of the security architecture), in practice some overlap often occurs. Regimes which cannot fully trust their own armies or which lack human resources to staff the officer corps adequately down to the lower levels are usually inclined to over-centralise and to limit as much as possible the autonomy of the lower ranks. In the Egyptian army, for example, 'each level has to query its superiors before approving an initiative, which tends to create a stiff and unresponsive command', resulting in very serious damage to its effectiveness in the battlefield. The same could be said of the Iraqi army, whose failures in the early 1980s have been attributed to over-centralisation of control in Saddam's hands; the army failed to exploit the opportunities which arose out of the initial surprise against the Iranians. Saddam's habit of punishing outspoken and successful commanders as well as incompetent ones further depressed any inclination to think or act independently.[60]

Although many aspects of bureaucracy in armies developed during the military revolution in Europe in the late sixteenth and seventeenth centuries,[61] some aspects of bureaucratic organization date as far back as the Assyrians in 1000BC.[62] The most developed example of early 'bureaucratic state' was of course the Chinese empire, the first state known to have introduced conscription under the Han.[63] In Europe the process of consolidating the monopoly of violence through the establishment of a bureaucratic system knew highs and lows. After the early success of the Romans, it took many centuries before 'bureaucratic solutions' were adopted again. Sub-contracting and tax farming were common options in Europe in the modern age. Only gradually, when attempting to develop more highly organised armies, were states forced to 'shift to a bureaucratic organization based on hierarchical monitoring and relatively weak incentives', featuring fixed salaries and dismissal for non-compliance. In this case motivation had initially to be provided to a much greater extent through coercion (such as shooting soldiers who deserted or failed to obey orders), but from the sixteenth century, armies started developing also 'non-instrumental motivations' such as the fostering of esprit de corps through repeated drills and the division of troops into smaller units to stimulate the creation of 'primary personal ties'. The same mechanism was identified by Durkheim in tribal religions: repeated participation in collective rituals creates a strong sense of group solidarity.[64]

The emotional resonance of daily and prolonged close-order drill created such a level of esprit de corps [...] that other social ties faded to insignificance.[65]

Political Commissars

A particular type of bureaucratised command and control which developed specifically in polities that drew inspiration from the Soviet model was the already mentioned 'political commissar'. The concept of 'political commissar' is an invention of the French Revolutionaries, who in fact introduced from 1791 two distinct figures: 'representatives on mission' and 'commissars', the former appointed by the political authorities and the latter by the Ministry of War. Their main task was to ensure the political reliability of the army, as well as to help maintain and improve the morale of the army. Friction between these two categories of commissars and the officers was often high; representatives on mission and 'commissars' often did not like each other too much either. The defection to the Austrians of General Dumouriez (the victor of Valmy) in April 1793 highlighted the continuing issue of political reliability in the army. It did not take long before the Committee on Public Health decided to take full control of the army and dismantle the Ministry of War; the Jacobins reduced the powers of the 'commissars' but did not touch the 'representatives on mission',[66] who were mostly Jacobins. The Jacobins succeeded in motivating the army to fight, but political interference and continuous purges gradually destroyed the fighting ability of the army. The 'representatives on mission' started losing power during Thermidor and eventually seem to have disappeared under Napoleon, who had sufficient confidence in the loyalty of the officers to his person not to need commissars of any kind.[67]

The conflict between former Tsarist officers ('military specialists') and political commissars and their respective supporters in the early years of Bolshevik power perfectly embodied the dilemma of combining loyalty and effectiveness, on which I focused in the first paragraph of this chapter. Bolshevik cadres used to accuse former Tsarist officers of disloyalty and the majority of the party definitely disliked them, but the political leadership and in particular Trotsky and Lenin were aware that the so-called 'military specialists' were badly needed if the army was to achieve victory on the battlefield. The massive expansion of the Red Army to 5 million men also demanded similarly huge numbers of officers to lead it, and the new Soviet power did not have the resources or the time to train a new class of loyal, indoctrinated officers. Lenin and Trotsky had to struggle to impose their views on a reluctant party and a number of compromise measures were taken, such as the screening of the 'specialists' and the creation of 'political commissars', an idea borrowed from their French predecessors despite a number of innovations. All military orders were supposed to be signed by both commissars and commanding officers, so that commanding officers were under close supervision all the time. The double chain of command evidently compromised military efficiency, not least because the commissars were *de facto* above the commanders in terms of power. Already by the end of 1919 the issue was being raised in some quarters of allowing commanding officers of proven loyalty to operate without the supervision of political commissars, the more so since the ranks of the party organisations in the army were growing and could play a monitoring role themselves. From 1922, the role of the commissars started effectively being reduced, initially marginally and then more substantially, as the Bolshevik-Communists grew more confident of the loyalty of the new class of officers being gradually created.[68]

However, following the Great Purges, the dual structure of command was re-established in 1937, as Stalin remained fearful of an army revolt. Stalin seems to have valued the disruption of the chain of command of the army as a way to prevent it from acting as a cohesive unit against him. However, the 'military commissars', as they were now called, had no longer any authority over the commanding officers. They were abolished again in 1940, as Stalin believed he had consolidated his control over the army, but they were once again reintroduced immediately after the German invasion. The military commissars were definitively eliminated in October 1942, as the Red Army started functioning smoothly and gaining confidence, and most importantly the party organisation within the army had been playing a growing role in terms of political socialisation and of ensuring the loyalty of the army; at this point it took over from the commissars. By the second half of 1941, there were 250,000 political workers in the Red Army. The system of political officers working through the party organisation remained the key tool for political control of the army after the Second World War, and it was constantly strengthened. According to Herspring, such was the importance of political organisations in the army, that 'in 1989 Soviet military leaders pleaded with the country's political leadership to keep them' in the military, because 'they served as unifying devices at a time when little else was left to hold the armed forces together'.[69]

However, the political workers in the army gradually lost their ability to guarantee the loyalty of the armed forces to the ruling party, by becoming an integral part of the army, with career paths merging, exchanges of personnel occurring and extensive personal contact with the commanding officers (see also chapter 5 on the 'rules' of bureaucratic functioning).[70]

Although complaints about the political commissars were still common during the Second World War and might in general be said not to be conducive to the optimum of military effectiveness, on the whole the system appears to have been remarkably successful in combining a degree of effectiveness with extreme political reliability in political structures which were neither inclusive nor based on 'free' fighters. Of course, adopting this system was not an option at everybody's disposal. Without a genuine mass political party geared towards the production of cadres, the system could not exist. Hence the costs (political and otherwise) of establishing such a system were considerable if not huge.[71]

The system was adopted wholeheartedly by communist regimes,[72] but few non-communist states managed to imitate it effectively, and when they succeeded they had to adopt many of the features of the Soviet-style party state. The Iraqi dictator Saddam Hussein was one of these few successful imitators. In his words, 'with party methods there is no chance for anyone who disagrees with us to jump on a couple of tanks and overthrown government'.[73] By 1970 3,000 Baathists had been granted military ranks, after intensive courses in the military college; they allowed the creation of a network of political commissars in the army. A Military Bureau was established to manage the commissars: one of its main tasks was guarding against a coup. As an Iraqi historian pointed out, 'the Baathists under Saddam Hussein managed to do what no party had done in Iraq's history: it brought the military under civilian control'.[74]

Nationalism

Bureaucratisation was not the last development in the process of building ever more effective and loyal armies. The introduction of mass mobilisation towards the end of the nineteenth century has been linked to the parallel changes in the organisation of politics. It has been argued that, in a sense, with citizen conscription states lost their monopoly over war making and had to surrender portions of power to ordinary people.[75] This process combined the expansion of urban agglomerations which:

made communication and political organization easy and effective. [...] [A]ristocratic retinues' power was rolled back, serfdom and other traditional forms of bondage were replaced by obligations of tax payment and military service, autonomous city institutions were built up...[76]

Mass armies also meant mass demobilisation processes after the war, which had important political implication in terms of the attitudes of ruling elites towards the population.[77] A linked process was the emergence of nationalist sentiments. Although symbols were widely used to motivate soldiers even before the appearance of nationalism, their impact in increasing their willingness to risk their lives was limited until they started being employed more widely throughout society, particularly in the educational process. The Hollywood-driven image of (enemy) nationalist combatants as mindless automatons willing to die but unable to adapt and innovate is not confirmed by such disparate examples as the *Wehrmacht*, the Israeli army and the North Vietnamese army. The ability to innovate and adapt seems to be related to the education and skills of the officer corps, which are not necessarily compromised by nationalist indoctrination; Pollack suggests in his study that Arab armies after World War II had more than sufficient will to stand and fight, but poor tactical leadership and limited technical skills.[78] Moreover, different kinds of nationalism might have a different impact. Extreme nationalism could also have the counter-productive effect of increasing the willingness of the adversary to fight to the last man; this was the Japanese and German case during World War II, as their enemies were pushed towards bitter resistance.[79]

Other benefits of nationalist indoctrination included an institutionalising impact: soldiers became as a result less inclined to follow their commanders regardless. When Dumouriez revolted against the Convention in 1793 and tried to march on Paris, his troops refused to follow and he was forced to flee to the Austrian army.[80] However, indoctrination (nationalist or otherwise) can only be credibly implemented by a regime with strong ideological credentials; moreover it is a long-term strategy with little short-term impact.[81]

Manipulative Techniques

If in the real world professionalisation and tying armies to civil society are often not viable options, as hinted above, political leaders and rulers obviously have nonetheless shown some ability to learn from past experiences and mistakes and gradually learned how to protect themselves from their own armies. The most obvious way to insulate a political system from the threat of a military coup or conspiracy is of course reliance on the secret police. This will be discussed in detail in chapter 4, but for the moment suffice it to say that complete insulation from an internal threat through policing can be very difficult and very costly, as shown by the case of Venice, which turned into a sort of totalitarian state in order to prevent coups.[82] This is why rulers often have made recourse to a variety of alternative techniques, which Quinlivan and others have categorised as coup-proofing, that is a set of techniques and organisational developments which are aimed at preventing military coups.[83] Sometimes these techniques achieved a relatively high degree of effectiveness. Many such practices in use today were introduced by the colonial powers and then inherited by post-colonial governments.[84]

Among these techniques, the manipulation of news and history in order to build an image of unblemished heroism for the army and therefore boost morale, has been in use since time immemorial.[85] Executions and corporal punishment for those who caused trouble are another old classic.[86] However, not in every context is it possible to enforce discipline by fear or coercion. In the Middle East, where tribalism still predominates as in Saudi Arabia, 'the

innate egalitarianism of the society mitigates against fear as the prime motivator, so a general lack of discipline pervades'.[87] Purging the officer corps, in
order to 'remove undesirables and demonstrate the regime's power and authority' and deter challenges, has also been practised for a long time and maintained in popularity in the twentieth century and beyond.[88] Typically, new
regimes would proceed to cleanse the army of clients of rivals and former rulers. In Uganda, Obote played off police against army and removed from
operational control officers who were politically unreliable or too authorita-
tive.[89] Of course all this has very negative repercussions on the effectiveness
of the army, particularly when it has previously achieved a degree of professionalism and skill.

The raising of indoctrinated slave armies (like the Mamluks, 'raised in barracks and infused with Islamic zeal, they became a fierce fighting force'),[90] has
not entirely fallen out of fashion if we consider the abduction of young children, who are then socialised as professionals of violence.[91] While this practice
is common in insurgent armies, it has not been recently reported in state militaries as far as I am aware.

Economic Strategies

A somewhat more sophisticated approach is ensuring the loyalty of army officers by granting them the *de facto* right to collect tax. The advantage of this
solution is that it can function in the presence of 'a non-bureaucratic organization', but the drawback is the low central control of military activities. The
feudalisation of the army was an ancestor to this solution; as Machiavelli
pointed out, centralisation is not always good, because once the central state
machinery falls, nothing else is left to oppose resistance.[92] Hence feudalisation
and the devolution of taxation rights can sometimes look attractive options
because of their intrinsic resilience. One example is that of Byzantium, where
the ruler deliberately opted to combine the existing strong urban tradition and
central state authority with feudalism. Because of its developed economic and
administrative structure, Byzantium was successful in keeping the feudal system in check.[93] A more modern version of this solution is the provision of
'corporate and private benefits' such as high budget allocations, high salaries
and privileged access to goods and services to army officers.[94] While offering
a higher degree of control to the ruling elite, this version is exposed to the danger of financial overstretching and the consequent need to downsize and cut
salaries.[95] Yet another version of the same solution consists in the permission

to become active in the economy of the country, usually with some monopoly privilege and forms of semi-tolerated corruption.[96]

To the chagrin of political economists, economic appeasement has not been particularly effective, as the example of the Pakistani army and its many coups suggests.

Divide and rule

The most readily available strategy for combining a degree of both effectiveness and loyalty has long been divide and rule. Keeping the army divided and making sure that at least part of it is effective can be achieved in a number of ways. As already mentioned, the employment of mercenaries from communities which were ferociously warlike, or skilled in the use of particular weapons, or from abroad was a solution widely used in the past and in the colonial era; it has been occasionally used in the contemporary era too, as in the case of the guards in Sierra Leone (Guineans and Palestinians) and in Uganda under Amin (Palestinians, Sudanese and Zaireans).[97] The same can be said of the recruitment of unpopular minorities from within the boundaries of the country, who would then be unable to revolt against the political authorities.[98] Another way of preventing a coup is to appoint commanding officers from despised or weak communities (as in the case of Siad Barre in Somalia).[99]

Another factor militating against expanding armies as a coup-proofing measure is the consideration that while coups might become more problematic to organise in a large army, maintaining full political control also becomes more difficult for the ruler, particularly if such control has to be maintained through a patrimonial system based on personal relations. Very common practices are:

- the periodical rotation of commanding officers, in order to prevent the formation of opposition factions and the development of personal power bases;[100]
- the strategic deployment of military units in such a way that those considered most loyal will be closer to the capital and/or have freedom of movement and relocation;
- the dispersion of units in order to make communication difficult among them.[101]

The habit of many regimes of discouraging communication among high rank officers, which is meant to make plotting more difficult, has obvious negative effects on coordination, unit integration, learning and improving the structures and practices.[102]

Organisational Strategies

A number of organisational strategies have also been tried. An army may be kept under control if the size remains small and it is staffed mostly or exclusively with loyalists. One example is that of Siaka Stevens in Sierra Leone (1971–85), who pursued a policy of restricting the size of the army to just 2,000 men, selected mainly from among his loyalists. This strategy has the benefit of being inexpensive, but of course is dependent on the absence of a major external threat. If a threat to the ruler then emerges, expanding the army quickly might become necessary, but fraught with difficulties. In the absence of a developed and refined recruitment system, the expansion of the Sierra Leonean army from 1992 onwards to over 6,000 and then to over 14,000 was done incorporating low quality manpower such as criminals, drop-outs, etc., further reducing its effectiveness and compromising its loyalty.[103]

Alternatively, an army may be blown up to a very large size, even in the absence of the ability to equip and train it appropriately, in order to prevent plotters from building a network sufficiently large to reach the critical mass needed to stage a successful coup.[104] This is a costly option and it is not clear whether preventing coups has ever been a key factor in leading to massive army expansion programmes. There is also a strong counter-indication that the expansion of the size of an army can compromise its effectiveness.[105] The huge expansion of the South Vietnamese army thanks to US support could not be matched by the training of sufficient numbers of officers to match it. Moreover, the military build-up on the eve of the American withdrawal undermined the South Vietnamese economy and accelerated inflation, eroding the purchasing value of military salaries.[106] Several other cases are known:

- the Colombian army from the 1990s onwards, when the huge expansion of its size led to an unprecedented shortage of officers, inadequate logistics and declining motivation;[107]
- the Afghan army trained after 2001;[108]
- the very rapid expansion of the Ethiopian army (a 1,300 per cent rise) from the mid 1970s to the late 1980s: social cohesion, development of officers, training and discipline were all compromised.[109]

Appointment Strategies

In order to prevent coups, the South Vietnamese government (particularly President Diem) splintered the military command system and promoted loyal incompetents. Divisions even rarely trained together, in order to keep the army as divided as possible; chains of command were duplicated and different agencies kept physically separate in order to slow decision-making and action-taking. Diem himself often issued direct orders to battalion commanders. The effectiveness of the South Vietnamese army in the field was affected very negatively; the situation got to the point where reports of military successes were manufactured to please the President and 'protect the reputation of the commanders involved'. Units were not committed to the fight because Diem had tasked their commanders to keep most of their forces in reserve and act as a counter-coup force, using rival generals to keep each other in check. Of course, all these efforts were ultimately in vain as Diem was the target of two separate coup attempts, of which the second was successful, but arguably delayed his fall.[110]

One of the most widely used divide and rule coup-proofing measures is establishing networks of personal loyalty among the officer corps. One particular version of this is the reliance on kinship ties.[111] In Sierra Leone the process of shifting away from professional criteria in recruitment and towards nepotism and political favouritism started under Siaka Stevens. The costs were soon to become obvious: when war actually reached Sierra Leone in the 1990s, the army was led by inexperienced officers, lacked ammunition, boots, uniforms, medical care, field kitchens and radios, weapons were rusty, etc.

In Nigeria this kind of favouritism soon led to a situation where there was little difference in age and experience between officers at the upper and lower levels of the hierarchy, resulting in a rapid weakening of hierarchies. Rapid non-meritocratic promotions prevented the adequate education of officers. Military rule further worsened the situation and had strong corrupting effects on the professionalism of the army, with many resignations of professional officers. In some cases the process reached extreme proportions, as in Uganda under Amin, when labourers, drivers and bodyguards became high-ranking officers, or in Equatorial Guinea. More generally, the widespread corruption of the appointment policy in almost all African armies inevitably reverberated on procurement policies too, with devastating effects. Soon the Nigerian army was even suspected of 'having shaped its military requirements in terms of equipment according to the opportunity for bribing, favouring heavy equipment and refusing aid programs which did not offer chances for corruption, including riverine training to secure the oil-rich delta'. By 1985, ships could not communicate to each other and the air force could not communicate to ground troops. Nigeria was not alone in facing the problems arising from indiscriminate patronage. By 1997 only seven of forty-six sub-Saharan Africa militaries were capable of deploying without significant augmentation a single battalion; only 9 states had a strong officers corps and 6 were able to perform engineering tasks; none was capable of sustained transportation of personnel. The Zambian army, for example, never did an exercise or tried to assess its capabilities *vis-à-vis* neighbouring countries.[112]

A personal relationship between the ruler and the officers can only work in practice in a small army; when the officers start numbering in the thousands it becomes unviable. In such cases an option can be entrenching a limited number of officers of proven loyalty in positions of power and keeping them there, allowing them to consolidate their power; usually this required that the officers be personally linked to the ruler(s) and at the same time be members of small and unpopular minorities.[113] This is the case in Saudi Arabia too, where privilege is accorded to 'royal family members' and 'others have close ties by marriage and other relationships. As a result, many important skills such as leadership, creativity, and knowledge of military affairs are in short supply.'[114]

Ethnic Favouritism

When even kinship cannot provide the required numbers, ethnic recruitment can also work as a coup-proofing technique; Horowitz describes how Kenyatta appointed Kikuyus to key positions and sacked Luo officers. In contemporary Africa, the practice of ethnic recruitment seems to have been quite common; the only army which during the 1970s seemed to be moving towards a balanced ethnic composition was Ghana's.[115] Obvious cases of ethnic recruitment were Burundi and Ethiopia, even if, at least in the case of the latter, with an eye to merit as well. Sectarian groups can fulfil the same role. In the Republic of (South) Vietnam officers were usually urban Catholics and the enlisted men rural Buddhists. Officers mistreated their men, who were conscripted for life, and 30 per cent deserted every year.[116] Another example of the negative impact of ethnically or tribally biased recruitment on army effectiveness is demonstrated by Saddam Hussein's Iraq.[117] While certainly not without some positive impact on the loyalty of the army, ethnic discrimination can be described as a form of inefficiency as 'it constrains the talent recruitment pool',[118] the more so in societies where skilled human resources are already in limited supply due to lack of education or insufficient mobilisation.

Another coup-proofing technique described by Horowitz is mixing officers of different ethnic and communitarian backgrounds, so that conspiracies can more easily be detected as they denounce each other or in any case are wary of cooperating; although not easy to establish in the first place (it could easily trigger coups if pushed too hard), such practice seems to have worked well in a number of 'civilian autocracies' like Guinea (under Sékou Touré), Kenya and Zambia, at least as far as the army was concerned. The tendency in the early post-colonial era was to slide towards greater and greater reliance on ethnically based coup-proofing techniques, as doubts over the loyalty of army officers grew stronger: it might be taken as an indication of at least some effectiveness.[119]

Manipulating the Security Architecture

All the coup-proofing techniques examined so far damage the military effectiveness of the army to a large if varying extent. A solution which might allow combining loyalty and effectiveness to a greater degree is the creation of parallel security forces ('counter-balancing forces').[120] In practice, this means that the 'security architecture' of the armed forces is tampered with, according to a rationale which is not so much military as political. Examples include Nkrumah's President Own Guard Regiment; Stevens' Special Security division; Obote and his two paramilitary forces; Iraq's National Guard and Popular Militias; Saudi Arabia's National Guard;[121] the Yemeni popular militia of Hafez Ismail;[122] Syria's many military establishments, and many others. Typically this takes the shape of the creation of a national guard or of its expansion, or the strengthening and up-arming of a gendarmerie, or again the creation of fighting units within the security services, the creation of a strong and heavily armed border force or of popular militias.[123]

It can however also take the shape of 'perverting' the original purpose of existing forces, as in the case of Diem's Special Forces, which instead of leading the counter-insurgency effort functioned as a palace guard and were staffed by untrained and incompetent loyalists.[124] In many cases, tampering with the security architecture clearly saved rulers from elimination: Afghanistan (1990)[125] and Kenya (1982) are two examples. Saddam Hussein is another one: in 1992 and 1996 the Special National Guard defeated coup attempts by the National Guard, whose officers had become increasingly critical of Saddam Hussein during the war with Iran. Although parallel military forces might not always be able to prevent successful coups by the regular army (as in the case of Madagascar 1972 and Congo Brazzaville 1968), they might have a deterrent effect as the post-coup stabilisation would appear too risky.[126] It is worth noting that paramilitary force, while not matching the power of armies, can be created quickly and staffed arbitrarily much more easily than an army where some professional requirements will continue to exist even in the most patrimonial of regimes, if for no other reason than their logistics and administration are more complex.[127]

In sum, the development of multiple agencies, each controlling only a modest share of the state's mobilisational capacity, offers the opportunity to keep centrifugal tendencies in check, because any rogue agency could be confronted by several others. The more acute the threat to state leaders, the greater the incentive to prevent the rise of large concentrations of power, particularly when these have their own mobilising capabilities.[128] We could add that the existence of overlap among agencies in terms of capabilities contributes to making each single agency less indispensable to executive power and therefore easily replaceable.

The main reason why the creation of parallel security forces is less injurious to military effectiveness than many other coup-proofing techniques is that it allows in principle for each one of the security forces to apply meritocratic criteria for the internal selection of personnel. Still, this technique has nonetheless negative repercussions on military effectiveness. To start with, parallel and overlapping security forces lead to increasingly difficult coordination and cooperation. Moreover, the creation of parallel military forces often implied that they were given priority over the regular army in the distribution of new equipment, in order to give them an edge in the event of a coup. The Syrian Defence Force and Republican Guard, for example, received the new Soviet-supplied T-72 tanks and anti-tank missiles in the 1970s and early 1980s, while the army, deployed in Lebanon and exposed to an Israeli attack, was left with older equipment, which the Israelis easily defeated in 1982.[129]

The very process of re-balancing the security architecture of a country is fraught with dangers. Changes in the architecture are likely to be perceived as controversial, particularly when one of the components grows at the expense of others. Nkrumah was overthrown by the army exactly because the latter disliked his favouritism for the Guard.[130] In Afghanistan too, the strengthening of the National Guard in 1988–90 antagonised the army and contributed to the 1990 violent confrontation.[131] When the Baathists in Iraq created in 1963 the first national guard, in fact a kind of popular militia, they alienated many army officers. Again the expansion of the National Guard in the 1980s created discontent among army officers.[132] The cost of creating parallel security structures also contributes to explaining why not every ruler indulged in it. In Egypt, for example, the presidential guard remained limited to just one brigade throughout the Nasser, Sadat and Mubarak eras, and no other parallel military force was created.[133] To go back to the previous discussion of paramilitary forces and the manipulation of the security architecture, creating a strong paramilitary force is likely to antagonise the army, the more so if the force is entirely new; on the other hand a weak paramilitary force would not be of much use.[134] Another useful example is that of Saudi Arabia: contrary to Iraq and Syria, Saudi Arabia never experienced any military coup, but the rulers were clearly fearful of Aran nationalist influences in the military and paid attention to coup-proofing nonetheless. The impact of coup-proofing on the security architecture of these three countries is obvious:

Table 1: parallel military forces in Saudi Arabia, Iraq and Syria

Country	Regular Ground forces	Parallel military
Saudi Arabia	3 armoured brigades	National Guard composed of: 3 mechanised brigades
	5 mechanised brigades	5 infantry brigades
	1 airborne brigade	Royal Guard regiment (army)
Iraq	3 armoured divisions	Republican Guard composed of: 2 armoured divisions
	3 mechanised divisions	3 mechanised divisions
	12 infantry divisions	1 infantry division
		Special Republican Guard composed of 4 brigades
		Special Forces composed of 2 brigades
Syria	6 armoured divisions	Republican Guard composed of 1 division
	3 mechanised divisions	Special Forces composed of 1 division

Source: Quinlivan, p. 142.

Keeping in mind what was said above about the dangers of altering the balance within the security architecture, it is interesting to note that the Saudis always rejected the idea of expanding their armed forces, and the size of the army and National Guard remained constant from the late 1960s, despite no lack of security threats in the region. Even as the historical enemy of Baath was dramatically building up its armed forces in the 1980s, Saudi Arabia did not follow up, and not because it did not feel threatened.[135] It preferred instead to buy huge amounts of weaponry which it lacked the manpower to use. Such an attitude was explained by a number of analysts as having to do with difficulties of recruitment, which is true to some extent but not because the population of Saudi Arabia is too small: it grew by several millions between 1970 and 2008, whereas the armed forces stagnated in terms of manpower. Even if it is true that the population mostly lacks adequate levels of education for a modern army, the actual number of educated Saudis has grown very much during these nearly forty years. Moreover, the fact that such numbers did not grow even faster is in turn the result of a lack of willingness to invest more of the country's huge resources in education. It is difficult not to link this reluctance to the fear that an expanding professional middle class (and officer corps) might represent a threat to the ruling dynasty.

Also, in the long run it is clear that even the best thought out security architecture can be subject to deterioration and crises. The emergence of a serious internal or external threat can never be discounted. Saddam Hussein had to reverse some of the coup-proofing he had indulged in after the Iranian counter-offensive in 1982, 'removing party officials from the command structure and recalling officers removed for political reasons'. The officer corps grew increasingly united as they fought together, often for survival; the development of a corporate identity across not only army officers but also among the National Guard restricted Hussein's room for manoeuvre, the more so as he had come himself to believe that the Iranian threat was more direct than the threat of a military coup. After the fall of Al Faw to the Iranians in 1986, 'he delegated control over military operations to his high command and allowed the generals to expand the Republican Guard with forces from regular units of proven skills and competence'. He also had to reduce the role of the Popular Militia, which had expanded into a force of hundreds of thousands and played a major role in the military effort. Once again, Tilly was right. Nonetheless Saddam at the same time built in safeguards by expanding the role and number of internal security forces, expanding the National Guard from a single brigade to seven and creating a Special National Guard as a protection against the old Guard. He also created the Fidayin Saddam, a militia mostly staffed by men from his tribe. After the end of the war, Saddam returned to his usual policy of weakening the army (and the National Guard) through purges, patronage, discrimination and fear.[136]

The Skills of the Security Architect

On balance, coup-proofing works within certain limits. The mix of coup-proofing techniques used by rulers varies according to the circumstances and their personal inclinations. The rejection of military professionalism is going to be stronger in contexts where the social composition of the army does not reflect the wider social structure, as in a number of African states following decolonisation, and where external threats are not perceived as strong. In such cases, rulers have an incentive to marginalise and weaken the army.[137] 'The end of colonialism and the subsequent sacking of white officers provided a blank slate for the first African rulers.'[138] Indeed, there is evidence that the politicians played a leading role in the decay of military professionalism, sometimes even facing resistance from the armies.[139]

Personal attitudes and ideological factors must also be taken into due account. Zaire's ruler Mobutu experimented with most of the coup-proofing techniques described here. Michael Schatzberg says of him that he feared an effective military.[140] Mobutu tried to buy military support by allowing officers to have private reserves for their own personal gain, even pocketing a percentage of their soldiers' wage; he replaced the command and control structure left in place by the Belgians with one based on personal loyalty, the 'politics of threats and rewards' and divide and rule tactics among the officer corps.[141] Lefever commented that 'Mobutu hires and fires and reassigns officers like Selassie but with less skill'; the result was that the chain of command of the army became weak and unpredictable. All this is in line with the theory, but Mobutu's own skills (or lack thereof) and weak beliefs have to be invoked when trying to explain why Mobutu did not try to improve his armed forces when faced with a repeated external threat. Three times his armed forces proved completely ineffective: in 1967 an army of 32,000 failed to cope with the mutiny of 150 foreign mercenaries and 900 Katangan gendarmes, despite committing half of its force to the task;[142] in 1977 he faced a close call in the first Shaba war; then again in 1978 his army had to be rescued from defeat by a foreign intervention, despite facing a numerically vastly inferior force. Mobutu had utilised the period between the two Shaba wars to purge the army, rather than improving its capabilities.[143] Ultimately Mobutu relied on foreign support to shore up his regime; twice he was saved by foreign troops. I have mentioned at the end of *The underlying dilemma* above, that external support is a deceptively easy and safe option for ineffective rulers, and Mobutu's case seems to confirm that. Once foreign support ceased to be forthcoming, his regime was doomed.

Coup-proofing did not always work even when used with moderation. Haile Selassie's coup-proofing techniques included keeping the Shoan Territorial Army close to Addis Ababa to counter-balance the increasingly professional and untrustworthy army, manipulating the chain of command of the army by encouraging army officers to bypass their superiors and approach him directly, encouraging officers to report on each other and reshuffling any officers whom he perceived to be a potential threat.[144] While these measures might have proved effective against a conventional coup, they did not work against a military revolution characterised by large participation of the rank and file; indeed by weakening the top officers and making them more remote from the rank and file, the Emperor made it more difficult to control the movement once started. Similarly, his splitting of the largest army units into battalions distributed throughout Ethiopian territory weakened the upper ranks of the officer corps, who were more loyal to the Emperor, and favoured the middle and lower ranks (lieutenants, captains, majors...), who were left in effective control of the fighting units.[145]

It is impossible, however, not to note that military coups have been a declining feature of world politics in the 1980s and onwards. Although this might in some cases be due to the development of stronger civil societies and political regimes and to a changing international environment (as in Latin America), there is a strong case to be made that coup-proofing has often worked. In the Arab world, where none of the trends against military coups identified in the previous sentence was very strong, military coups passed from being a regular feature until the early 1970s to almost disappearing from the second half of 1970s. This was certainly the case in Syria and Iraq. After an endless series of coups, Hafez al-Assad seized power in Syria in 1970 and invested heavily in 'coup-proofing'. Saddam Hussein did the same in Iraq from 1979 onwards.[146] With minor exceptions, such as Mauritania, this is still true to date (2010).

The first hypothesis of this book, that *institution-building is a key aspect of any process of taming violence*, is partially confirmed by the review of the literature. However, we have also seen that institution-building is just one strategy among many, and is far from suitable for all ruling elites in all situations. From the perspective of a ruling elite whose monopoly of violence is not under immediate threat, a strongly institutionalised security sector might well look like a 'Frankenstein' which could represent the more direct menace to the regime. As a result, it is to be expected that ruling elites might show no enthusiasm for institution-building, particularly in the security sector. It should also be expected that ruling elites, if coerced or convinced to sponsor institution building, might not be committed to the process and even try to sabotage it, or turn it into a façade deep enough to satisfy casual observers, but hiding a patrimonial substance.

This chapter has also highlighted how not all the paths to institution-building are equally counter-productive in the long term; some of them can deliver stability and solid control over the army, even in the absence of the development of solid political settlements based on 'open access orders': think of the political commissar system, for example.

3

MAINTAINING THE MONOPOLY

WHEN RUTHLESSNESS IS STILL NEEDED

'People, meanwhile, continue to adopt ever newer forms of luxury and sedentary culture and of peace, tranquillity, and softness in all their conditions, and to sink ever deeper into them. They thus become estranged from desert life and desert toughness. Gradually, they lose more and more of the old virtues. They forget the quality of bravery that was their protection and defence. Eventually, they come to depend upon some other militia, if they have one'.

Ibn Khaldun, *The Muqaddimah*, Princeton: Princeton University Press, 1967, p. 135

The best demonstration of the impact of ruthless violence in state formation may perhaps come from an extreme situation. What could be least appealing in an effort to 'make a state' than the recourse to ruthless violence at the hand of an occupying army? It was long believed by 'many Americans' that 'the escalating violence of the village war' would 'turn villages against the [South Vietnamese government] or endear the [Viet Cong] to them'. Interviews with surrendering and defecting Viet Cong cadres instead indicated that:

when powerful Allied attacks commenced in the villages whose residents supported the [Viet Cong], the populace's willingness to cooperate the [Viet Cong] usually dropped off rapidly. A former district level cadre, for example, recalled how he and the other cadres appraised the situation after high-intensity warfare had arrived in their area: "All of us agreed that the people were then very tired of the war and that they were very afraid of it. That is why all the policies of the Front have run into difficulties.

The amount of tax collected and the number of conscripted youths diminished notice-ably, although the cadres did their best to cope with the situation. The increasing inten-sity of the war, the intensive and frequent shelling and strafings were considered the real causes of the deterioration of the people's enthusiasm". [...] The villagers did not assign much blame to the Allies for the attacks because they respected the power of the Allies and believed that Allied forces had no realistic choice but to use powerful weapons against the Communists wherever they could find them. They faulted the Allies only when they unmistakenly unleashed heavy weapons on hamlets not contain-ing Communist soldiers.[1]

Note that American violence was ruthless, but increasingly selective. Although Moyar might have extrapolated too much out of interviews with defectors, who by definition cannot represent an unbiased sample of the views of Viet Cong activists, the problem faced by the Vietnamese communists was one typical of all insurgents. It explains why insurgents cannot go on fighting a guerrilla war indefinitely, but as Mao was well aware have at some point to upgrade their operations into a direct challenge to the government:

Because the [Viet Cong] forces repeatedly failed to win tangible victories over Allied forces in areas of heavy military activity and because Allied activity made life as a mem-ber of the [Viet Cong] harder and more dangerous, service with the [Viet Cong] seemed less attractive to young villagers and the parents who heavily influenced their decisions. [...] If the Communists continued to come under Allied attack in the ham-lets and flee each time, the villagers reasoned, they were not accomplishing anything but adding to the people's woes.[2]

As we are going to see in this chapter, ruthless violence re-emerges as a key tool in the hands of the ruling elite whenever the monopoly of large-scale vio-lence is in crisis. The ill fate of the American adventure in Vietnam does not diminish this point, as the eventual failure was due to other factors.

Understanding is Not Enough: Why the Military Predominates in Counter-Insurgency

The Limits of Political Pre-Emption

In the previous chapter we discussed how rulers maintain control of their own armies; this is of course not the only way by which the monopoly of large-scale violence by a ruler can be challenged. Any monopoly of large-scale violence can always be challenged in principle by an insurgency. Skilled coalition-mak-ing among elites (see *The unsustainable lightness of police reform* below and *The underlying dilemma* above) can reduce the risks, but there are several examples in history of insurgencies started by groups which had hitherto been completely marginal. No coalition-making effort at the centre, however enlightened, could guarantee the establishment of a political order that would incorporate extremist or marginal elements; indeed any effort in such a direction would be bound to fail or even backfire, as incorporating groups too disparate and whose importance is controversial might well sink the whole effort. The presence of a 'filter' (such as a political organisation) capable of mediating incorporation into the coalition on the basis of a more or less objective assessment of their representativeness is likely to favour the process, particularly if run by a capable leadership.

However, no ultimate guarantee exists. In the presence of the right mix of social conditions (primarily a numerous, frustrated youth), any regime might be vulnerable to any opposition group which finds the right mix of ideology and organisation (see chapter 1). Moreover, forming inclusive regimes when economic and power accumulation is going on is not easily implemented in practice; rather than redistribution, political regimes in these circumstances are more likely to be concerned with how to squeeze more out of the population. This is one reason why even in maintaining the monopoly of large-scale violence the role of coercion may remain predominant. The character of that coercion, whether ruthless or tame ('velvet glove'), selective or indiscriminate, whether linked to a wider political strategy or not, depends on a number of circumstances.

As pointed out in the introduction (*The crucial importance of selective violence*), the main problem associated with the coercive element of counter-insurgency is that indiscriminate violence causes resentment and fails to generate a clear structure of incentives for non-collaboration with rebels, and may even produce strong incentives for collaboration with them, allowing insurgents to solve collective action problems by turning the protection of the civilian population into an incentive to side with them.[3] In other terms, coercion works best if it is carefully targeted; hence scholars argue for the need to rely on strong intelligence[4] and on disciplined and well behaved armies.[5]

In the world of implementation, nothing is of course that simple. The institutions developed for the handling of selective violence might be affected by the emergence of a state of civil war and their functionality might be compromised. The system of incentives and bureaucratic control which operates in a state of peace can be shaken by civil conflict; the loss of faith in the ruling elite and the emergence of private interests can be difficult to control. Within the elite, different interests might emerge, as well as different definitions of the enemy. The very fact that the monopoly of large-scale violence is seriously challenged is likely to invite components of the ruling elite to try to renegotiate the elite bargain, which therefore comes under stress. The race to accumulate the means of coercion may start again, undermining the very basis of the institutions built during the previous consolidation.

The following chapters instead deal with the various issues related to 'taming the violence'. Here we are going to discuss three other issues:

- the relationship between elite bargaining and ruthless coercion in civil war;
- whether ruthlessness can be mitigated in civil war;
- the risk of an internal crisis of the elite bargain and of the monopoly of violence in the presence of a military challenge.

The Rationale of 'Political Counter-Insurgency'

Much of the current debate on counter-insurgency is about the merits of the 'political' approach, which is deemed to be much more effective.[6] What is meant by that term is a counter-insurgency that incorporates redistribution of resources and/or political accommodation of the constituency of the insurgents, if not of the insurgents themselves. A political strategy of preservation of the monopoly of violence is logically most closely associated with the use of the 'velvet glove' in the repression. Often, however, it has to operate in association with military repression because other options are not available, or because the insurgency has progressed to the stage where the monopoly of large-scale violence is seriously compromised. Targeted violence is then very difficult to practise, even if the agents of coercion are aware of its benefits. In environments more conducive to the deployment of the political approach, there is evidence that when successfully implemented it has a positive impact. Even in such cases, however, there are a number of problems with the successful implementation of a political approach in counter-insurgency.

The most notorious example of merely coercive counter-insurgency pertains to the German army in the Soviet territories and in a number of other European countries, chiefly Yugoslavia, in 1942–5. The Nazi government in Germany was already stating its belief in physical extermination as the decisive tool in counter-insurgency in internal documents dating 1936, that is long pre-dating the start of war and the experience of the Eastern Front. During the war, the Germans developed the idea that 'gaining the trust of the population, treating it reasonably' would provide substantial support in counter-insurgency. They also had the skills and the understanding needed to adapt tactical operations to the new context: the Germans were drawing conclusions that resembled the post-war consensus on counter-insurgency: they were resolutely convinced that a passive attitude, a 'garrison mentality', was disastrous in counter-insurgency and that the initiative had to be taken away from the enemy. From 1944, German manuals started advocating restraint in the recourse to reprisals and executions, although with little impact on the ground. Large formations of regular troops were deemed to be useless, due to their inability to surprise the enemy: what mattered were speed, mobility and secrecy.[7] However, the possibility to exploit divergences between population and partisans was never fully developed, despite the awareness of the existence of anti-Bolshevist feelings among the Soviet population. The stress was always on the psychological impact believed to derive from the perception of strength of the German troops by the population; hence a lot of energy was invested in propaganda operations to convince the locals of the invincibility of the *Wehrmacht*.[8] Given that the context was definitely one of state formation (in fact *empire* formation), there was a rationale for relying on the assertion of domination in the most ruthless *and* indiscriminate way. Mass reprisals against civilians were supposed to deliver such assertion.

Even in the context of the orgy of violence which was Nazi Germany's Eastern Front campaign in the 1940s, the need for a political approach came to be understood. Interestingly the latest theoretical documents produced by the Germans show some awareness of the limitation of not having a positive political project to propose to the population.[9] As in most other cases when the need for a 'political approach' was raised, it came to nothing, because the political costs would have been such as to nullify the original *raison d'être* of the war. We see here a first confirmation of the fourth hypothesis of this book: that *sophisticated military-political actors clearly understand what kind of violence is counter-productive*. However, they are not always in a position to implement.

The evidence indeed suggests that some political counter-insurgency efforts at least might have a major positive impact on state-building, because it might strengthen the state structure per se, and the political settlement at its roots. There is indeed evidence to contradict the theory that internal wars are necessarily detrimental to state-building (in contrast to external wars).[10] This was the case for example of Malaysia:

The strategy of political counter-insurgency, addressing grievances of the rural population, paved the way for the centralising of power. Autonomy and capacity of the central federal state increased. [...] It became increasingly recognised that a more centralised, co-ordinated implementation of the government's counter-insurgent policy would be necessary in order to finally defeat the communists.[11]

The same can be said of Peru under Fujimori:

The Fujimori regime made significant progress against Sender Luminoso by addressing some of the fundamental weaknesses of the Peruvian state. [...] Much of this effectiveness was the result of a more efficient use of state resources and a sustained effort to increase those resources through changes in macroeconomic policy.[12]

The Philippines witnessed a similar attempt 'to strengthen state capacities and steer the state away from its weak decentralised form' in order to crush the Muslim and Maoist insurgencies under Marcos, even if in part such attempt was offset by the Maoist (NPA) decision to 'decentralise revolution'.[13] In several other cases it may be argued that:

the prospect of such insurgency has in some cases been as powerful a stimulus to state-initiated schemes of development as the rather blander economic development schemes favoured by civilian bureaucrats.[14]

Difficult Implementation

However, while there is merit in arguing that a 'political approach' might be the most appropriate counter-insurgent answer, in reality it is not easy to implement for a number of reasons:

- it can be very expensive as it may require some kind of distribution of rent and resources;
- it requires a high degree of administrative coordination and commitment;
- governments which face a guerrilla threat are also likely to face a major shortfall in revenues and do not have access to the funds needed to implement a comprehensive political approach.

Political counter-insurgency, if applied consistently, amounts to nothing less than the formulation of a new elite bargain. The very process of its formulation is inherently controversial: who is in and who is out? How does coercion shape the elite bargain? (See *The political dimensions of the monopoly* in the introduction.)

Counter-insurgency in the Philippines is a typical example of how difficult it can be in practice to apply a complex strategy, even when the conviction exists among the policy-makers that the approach is the right one. Against the Maoist NPA, the new strategy adopted in 1989 envisaged a mix of military pressure and social reform, but successive governments all failed to introduce genuine land reform. A typical example of the difficulties in coordinating complex counter-insurgent efforts comes from South Vietnam, both among American agencies, South Vietnamese ones and between American and South Vietnamese ones.[15]

As a result, coercion usually remains absolutely predominant in counter-insurgency efforts, at least for most of their duration. The nature of specific political regimes can itself be a major constraint to the development of the tactical capabilities demanded by 'velvet glove' repression. The Chinese Ching dynasty, like the KMT after them, had some effective generals, but lacked effective field grade officers. Peasants could not become officers, and the cultural values of the upper classes prevented these from becoming effective field commanders.[16] Therefore, not every army can be turned into an effective counter-insurgent force. Indeed even in societies which recruited their officers from all strata of society, an army which successfully copes with large-scale regular warfare might still not be able to cope with counter-insurgency: the rules of engagement are very different. The struggle of the NATO command in Afghanistan to implement rules of engagement more appropriate to a counter-insurgency are clear evidence of this.[17]

The problem is that even when the understanding of what type of army is needed is achieved, mobilising the political will to transform the army is difficult and takes time; moreover once the political will exists, re-tasking large armies is not easy.

Disinclination to Implement

In addition to the points raised above concerning the difficulty of implementing a political counter-insurgency, political elites might be wary of ceding some political and economic power to the very people whom they blame for the prevailing violence and lawlessness. Even when effective and disciplined instruments of coercion are available and they faithfully implement the directives of the political leaders, reaching a political settlement of a conflict is far from guaranteed because the temptation to opt for extreme coercion is always present. The dream of completely wiping out an insurgency without some political compromise is inevitably attractive. In other words, political leaders are not necessarily less war-mongering than their generals; sometimes they are more. Political and military leaders might be ideologically motivated to pursue ruthless coercion.

Even in the absence of ideological inclinations towards ruthless coercion, there might be resilience towards combining military and political strategies, because initial reactions to insurgencies:

are likely to be close to the military pole of the continuum. [...] The army, as the lead agency in the fighting, rapidly expands and gains in power. The careers of military officers, politicians and bureaucrats become tied to the military policy. Any inability to reduce the guerrilla threat is seen as a failure of implementation rather than a failure of policy. A major change in strategy usually has to await a general recognition of the limitations of the military approach and change in key top political and military personnel.[18]

The repression of the revolt in the Vendée in the 1790s clearly exemplifies this pattern, at least until the fall of the Jacobins; it was relatively successful just because of Paris's ability to deploy overwhelming force.[19] During the Napoleonic period, French generals once again demonstrated an inclination towards purely coercive solutions, particularly but not only in Spain. The main exception was that of General Suchet in Aragon, who tried his best not to antagonise the population. While the military option proved successful in parts of Italy like Calabria, it mostly failed completely in Spain, where the odds were different. Suchet was the only French general to have a degree of success in the Peninsular wars.[20]

In Iraq, until 2006 the Americans insisted on a 'coercion and enforcement' counter-insurgency approach, refusing to engage politically with the insurgents. In such cases some ideological/cultural attitudes might also combine to play a role: in Iraq the Americans might well have been initially influenced by old British assessments that 'the Arabs of Iraq respect nothing but force'. As a result what initially had been a modest insurgency, which could probably have been contained easily with the 'velvet glove' approach, escalated into a major problem.[21]

The fact that a preference for ruthless coercion resurfaced periodically in states confronted with insurgencies, even when the consensus had already incorporated the point that solutions to internal wars can only be political and that coercion has to be as targeted as possible, might in part at least be the result of the tendency of insurgencies to become more sophisticated after World War II, both due to the Cold War environment and to the perfecting of new organisational tools by non-state organisations (see chapter 1). Political, economic or social counter-insurgency tools lost importance when the insurgents were not local communities, which could more easily be appeased with limited political or economic measures: 'there has to be less carrot and more stick', argued the Rhodesian intelligence chief.[22] This might not be a mere observation concerning the radicalism of the opponents, but a reflection of the greater disinclination of the ruling elite to compromise with a national counter-elite. An indication of this may come from the fact that even when foreign advisers advocated greater attention towards soft counter-insurgency policies, host armies were often reluctant or uninterested.[23] To the extent that the strategy of political counter-insurgency turned out to be more acceptable to the ruling elite, it was in the case of insurgencies where the new ideological element was weak or non-existent, as in a number of wars on the African continent after World War II.

Because of the political dynamics described in this last paragraph, historical evidence seems to indicate that the type of 'political approach' more likely to be acceptable to a ruling elite and to be implemented (hence in some cases at least to succeed) in counter-insurgency is not focused on appeasing the grievances of the insurgents and their supporters, particularly if these have a claim to being a national counter-elite. Instead, it is typically based on mobilising and consolidating support among their opponents or on co-opting the base of the insurgents piecemeal: no entitlements as a social or identity group, but individually tailored patronage agreements. This type of 'political approach', if it can still be called such, is linked to the reliance on militias in military counter-insurgency. The last paragraph of this chapter deals with this aspect and with its implications for state-building in detail.

Back to State Formation I

When the challenge raised by an insurgency becomes strong enough to demolish the monopoly of large-scale violence, the task of the counter-insurgent resembles the original task of establishing the monopoly, at least in part of the territory of the state. In such cases, there are not likely to be alternatives to ruthless repression. Establishing the boundary between situations requiring ruthless coercion and others where the 'velvet glove' would work better, is of course a difficult judgement; in practice it is going to be an arbitrary decision of the policy-makers. This is why the personal inclinations of a particular ruler are important. Other factors might influence the decisional process as well, at times in unpredictable ways. The availability of external support, for example, could sometimes favour the adoption of the 'velvet glove', and at some other times push a ruling elite to unleash a full repression even when the 'velvet glove' would still be an option. Communication between ruling elites and external supporters, and the constraints deriving from the international environment are factors which may account for either decision.

The factors just mentioned are context-specific and are best left to detailed case studies. Some more structural reasons favouring ruthless repression can, however, also be identified. One of these is that insurgencies historically proved difficult to deal with in a bureaucratised way, even if the evolution of 'Western' warfare in the late twentieth century has probably made armies more suited to this type of engagement, at least with regard to the ability to fight in small units (see end of previous chapter). The historical records show examples of states which had already undergone a fair degree of bureaucratisation and 'military revolution' at the centre, but were still relying on the old tools of territorial control in remote and unruly regions. For example, the British in Ireland relied very much on divide and rule against a disorganised but persistent insurgency:

In 1697 a law was passed by which any tory who could show that he had killed two others was to be granted a pardon. Between 1717 and 1776 the statute books included the provision that any tory who brought in the head of just one other was also to receive a pardon.[24]

Militias and Oil Spots

In terms of the contemporary debate, the swing of the pendulum between reliance on regular armies and irregular forces can be illustrated with reference to the militia and oil spot strategies.

States have been relying on militias even when they had large and powerful regular armies at their service. This is the case of the French in North Africa in the early twentieth century, who relied primarily not on bureaucratised military force, but on locally recruited forces and on utilising divisions and rivalries between tribes and between their chiefs.[25] In Vietnam, the Montagnard irregular units were most appreciated by the Americans in the counterinsurgency effort, and large militias were developed throughout the south.[26] The Soviets too, for all their propensity to build large conventional armies, already during the 1920s and 1930s developed an understanding of the need to employ local forces against the insurgents.[27] Even as late as the later twentieth century through to the early twenty-first century, the most modern military forces of the world regularly ended up employing patrimonial militias to reach out where they could not. The example of the Soviet army in Afghanistan is well known,[28] but the same experience is being repeated by the American and British armies in Afghanistan since 2001.[29]

In modern terms this is described as the 'importance of local defence': it allows armies to maintain a constant presence at village level, separate rural civilians from guerrillas and protect village officials; civilians might then develop a bond to the government. Moreover, regular troops are released for other tasks. A number of counter-insurgent efforts are claimed to have succeeded or anyway achieved important results thanks to the massive mobilisation of villagers in local militias: Thailand, South Vietnam, Peru, Guatemala, Western Ukraine and the Baltic Republics.[30] In South Vietnam it was even claimed that the local militias were far more effective (in terms of dollars spent per enemy killed) than the regular army. Although these financial comparisons do not make much sense,[31] it is true that one advantage of militias is that they are cheap, because they live off the ground and do not need a sophisticated logistical system to support them, nor need a leave system and other features of regular armies.

In this interpretation, the problem in a sense boils down to territorial and population control: 'once a civil war is on, the military requirements for the establishment and preservation of control over the entire territory are staggering'.[32] Only local militias can provide sufficient manpower to establish a presence in every village. There is a consensus among scholars and practitioners on this point:

never abandon a village after letting civilians rally to your standard;[33]

there must be absolute determination to establish and maintain a government police post intact and uncorrupt in every inhabited village.[34]

A major problem of any counter-insurgent effort is that civilian populations tend to respond to power and authority and 'control may trump the political preferences of the population in generating collaboration'. One reason is that control 'lowers the cost of collaboration with the established authority by shielding the population from competing sovereignty claims'; another that 'control signals credibility [...] of benefits and sanctions'.[35] American officials operating in the Vietnamese field often recognised that '...local inhabitants judged the GVN and the Front above all on their respective ability to provide security'.[36] The French in Algeria achieved military success chiefly through saturation, at one point deploying one French soldier to every twenty-three Algerians and an additional Algerian auxiliary to every sixty-nine civilians.[37]

A partially alternative model of counter-insurgency involves the creation of strongholds in enemy territory and the gradual extension of control from there outwards, a concept first theoretically elaborated by the French as the 'oil spot'. Tsarist Russia's counter-insurgency followed this model and relied on the deployment of large numbers of troops, isolating the target area from external assistance, establishing tight control of cities and towns and then extending domination outwards, building forts to constrain movement of rebels, as well as drying up the spring of resistance by destroying settlements, crops, etc.[38] Both in the cases of the French and of the Russians, such a model was usually successful against resisting communities, not organised in well-structured non-state armed groups. One characteristic of the oil spot model which makes it in practice a possible alternative to the militias is that it can be implemented by a regular army. Because it concentrates force in limited areas, it can be applied with relatively limited numbers of troops. Therefore, militias are not strictly necessary even if there is no particular reason why they cannot be integrated into the oil spot strategy.

Against sophisticated organisations, modelled after the Leninist, Maoist or Islamist examples, and served by tested ideologies with a widespread appeal, the local militia model proved more effective because oil spots are vulnerable to infiltration by determined and well organised opponents. Here we have a paradox: the more sophisticated the insurgency, the more primitive the response. The implications for state-building are important. If, as argued in chapter 1, ideological groups with sophisticated organisations are prime candidates for state-making, countering them with irregular forces may achieve short-term tactical success at the expense of the viability of the state built around the existing ruling elite.

It is worth pointing out that one of the characteristics of militias is the weak bureaucratic supervision and their inclination towards ruthless behaviour. It is telling that the more conventional armies struggle to defeat an insurgency, the more they look at militias as the solution. One reason might be that militias can more discreetly use violent tactics that could send officers of a regular army to the court martial. The Soviet army in Afghanistan tried 2,000 of its men for abuses and misbehaviour, including several who were executed, but tolerated much worse behaviour from the militias it had helped to establish.[39] The need for 'ruthlessness' resurfaces as state formation turns into the priority task again. However, that also means that all elements of the state in place, if any, will decay further as a result of the corrosive action of the militias.

In principle, it is possible to develop counter-measures which limit the indiscipline and unreliability of the militias. In order to maintain a degree of control over them, the regular army itself has to be able to operate in small units and be spread around, as opposed to being concentrated to achieve overwhelming superiority as demanded by the Clausewitzian orthodoxy. The Marines experimented with such tactics in Vietnam (the CAPs): small teams of regulars deployed in the villages to give confidence to militias and control them. They also deployed teams of advisers regularly visiting the villages. One key aspect of relying on local militias is the ability to deploy relief forces quickly when needed.[40] In the last section (*Decaying monopolies*) we shall deal in detail with the problem associated with the use of militias on a large scale.

The Small Unit Alternative

As argued in the previous paragraph, oil spots have limited application against sophisticated insurgencies. The only other solid alternative to using irregular forces is the development of armies based on the deployment of an autonomous small unit. Small units of regular troops are essential to pursue the insurgents effectively. The historical evidence suggests a record of success.

The Huk guerrillas resisting the Japanese during World War II, for example, acknowledged after their defeat that they never felt threatened by the 'ponderous multi-battalion-sized sweeps by the Filipino army' and were able to 'predict the direction and duration of large-scale operation'. It was the small 'hunter-killer' teams that stayed into the jungle that caused most grief.[41] The Portuguese army, when faced with escalating insurgencies in the colonies of Guinea, Mozambique and Angola, completely restructured to operate in small units. This was a key to its relative success in containing the insurgencies, despite its limited means and manpower.[42]

However, the use of small autonomous units in counter-insurgency has important implications for the internal security architecture of armies. As pointed out in a paper from a US presidential study committee:

tailoring a military force to the task of countering [...] another military force entails some sacrifice of capabilities to counter internal aggression. The latter require widespread deployment, not concentration. It requires small, mobile, lightly equipped units of the rangers or commando type.[43]

Nagl argues that 'the demands of conventional and unconventional warfare differ so greatly that in extremis it may be very difficult, if not impossible, for an organisation optimised for one to adapt to the other, all the more so when it has a strong organisational culture attuned to its original role'.[44] Conventional armies tend not to believe that small units can survive in a hostile environment and obtain results.[45] We should add that small units operating in a dispersed fashion are also very difficult to control from the centre; if the US army (with its very advanced communication technologies) experienced difficulties in this regard in Afghanistan after 2002 when applying such tactics on a relatively limited scale,[46] we can imagine what order of problem less technologically endowed armies must face.

As a result, many armies have historically displayed considerable reluctance to devote substantial resources against counter-insurgency in the long term. In their efforts to contain the partisans of various occupied countries in World War II, the Germans increasingly placed a stress on small, mobile units, and achieved tactical success, but were of course hampered in implementing any massive shift in this direction by the predominant preoccupation with fighting the Red Army.[47] Less understandably, the US army had, at the beginning of the twenty-first century, a structure still largely targeted at fighting large wars with regular armies, despite the end of the Cold War. Earlier, the legacy of the Philippines and of various interventions in Latin America had had little impact in Vietnam,[48] while in turn the lessons of Vietnam had only a major impact on the Special Forces but not on the army itself and little on the marines either.[49] The reaction of the US army to the defeat in Vietnam was markedly different from that of the French at the time of their surrendering of Indochina. The French developed a new counter-insurgency doctrine, which proved militarily rather successful in Algeria; the Americans 'all but abandoned counter-insurgency'. US military schools after Vietnam paid only 'lip service to counter-insurgency' and the subject was regarded as unimportant.[50]

We put an Army on the battlefield that [...] doesn't have any doctrine, nor was it educated or trained, to deal with an insurgency... After the Vietnam War, we purged ourselves of everything that had to do with irregular warfare or insurgency, because it had to do with how we lost that war. In hindsight, that was a bad decision.[51]

The Soviet army was even more reluctant to absorb the lessons of counter-insurgencies. During Stalin's time, the ruthless repression in Ukraine and Lithuania from 1944 onwards was carried out by the NKVD (or later MVD and MGB) more than the Soviet army, which was judged as ineffective for the task.[52] When it could not shy away from them altogether, like in Afghanistan from 1979 onwards, the Soviet army eventually shed the experience gained as quickly as possible. The subsequent war in Chechnya, with its disastrous start for the Russians, seems to demonstrate this point eloquently.

Another example is that of the Indian army, which despite being constantly involved in counter-insurgency campaigns from the 1950s onwards in Nagaland and Mizoram, remained bound to conventional tactics even in what it called its 'counter-insurgency theory'. Of British experiences, the Indians keenly adopted the resettlement of villagers into strategic villages which they could control, even if they failed to implement the strategy consistently enough. But they never developed the autonomous small unit on a significant scale, continuing to operate at the company and battalion level, even if from the 1970s theoretical writings in the army's publications began to show an appreciation for the importance of small units in counter-insurgency. Clearly the Indian army was not keen to fully convert a significant number of its units to non-conventional warfare.[53]

Perhaps most surprisingly of all, the Israeli army showed a reluctance to re-focus on counter-insurgency operations; the lessons learned in Lebanon in the 1990s[54] seemed to have been forgotten by 2006, when the army was called upon to enter Lebanon again. Exceptions to this pattern include, to an extent, the already mentioned French army, which maintained a component specifically designed to deal with local wars, and the British army, to which fighting small wars has long been the institutional priority even if it often indulged in self-complacency after Malaya.[55]

The explanation for this widespread pattern could be that fighting small wars could hardly be considered a priority by the armies of superpowers. That the international context and the international ambitions of a country might be a determinant is confirmed by the fact that small countries have sometimes shaped their armies to become almost exclusively focused on counter-insurgencies, which in some cases were perceived as mortal threats to rulers and governments. The Portuguese Army adapted well to counter-insurgency, adopting it as its key task to be tackled with long-term strategies and low-tech resources. As of 1975, it had been quite successful in containing the insurgencies of Lusophone Africa, although at an intolerable financial cost (see also *The underlying dilemma* in chapter 2).[56]

Another example is that of the Sandinista army in the 1980s, which had first relied on conventional tactics and static defence of valuable assets and population centres, leaving little for search-and-destroy patrols. During 1983–4, perhaps on advice by Cuban adviser General Ochoa, it however developed its own small unit tactics, building an army largely composed of light irregular warfare battalions, divided into *batallones de lucha irregular* (BLI) staffed by conscripts and locally recruited *batallones ligeros cazadores* (BLC) staffed by volunteers, which managed to contain and strategically corner one of the best resourced insurgencies in history (the so-called Contras). The Sandinistas managed to keep the roads open and prevent the Contras from holding any Nicaraguan territory for any length of time.[57] Between 1984 and 1985 the ability of the Sandinistas to use their forces effectively increased significantly and morale improved accordingly.[58] The *cazadores* were an interesting innovation, in that they were drawn from the popular militias, being in fact the youngest and fittest militiamen, while the older and not so fit played a merely defensive role. By 1986 special units operating in small teams such as the 'Special Mobile Units' and the 'Special Assignment Groups' had also been established.[59]

The Role of Technology II

When an incumbent or a foreign army enjoys a significant technological edge over opposed non-state armed groups, the temptation to abstain from the troublesome tactical adaptation discussed above is particularly difficult to resist:

It is, on the face of it, quite logical in a force with unparalleled access to high technology, to seek to use technological solutions to compensate for shortages in manpower. [...] In an environment where, above all else, it is imperative that the occupying force be seen as a force for the good, it is counter-productive when technological solutions are employed that promote separation from the population. Furthermore, a predilection with technology arguably encourages the search for the quick, convenient solution, often at the expense of the less obvious, but ultimately more enduring one.[60]

The American belief in the resolutive value of technology had repercussions in a number of countries which received US assistance. Already at the time of the Chinese civil war, Washington focused its support of the KMT (GMD) government on advanced military technology, but 'the American weaponry proved to be a handicap to the GMD army, [...] the American artillery was, in many cases, a logistic drain to the GMD forces'. American equipment stretched the GMD army logistics beyond its limits; its units performed far better when acting as light infantry without much support. The same applied to tanks, 'without taking into account the importance of allowing their armies time to adapt to the armoured warfare tactics'.[61] The Americans were merely exporting their own inclination to 'excessive use of firepower', which would later impact negatively on their own counter-insurgency effort in Vietnam.[62]

Similarly in El Salvador, if on a smaller scale, American training turned out a reasonably performing Salvadoran conventional army, which as such had serious problems in facing the rebels once the latter reverted to guerrilla tactics in 1984–5:

The Army never fully embraced counter-insurgency tactics and remained obsessed with large conventional operations, movement by truck or helicopter, and excessive use of firepower throughout the remainder of the war. The emphasis on firepower led Salvadoran infantry units to carry 90-mm recoilless rifles, 81-mm mortars, and 0.50-caliber machine guns on many missions for which assault rifles and medium machine guns would have been sufficient. Carrying such heavy weapons and ammunition in rugged terrain meant that when contact [was] made, they [didn't] have the foot mobility to manoeuvre around and cover the ground fast enough to cut the guerrillas off. They [were] simply far less mobile than the guerrillas.[63]

Another similar situation had already been experienced in South Vietnam, where even after having been re-equipped and retrained by the Americans, the new army remained largely road-bound; in particular Vietnamese officers would not operate beyond the range of their artillery, which itself was dependent on good roads for movement.[64]

The inclination to use technologically-driven coercion became more pronounced once air power started playing a major role in counter-insurgency. Theoreticians consistently argued that air power should be applied with restraints in counter-insurgency, both because of collateral damage and because of the political implications of the latter.[65] However, its mere availability always represented a temptation to indulge in massive displays of power. One can understand why: if the issue in state formation is to destroy or intimidate the enemy into submission, air power must look a particularly easy way to do so. As argued above, telling where state formation ends and where maintaining the monopoly of violence starts is a somewhat arbitrary matter, so indulging in 'coercion from the air' can be somewhat justified in political terms. The case of Israel is the most obvious example of 'coercion from the air' applied contexts, where a political approach would, in all likelihood, have borne more fruit.[66]

The risk (from the counter-insurgent's point of view) is a double one: indiscriminate impact and being lured into a false sense of confidence in one's own capabilities. Even when aircraft were provided in relatively modest numbers and of outdated models, the impact on armed forces of limited skills and know-how could be massive. In El Salvador, for example, the American-equipped air force had a major impact in the early stage of the war (1980–84), when the insurgents were mounting large-scale attacks, but it declined in effectiveness once they shifted to asymmetric tactics. The multiplicative impact of a relatively large air force on the capabilities of the army was not as great as imagined: even with equipment dating back to the 1960s, the Salvadoran air force had major maintenance problems and low serviceability rates, because of the excessive number of aircraft taken into service and the large number of different types being utilised. It proved impossible to find sufficient numbers of qualified recruits to expand the air force fast enough.[67]

Other examples can be found. The Ethiopian armed forces, well equipped with Soviet assistance, developed major maintenance problems and a shortage of skilled personnel, such as pilots. The situation was compounded by the Soviet tendency deliberately to restrict the supply of spare parts and ammunition, presumably to create a situation of dependency (see also *The role of technology I* in chapter 1).[68]

The theoretical justification for adopting 'coercion from the air' in almost every conflict was quickly developed: it was meant to 'reassure the masses that powerful military force can be quickly brought to bear against insurgents', making them 'less eager to harbour fanatical terrorists, especially if the insurgents are using fear or intimidation against them and disrupting their day-to-day life'.[69] As the remotely-piloted drone technology reached maturity in the twenty-first century, the argument that counter-insurgency should rely on air power was strengthened further.[70] Modern air forces have made use of Show of Force operations with no expenditure of ordnance in a number of cases in recent conflicts such as Afghanistan,[71] but controversy over collateral causalities continued and indeed reached new heights in Afghanistan itself in 2008–9, despite the new technologies. Despite the fact that the latest version of the US army counterinsurgency manual (FM 3–24) advocates a 'velvet glove' approach, in Iraq during the tenure of one of the 'architects' of the new doctrine air strikes increased five-fold (2006–7).[72]

In recent years experiments have been carried out with technologies that should in principle allow a targeting of violence more precise and potentially more careful than ever: surveillance technologies, identification technologies like iris scanning, etc. It is too early to assess their impact, but it is clear that while they might deter opportunistic adversaries, they will struggle to raise the costs of operating to non-state armed groups, to the point where ideological groups would be definitely discouraged from raising a challenge.

Decaying Monopolies

Shifting Correlation of Forces

The emergence of a threat to the monopoly of large-scale violence is not necessarily an indicator of a regime's growing weakness: the circumstances leading to such emergence might be completely out of the control of the regime and be related to wider cultural and intellectual developments, or changing international alignments. A decaying monopoly can be the result of external causes as much as of an internal crisis of a regime. The most classical and widely discussed case of decaying or collapsed monopoly of large-scale violence is of course insurgent challenges to the state. The large majority of efforts by radical and extremist groups to mount insurgencies have failed, mostly at an early stage, to the point that often they do not even get counted in quantitative studies of insurgencies and counter-insurgencies. Still, even when failing, insurgencies in several cases have broken the monopoly of large-scale violence of the state for at least a significant period of time. One obvious reason why this may happen is that the correlation of forces is altered, for example through the newly arising willingness of a foreign source to support financially an opposition group. In other words, previous successes of the central government in establishing a centralisation of patronage can be undone, making it possible to raise challenging armies.

Episodes of this kind have not been uncommon, particularly during the Cold War. The PKK in Turkey benefited both from a Soviet willingness to help and from smuggling opportunities.[73] Several insurgent movements in Central America also benefited from the rivalries of the Cold War (El Salvador, Honduras, Guatemala, Nicaragua). In Mozambique and Angola, Renamo and UNITA were, at least for a period of their existence, largely dependent on South African handouts, and the anti-Vietnamese Cambodian guerrillas would not have got very far without Chinese support. More recently, non-state organisations have been supporting Islamist insurgents in a number of Islamic countries. Examples like this can multiply.

Indeed, there is a growing stream of studies arguing exactly that insurgencies rarely win without external support and the availability of a sanctuary in a neighbouring country.[74] However, it would be misleading to overstate the case: support of insurgencies cannot be viewed in isolation. In most cases, there was no such thing as a 'level playing field' before external support to the insurgencies started: governments targeted by the insurgents were already recipients of external support themselves, a fact which might well have been instrumental in driving insurgents to seek external support. In many cases, external support to governments exceeded the defence budget by several times, creating an environment where an insurgency would find it very difficult to succeed without external support. It is appropriate to ask how many governments would have survived even an autochthonous insurgent movement in the absence of such external support.

Moreover, not all major insurgencies have received external support. The discovery of a new source of funding, for example through the development of new smuggling routes or the emergence of a large and supportive diaspora or refugee community abroad, were in some cases sufficient to fund insurgencies even in the absence of support from foreign states. A notorious example of this is the Tamil Tigers of Sri Lanka.[75]

Another reason why mounting insurgent challenges can get easier at some point in time was pointed out initially by Theda Skocpol and her contributors.[76] The appearance of fissures and cracks within a ruling coalition, or even more so in open conflict among former partners, can provide an opportunity for the 'underdogs' to undermine the monopoly of large-scale violence. Examples of this include such disparate cases as Italy and Germany after World War I, China in the 1920s, Iraq after 2003, Burma (Myanmar) after World War II, etc. The weakening of the security and political institutions of a state could also often lead to 'warlordism'. The most typical instance in which warlordism arises is when political power collapses, but the military forces on which it rested survive, at least in part. In this case one could talk of 'orphan' warlords, mostly former regional commanders of the central state army who, faced with a political crisis at the centre, opted to set up their own fiefdoms.[77] A typical example of orphan warlordism might be White Russian generals after 1917.[78]

A third reason why the monopoly of large-scale violence can become vulnerable derives directly from the dilemma discussed in chapter 2. Because some rulers might see effective armed forces as a greater threat than any challenge external to the regime, often the level of efficiency of armed forces is (to say the least) less than optimal. Indeed this dilemma can lead to extremely dysfunctional armed forces. Extreme examples such as Mobutu's in Zaire were discussed in chapter 2; we can add Batista's in Cuba[79] and others.

Yet another reason for the decay of monopolies of violence is the increasing availability of guns in specific regions, as a result of conflicts in neighbouring countries. In sub-Saharan Africa it is estimated that 5 million weapons lay in the hands of private citizens or non-state armed groups.[80] Governments themselves might in some cases be responsible for small arms proliferation, as in the case of Angola in 1992, when an estimated 1 million weapons were distributed to civilians,[81] but 'innocent' neighbours will be affected too. While the availability of weapons is, of course, a necessary condition for the emergence of a threat to the monopoly of large-scale violence, it is important to highlight here that it is not sufficient: collective action has also to be enabled for weapons to become a threat. Indeed, once UNITA was defeated on the battlefield and its leader killed, no major threat to the Angolan state emerged despite the huge availability of weapons. The same could be said of Mozambique or South Africa after the end of the wars in southern Africa. For this reason, I am not going to discuss the proliferation of small weapons in greater detail here.

A fifth reason is that organisational and mobilisation techniques evolve and improve, as do military techniques and technologies. A monopoly of large-scale violence is therefore a dynamic process and not a condition acquired once and for all. The emergence of Leninism, Maoism and Islamism are all clear examples of innovations that altered the correlation of forces between the holder of monopolies of violence and radical opposition groups, with consequences which are well known. I have already discussed this aspect in chapter 1.

Civil War and the Re-Negotiation of the Elite Bargain

In this chapter, instead, I am going to deal with a sixth source of threats to the monopoly of large-scale violence, that is internal contradictions to the very effort to maintain the monopoly itself. These contradictions can more effectively be described as a dilemma between the need to fight off insurgent challenges on the ground and the need to maintain an effective chain of command and control within a regime's own forces. While this may apply to external (state to state) challenges as well, at least to some extent (as discussed in chapter 2, *A special kind of bureaucracy*), it is particularly problematic when facing an insurgency because it has to be dealt with in a decentralised way, compounding the issue of command and control and potentially turning bureaucratic structures, by their own nature inflexible and slow to adapt, into a liability.

Teitler argues that the formation of a professional officer corps requires standardisation of the combat conditions; hence a tendency to agree honour codes among professionals of violence. From this derives the unsuitability of professional soldiers to fight out in conflicts which involve non-professionals, such as insurgencies.[82] One of the points emerging from chapter 2 was that institution-building strategies, such as bureaucratisation, can combine effectiveness and loyalty in the long run. However, institution-building is a costly process, not just in financial but also in political terms. Confining professionalisation and institution-building to one or few sectors of the state apparatus is extremely dangerous for patrimonial rulers. In order to work effectively, the strategy has to encompass the whole of the state apparatus and of the political system.

History has demonstrated that a combination of institution-building and of concession of political and social entitlements works well in ensuring mass mobilisation behind the ruling elites from the threat of conventional attacks from an outside power. However, it is evident that in a context of internal strife this strategy is extremely difficult to implement. The most obvious reason for this is that building institutions in the middle of a civil war is hampered by the difficulty of mobilising human resources of adequate skill level; the educated class is likely to avoid involvement in the conflict by taking sides, except if motivated ideologically. Resources will be in short supply and mostly directed at the war effort as such. Finally, intimidation and violence make implementation difficult. There are disincentives to building institutions, even when the capacity to do so is present. Fighting an internal enemy, particularly once the threat grows beyond a certain threshold, is not easily compatible with strong institutions, particularly autonomous and law-bound judicial systems. In this sense, Schmitt had a point when he argued against the 'ultimate rule of law' and the bureaucratisation of the state, which could allow the latter to be over-taken by events at some unpredictable point, particularly in the event of an emergency.[83]

We shall deal in greater detail with these issues in the following chapters. The issue to be discussed here is that of the impact of specific policy choices (made by a threatened ruling elite) to re-patrimonialise in order to confront insurgent challenges more effectively. The hypothesis (the sixth in the intro-duction) is that such a strategy amounts to nothing less than a renegotiation of the terms of the old political settlement or elite bargain and that it can have longer-term consequences and lead to internal decay. It undermines the insti-tutional machinery of the state and/or delegates control of parts of the state apparatus away from the ruler. Reno repeatedly stressed the point in his writ-ings, that in West Africa warlords (and military-political entrepreneurs) are often former members or collaborators of the ruling elite, who are trying to maintain or increase their influence through 'non-conventional' means once the old system becomes increasingly inefficient in building at least a degree of consensus; they often maintain links to the state apparatus or to the rival coalition even when they are formally opposed to it.[84] An internal conflict can be the typical situation where this occurs. In North et al.'s terms, the weak or decaying institutional framework brings back to the surface the need of political actors to maintain an armed retinue in order to secure political representation.

There are a number of reasons why a particular regime might decide to allow a partial loss of control over its security establishment through the creation of semi-autonomous forces (usually irregular militias). One reason has been men-tioned already above and derives from the need to counter certain specific types of opposition. Insurgencies and particularly decentralised ones (but not only) might demand decentralised counter-insurgencies in order to be con-tained or defeated (see also *Back to state formation* below). There are examples dating back many centuries ago. The Chinese empire, for example, developed mounted archer forces to fight its nomad enemies in 307 BC.[85]

More recently in the Philippines, the re-empowerment of the caciques after the fall of Marcos in 1986 seems to have worked well in marginalising the Maoist NPA, at the same time however weakening the hold of the central government.[86] Not always were such strategies successful. For example, Sri Lanka's Home Guard, which at one point also included Muslim Tamil speakers alongside Sinhalese members, contributed to igniting ethnic conflict by resettling Muslims in territories vacated by Tamils. Similarly it has been argued that the Guatemalan village defence forces, created in 1982, might with their abuse have helped the leftist guerrillas in their recruitment effort.[87] In Sudan the indiscriminate targeting of African ethnic groups by the pro-government militias seems to have been counter-productive, pushing even those not initially aligned with the insurgents over to their side.[88]

Notwithstanding a number of counter-productive effects, on the whole it seems that irregular forces played in general a role useful to government in the repression of insurgencies, fulfilling tasks that bureaucratised armies were unable to fulfil (see previous paragraph). In a sense it could be argued that the creation or strengthening of 'big men and their retinues' by central governments can be an effective counter-insurgent strategy in preventing mobilisation efforts by groups and movements who target individuals in their recruitment efforts, not least because their patronage networks can absorb many youth who might otherwise have joined the insurgency. By establishing a local armed force, it can also counter-balance the mobilisation carried out by the insurgents if it is too late to prevent it, allowing some breathing space for government supporters. There may be an element of social engineering in these strategies, despite the tendency of policy-makers to legitimise them with talks of 're-empowering traditional elders': in practice these strategies often envisage the passage from communities of autonomous small farmers or egalitarian tribes to hierarchical structures based on social dependence.[89]

Mercenaries

Focusing on the re-emergence of mercenaries and particularly private military companies in Africa as a state strategy leading to the decay of the monopoly of large-scale violence, has been quite popular in recent years. Their impact seems to have been exaggerated, both in terms of their impact and in terms of their peculiarity: they only played a significant role in Angola and Sierra Leone, and in the case of Angola even that was more at the level of training and intelligence than of direct fighting. The intervention of Sandline in Sierra Leone was accused of compelling the RUF to 'adopt butchery of civilians as its only, albeit counterproductive, means of retaliation'.[90] However, the same could be argued of any international intervention against technologically inferior non-state armed groups. Similarly it has been argued that the intervention of Executive Outcomes lessened the legitimacy of the Angolan government, but again the same could be said of any external intervention, including peacekeeping. Older kinds of mercenaries, recruited individually or in any case not as part of a 'package', were also reported to be active in the two Congos and possibly Angola too, with an estimated total in 1999 of about 1,000. The profile of mercenaries has been much lower in recent years than it was in the postcolonial era when the tendency was to engage them in small groups, but mercenaries from abroad were still preferred because of the assumption, they would neither care nor understand local politics and therefore would avoid interfering.[91]

Overall the impact of mercenaries of all kinds on the monopoly of violence and the legitimacy of governments from the last quarter of the twentieth century onwards seems to have been very limited. Such mercenaries did not operate on their own turf and remained dependent on local political support, a fact that restrained any political ambition they might have developed. A different case is that of private *security* companies accompanying external intervention, which we shall discuss in chapter 6.

Militias

A more serious threat to the state monopoly of large-scale violence came instead from locally rooted irregular forces. They might cooperate with the central government for mercenary or other reasons, but the key point distinguishing them from genuine mercenaries is that being tied to a local reality, they cannot avoid being political. During the 1990s, irregular militias experienced a wave of popularity in a number of African countries, in response to the ineffectiveness or untrustworthiness of the regular armies. Sometimes, as in the case of the Kamajors in Sierra Leone, such militias initially developed at the community level and then started enjoying state sponsorship. The Kamajors even developed a command hierarchy, organising battalions and companies and administrative structures, but always maintaining their allegiance to local leaders. Their relationship with the Sierra Leonean army was difficult and they even clashed with it. Once the army took power in 1997, possibly motivated by the rise of the militias among other reasons, the military 'junta' tried to disband the Kamajors who, however, refused to surrender their weapons. The formation of irregular forces, outside any system of bureaucratic control, left the door open to the risk of a personal feud being created: 'many Kamajor leaders became petty tyrants and little judges'.[92]

In other cases the state played a direct role in the creation of militias. In Sudan the Janjaweed and Murahaleen militias were organised to fight insurgent groups. The former in particular were organised in brigades and integrated into the army, usually led by emirs of Arab tribes who had served in the state administration. Despite this, gradually Khartoum lost control.[93] In the south too, the Sudanese state had difficulties managing the militias it had recruited.[94] Another example might be Tajikistan during and for some time after its civil war.[95] Historical examples include post-Carolingian western Europe, the Byzantine Empire in the late tenth century and the late Roman Empire. In other cases where the state was strong enough to prevent the formation of feuds, there is nonetheless evidence that reliance on militias led to the formation of mafias and other similar 'interest groups', such as in Turkey.[96]

The decay of the state monopoly of violence was particularly dramatic in the cases of Chad, Afghanistan and Tajikistan. In Chad the process of decay of the 'national' armed forces started not long after independence. Even after the multiple civil wars seemed to have been decisively won by Deby, the military remained:

fragmented, unorganised, undisciplined, and uncontrollable. [...] Erosion of discipline at both higher and lower levels within the ranks of the Forces Armées Nationales Tchadiennes (Fant) seriously undermined the principles of civilian governance and rule of law. Battalion commanders exercised executive and judicial powers within their individual jurisdictions without consulting the properly designated authorities, whilst extra-judicial exactions by army units terrorised the civilian population in many areas of the country. The violent confiscation of goods was a common practice. The line between the elements of the 'regular' army, whether or not in uniform, and shake-down extortionists (the so-called 'road cutters') was often blurred. Discipline among the much-vaunted Garde Republicaine has also frayed. Its members have suffered (as have many in Fant) from salary arrears. Funds earmarked for the maintenance of their facilities and equipment were regularly skimmed off at the top; soldiers, in turn, fed off the population.[97]

The attempt to downsize the army resulted in the mid-1990s in defections to rebel groups.

In Afghanistan, the pro-government militias mostly revolted against the central government in 1992, leading to a *de facto* collapse of the state, from which it proved then extremely difficult to recover.[98] In Tajikistan, the need to organise irregular militias was in this case dictated by the inexistence of a

Tajik army in the early 1990s, as a result of the sudden disintegration of the Soviet Union.[99]

In the three cases just mentioned, as well as in the case of Sudan, we can talk of abandoned monopolies of large-scale violence, since the state more or less willingly presided over the transfer of parts of its claim over the monopoly to groups which maintained some relation with it. In this sense it is fair to say with Salmon that:

privatisation is [...] neither necessarily permanent nor imposed, but renegotiable and voluntary. It provides the state with a means of reducing demands on its military, administrative and extractive instruments, and thus frees up resources that can be reinvested in consolidating core functions. The resulting system is thus not a static picture of 'failure' but an often fluid realm of transactions between state and non-state actors.[100]

Reclaiming the Monopoly

The examples above also show how once surrendered, monopolies of violence are difficult to capture back. The process of decay of monopolies of large-scale violence is not necessarily irreversible or irresistible. In some cases, struggling governments realised how the risks of surrendering the monopoly of forces to militias can be counter-productive. Pincus provides the example of James II's England:

Soon after his accession to the throne in 1685, James began to implement his longheld desire of creating a military force that would rival Continental armies. [...] The failed rebellion of his nephew the Duke of Monmouth, James openly declared, "had rendered an essential service" by demonstrating "that no reliance" could be placed on the traditional militia. The rebels "had thereby given reasons for levying and maintaining troops." [...] The dramatic growth in the size of the army does not capture the impact of James II's standing army on English society. James transformed England's twenty-seven garrisons from dilapidated and almost abandoned stations into military strongholds.[101]

The opposition he faced was very strong from the beginning:

The lifelong Tory Sir Thomas Clarges "set out the great consequence of melting the militia and establishing a standing force," adding that James's decision to employ Roman Catholic officers was "illegal." The political maverick Sir Thomas Meres, a number of army officers, and servants of the royal household soon joined Clarges in opposing a standing army. Sir John Thompson was probably typical of the Whigs in being "very violent" against "keeping a standing army." In the Lords the Whigs Viscount Mordaunt, Charles Paulet, Earl of Winchester, William Cavendish, Earl of Devonshire, and the moderate George Savile, Marquis of Halifax, were all conspicuous in their opposition both to the employment of Catholic officers and to the creation of a standing army. Both houses made their opposition to James's plans to create a modern army clear.[102]

More recent examples are abundant. The Philippine government under Magsaysay after World War II, for example, disbanded the militia, a source of abuse in the countryside; later former Huk guerrillas recognised that this had been a winning move that undercut their support.[103] Iraqi Prime Minister Al Maliki in March 2008 sent the army to Bassora to disband local militias by force with whom he had entertained relations earlier, in a demonstration of strength meant to assert the central state against centripetal forces.[104] By contrast, in Colombia, the decision to move against the paramilitaries was mainly driven by international (US) pressure.[105] In South Vietnam under Diem, some army commanders in more remote regions had set themselves up as warlords and had started collecting taxes, but American intervention at least had the effect of stopping this process of disintegration.[106]

Perhaps the most interesting cases of recovered monopolies of large-scale violence are Tajikistan, where by 2001 Dushanbe had fully re-established control,[107] and Georgia, where Shevardnadze also succeeded, although he did not manage to enjoy his success for long. The nuts and bolts of re-centralisation are worth a more detailed look. When Shevardnadze took over Georgia in 1995 he was at the mercy of the Mekhedrioni militia leaders, but he successfully re-centralised authority by playing divide and rule among them and guaranteeing their economic interests while undermining their political and military power. The steps he took to reassure the militia leaders that their traffic would not be challenged included the distribution of formal and symbolic titles, public statements of friendship, distribution of military hardware, the right to staff key security institutions with clients and even veto power over the decision-making process. In order to undermine them later, he had patiently to develop relations with lieutenants and rank and file and slowly separate them from their leaders, establish new security agencies with overlapping mandates, creating his own clientele by co-opting people into the state administration. When observed from the exterior, the process appeared contradictory, as Shevarnadze tried to increase his political leverage by accepting to maintain the state:

extremely weak in certain areas, especially public administration and taxation, was made credible by handing entire bureaucracies over to incorporated militia members, as explicit side-payments for their loyalty.[108]

Again we see here Schmitt's 'sovereign' at work, succeeding where mechanical institution-building failed (see chapter 6). Shevarnadze did not reap the benefits of his work, but his successors did.

A case similar to that of Georgia under Shevarnadze was Rakhmonov's Tajikistan. Another master of divide and rule, Rakhmonov 'realigned domestic institutions and economic policy to make it more difficult for elites from different regions to cooperate with each other'. He also secured external support, allowing Russia to control the national borders. At this point he could proceed to isolate first the Hissori clan, who had been the original pillar of the pro-government militia coalition ('Popular Front'), and then the Khojandis, who had been dominant in Soviet times. He then consolidated Kulobi support by giving them dominance over the richest lands of the south-west, separating the grassroots of the faction from the leaders, whom he proceeded gradually to eliminate or marginalise. The UTO armed opposition was similarly co-opted with the promise of personal rewards, separated from its base and then progressively marginalised.[109]

If the role of political leadership and brinkmanship is undeniable, the recovery of the monopoly of large-scale violence from processes of decay can also be favoured by social and economic processes, independently of any political player's will. Internal war is also an opportunity for capital accumulation.[110] In its context, political and military players may also team up with war profiteers and 'rogue capitalists' in order to develop their own shadow logistics and financial services. Could a relationship of this kind represent an early form of the marriage of capital and coercion which in Tilly's interpretation 'made' Europe? It can be argued that the Tillyan model no longer applies, because the process of state formation is over-determined by international constraints.[111] As a result, the relationship that would-be rulers might be able to build with rogue or shadow capitalists would be difficult to consolidate and legitimise, particularly in the long term. The financial cooperation between warlords and rogue capitalists tends therefore to be limited to war situations and the immediate post-conflict period. After that, 'insurgents' either turn into 'mafiosi' or are forced gradually to drop their dangerous liaisons and clean up their act if they want to reinvent themselves as politicians or statesmen. The rise and fall of Charles Taylor of Liberia is exemplary in this regard; his failure to clean up led to his quick downfall.[112]

From the perspective of state-building, for the potential of a cycle of this kind to be successfully harnessed, what matters is that some agent able to claim the role of a central ruler emerges or is consolidated. Such an agent has to reassure the new capitalists that the successful accumulation of capital during internal war will be protected.

In conclusion, this chapter has shown why coercion remains a key ingredient of the state even when the problem is maintaining the monopoly, not establishing it in the first place. The risk of a challenge to the monopoly, however remote, can never be completely discounted. When the challenge does arise, it cannot always be met by coercion in 'velvet gloves'; often there is no alternative to ruthless coercion; even if it could, the ruling elite does not want to face the costs associated with tame coercion and with a political approach to containing opposition. Hypothesis 3 concerning the need for ruthless violence in state formation re-emerges again here. The challenge can be strong enough to roll back state consolidation to state formation, smashing the monopoly of violence; perhaps more often, it can be the clumsy reaction of the coercive apparatus of the state which turns a modest challenge into a much more substantial one. This is not necessarily because of simple stupidity or incompetence, but also because of political dynamics within the ruling coalition and because of genuine dilemmas arising from the type of challenge a state might face. The very effort of fighting off an insurgency can create cracks within a ruling elite, calling into question the political settlement which had allowed state formation in the first place, confirming hypothesis 6:

the re-negotiation of the terms of the political settlement, which may include changes in the command and control structure within the coercive apparatus, can weaken the ability of the ruling elite to operate in a coordinated fashion and endanger the monopoly of violence.

4

MAINTAINING THE MONOPOLY
THE ROLE OF POLITICAL POLICING

'The Sovereign can punish immediately any fault he discovers, but he cannot flatter himself into supposing that he sees all the faults he should punish'.

de Tocqueville, *Democracy in America*, 1835

As already stated in this book, the personal inclinations of leaders matter. However, in case any reader should be tempted to dismiss Stalin's and Hitler's orgies of violence as mere psychopathology, one should consider the Phoenix programme, adopted after much hesitation by the Americans in Vietnam. The programme is still the object of substantial controversy, in particular concerning the role played by targeted assassination. This account by a Vietnam veteran is particularly grim:

The problem was, how do you find the people on the blacklist? It's not like you had their address and telephone number. The normal procedure would be to go into a village and just grab someone and say, 'Where's Nguyen so-and-so?' Half the time the people were so afraid they would not say anything. Then a Phoenix team would take the informant, put a sandbag over his head, poke out two holes so he could see, put commo wire around his neck like a long leash, and walk him through the village and say, 'When we go by Nguyen's house scratch your head'. Then that night Phoenix would come back, knock on the door, and say, 'April Fool, motherfucker'. Whoever answered the door would get wasted. As far as they were concerned, whoever answered was a Communist, including family members. Sometimes they'd come back to camp with ears to prove that they killed people.[1]

Another veteran, despite his own pacifist inclinations, stated that:

If you accept the need to have a war, then I think an effort like Phoenix is necessary. You go after the political underpinning of the other side.[2]

The point being made in this book is not about how bad (or not really so bad) the Phoenix Programme was; instead the point is about the comparatively soft context in which this occurred. Phoenix was taking place in what was for the United States still a 'small war' which had grown too much; the monopoly of violence in the homeland was never challenged and the Americans could afford to look at the issue of state formation in South Vietnam with relative cool. As discussed in the case of the colonial wars above (chapter 1), liberal regimes often proved ready to compromise on the rule of law standards they had developed for the homeland when faced with a local challenge to their monopoly of large-scale violence overseas.

In Phoenix's case the Americans decided to abandon any pretence of rule of law and embarked on this operation to destroy much of the Viet Cong cadre structure. The CIA was deeply involved in the programme, at whose core were methods of improved information gathering on suspects and their 'fast track' processing. Guidelines to avoid torture and needless killing were in place, but were rarely respected in the context of the ruthless confrontation. The Viet Cong suffered serious damage, although at the price of substantial human rights violations which compromised political support back home.[3] What to expect, then, from new states, short of financial and human resources to achieve any rapid success in the taming of the violence?

Uses of Political Policing

Internal security services have from the perspective of state-building multiple uses. The most obvious one is physically protecting the rulers from secret plots. For this purpose, they do not need a very sophisticated structure or deep reach, as they just need to secure the immediate surroundings of the 'prince', such as the court or maybe the capital. The next use is to control the state's own organisations and institutions, starting from the armed forces. Finally, they can be used to keep an eye on the country as a whole, infiltrating society and spying on virtually anyone, a particularly useful role in the presence of active opposition or of an insurgency. Intelligence in this case becomes 'the link connecting one side's strength with the other side's weakness'.[4]

Depending on the nature of political regimes, different priorities have been adopted at different times by different rulers. Most contemporary Arab regimes have, for example, prioritised control over the army, mainly because of the expansion of Arab armed forces from the 1950s onwards and a long series of military coups.[5] The Soviet regime's attitude varied widely during its existence, from being the most ruthless police state in Stalin's time, to a much more restrained policy later (see below). In such cases, the secret police was a very well defined presence in the life of these societies. In the 'Western democracies' the security services have been as discrete and low profile as possible, almost pretending not to exist.

State-Building

The first 'modern' political police system is generally considered to have appeared under the reign of Joseph II of Austria. It was 'modern' in its systematic penetration of all classes of society and in the lavishness of its resources, as well as the fact that it was not created to watch for court intrigues or desperate revolutionaries, but in order to maintain surveillance of the official classes, the army, the bureaucracy, the judges and the clergy. Among its tasks were also the prevention of corruption and keeping a more general watch on the state of the nation. Joseph's intention was to facilitate his aim of modernising the state: his intelligence system allowed him to supervise the 'work in progress.'[6] In other words, the secret police was in this case functional to a project of state-building. Arguably there was an element of 'state-building' in Ivan the Terrible's Oprichnina, at least in the beginning, but the case is not as clear cut as Joseph II's, because the Oprichnina degenerated into a reign of terror, with negative consequences for the stability of the state. The role of the secret police in the state-building projects of the twentieth century cases is recurrent, as we shall see later.

Already what might have been the first effective intelligence service based on historical record, in the Egyptian empire under Pharaohs Amenphis II and Amenhotep II, seems to have had a similar task. It does not appear that the Egyptian monarchy had a sophisticated and organised secret police dedicated to maintaining internal order; this was mainly achieved through the clergy, a privileged class who succeeded in inculcating belief among the people. It is of particular importance to this study, however, that a kind of internal intelligence system existed, centred around the *vizir* and a high official known as 'the eyes and the ears of the king'. Its purpose seems to have been mainly to control the state bureaucracy. Even the Assyrians appear to have had a 'service', with agents reporting on the mood of the people in the streets and exercising constant supervision of the loyalty and efficiency of royal officials. Suspicious conduct was reported to the court and special 'messengers' were dispatched to investigate.[7]

The Persians also had an office called 'Eye of the king', which controlled all the satraps and the royal functionaries. Cyrus advertised the fact that he was recruiting agents through the offer of considerable financial rewards and that he listened personally to them, presumably to prevent people from speaking against him. On the other hand, royal commissioners were used to check the administration, and the Minister of the Royal Post was akin to a minister of intelligence. The system appears to have been later adopted by Alexander, after his conquest of the Persian Empire.[8]

The internal intelligence of the Arab Caliphate presented some similarities with the examples above. The postmaster general (called 'Eye of the Caliph') was at the same time the chief of the intelligence service and acted as supervisor of the state bureaucracy and judiciary, as well as a supplier of information about the political tendencies of citizens. Again rather than focusing on direct threats to the regime, the 'Eye of the Caliph' also reported on the situation of farmers and the prospects for the harvest, as this had obvious political implications. The Caliph also had a separate agency employing informers and spies, sometimes numbering in the thousands. It appears to have been run by a special director of intelligence called the Khaibar, independent of the postmaster general.[9]

In countries with weak or corrupt bureaucratic structures, the security services have played a supervisory role even in more recent times, to make the state machinery more accountable to the ruling elite. In Brezhnev's Soviet Union, for example, the KGB was, during the 1970s, tasked with fighting economic crime and corruption, under Andropov's leadership, because of the failure of the Ministry of Interior to act in that regard. The police was poorly paid, and corruption within its ranks was common. The KGB had a deserved reputation in Soviet society for being largely untarnished by the corruption which was affecting other agencies of the state. The KGB had been involved in fighting corruption and economic crime even before that, particularly in the Caucasus where such 'malpractices' were endemic. The mandate to fight corruption was strengthened in 1980–81, after the KGB itself reported to the Kremlin that the Polish revolt (Solidarnosh) had been primarily motivated by corruption. In general, it seems that the KGB really believed that widespread corruption was one of the main causes of popular dissatisfaction in all socialist systems. From 1982, as KGB head Andropov became President of the USSR, the fight against corruption became more repressive, even infringing civil rights. It never succeeded in stamping corruption out of the system, however.[10]

Policing the Ruling Coalition

Contrary to the cases discussed above, the Romans were slow in developing a proper intelligence service and always kept its role more limited, while the senate and factional competition played the role of supervising the state administration. The republic relied on the goodwill of allies to supply external information and intelligence; this system was vulnerable because if the alliance broke up, the Romans would be left without reliable information.[11] The use of private spies expanded greatly during the period of the civil wars and from the early days of the Empire. During the civil wars, Octavian used agents for political propaganda and to gather information about the mood of the population, as well as for more 'operational' uses such as dispatching 'undesirable' individuals. He also used agitators to undermine Mark Antony's status among his soldiers. The use of intelligence agents attached to the imperial bodyguard then became common under the empire, at least from the second century AD, with spying on the army, the bureaucracy, members of the court and religious sects, as well as carrying out targeted assassinations. The system was very weakly supervised and easily subject to abuse: the so-called *frumentarii* often misused their information and got involved in intrigues. Eventually Emperor Diocletian abolished them and created a new corps of intelligence, the *agens in rebus*, now forming a special department in the imperial service and hence subject to stronger supervision.[12]

The *agentes in rebus* did not function very smoothly either. Byzantium later maintained the system, but under Emperor Julian their number was cut to 17 from the previous several hundred, because of complaints from the provinces about their misbehaviour. Soon their numbers started rising rapidly again, reaching over 1,000, but recruitment this time was made very selective. Both in Rome and Byzantium they were put in charge of supervising the execution of imperial orders and the regular functioning of the administration,[13] but they too had the tendency to become corrupt. Emperor Constantinus Augustus in around AD 355 several times issued laws which required the *agentes* to avoid imprisoning people without proof and threatened them with punishment in case of transgression.[14] The *agentes in rebus* and another group of officials known as *notarii* were also used to supervise the army deployed in the provinces. Finally the Romans developed from the time of Domitian (AD 51–96) a sophisticated system of 'counter-intelligence' in the army, building a database of files on every centurion, which were then used to control appointments, promotions and transfers.[15]

The relatively modest role attributed to political policing in Rome was echoed in most of modern age Europe. Elizabeth I's spymaster Francis Walsingham did not really have an organisation to rely on and was paying his spies out of his own pockets.[16] In France, until the Revolution the model remained the one created by Richelieu, that is the 'high police', the *Cabinet Noir*. It was however a very small organisation, never employing more than fifteen individuals full time.[17] The focus was on political machinations in high places, or in any case prominent dissident exiles, which the political police of the monarchy tried to silence, kidnap and possibly even murder,[18] as opposed to the danger represented by the mob. The largest secret police of the modern age in Europe was probably Ivan the Terrible's Oprichnina, with around 6,000 members.[19] It is telling that even the Russian Oprichnina relied primarily on individual denunciations, rather than on its own investigative efforts.[20] The Oprichnina was soon disbanded and nothing resembling it was re-established for a long time. Peter the Great's Preobrazhensky Office started off with just two clerks and eight assistants.[21] The primary role of these secret police was to keep in line the various components of the ruling elite, hence their modest size and aims.

This type of political policing relates to what was discussed in *The political dimensions of the monopoly of violence* above, and particularly coercive coalition-building. Although this use of political policing has continued into the twentieth century and arguably into the twenty-first century, it is not discussed very much because it has been overshadowed by other purposes of political policing, which absorb much greater energy. See also *Coercive coalition-building* below.

Policing the Opposition

Political policing as a system to prevent challenges from outside the ruling elite also had a long history. The Chinese empire, always a leader in terms of sophistication of government, experimented with different types of internal espionage. In the fourth century BC, villages were grouped into larger units and a system of mutual espionage introduced: every household in each group of villages was responsible for the behaviour of every other household. A more bureaucratised secret service appeared under the Han, although it does not seem to have been as efficient, and the system of collective responsibility and mutual spying was re-established in the tenth century AD.[22]

From Joseph II onwards, the model of an intelligence system capable of monitoring what was happening in society became increasingly common throughout Europe, although not necessarily with the same transformative aims as the original. His model would later provide a 'solid foundation' to suppress Jacobinism, even if it had not originally been meant for such a purpose.[23] It was indeed the French Revolution that ushered in a new era of 'deep' political policing. The old, narrowly focused political police was demonstrated to be anachronistic by the late eighteenth century. The argument that the French crown succumbed in 1789 because of the inefficiency of its police might or might not be true, but successive governments took it seriously, as I shall show below.

Under Napoleon's chief of police, Fouché, every branch of the administration was subordinated to the police. This does not mean that the period could be described as a reign of terror: the experience of the revolutionary years with terror inclined Napoleon and Fouché to adopt whenever possible softer approaches: co-option became the rule.[24] Even the governments of the reactionary era avoided excesses and bloodshed to a large extent. Growth notwithstanding, their political police was still mostly small in number by the twentieth century's standards, and agents were usually part-time informants, payment being by results.[25] For all his reputation, Metternich only had 700 agents at his service.[26]

Even the Tsarist intelligence of the years following the French Revolution (known as the Third Section) started with just sixteen full-time officials and had only grown to forty by 1846, although it had a wide network of informers and controlled the gendarmes.[27] It was not until the establishment of the Okhrana (1880) that the secret police of Russia reached a membership of thousands again. The Okhrana had 20,000 staff and a big budget, but its experience demonstrated that high levels of staffing and good funding are not necessarily what are needed to make a secret police function: skilled staff are essential.[28] Given the social and educational development of Europe at that time, there were structural constraints on how big a functional secret police could grow. The Third Section had been staffed by more qualified people and had proved more effective despite its small numbers. Thanks to its analytical capabilities, it developed an awareness of the problems facing the empire and developed proposals for alleviating them, which were often not very different from those of the liberals. For example, it produced reports sympathetic to the idea of freeing the serfs and softening the censorship.[29] The Third Section had the opposite problem to what the Okhrana experienced later: it was actually quite burdened by its information-gathering and welfare tasks, ending up overworked and not very effective at combating political dissent.

All this suggests that the task of policing political opposition, once elite bargaining and the monopoly of violence are in place, is manageable with limited resources if there is limited violence.

Coercive Coalition-Building

At various stages of the consolidation of a regime, *pre-empting hostile collective action through co-option, alliances, manipulation and intimidation is as important as the mere accumulation of the means of coercion* (hypothesis 2). Above we have discussed how political policing can serve the purpose of maintaining a coalition formed on the basis of coercion; we are now going to look at how political policing can bring about a coalition of this kind in the first place. In modern terms, this task of the political police often takes the shape of 'controlled democracy'. This is the case for example in South Korea, where:

the political system is still [in 1998] managed by existing (state) elites who employ the security services as part of their strategy of control. [...] In this corporatist system state elites have the deciding voice in matters of social concern and national policy, over the wishes of business, organized labour and other civil society groups. Democracy in this sense, whilst tangible and genuine, is also a system in which existing elites seek to maintain control. The security services are a part of this process: the [services] is thus embedded in a bureaucratic and politicized system of government which influences its priorities and operations.[30]

Apart from the fact that the South Korean intelligence '[displayed] the self-interest of all (powerful) bureaucracies in preserving its position and resources', thereby complicating its long-term role in managing 'controlled democracy', the main risk, of course, is of the process getting out of control. The South Korean story was eventually one of successful transition to democratic government, with the security service seeing most of the commanding staff replaced and many laws changed in the direction of greater restriction to its domestic activities. Later the intelligence service played an important role in securing the victory of Kim Young Sam in 1992, a moderate reformer acceptable to the establishment. The transition was not completely smooth, however, with some of the reforms of the early 1990s being revoked in 1997, before being re-implemented shortly afterwards. At that point the agency's role in Korean society was being undermined by a series of scandals, in which the agency was involved alongside the country's political elite. Allegedly, the security agency continued being involved in South Korean politics even after that, but had clearly lost the ability to manage political developments.[31] The Korean example once again suggests that in the long run 'limited' or 'controlled' democracy might be an oxymoron.

The Iranian system of competitive but restrained elections (2009) is a good example of derailment. The role of the security services in intimidating the intellectual opposition to the Islamic regime and the more radical wing of the reformist movement has been alleged by various sources; Iran's judiciary found some involvement of intelligence agents in the murder of several dissidents. The fact that a number of agents were arrested suggests that not everything went according to plan.[32]

In Algeria, the security services have been accused of engineering a 'strategy of tension', favouring the emergence of Islamist insurgent groups to discredit the Islamic Salvation Front before the 1991 elections, and then to manipulate public opinion after the military coup, as well as to motivate the state apparatus. The infiltration of political parties was also widely practised. The Algerian services, however, lost control of their agents within the insurgency and had to re-infiltrate it from scratch as well as set up a very violent repressive effort.[33]

The best known case is that of Peru under President Fujimori, when the chief of the secret police, Montesinos, subverted the political system, 'methodically' bribing judges, politicians and the news media.

Montesinos and Fujimori maintained the facade of democracy—the citizens voted, judges decided, the media reported—but they drained its substance.[34]

Montesinos tried to reduce the recourse to violence to a minimum, particularly against prominent individuals, although he did employ death squads against farmers and students. Montesinos developed a sophisticated system to gather the financial resources to fund his system of bribery and corruption, well beyond the bare budget of the Peruvian intelligence, as well as using his position at the centre of the state to distribute favours, including promotions, judicial string-pulling, support in election campaigns and congressional votes. He also used blackmail against more resilient individuals, for example filming military officers in a brothel. The Montesinos system is of particular interest because it shows how it was possible heavily to tweak a formal democracy in the interest of a power group by using money to buy the free media. However, the weakness of the system is shown by the fact that the system lasted ten years, a relatively short time span for a political regime, before being brought down in a scandal.[35]

This again raises the issue of the risks implicit in subtle systems of control and 'limited democracies': how long can political dynamics be controlled? The examples brought up in this paragraph are mostly failures; indeed the evidence suggests that complex societies, with dynamic social groups and organisations, are only susceptible to limited amounts of coercive coalition-making. However, political policing serves the purpose of moderating the demands of new partners in elite bargaining, for example, convincing them to drop demands of justice and retaliation against the abuses of the coalition previously in power, or dropping their more radical social and political demands. See also *Controlling the controllers* below.

Taming the Coercion

The earlier example of the Third Section in Tsarist Russia illustrates well how 'deep' social control through the political police is not simple to implement for a government which does not have deep roots in the educated class. How could a 'reactionary' government create a secret police large enough to monitor and supervise the activities of the expanding intelligentsia, without extensively recruiting within the ranks of the intelligentsia itself? And if it did recruit, how could it insulate the secret police from the influence of subversive ideas circulating within the educated class?

This might go some way to explain why the option of establishing at least a degree of rule of law has often been taken into serious consideration even by regimes which in the end followed another pattern of evolution. The attraction was not the rule of law per se, but its potential in terms of taming the coercive side of ruling, as a strategy of pre-empting the rise of challenges. This is reflected in the ambiguous 'philosophical' grounding of nineteenth century secret policing. Throughout the nineteenth century it was relatively easy to classify liberal countries, more discrete and respectful of the rule of law (within certain limits), as distinct from authoritarian regimes, which increasingly looked like 'police states'. Still, the separation was never complete, as most authoritarian regimes did not in principle rule out an evolution along more liberal lines. Even the Tsarist Okhrana maintained a reluctance to use violence in its repression, which one author described as the result of a 'conflict between desire to create a Rechstaat and fear of relinquishing domination over political and legal functions.'[36] Metternich, despite his reputation, was not interested in ruthless repression; for example he opposed the radical attitudes of the Prince of Canosa, an ardent Catholic and royalist who in 1815 was appointed by Ferdinand of Naples as chief of police. Canosa's purges and his sponsoring of the Catholic secret society of the Calderari were somehow seen as having contributed to the 1820 Neapolitan rising, and Metternich insisted on his sacking.[37]

The rule of law seems therefore to have tempted European rulers, at least in so far as it seemed to offer a way to manage the security establishment and prevent excesses and disloyalty. Indeed as the threat of social revolution receded and 'high police' or internal intelligence started (again) playing a major role in the running of the state and in protecting rulers from a narrower ring of enemies, the issue of the loyalty of the agents of coercion became important. Napoleon appears to have been wary of Fouché: he never granted him the full powers he demanded, and created counter-balancing organisations under Dubois, the prefect of Paris, and under General Savary. In 1810 Fouché was dismissed for acting too often on his own initiative and for maintaining contacts with the British. Savary was loyal but unimaginative, and could not prevent the coup of General Malet during the Moscow campaign, which came close to toppling the regime. Although there are no examples of security services directly taking over power in a country before the twentieth century, plots and manipulation were much more common. For example, there is some evidence that the Tsarist secret police, Okhrana, might have been involved in the 1911 assassination of Stolypin, the Prime Minister of the Tsar.[38]

The value of reading the taming of coercion not as the result of liberal convictions of a particular set of rulers, but of a specific strategy to tackle the problem of how to maintain monopoly most effectively is reinforced by another consideration: the 'liberal' states continued to use a variety of techniques of coercion, including torture, on a very large scale against those excluded from the privilege of being part of the political settlement. This happened particularly in their colonies but not only there. As Rejali points out, many clean torture techniques first appeared in the context of British military punishments and of French and British colonial operations.[39]

An additional reason for ruling elites having an interest in keeping the political police under control is that there is evidence that the reliance on torture in interrogation has been inversely proportional to the success in defeating insurgencies. The British Special Branch in Malaya did not use torture, but relied instead on turning around communist insurgents and using them to convince others like them to surrender. It used strong rewards as an incentive and offered a new life to the deserters.[40] The Iranian SAVAK, while using torture extensively, also relied primarily on turning around opposition activists, enjoying a particularly high degree of success with communists, who were more susceptible to being convinced of the value of the Shah's programme of modernisation.[41]

The first half of the twentieth century, with its radical clash of ideologies and wars of annihilation, was not particularly suited to the evolution of internal intelligence towards a 'velvet glove' approach, nor for that matter towards accurate targeting. However, even in those not very conducive circumstances, a trend in that direction could be noted. The German army on the Eastern Front, for example, began to develop a relatively sophisticated policy of promoting internal differences in the ranks of the partisans and of targeting the leadership, as well as creating local counter-insurgent militias around local leaders.[42] Soviet views evolved in part in similar directions, promoting the targeting of insurgent leaders while still indulging in the imposition of collective guilt, hostage taking and mass deportation.[43] As we see, tame coercion and selective targeting often go hand in hand, but let's not forget that they are not the same.

A traditional, effective way of gathering information in counter-insurgency has usually been reliance on local militias, local police forces or the local administrative structure. The drawback of militias is their tendency to apply indiscriminate repression, which is likely to make the information gathered not very reliable.[44] A relatively disciplined police force usually works better, but as the chapter on policing has shown, often the rural areas of a poorly developed country are very thinly and ineffectively policed. I discuss the role of local government in chapter 5, but usually its reach to the rural areas is limited. This is why professional intelligence services, capable of acting discretely and of accurate targeting, are a major asset in any internal conflict. Indeed the creation of the famed Special Branch in Malaya was a consequence of the ineffectiveness of the police in gathering information locally, not least because few rural policemen spoke any Chinese (the language of the large majority of the population in the areas most affected by the insurgency) and because of the long distances involved.[45] This was not always understood by 'counter-insurgents'. In Vietnam, the CIA was originally in charge of the formation of the Civilian Irregular Defense Groups, a successful programme, but the army took it over in 1963.[46] As Kalyvas puts it, the very presence of local agents signals an organisation's willingness and potential capacity to be selective in its repression, and therefore discourages hostile behaviour. This was for example how the Viet Cong viewed the presence of enemy informers.[47]

Back to State Formation II

We have seen above how the French revolutionary wars momentarily disrupted Europe's pattern of taming coercion. They were not the last episode to cause such disruption. As Europe entered its most violent century, the development of intelligence services accelerated and radicalised. In the new context, the idea of a world without political police was going to be *de facto* reneged upon by the reformists and revolutionaries who had earlier propagated it. The German Social Democrats after World War I abolished the political police, but operational realities soon led to the secret re-establishment in Prussia of a political police; in order not to offend the political principles of the Social Democrats, it was disguised by nominally attaching it as a sub-section of the general police department.[48]

A much more dramatic revision of earlier ideological statements characterised Russia. Soon after conquering power, the Bolsheviks established the Cheka as a 'temporary' organ to face the peculiar situation of the civil war and to 'wage war against the class enemies'. Terror was used on a scale much greater than under the Directory in revolutionary France. Whether terror on such a scale helped the Bolshevik cause or not is still a matter of debate, but the context was one that rewarded ruthlessness: the Bolsheviks were bringing to life a new state. The Cheka already had a staff of 37,000 in January 1919 and reached 260,000 at its peak in mid 1921.[49]

Even in these days of civil war, however, the tasks of the Cheka were not limited to terror. In December 1917 the Cheka established a department to combat speculation, which did not prove very effective because at the time the priorities were other. However, soon the Cheka also began to establish close surveillance on personnel of the Soviet economic and trade agencies. In the autumn of 1919 the Economic Administration was created within the Cheka, to combat abuse and sabotage in institutions administering the national economy. The Special Inter-departmental commission followed, with the task of investigating and combating speculation and abuse of office. It played an important role in studying and understanding the defects of the economic structure, through the collection of information and statistical data.[50] In other words, the Cheka already played some role as an agent of the building of a new state.

That the ruthlessness of the Cheka was the result of the military/political environment and not just of the ideological inclinations of the Bolsheviks is, in a sense, demonstrated by the German case. The National Socialists were capable of even more extreme violence, as is demonstrated by what they did on the Eastern Front. In Germany, however, they were never seriously challenged and could always depend on the effectiveness and reliability of an undisrupted state bureaucracy. The Nazis did not need to create a very large Gestapo, being well served by the German state machinery and not needing to terrorise it into action. Their plans for transforming Germany were modest compared to those of the Bolsheviks for Russia. In January 1934 the Gestapo had only 1,329 employees and at its pre-war peak just 7,000 (cf. the considerably higher figures in the Stasi, below).[51] A certain residual respect for the rule of law continued to exist into the first few years of the Third Reich, when many arrested suspects were still being freed for lack of evidence.[52]

The impact of a crisis in the monopoly of violence on the role and functioning of the political police is also demonstrated by the rapid growth of its role even in the context of the wars fought by 'liberal' colonial powers in the late nineteenth to early twentieth century (the Boer War, and the Philippines). Callwell famously declared that 'in no class of warfare is a well-organized and well served intelligence department more essential than in that against guerrillas.'[53] The use of torture techniques by Western democracies in counter-insurgency efforts is documented throughout the twentieth century and into the first decade of the twenty-first.[54] The ruthlessness of these repressions was not on the same scale as the Bolsheviks' violence, but neither was the nature of the threat: these were 'small wars' fought away from home.

Intelligence-gathering is of great importance to insurgents too, even if some of the early classics of counter-insurgency under-estimated its value. Callwell, for example, believed that the insurgent would suffer little from lack of intelligence, due to his knowledge of the land, the population and his ability to monitor the movement of the enemy.[55] As insurgencies started to be populated by sophisticated organisations during the twentieth century, a consensus started to emerge that intelligence played an essential role on both sides of a conflict. In reality it was not just a matter of gathering information, but also of preventing the enemy from gathering it:

Intercepting enemy couriers often provides priceless information; the capture of such persons also disrupts the enemy's internal command system. [...] Proactive counterinsurgent tactics also damage the enemy's intelligence capability.[56]

A guerrilla band which is constantly harassed and driven from place to place soon loses contact with its own sources of information; it becomes confused and its intelligence system breaks down.[57]

A keen sense of the value of political policing was often maintained by former insurgents once in power, as shown by the tight population control implemented by the Chinese Communists after their conquest of power, particularly in areas exposed to Nationalist counter-attacks.[58]

How Much Control?

The management of an internal intelligence system is always going to be problematic in a number of ways, whether it is called political police and dominates the life of the population or it is remote from the public eye and discreet in its activities. The first dilemma is how far the attempt to control the political life of a country from above should go.

The need for a centralised intelligence effort, 'collecting, processing, analysing and collating/assessing the intelligence from all the disparate sources', firmly established itself and became a matter of consensus among 'counter-insurgents'.[59] The British police Special Branch in Malaya was granted the exclusive right to have secret agents and became a recipient for all raw information on the insurgency, to good effect.[60] Particularly when regimes were freshly established and subject to strong challenges, the need for a centralised intelligence effort did not need much persuasion. The new state of the Viet Minh moved quickly to create an original, unified national security at the beginning of 1946, being under pressure from both the pro-Chinese nationalists in the north and the French in the south. Although the Vietnamese communists had for tactical reasons to surrender the top posts in the security to non-communists, they took care to maintain all the real power in the hands of party men.[61]

In the absence of an open and serious challenge to the state, political policing is bound to be controversial, and the more so if it is highly centralised. As the author of *Police State* pointed out, 'no matter how much police powers are formally controlled by an insistence of due process, objective expert evidence or independent arbitration, their application, which is the work of the police services, is essentially arbitrary'. Moreover:

the complexity of administration in modern societies is such that if all laws and police ordnances were to be universally enforced, all citizens would be criminals. [...] The more societies make this anti-social behaviour technically illegal, the greater the discretionary powers vested in the police authorities.[62]

In authoritarian regimes the centralisation of the political police was of course easier to implement. The KGB remained to the end the most centralised of Soviet institutions. In the republics, ministries as a rule were less centralised than all-union ministerial agencies, but not the KGB, which remained highly centralised and controlled from the top.[63] One problem that even authoritarian regimes have to face, however, is the sheer cost of establishing a structure able to control society fully in the face of widespread dissatisfaction. The East German Stasi, not even the most extreme example, employed 274,000 full-time staff and 174,000 informers, for a country of 18 million.[64]

Even if the impact of civilian oversight cannot therefore be minimised, it is also true that the dilemma cannot be reduced to the different options taken by 'democracies', 'authoritarian' governments and 'totalitarian' ones, either.[65] Hans Frank, a loyal member of the National Socialist party and governor general of occupied Poland, commented that in Germany in the early 1940s:

unfortunately the view appears to be growing, even among leading National Socialists, that the greater the uncertainty regarding the legal position of the ordinary citizen, the more secure is the position of the authorities.[66]

In other words, even among the Nazis there was no obvious consensus on how far the police state should go.

The case of the intelligence services of the Soviet Union is worthy of examining in some depth, to illustrate this particular dilemma. While as illustrated earlier the Cheka had extra-legal status and was conceived as a temporary organisation for the time of civil war, the problem of a more institutionalised approach to political repression and control emerged in the early years of Soviet power. The People's Commissariat of Justice, for example, turned hostile to Cheka because instead of turning offenders over to revolutionary tribunals, it tended to rely on summary justice. Complaints about the excesses of the Cheka led to the establishment of 'definite procedural requirements' concerning arrests when the new GPU was launched in 1922; it was only authorised to investigate, and summary justice was not allowed. The new style of political policing was somewhat ahead of the reality of the new regime, and already within a few months the GPU was given broad powers to exile, imprison or even in some cases execute. By the time the inter-party clean-up was underway in 1929, special regulations were issued to deprive the procuracy of any control over the investigative activities of the political police. After the orgy of executions and sentencing of the first half of the 1930s, again the need was felt for a stabilisation and some form of institutionalisation of the repression, although arbitrary behaviour continued every time it was needed. By 1939 the situation had stabilised to the point that Party members were given some protections from indiscriminate purges. The end of the terror was signalled by the fact that the political police was made into a scapegoat of the past excesses.[67]

The system however remained extremely repressive and coercive, even by the end of World War II, when the Soviet regime was riding on a high wave of support. A US military intelligence assessment of the Soviet counter-intelligence in the first half of the 1940s commented that the:

constant emphasis on repression and coercion breeds resentment and disaffection even in normally loyal persons. [...] The very comprehensiveness of espionage regulations and security measures disperses the efforts of counterintelligence agencies and forces them to depend primarily upon routine and stereotyped methods. Consequently, while inexpert agents are easily detected, skilled foreign agents with authentic credentials can operate with considerable impunity.[68]

The deportations of the 1940s still fell short of a professionally nearly blood-less operation, even if the Soviet propaganda of the time tried to describe them as such.[69] Deeper reforms only started with Stalin's death:

Stalin's successors arrived at the same conclusion as that reached by the French at the close of their revolution: the police are the enemy of democracy. This view held that the police, while a necessary and inevitable institution of society, must be firmly con-trolled. The Party thus took various steps to ensure that the militia apparatus provided no further threat to its preeminence. Among the most visible of these steps was the appointment of trusted Party personnel to posts in the militia leadership, a policy that reinstated Party dominance over the institution in the short term, but led to crippling corruption in the long term. Another key step was the reshuffling of the entire law enforcement apparatus in order to prevent the reemergence of a hegemonic police [...]. In 1954, for the first time in three decades, the KGB (Committee on State Security, or security police) was separated from the MVD (Ministry of Internal Affairs, or the regular police)—a major achievement of the de-Stalinization process.[70]

The KGB, formed in 1954, was meant to incarnate the new post-Stalinist ethos of the secret police, although the laws which had allowed the terror were only repealed in 1956, after having been used to eliminate Beria. The legal reforms of 1955–61 offered some substantial protection to the Soviet citizen against police persecution: procurators were given powers to control political police investigations, punishment could only be imparted by courts and the concept of political crime was narrowed. However, legality was still conceived primarily to protect the state, not the citizens, and as the Khrushovite liber-alisation started to falter, the jurisdiction of the KGB in investigating crimes started to expand again. The institutional role of the KGB was never well defined, but there was certainly a change of style in the 1970s, with the adop-tion of softer approaches. KGB officers started dealing with misbehaving citi-zens through 'friendly chats', which warned them of the risks they were taking. As of the early 1980s, the number of political arrests rarely exceeded 200 a year. In sum, while coercion became gradually more sophisticated and carefully tar-geted, institutionalised limitations on police powers were never fully estab-lished. While Khrushchev downgraded the status of the political police and put an end to widespread police violence, he did not close the legal loopholes that enabled the KGB to infringe individual rights.[71]

The dilemma of how much control may be most effective in perpetuating the monopoly of large-scale violence is made all the more complex by the fact that investing in intelligence-gathering ad hoc, that is when a clear threat emerges, might not work. In their incubation phase, guerrilla movements tend to be disregarded by the authorities and particularly by armies, which do not consider it worthwhile to deal with minuscule developments such as low-scale propaganda and infiltration.[72] As Galula puts it:

until the insurgent has clearly revealed his intentions by engaging in subversion or open violence, he represents nothing but an imprecise, potential menace...[73]

In Oman in the 1960s the intelligence service was reportedly slow in adapting to the new threat of the nationalist movement based among young Omanis, as opposed to the supporters of the old theocracy in exile, who had been the main threat in the 1950s. The sultan was hostile to recruiting younger Omanis; nobody dared contradict him and therefore the service had to continue to rely on old informers. Typically little attention was paid to 'discussion groups' in Muscat, even if evidence was emerging that they were linked to the rebels. The sultan claimed to be monitoring the capital with his own sources, even if this had already proved ineffective in the past.[74] In a completely different context, during the first half of the 1980s Israeli intelligence ignored reports from its informers on the ground about the growth of Hezbollah as a major force. By 1986, when the challenge presented by Hezbollah became clear, Israeli intelligence did not have a single agent inside that organisation.[75]

As in the case of the 'oil spot' counter-insurgency strategy described in chapter 2, the ideological insurgencies of the twentieth century have proved particularly difficult to crack for intelligence services. An Israeli intelligence officer remarked how in the 1970s and early 1980s it had been easy to recruit informers among the Lebanese Shiites, who lacked a national identity and felt rejected by their compatriots. The appearance of Hezbollah on the scene changed everything: 'suddenly, they have a framework to identify with, to strengthen their backs. For people like this it is much more difficult to betray their community'.[76]

On the other hand the temptation to indulge in a massive pre-emptive screening of suspects can be counter-productive. Fear of denunciation is a strong motivator to join insurgent movements, exacerbated by the fact that bad tips usually present a major problem. In Kalyvas' words, part of the problem is that individuals are generally more practised at deceiving than at detecting deception. Various 'institutional' mechanisms have been devised over time to tackle the problem, such as the appeal procedures used by the Chinese communist insurgents. A more widely used and perhaps more effective system is cross-checking which, however, requires a high level of control and an efficient bureaucracy. Some authoritarian governments have proved successful at using it on a large scale. A cheaper system which has been used on a large scale, particularly in contexts of civil war where resources are limited, is secondary profiling ('visible features that may signal disloyalty'), which has obvious counter-indications from the perspective of 'taming violence'.[77]

Controlling the Controllers

The Risks

The second dilemma that we are going to discuss concerning the secret police is how the political authorities can maintain control over their own intelligence services. As mentioned already, even Napoleon could not fully trust Fouché, who indeed from time to time plotted against him with Talleyrand and Murat.[78] Chapman remarked that 'the full blossoming of police powers and abuses can only occur in authoritarian regimes', although he also recognised that 'several types of authoritarian regime also manage to keep them under control'.[79]

The conventional wisdom is that in the liberal democracies of the twentieth century the picture is 'very different' from that of authoritarian regimes, whose 'structure, processes and values [...] are symbiotically compatible with a strong, intrusive intelligence apparatus'. This is undoubtedly true to a large extent. However, scholars have recognised that during much of the Cold War no Western democracy apart perhaps from the US 'established effective, independent oversight of its intelligence services. [...] Obvious and difficult questions exist as to whether an institution dedicated to free debate and wide-open public access can ever be a reliable custodian of the nation's most sensitive secrets'.[80] In fact:

there is virtually no domestic intelligence agency, including MI5 in Great Britain, untainted by scandal, political spying and dirty tricks, activities that threaten not only individual rights, but the proper functioning of democratic government. In 1976, the Church Committee documented and catalogued the abuses committed by the FBI, CIA and other intelligence agencies against Americans: violations of and lack of regard for the law; overbroad domestic intelligence activity; excessive use of intrusive techniques; use of covert action to disrupt and discredit domestic groups; political abuse of intelligence information; inadequate controls on dissemination and retention of information about individuals; and deficiencies in control and accountability. Risks to civil liberties are inherent in the very nature of domestic intelligence.[81]

Indeed, examples of intelligence services getting out of institutional control are common even among (relatively) established democracies. Post-1945 Italy provides several examples of that, starting from 1966 when a commission of inquiry found that the service had always operated free of all control, and then continuing into the 1990s with similar accusations. Although the security services were involved in at least one alleged attempt to organise a coup, their activity does not seem to have been aimed at subverting the government of the day, but at manipulating the political environment and public opinion in order to keep leftist parties out of government and push the ruling coalition further to the right. Contingency plans for intervening in the event of a leftist drift also appear to have been prepared. Although there is no definitive evidence on these points, the information available suggests that some manipulation of subversive groups of the right and of the left might have taken place, particularly in the 1970s. The intent could have been to intimidate the Communist Party, at that time scoring high in the polls, into collaborating 'constructively' with the Christian Democrats (the party of government), without any direct reward or participation in the government (see *Coercive coalition-building* above).[82]

In a context of relatively strong institutions, strong civil society, but some oversight, the political police can only be used for coercive coalition-building if there is plausible denial of the involvement of the ruling elite; letting the political police loose allows for this denial, but also implies the risk of excesses and of them going astray. In the presence of power struggles within a ruling elite, the expansion of the role of the security services is facilitated. In the Soviet Union, for example, during the Brezhnev period the KGB was drawn into Kremlin power struggles, playing an important role as the one organisation having enough information on party and state officials to damage or destroy their careers (see also *Policing the ruling coalition* above).[83]

As in the case of armies, discussed in chapter 2, in the security services too, friction between increasingly professional operatives and analysts and patrimonial regimes can affect the stability of political systems and the effectiveness of the security forces. In Oman the intelligence grew increasingly professional over time, but this put it at odds with the regime:

In the late 1950s, when the service was still in its formative stages, most reporting was directly related to imminent military operations and defined targets such as shipments of arms and explosives. Reports were often delayed by days because of primitive communications. By the early 1960s, there were more sustained accounts of rebel organizations and objectives, appreciations of the susceptibility of specific tribal notables and others to support the rebel cause, and suggestions of administrative reforms and possible 'hearts and minds' developmental measures that could be pursued by the sultan, who consistently showed a singular lack of interest in such measures. [...] Living in Omani towns that were deprived of schools, adequate medical facilities, and other basic necessities and encumbered by multiple petty restrictions imposed by the rulers, intelligence officers had few illusions concerning the quality of the regime they served.[84]

There is no record of intelligence services ever having staged a coup, as they usually do not have the military strength to carry one out on their own. However, when the political regime is weak, the possibility that the political police might actually gradually take power in a stealthy way should not be discounted. Some analysts contend that Russia too fell under the control of its intelligence services in the 1990s.[85]

The case of Pakistan is also well known, if not in depth. The military intelligence known as the Inter-Services Intelligence Directorate (ISI) started acquiring domestic intelligence tasks in the late 1950s, as military ruler Ayub Khan used to control social organisations and the clergy. Its involvement in East Pakistan to prevent Bangladeshi nationalists from gaining influence was a complete failure, but this did not prevent President Zulfikar Ali Bhutto from adopting ISI in the fight against the Baluchi nationalists during the 1970s. ISI was extensively used by dictator Zia ul-Haq in the 1980s; when Benazir Bhutto came to power in the late 1980s, she tried to bring ISI under control, mainly by strengthening the two other intelligence services, the Federal Investigation Agency and the Intelligence Bureau, but by then the ISI and army were closely intertwined and as of 2009 the civilian government was still struggling to reduce ISI's power and influence; Benazir had by then been assassinated in unclear circumstances.[86]

The Attempted Solutions

Unstable regimes, or regimes which feel insecure and threatened, have been particularly inclined to purge their intelligence services periodically and replace key personnel, negatively affecting their operational capabilities and disrupting the intelligence network. Stalin notoriously savagely purged the NKVD twice, each time putting to death 85–95 per cent of the top officials.[87] The existence of divisions within a regime is a typical situation which can favour the participation of the secret police in the power struggle. In South Korea, the directors of the Korean Central Intelligence Agency (KCIA) were routinely trying to take part in the power struggles of the 1960s and 1970s, until in 1979 the then head of the KCIA, Kim Chae Kyu, killed President Park Chung Hee. The

KCIA at its height was a huge structure with 370,000 employees. Following that the Agency lost its autonomous power and underwent a deep reform, being renamed the Agency for National Security Planning.[88]

The personal inclinations of the ruler are however a decisive factor here: Asad of Syria, for example, never purged his security chiefs after the initial round of appointments, in contrast to the constant purging that had characterised the previous 20 years.[89]

As in the case of the armed forces, a typical tactic applied by regimes fearing plots and betrayal has been the multiplication of security services, usually with overlapping agendas and tasks. Even among Arab military regimes, differences are noticeable in this regard. Egypt was not characterised by any proliferation of security services and they remained limited to three: General Intelligence, Department of Military Intelligence and State Security Investigative Service.[90] Since practically every country has at least two such services, Egypt remained fairly close to the norm. In Syria, by contrast, the number of security agencies reached five, without counting the private security networks maintained by key dignitaries of the regime: Presidential Security Council; General Intelligence Directorate; Political Security Directorate; Military Intelligence; Air Force Intelligence.[91]

Saddam Hussein brought the art of playing divide and rule with security services to new heights, through a series of reforms which started in 1973 when the head of General Security attempted a coup against the Hassan al-Bakr/ Saddam Hussein regime. By the 1990s there were five major security agencies in Iraq: *al-Amn al-Khas* (Special Security), *al-Amn al-'Amm* (General Security), *al-Mukhabarat* (General Intelligence), *al-Istikhbarat* (Military Intelligence) and *al-Amn al-'Askari* (Military Security). In the case of this latter agency, the concern with protecting the regime from its own armed forces reached the point that Iraqi military intelligence remained focused on internal security even during the war with Iran, with the result that it failed to provide adequate information about Iranian plans.[92] As Saddam allowed more autonomy to the army in the second half of the 1980s to face the Iranian threat, he built up safeguards in the shape of additional security agencies.[93] According to one specialist, some agencies were specifically created to 'monitor the activities of the others'. The Iraqi services were staffed by relatives or tribesmen of Saddam, or in any case Sunni Arabs. All the agencies reported directly to President Saddam, rather than to the ministries from which they formally depended. Even the National Security Council, created in principle to coordinate the activities of the various agencies, served rather the purpose of supervising their activities. Information exchange among the agencies remained rare, as the system was designed to encourage competition.[94]

Examples of this kind abound. Despite American aversion to the manipulation of their security architecture for political reasons, South Vietnamese ruler Diem not only refused to reduce his number of agencies but even created a few new ones. There were at least six major intelligence agencies and four minor ones, according to the CIA 'competing, duplicating, thrusting and nullifying each other's efforts through lack of centralized co-ordination'.[95] The rule of centralisation only applied in Diem's case when he felt he had complete control over an agency. Otherwise, he would try to undermine the upper layer of officials to the benefit of the lower layers.[96]

Even when the security architecture is not openly manipulated with the creation of parallel agencies, insecure regimes tend to rely on personal networks as tools of control and supervision, bypassing institutional roles. In Ghana, for example, the different intelligence services were extensively subject to purges in the late 1970s and early 1980s. After Rawling's coup, he completely restructured them and increased the level of professionalism, but his Chief of National Security still maintained control through informal networks, which allowed him to 'nerve centres of security entities'.[97]

How Much Violence?

The third dilemma to be discussed here is how violent the political police should be. It appears easy to argue that violence should *always* be as contained and as targeted as possible. As I have pointed out in the introduction, there is a basic distinction to be made between state formation and the maintaining of the monopoly once established. Rulers busy trying to complete the primitive accumulation of coercive power have indulged in violence wholeheartedly, and not just because they had no time for developing a greater sophistication. Stalin for one seems to have thought that violent purges would have strengthened his power by intimidating rival factions in the party; he spoke admiringly of Hitler's Night of the Long Knives.[98]

While indiscriminate violence is only useful in the context of the primitive accumulation of coercive power, the contrary is not necessarily true. Sometimes the principles of tame and targeted coercion are accepted as politically convenient even in the absence of a monopoly of violence, as long as an organisation has the capability to implement it effectively. The Viet Minh, for example, was very concerned to contain its terrorist efforts against the French occupiers and the collaborationists and avoid a 'spiral of counter-productive violence', aware that excessive or indiscriminate violence was bound to create a backlash among the population.[99] Later, faced with a massive 'heart and minds' effort from the Americans and the latter's lavish support for the Saigon government, the Viet Minh's heirs (the Viet Cong) indulged instead in systematic retaliation against civilians collaborating with the South Vietnamese government.[100]

The Viet Minh would certainly have ranked very high in any scale measuring the capabilities of insurgent organisations. In practice to implement coercion with a 'velvet glove' in the absence of a monopoly of large-scale violence is very difficult, as has been repeated several times already. Even in the presence of an awareness of the potential gains to derive from the velvet glove approach, reducing coercion to the point where it is no longer counter-productive is not so easy. For example, in the 1980s the Sandinista State Security seems to have followed Cuban recommendations and have abandoned physical torture to shift towards more sophisticated methods of depersonalisation and psychological torture; it was also quite accurate in targeting informers and civilian supporters of the Contras, but several of those arrested or interrogated and released then joined the Contras as active fighters. The harsh conditions of the prison often sufficed to convince sympathisers to turn into active insurgents.[101] The parallel judiciary set up to deal with the insurgency, the Special Courts, had little option but to arrest and imprison people on the basis of mere hearsay and flimsy evidence, then release them and probably drive recruits to the Contras.[102]

In this chapter we have examined a range of uses for political police, all related to maintaining the monopoly of large-scale violence, or establishing it. Perhaps the least obvious points to be made concern:

- the role of the political police in state-building;
- the co-option of individuals and groups around the ruling elite (a kind of coercive coalition-building);
- the difficulty of keeping violence within certain limits.

Most if not all state agencies involved in the use of coercion have found the ability to use violence in repression and interrogation necessary, including in the contemporary era; the main difference has been one of sophistication. As pointed out, even authoritarian regimes tend to refrain from large-scale use of violence and become more subtle, using coercion primarily to back up persuasion. This seems a resounding confirmation of hypothesis 4: *sophisticated military-political actors clearly understand what kind of violence is counter-productive*. At the same time the professionals of intelligence-gathering seem to have reached a consensus that torture, even in its most stealthy and sophisticated forms, is not very effective in producing good quality intelligence.[103] Although incompetence and hatred might account for some of the resilience in insisting on the use of torture techniques, their almost universal use across time and space suggests other reasons as well. In this chapter we have examined the use of both tame and ruthless (but selective) violence as a method of intimidation, not the most attractive aspect of state-building, but one without which the understanding of the functioning of the state would be incomplete.

5

MAINTAINING THE MONOPOLY
THE POLITICAL MICROMANAGEMENT
OF POPULATION CONTROL

'Whoever becomes prince of a city or state, especially if the foundation of his power is feeble, and does not wish to establish there either a monarchy or a republic, will find the best means for holding that principality to organize the government entirely anew (he being himself a new prince there); that is, he should appoint new governors with new titles, new powers, and new men, and he should make the poor rich. [...] In short, he should leave nothing unchanged in that province, so that there should be neither rank, nor grade, nor honor, nor wealth, that should not be recognized as coming from him'.

Niccoló Machiavelli, *Discourses on the First Ten Books of Titus Livius* (1531), chapter 26, translated by Christian E. Detmold

Among the first independent rulers to follow the European example of implementation of the rule of law and participation in local administration was the Ottoman Empire. Already with Mahmut's reforms of 1831–8 the governors and other provincial officials were to end their exactions and 'rule justly', according to the law; relatively independent financial and military officials were sent by the relevant Istanbul ministries to supervise and to prevent the 'absolute and unlimited misrule that had been inflicted on the subjects in the past'. The Tanzimat reforms started in 1839 saw a further weakening of the powers of the governors, in part because more officials were sent from the centre and in part because their control over military forces was completely ended.

The governors were weakened also by the establishment of advisory councils of representatives of the ruling class and local population groups. The aim was 'protecting and promoting the lives and properties of the subjects'. In part at least the reforms were successful:

> More money was collected for the treasury. Security improved, and the courts and administrators protected the subjects more effectively from misrule and oppression than had been the case in the past. The representative councils in particular were the first means provided for subjects to participate in the process of rule beyond the local level.[1]

This enthusiastic acceptance of some principles of reform coming from the West proved somewhat far-fetched and later the powers of the governors were restored. Over-reliance on Western models coupled with a lack of resources to pay adequate salaries consistently and a lack of sufficiently trained personnel ensured that the reforms would not be successful.[2]

> Certain basic problems inherent in the very concept of borrowing from one culture to another [...] combined to give even the most carefully planned reforms the air of imitative shallowness and incongruity with the Ottoman setting [...]. Such efforts always encountered obstacles [...], either in pre-existing vested interests, or in the opposition of principle emerging from the growing sense of cultural cleavage [...] or from the self-contradictory character of the imperial supranationalism'. [...] The difficulties [...] demonstrated how lacking they were in subordinates prepared to understand and support their efforts. [...] Rational-legalism was coming to exist in the minds of Ottoman statesmen as a myth and an ideal [...]. We could cite a long series of dramatic incidents in which Ottoman statesmen and their republican successors have risked their careers and sometimes their lives for the sake of this ideal. In the nineteenth century, they were sometimes denounced for their pains as excessively Europeanized [...]; one of the things that made them politically vulnerable [...] was that there was little popular appreciation for the values that lay behind their behaviour.[3]

Finally, 'as deviations from patterns sanctioned by tradition, the innovations of the era of reform were inherently controversial'.[4] As the new sultan, Abdulhamit II, stated:

> I made a mistake when I wished to imitate my father, Abdulmecit, who sought to reform by persuasion and by liberal institutions. I shall follow in the footsteps of my grandfather, Sultan Mahmut. Like him I now understand that it is only by force that one can move the people with whose protection God has entrusted me.[5]

What we see here is that although the idea of local administration geared up to treat the population fairly and protect their rights would seem absolutely uncontroversial, nothing is so simple. This chapter is about underscoring the origins and rationale of local government.

What Political Micromanagement of the Population is About

Hypothesis 2 raised the issue of the preventative dimension of coercion, particularly in a context of state-building and 'taming of violence': *pre-empting hostile collective action through co-option, alliances, manipulation and intimidation is as important as the mere accumulation of the means of coercion*. In the previous chapters, I examined one dimension of this prevention: political policing. A third dimension which I am going to discuss here is the political micromanagement of population control. This differs from political policing in that it is open and not secret (at least in principle) and it does not directly involve coercion, even if, as we shall see, political micromanagers can invoke the support of the forces of coercion to 'smooth' their work and are often expected to manage coercive effort at the local level. In the words of a 'counter-insurgent':

close cooperation between local civil administration and the Army deployed in its area is the sine qua non for successful counter insurgency operation.[6]

There is of course a more general dimension of political management which is related to the prevention of conflict, and has to do with the functioning of the political system as such and the processes of coalition-making and political organisation. Sub-national administrators may or may not be involved in this, but it is useful to bear in mind that these dimensions are related.

Much of the work of building local government is about the co-option of local notables to cooperate with the government and control the population; indeed the measure of success of such an operation is the degree of dependency from the state which is created among the notables. As one author pointed out for Chad, although this was certainly not the most successful example of state, 'the traditional chief needs the administration more than the administration needs him and suffers from the crisis of the state like any other official'.[7] The legacy of the colonial experience is evident here.

In state consolidation, locally influential individuals and groups have to be managed carefully, particularly when the monopoly of large-scale violence is still precarious. This does not mean that any new state can afford to leave local communities and notables as it found them:

the [early] state won support by leaving large amounts of decision-making and regulatory authority in the hands of family, kinship, local, and occupational groupings and interfering in the activities of these groups only sparingly. [...] Nevertheless, the existence of the state promoted the internal restructuring of these groups by supporting the development within them of hierarchical authority structures that could not exist without its ultimate support.[8]

In other words, states made communities dependent on their support by encouraging hierarchical structures within them and positioning themselves as ultimate guarantors of the new social order.

In a sense this process of co-option of local communities and leaders could be described as subaltern or coercive coalition-building, depending on the role of coercion in the process. Genuine coalition-building is an alliance among peers; in subaltern coalition-building the implicit threat of violence by the ruler gives a strong incentive to groups and individuals to ally with him in a subordinate position, although not without some rights and entitlements. In coercive coalition-building, the ruler actually forces groups to establish relations with him, so that their bargaining position is weaker even if the ruler avoids establishing a true dictatorship (in which case it would be inappropriate to speak of a coalition altogether). The relationship with local communities and groups established through these types of coalition-building could not in general be managed directly from the centre, at least in large states: this is the origins of local administration.

Dilemmas

The Benefits and Dangers of Decentralised Systems

The range of systems of sub-national government adopted by various regimes to control and manage their territories has historically varied hugely. The essential dilemma of local administration was summed up by Finer this way:

unless officials can win a measure of popular acceptance, they must use coercion and threats, and that to do that unremittingly over a long period of time is highly expensive, time-consuming, distracting, and ultimately self-defeating. [...] A governor or a mayor who provokes tax revolts or riots is not much use to his superiors [...]. Hence these officials have to get on with the local population. But if the only way to do this is by espousing local interests, this too is a reason for the government to get rid of them.[9]

Similarly, rotating governors prevents them from getting too cosy with the locals, but also prevents them from getting to know their region of responsibility really thoroughly. The problem did not just affect pre-twentieth century polities; FitzGerald noted in South Vietnam that '...it was in the interests of those who held power in the provinces to engage in the contrary attempt to assure that the central government held as little power as possible'.[10]

One obvious way of classifying the different systems is in terms of centralisation and decentralisation, but this risks being anachronistic. As Samuel Finer pointed out, it was impossible to have a genuinely centralised system of government before the twentieth century and its technological achievements. As a result, states had an 'architectonic' function: they were providing the most basic frameworks for an 'ocean of self-regarding activities'. In these conditions, corruption was inevitably endemic, distorting and frustrating the aims of government, and no concept of a 'selfless, devoted public service' could develop. The 'centralised' Chinese empire, for example, was dependent on the cooperation of local elites in order to carry out its policies. Still, in comparative terms, it makes sense to distinguish between the Chinese imperial model, which tried to bring uniformity and impose a single system throughout the empire, and the Ottoman model, which tendentially allowed the conquered territories to keep their own administrative arrangements. To exercise control the Ottomans used powerful governors, who however were sent from the Palace and selected from a narrow, palace-educated elite and tended therefore to identify with the centre. At the same time the Palace was fostering loyalty by creating its own military class of 'petty knights', by assigning them land (timars). The Byzantines had used a somewhat different system, with military and civilian functions concentrated in the hands of a *strategos*, but kept finances separated, with an official (Chartlarius) who responded directly to the capital; similarly judges answered to the centre. The system adopted by the Mughal Empire was more similar to the Ottoman than to the Chinese: it relied on strong control of the governors, who were shifted around often, spied on by secret agents and controlled by inspectors. To limit corruption, the treasurers were appointed directly from the centre and the governors were given no control over them.[11]

The most decentralised systems were the Persian Empire and the Caliphate (apart from the early period). Governors had full powers and made all other appointments, including police chiefs and judges; there was little to balance them. There was no institutionalised system to control them, although kings and caliphs would use spies and informants to figure out whether they were loyal (see chapter 4). The centre used to play divide and rule among governors and satraps, in order to make alliances among them difficult. Sometimes governors in remote provinces could even afford to resist the appointment of a replacement. In practice these empires looked like 'confederations' of governatorates; there was no interference with local cults, local legal traditions and processes, social or political structures. Government officials were spread so thin on the ground that the cooperation of local leaders and notables was essential to the function of these extremely decentralised systems. Militias had to be used often, to maintain order locally.[12] As long as they were obedient and paid tributes, the centre would not have objected. Several methods were used to guarantee the loyalty of the governors, including the retention of family members at court.[13] The Roman Empire was closer to these decentralised systems, essentially a 'mere superstructure' added to self-governing communities. The advantage of these decentralised systems was their simplicity, but loss of control to unfaithful governors was a frequent occurrence.[14]

Until the Italian invasion of 1935, the Ethiopian monarchy was also highly decentralised. Even a 'centraliser' as Emperor Tewodros often deferred to regional power; his successors mostly contented themselves with the collection of tributes and avoided direct intervention in local administration.[15] The monarchy had a strong feudal character: nearly all important government posts had a military origin and the principal task of the governor was to raise an army; the administrative tasks were subsidiary to that. The provincial governor was paid no salary; he had to raise a tribute to pay himself, his entourage and his soldiers. Each had a court of his own and a circle of officials of his own appointment. Governors from traditional divisions with a tradition of autonomy and governors from the royal family were usually allowed to rule with little interference from central government. They tried to maintain some control over their own regions by preventing lands and offices that they distributed from becoming hereditary, and aimed at unsettling their holders from time to time.[16]

In contemporary terms, decentralisation is seen as a recipe for good governance because it allows, in principle, for local communities to take decisions for themselves or in any case influence decision-making. In the absence of a strong, supporting structure of central government, however, decentralised local government tends to go astray. Post-independence India, for example, had several layers of government and was, in principle, highly decentralised, but was unable to deliver dispute resolution effectively at village level. The panchayat system of village councils was recognised in the Constitution, but not effectively implemented. As two authors pointed out in 1996, 'despite fifty years of independence, the power structure at the village level remains oppressive'. A World Bank study found that educated people and higher castes controlled the panchayats, leaving others marginalised. The Indian federal government decided to address the situation by establishing People's Courts (Lok Adalat) and debating a system of Alternative Dispute Resolution based on village councils (Nyaya Panchayat), but the government was divided over those who advocated the latter and those who advocated a system of centrally run rural courts. The debate acquired a degree of urgency as the Maoist insurgents escalated their activities in a number of districts; there was a strong feeling that the Maoists were gaining support among the tribals and the lower castes by establishing their own community councils and managing a dispute resolution system more effective than that of the state.[17]

The Difficulties, Benefits and Dangers of Centralisation

The Assyrians represented one of the first attempts to establish a firm hold on their territories. They used their intelligence system as a 'neural network' that kept the empire together. They made it compulsory for every citizen to report everything that touched the king, and local officials had to give priority to passing intelligence upwards without delay. The governors were controlled by a grand official who led a corps of inspectors, and these travelled to the provinces to check and control the activities of the governors.[18]

The Chinese T'ang empire belonged to the same category of governments more concerned with controlling the periphery; it maintained a very firm central control on the prefectures, through the Mandarinate bureaucracy, a thorough system of legislation and regulation and a constant rotation of officials. Prefectures had a degree of autonomy because revenue was raised locally and could be spent at the discretion of the prefect, as supervision from the capital was lax. But prefectures were too small for a prefect to mobilise sufficient forces to defy the capital, and the military in any case responded directly to the capital, not to the prefect. The Ming empire was also comparatively centralised and in particular developed a perhaps unprecedented concern for record-keeping and bureaucratic record-checking. As a system of control it would have had immense fortune later on, but for the time it was too expensive, so that officials were underpaid and had to be corrupt. Inspections could only be limited to spot-checks, as a typical inspector was responsible for a region populated by 7.6 million people. It also encouraged officials to be very cautious in their actions. Like other similar empires, the Mings had to rely on the co-option of the local gentry. The Han empire reached a new level of centralisation thanks to the high number of officials and their intrusiveness, which allowed it to ban any form of self-government. It also built on the Ming experiments with record-keeping so that it could rely on written documents to facilitate the task of supervision and control. Still, the fact that emperors rarely moved around and that inspections were irregular and rare made the system not very effective.[19]

Such centralised systems were periodically subject to crises of central control, which would lead to concessions of growing autonomy, in turn allowing local officials and notables space for more corruption and abuses.[20]

Establishing centralised governments was not just difficult, but also danger-ous. The most centralised systems of government, like France's, took a long time to develop and often faced revolt in the periphery.[21] By the nineteenth century many of the limitations of the past were still constraining the establish-ment of a truly centralised government. In Tsarist Russia the balance of power between centre and periphery shifted regularly in accordance with a number of factors, among which the most important was probably the personality and capabilities of the Tsar. Peter the Great had created an 'activist style of govern-ment', centred on the provincial chief who became an official with wide pow-ers, derived from his personal connection to the autocrat. His reliance on Western administrative models, however, proved not to be very suited to Russia's environment.[22]

Catherine the Great went even further and declared the governor to be the master of the province. Her solution to the dilemma of combining personal autocracy with regular institutions and procedures was to turn the governor-general into a true viceroy. The patrimonial element started to be gradually reduced during the nineteenth century, as governors came under the control of the Ministry of Interior, which could select, reward and punish them. Police districts were created under the direct control of the governors. In reality, ultimately the governor remained under the control of the emperor, and gov-ernors reportedly felt that the ministries had too much power and they were too limited. Favouritism and connections had a wide impact on the selection of governors, but between 1880 and 1914 the ministry developed and refined criteria for holding office, taking career background and education into serious consideration.[23]

On the whole, the Tsarist system of territorial management was not too inef-fective in comparative terms, considering how difficult supervision was because of the huge territorial extension of the country and the limited staffing: offi-cials eager to make a good impression frequently stage-managed encounters, such as the eponymous Potemkin village, but in general governors would travel to trouble spots in the districts in the event of strikes and other disturbances, leading the troops; inspections were carried out frequently by most governors, even if some shirked this responsibility whenever possible. The Ministry of Interior was trying to oversee the governors as it could, including by getting provincial agents of police to send regular reports about governors to the min-istry. The priority was clearly to ensure social order: often the ministry toler-ated very questionable activities of the governors, such as corruption and involvement in pogroms, frequently just punishing them by transfer from one province to another. Apart from the police, the other branches of government were 'irresponsible' and not fully subordinated to the governor, limiting his influence. However the governor could appoint the chief of police and his deputy, but police as such represented a rather thin layer in comparison to the population and territory to be controlled: in theory there was a policeman for every 2,500 villagers, but in practice the ratio was much worse. The governors had no control over the gendarmerie and had actually to busy themselves managing the rivalry between that and the police. The gendarmerie also expected stronger help from the governor towards suppressing dissent. Improving on this situation proved very problematic, not least because of the difficulty in recruiting adequately trained staff to man the administration. Moreover, efficient governors were not necessarily going to be respected, as personality and tact maintained their full importance. Keeping good relations with the clergy was paramount.[24]

Facing Decay

As appears clearly from the rapid historical survey above, handing over land rights in exchange for government service was a common practice to mobilise local support in ancient empires. In some cases it was more deliberate than others. In pre-colonial Vietnam, for example, the policy was to reward officials whose regions were trouble-free and punish those who encountered trouble. Inevitably, therefore, district mandarins tended to form:

discreet alliances with local influential families. In periods of dynamistic vitality, the imperial authorities worked hard to eliminate or circumscribe the power of clans or lineages. At other times there was no choice but to accept the existence of substantial political alignments beyond imperial control. [...] Wise monarchs avoided interference in village affairs without due cause, realizing the impossibility of their civil or military officials forcing compliance with every edict emanating from the court.[25]

However, often this practice led to the rise of a provincial aristocracy, which ended up representing a major constraint to central rulers. If a stranger was appointed over their heads, they could frustrate him by using their influence or forcing him to accommodate to their pressure. If the central government appointed the most influential local landlord as its officer, it would probably lose all control.[26]

Systems of control such as the frequent rotation of appointees were also subject to decay relatively easily. In the Caliphate up to 1200, for example, governors' appointments were limited to a very short term and then rapidly rotated to prevent them from developing local support, so that their careers would be entirely at the mercy of the caliphs. However:

the ideal of frequent rotation of governors, separation of civil and military power and inspection by the *barid* was hard to implement. Governorships were often awarded in payment of political debts to warlords, generals and members of the royal family,

to the point that by the Seljuq period the central government had grown unable to maintain control. Among the reasons was the decline of central checks on the authority of provincial governors.[27]

In order to contain this tendency to lose control of the provincial aristocracies, various solutions were developed. To return to pre-colonial Vietnam, for example:

In 1488, Le Thanh Ton authorized district mandarins to choose commune heads (plus two assistants) from among the local neo-Confucian literati. Undoubtedly Le Thanh Ton aimed to build imperial links to commune heads that would help check the power of local clans.[28]

In the twentieth century sub-national administration in developed countries underwent a change similar to that described for the police and rule of law: it acquired autonomy and was completely institutionalised. The reasons which led to this evolution are likely to be very similar to those already discussed in chapter 4.

Old and New Tools

Imitation or 'Contagion'? Professional Bureaucracies

Administrative systems do not have as strong a tendency to imitate each other as armies have, as they are not in direct competition. They have nonetheless been influencing each other throughout human history. In Europe, the French administrative model was imitated in several countries after the French revolutionary and Napoleonic wars.[29] In the East, the Chinese model was attractive to neighbouring countries. The 1490 administrative reform in Vietnam, for example, was in part inspired by the Chinese example.[30]

Gradually, but more markedly from the nineteenth century, sub-national administration underwent a number of unprecedented changes. Some of them were technological in nature; others were the result of the expanding fiscal resources of some states, itself a consequence of the industrial revolution. As we have seen in the previous paragraph, bureaucracies as 'organizational forms that make it in the instrumental interest of officials to comply with the orders of rulers (by using appropriate forms of monitoring and sanctions)'[31] had been developed with mixed results long before the modern age. Efforts to professionalise the bureaucracy (i.e. adopting meritocratic criteria in staffing) had also been practised in China for several centuries. However, the new fiscal buoyancy allowed the expansion of professional bureaucracies to levels of staffing where they could actually start to manage territory relatively efficiently. That meant that in wealthy countries the sub-national administrative layer became thicker and thicker; offices started being established at ever lower levels, including eventually in all small towns and in many villages.

Because of the degree of control and management that the new professional bureaucracy allowed, this rapidly became a standard of reference and a model to be imitated everywhere; the colonial expansion of European powers greatly facilitated this 'contagion'. The case of the Ottoman Empire and Turkey was discussed at the beginning of this chapter. In most other cases, there was no major impact until the twentieth century. Reza Shah's reforms in Iran during the 1920s and 1930s envisaged the bureaucratisation of provincial administration and police, the secularisation of the courts, the deployment of army and gendarmerie in the provinces. Community political and administrative institutions were dismantled and replaced with central government's bureaucracy. A national gendarmerie replaced local gendarmeries.[32]

In Ethiopia Haile Selassie had already shown centralising tendencies in the early years of his rule, introducing the rule of having imperial appointees to all provinces except Tigre and Wollaga. However, the real reforms started in 1941, following liberation from Italian occupation. Thanks to the creation of a large standing army and the increased control of the government over economic resources, it became possible for the emperor to alter the balance of strength between centre and periphery. Haile Selassie now advocated the right to 'make and revoke appointments almost at will to any of the provincial governorships'. Only in the key province of Tigre did Selassie compromise and keep appointing governors from the established ruling house; elsewhere local elites had to satisfy themselves with the position of deputies to Shoan governors. In northern Ethiopia Selassie kept appointing natives of the province as sub-governors, but not in the south, which was more suspected of disloyalty. As a result, centre-periphery relations changed from a 'relationship between Emperor and provincial lords' into 'a confrontation between national government and regional pressures'.[33] As the reform proceeded during the 1950s, provincial governors started losing their direct channel to the emperor and began dealing with the Ministry of Interior. They were still appointed primarily because of their loyalty, but ability to carry out a policy was held in high regard and a strong degree of competence was desired. Moreover, the governors were no longer able to appoint or dismiss and could only recommend to the ministry. They were still authorised to call in the army if the local police was not able to handle disturbances.[34] The aristocrats' militias were banned, as was their right to maintain relations with foreign powers.[35]

The Ottoman case in particular illustrates how the process of imitation could often take the shape of a 'contagion' spreading from more successful countries (economically and militarily) to others not so successful, as discussed in the introduction (*The counter-productivity of intervention*).

How Bureaucracies Work

We have seen that, although the power of bureaucratic systems of management is unquestionable, whether they are always suitable is doubtful. Another issue is that handling them has always been far from easy. Bureaucracies can be described as live machines. The development of 'bureaux' itself was a gradual process, involving primarily the 'routinisation of charisma':

a group of men brought together by personal devotion to a charismatic leader may transform itself into a bureaucratic structure in order to perpetuate his ideas.

A bureau may either 'be deliberately created by a group in society to carry out a specific function for which they perceive a need', or split from an existing bureau, or again 'be created out of entrepreneurship if a group of men promoting a particular policy gains enough support to establish and operate a large non-market organisation devoted to that policy'. In Dows' interpretation, bureaux are usually created not through top-down interventions of the state, but are:

initially dominated by advocates or zealots. Spontaneous entrepreneurship means the aggressive agitation and action by a small group of zealots who have a specific idea they want to put in practice on a large scale.[36]

Once they are established, bureaucracies need formal rules, 'because there is no clear linkage between the nature of an action and its value or ultimate end' and 'there is no other way to help individuals decide their behaviour'. 'Formalised rules are also efficient ways of coordinating complex activities'.[37] Even in such formalised environments, however, political and personal relationships to officials remain important. 'Virtually all political systems have some level at which appointments are quite clearly political—frequently referred to as "policy-making" positions'.[38] Moreover, bureau leaders value personal loyalty because they are almost certain to 'become embroiled in scandalous acts', as one cannot be fully informed of the behaviour of his subordinates; moreover uncertainty may cause unavoidable errors. Sometimes pressure to produce results sooner rather than later also contributes to creating problems. Finally, the tendency of officials to distort the information they pass to their superiors is nearly universal.[39] 'Subunits cheat in the hope of getting more rewards [...] or of being burdened with fewer responsibilities. [...] Centralized organisations therefore need to develop monitoring organizational structures that parallel the rest of the organizational structure'.[40] From this derives the need to develop a strong monitoring capacity, otherwise bureaucratic structures can actually turn out to be a liability rather than a source of efficiency:

Since bureaucracy relies on fairly weak positive and negative sanctions, (fixed salaries and the threat of dismissal), it will be efficient only when monitoring capacity is well developed. When monitoring capacity is poor, two types of patrimonial systems will outperform centralized bureaucracy: (1) forms that include the stronger sanctions necessary to induce agents to comply, such as tax farming [...] or severe negative sanctions [...]; and/or (2) a decentralized administration that makes central monitoring less important, such as feudalism or prebendalism (payment in land or the profits from land).[41]

Controls from the top are implemented through written reporting; even if the amount of paperwork produced is unmanageable and could never be thoroughly checked, written reports still serve the purpose of reminding subordinates that they have to meet certain standards of performance. However, inevitably 'subordinates react to effort to control from above by trying to evade or counteract such controls'; therefore personal inspections, preferably without prior warning, are also important. Subordinates of course try to minimise their impact by relying on tipping off, motivated by the expectation of similar favours in the future.[42] In this regard the importance of separate monitoring agencies becomes obvious. A monitoring organisation can function effectively only if there is a fundamental conflict of interest between it and the operating bureau it surveys. The effectiveness of monitoring agencies can be maintained only if a definite tension exists between their members and the members of the operating bureaux they monitor. Tension depends on: 1) surveillance of operators being clear and their sole task; if operational responsibilities are shared, performance will take precedence over zeal in reporting deviations; 2) no exchange of personnel between monitoring and operating agencies; 3) monitoring officers should be furnished only with the knowledge suited to their surveillance task; 4) there should be a minimum of personal contact between the two agencies.[43]

Although this might seem counter-intuitive, bureaucracy can develop a kind of soul:

Values and emotions will be especially important when highly motivated agents are necessary (due to poor monitoring capacity) and when instrumental motivations are ineffective. When the costs of compliance are high and the benefits of compliance are low [...], principals will seek non-instrumental ways to motivate agents.[44]

Motivation can be achieved 'by recruiting agents who already hold values or emotions consistent with the principal' or by making agents acquire value and emotions through training and job performance. It has for example been argued (somewhat controversially) that one of the reasons for the efficiency of the Prussian and Dutch administrations lay in the fact that rulers selected agents on the basis of religious affiliation. Similarly it has been argued that because the Chinese bureaucracy was 'permeated by factional and patronage ties that inhibited monitoring and created widespread collusion', pro-state Confucian values were instilled in the bureaucracy, although scholars have not reached a consensus on this either.[45]

Particularly when a bureau is asked to behave in a way incompatible with dominant social customs, indoctrination can be a useful and even necessary tool to ensure the performance of the bureaucracy. Because indoctrination tends to be very expensive, usually selective recruitment is preferred as far as possible.[46] This can go as far as the development of an ideology by top level officials. Ideologies are:

efficient means of communicating with certain groups both inside and outside their bureaus. [...] They are used to convince external agents with control over funding of the fact that the bureau deserves continued funding. The need of an ideology is particularly strong when bureaus are engaged in highly controversial activities, or when their benefits are mostly indirect.[47]

Bureaucratic 'Churches'

The waning of the original 'revolutionary' commitment is a problem that all regimes face sooner or later. The space between a fully-fledged, functional bureaucracy and complete patrimonialism cannot therefore be occupied by the zeal of newcomers for any length of time. If bureaucracies can have 'souls' (see above), there has to be a 'church' in place that takes cares of them. Political organisations represent such 'churches' and can play an important role in supervising local government from within and from without. The Viet Minh for example, adopted instead a very determined attitude towards local communities in areas under its control. As early as November 1945 it issued a decree on the formation of People's Councils and administrative committees, which implied a high degree of control from above of the elected councils. Not only did the results of council and committees elections have to be ratified, but contradicting decrees or instructions from above brought punishment, budgets had to be submitted and approved, and if the people's council refused to comply with directives from above, it could be dissolved and new elections ordered. With that and with its well-developed structure, 'the Communist party succeeded in penetrating the village to a degree impossible under former rulers'; it also managed to control local conflicts by implementing a balance of power among villages in the communes. The Communist party had difficulties in controlling party members: the embezzlement of funds in agricultural cooperatives was documented and the low pay to cadres contributed to corruption becoming widespread, but control remained nonetheless very solid.[48]

As argued in the case of political commissars in armies (chapter 2), not all regimes have at their disposal a viable political organisation to take over this type of task. As in the case of Chad mentioned above, a weak political organisation put in charge of administering a country is likely to turn into a liability. Still, it would be wrong to assume that only sophisticated political organisations with strong roots among the population can deliver a measure of administrative control and supervision. In Ethiopia, the Derg regime relied on urban and rural neighbourhood associations first, and then from 1984 on the local organisation of the Workers Party of Ethiopia and the mass organisations set up in the various sectors of society to tighten control even down to village level. In this way it created a new, parallel party hierarchy to the state one.[49] Although the Workers Party had weak roots, the system still delivered a fair degree of administrative control until its collapse in 1991.

Handy old Tools

The purpose of highlighting the difficulties of building and maintaining an effective bureaucracy is to explain the persistence of the 'classical' tools of control of administrative and bureaucratic structures. Nepotism, for example, is a 'very efficient way of control under certain circumstances', despite obvious drawbacks:

• relatives are difficult to control and enjoy great leeway regarding matters not vital to the interest of the sovereign;

- appointing relatives tends to discourage ambitious bureau members from striving to attain such positions.[50]

In Migdal's words:

the unique propensity any state agency assumes creates in it centrifugal tendencies, pulling it from the views of other agencies and the executive state leadership. Such particular views are created and reinforced in any number of ways, including shared socialization [...], the repeated representation of the agency's interests in wider forums (as in the competition for funds), daily personal interaction, the effective allocation of resources and status within the agency, and so on.

These particular views 'threaten the coherence and, indeed, the stability of the state'.[51] It is imperative for state leaders, therefore, to 'find centripetal forces to counteract the centrifugal tendencies of their agencies if they are able to keep the state organization as a whole together, acting more or less cohesively'.[52]

Since the era of decolonisation there may have been a learning curve for leaders on how to survive in the churning waters of politics where states have had relatively little social control over broad segments of their societies. Leaders and future leaders may have noticed the risks involved in rushing headlong into ambitious programs of social change. They may have witnessed the dangers inherent in pursuing full social agendas through their agencies to carry out far-reaching policies of change.[53]

In such cases, nepotism continues to represent a strategy for 'mitigating powerful centrifugal forces' even in bureaucratised contexts. Nepotism can take several shapes. The 'most popular' method has been to 'appoint top agency officials having deep personal loyalties to the state leaders'. These loyalties might be due to kinship, shared regional origins, shared ethnic, tribal or sectarian backgrounds, or school connections. Mexico's Revolutionary Institutional Party (PRI) is an excellent example of this, because its leaders were not merely a conservative elite trying to protect their own power, but had an agenda of change as well.[54] A policy of appointments can also be used to forge political coalitions, which in some cases can take the shape of 'ethnic bargaining' when 'critical elements of the population' are bound to the state through the appointment of some of their number. In such processes of ethnic co-option, a high degree of political mastery on the side of the rulers is needed, as controversy can easily arise.[55]

Particularly in 'less developed countries', where the technologies of control applied to bureaucracies are 'more like those in early modern states that those in contemporary developed states', the adoption of administrative systems modelled on twentieth-century Western ones only increased the costs of the administration without decreasing corruption or increasing efficiency.[56] At the sub-national level:

implementors are usually far from the sight of state leaders, often even far from the sight of the top personnel in their agencies, and they pose little danger of creating power centers that could threaten the position of state leaders. Nonetheless, they have been crucial in determining whose authority and rules will take hold in region after region, the state's or the strongmen's. [...] Their leading role in changing the rules of the game has subjected them to pressure and risk from four groups. First [...] they have needed to consider their supervisors. [...] Second, the intended clients of the program. [...] Third, regional actors from other state agencies and from the state-sponsored party, if existing. [...] Finally, nonstate local leaders, strongmen such as landlords, moneylenders, local businessmen.[57]

The ability and willingness of state officials to implement policies depends therefore on the balance of these factors, as well as the willingness of the organisation to protect them from all kinds of opposition, and the compatibility of those policies with the desire of career advancement. Other factors affecting the implementation of policies are non-merit appointment at the head of agencies and the frequency of the shuttling in and out of agency heads. Migdal believes that 'the structure of society has an important indirect effect on policy implementation'; the fragmentation of social control leads to the 'politics of survival', which is deeply disruptive of the effectiveness of implementing agencies. There is always some leakage of authority as a policy moves through an agency; the weaker the state, the more likely such leakage is to turn into haemorrhage. Only in extreme cases of state weakness does the failure of the state to implement its own policies have no effect whatsoever; often the impact remains substantial, even if quite different from official laws and policies.[58]

A typical result involves some kind of accommodation among officials and between officials and strongmen, shaping the 'nature of the insinuation of state agencies into village and town'. Often, therefore, state policies of radical change and reform can coexist with local realities which contradict those same policies. An extreme example was Tanzania, where 'supervision was so lax that one observer found an alarming number of cases in which he could find no record of project implementation at all'. The local strongmen 'would like to enhance the state, or at least the resources it can make available to them, but they must also thwart the state from [...] being in a position to offer viable strategies of survival to the population directly'.[59]

Moreover, even aside from the difficulties of handling sophisticated bureaucratic machines, not all ruling elites who adopted at least in part the new system were similarly committed to it, or had sufficient resources to manage it effectively. In fact, even in wealthy countries often the old practices of the past, the non-bureaucratic control 'tools' illustrated above, did not disappear altogether. In fact for centuries even in Europe the transition from a situation in which 'functionaries were still essentially the servants of the ruler to one in which they became governed by the impersonal rules of the state' was not complete until the nineteenth or even the twentieth century.

In the early phases of [the evolution of the bureaucratic state], rulers undermined other forms of participation, centralized jurisdiction, created a more hierarchical relationship to authority, and employed a larger number of permanent officials who were better trained and paid for state service, and who were also presumably more impersonal in exercising their duties. But growing states were obliged to compromise with existing institutions and with the social groups over which they were establishing control. The officialdom of the new bureaucracies was part of the social context of state-building, and in a stratified society it was difficult to escape the influence of family and group solidarity, which affected both the functioning of government and protected established elites within the state's expanding authority.[60]

I summarise here the most important old administrative tools used throughout history:

- Complete local autonomy in exchange for tribute and political loyalty;
- Selection of governors tied by kinship or training to the court;
- Feudalism: distribution of land in exchange for military service;
- Parallel financial system, independent of local administrator and directly responding to the centre;
- Rotation of governors;
- Surveillance by the political police;
- Inspections carried out by specialised functionaries;
- Divide and rule among local administrators;
- Retention of family members of governors at court;
- Punishment and rewards system;
- Appointment of personal loyalists.

Implications for the Management of Coercion

As mentioned at the beginning of this chapter, the importance of sub-national administration to soften the impact of naked coercion is particularly evident in counter-insurgencies. Often, the military establishment of countries involved in counter-insurgency campaigns recognised the need to adopt a 'concerted military and political response' only after some years of attempts at winning an outright military victory. The French gradually refined their approach through a series of colonial wars, increasing their reliance on political tactics and then also beginning to offer services to the civilian population, even though they remained ready to resort to extreme coercion when they believed it was needed.[61]

The Soviets too, for all the propensity to violence shown in their civil war, rapidly developed an understanding of the opportunity of showing consideration for local culture and religion as well as for employing local forces against the Central Asian insurgents.[62] During Stalin's time, such considerations had little influence, but even the ruthless repression in Ukraine and Lithuania from 1944 onwards displayed some elements of a political strategy: attempts were made to use Catholic priests in Lithuania to invite rebels to lay down arms, etc.[63] As already discussed, the Germans had an extremist attitude towards counter-insurgency on the Eastern Front in World War II, focused as it was on the psychological impact believed to derive from the perception of strength of the German troops by the population. They too, however, realised that they needed an interface to deal with the local population and tried to use local mayors to this end.[64]

The Unbearable Lightness of Technocracy

Conversely, weak or badly managed administrative structures have arguably often been a source of friction and worse. Chad, one of the worst administered countries in the world, is a good example of this. In the 1960s the country was under-administered, with administrative units too large, prefects who could not reach out or had to travel hundreds of kilometres to reach the area of their competence. It also lacked trained cadres and was burdened by an ineffective single party system with almost no reach in the provinces. Northern Chad in particular also suffered from the exactions of the hostile and misinformed southerners who staffed the administration, a situation compounded by the weak presence of the military in the north to contain any outburst of protest. The importance of patronage as a source of bad governance is highlighted by the fact that the government was long reluctant to identify the causes of the revolt, even if internal reports correctly identified the administrations' excesses as the cause.[65]

According to Decalo:

Contemptuously maladministered by both civil and military officials since the withdrawal of the French garrison in B.E.T. in January 1965, a dancehall brawl in Bardai that saw the death of one Chadian soldier provoked gross military 'retaliation'. The entire village, men, women, and children - including the Derde of the Toubou and his household - were paraded, many naked, amid jeers and insults, and arbitrary 'fines' were imposed for a variety of offences, such as wearing turbans or beards. Though the brutalisation of the population was eventually curtailed, the damage to Toubou pride had been done. The Derde slipped away into exile in Libya, while his sons raised the banner of war. [...] The replacement at independence of Arabophone and Arabophile French administrators, respectful and familiar with Muslim life and social hierarchy, by inexperienced officials with little understanding of the 'uncivilised' stratified society in the north, created the basic potential for a series of explosive confrontations.[66]

The gradual build-up of the rebellion after a number of incidents, and the inability of the central government and its administration to cope effectively with what initially were a string of local incidents strengthen this image of an incompetent administration.[67]

The case of Chad also highlights the flaws of the administrative systems inherited from the colonial powers, which the new local elites failed to adapt.

The African political leaders did not have remotely adequate ideas of their own for the organization of politics and the state because they were inadequately prepared for the task.

As a result:

it was perhaps inevitable that the traditional elites should oppose the new men. [...] Regionalism was a strategy for the defense of privilege and position or, for each party, an attempt to exclude rivals.[68]

The failure of French-inspired reforms in 1968 is also very significant because it illustrates that 'treating political problems as administrative ones' does not work, and the delusions of basing post-colonial administration on deals with the 'traditional' authorities. In the end the rebellion of FROLINAT was the result of the alienation of 'non-traditional' strata in the north, whose interests had been ignored.[69] Once even the thin crust of state territorial control had been broken with the start of the rebellion, re-establishing it required a strong dose of charismatic leadership. In the absence of that, there appeared to be no other solution but co-opting regional warlords as Goukuni did:

they were allowed to keep their separate armies and, for a time, to be separately sup-plied'. [...] They were free to exercise a considerable measure of local self-government that was not regulated by any national constitutional instruments.[70]

A similar example of the misplaced hope that relying on the old notables would deliver stability is that of French administrative reforms in Vietnam, which meant to introduce a fairer system and avoid the arbitrary behaviour of local notables, working for the administration in raising taxes. The French remained prisoners of the old notables, who could sabotage the reform effort because the French regime was too moderate to undermine their power.[71] The French had themselves set in motion the decay of the old order when they colonised Vietnam, but ended up placing their hopes of retaining control on the very 'old society' that they had undermined.

The pattern of shifting back and forth between reliance on technical solu-tions and hope in the miraculous involvement of local notables in some kind of subaltern coalition-making has not been a French peculiarity. In their adven-tures abroad, Americans have often done the same. In Vietnam technical solu-tions were still the big thing:

Since the days of the Diem regime, the Americans had assumed that technical changes such as a retraining program, an increase in aid, a change of priorities or province chiefs, would change the nature of the [South Vietnamese government] and start it on the road to improvement. But year after year those administrative reforms were attempted, if not achieved, and they made no difference at all.[72]

By the time they got involved in Iraq from 2003 onwards, the pendulum had gone all the way:

The subcontracting of governance and the benefits of patronage to local agents is hardly a novel tactic in cases of foreign occupation. Nevertheless, by placing a high degree of reliance upon specific individuals who were engaged in local struggles for pre-emi-nence, the Coalition found itself sucked into entrenched contests over which large portions of the governatorate's population could be mobilised. [...] This approach ensnared the Coalition within local struggles which were often unanticipated and poorly understood by them. [...] The result has been an ongoing set of conflicts, often violent in nature, which are unlikely to be amenable to solution through the passing of laws or constitutional provisions, but can only be resolved through one set of institu-tions effectively supplanting the other as the site of ultimate authority.[73]

It should not be surprising, in the context of the above, that the concern of many new rulers in the post-colonial era would have been to overhaul the inherited administrative system, in most cases with the intention of increasing their control over territory. As soon as Siad Barre came to power in Somalia, he replaced provincial governors with military men; only from 1971 did these military men start to be assisted by regional and district revolutionary councils, which in any case had no power. Attempts by councillors to advise the governors, who were also chairmen of the councils, were usually rejected.[74]

What then drives the development of a different system of local government, more concerned with the welfare of the population? As argued by Tilly and North among others, the greater the need a government has for its population, the more sophisticated the taming of violence and the more advanced the granting of entitlements and rights is going to be. Vice versa, a government relying on rents of any kind will have less of an incentive to move in the same direction. This seems to apply to local government too. Fitzgerald discussed the case of South Vietnam:

…bureaucrats, the police, and all the various groups of cadre. The CIA trained them to use many of the NLF techniques, but the cadres saw no reason to use them. Unlike the NLF they did not depend on the support of the villagers for their lives and they did not feel that their efforts would be rewarded by those in authority. […] In the days of the Diem regime the desire for profit persuaded at least some of the officials to try to keep the peasants alive and productive, and only moderately discontented, but now they could forget the peasants entirely and concentrate on filling out forms. The aid program had, in other words, relieved them even of their desire to exploit the peasants.[75]

The Americans in Vietnam never captured these dynamics and instead continued pouring in more and more money. FitzGerald relates a revealing anecdote:

Just before his departure for a two-week tour of Vietnam in 1967, the defence analyst, Herman Kahn, listened to an American businessman give a detailed account of the economic situation in South Vietnam. At the end of the talk—an argument for reducing the war—Kahn said, I see what you mean. We have corrupted the cities. Now, perhaps we can corrupt the countryside as well. It was not a joke.[76]

Shadow Local Governments

A particular case, which highlights the importance of political management at local level, is that of insurgent movements and their handling of local 'government'. Insurgents typically form shadow local governments once they establish their monopoly of violence over securely held areas. The first concern characterising insurgent movements was a degree of inclusiveness: while it would have been much easier in the short term for both Tito and Mao to rely on ethnic, local or class conflict to mobilise fighters in their ranks, they also realised that such tactics would have heightened their vulnerability *vis-à-vis* their enemies. Mao was particularly keen on mobilising whole sections of the rural population and not practising class war, as the CCP had been doing in its early days. Tito for his part formed ethnically mixed units in order to forge national unity and avoid the impact of traditional animosities.[77]

In general, regimes arising of insurgent movements have shown a high degree of concern for securing territorial control; they also had the knowledge of what was needed to achieve that. Often the emergence of a 'new state' from the fresh ashes of a rebellion presented particularly acute problems to the would-be administrators. In Chad, for example:

the "liberated areas" brought into being new political fields; the restructuring of authority in these areas proved an extremely complex and delicate operation as it released competing claims among presumptive leaders, and on occasion led to violent confrontations; defections, double-crossings, and settlings of accounts figure prominently in the annals of the insurgency. Local disputes provided the seedbed of factionalism.[78]

When the new rulers had the skills and the human resources, however, they often established very effective and thorough systems of local administration. The RPF regime in Rwanda relied on informal local government for territorial control, giving wide responsibility to the lowest levels of local government:

- mobilisation and sensitisation of the local community in law and order matters;
- night patrols;
- law enforcement;
- promoting the functioning of the local (gacaca) system of justice to deal with minor anti-social behaviour, disputes and crimes (or directing them upwards);
- recording strangers to the neighbourhood; reporting deviant behaviour;
- punishment for misbehaviour; the establishment of bylaws that reflect local needs;
- control over local defence forces.

In practice, the system allowed central government to gather detailed information about local communities, including potential trouble-makers, but not only that. Baker believes that 'the structure has provided an effective ordering of social life' and that 'local leaders take their work seriously'. Because the system is 'driven by civic responsibility and a desire to rebuild a shattered nation', its long-term sustainability is a problem, as highlighted by Baker himself:

How long can the spirit of voluntarism be sustained? Will future generations, that did not fight to stop the genocide or suffer as victims of it, be driven by the same strong desire to eradicate injustice for no recompense?

Indeed there were signs that the RPF government itself might have already started pushing for a structure more responsive to pressure coming from the top, and less dependent on popular support, as it started interfering in the choice of local leaders.[79]

This chapter has shown how the second hypothesis of this book, about the political pre-emption of challenges to the monopoly of violence, is confirmed by the literature. Hints on the ways in which governments manage their monopoly and co-opt groups and individuals exist in the literature, but on the whole this is quite a neglected field of study. We certainly need more evidence of how states promote change and restructuring within local communities, creating a new social order of which it is the guarantor. The process of expropriation of the autonomous capability of the communities to rule themselves (administer justice, police, educate children, defend against external threats) has also been studied in only a very limited number of cases.

This chapter nonetheless contains sufficient evidence to question the growing consensus among international assistance policy-makers that decentralisation is good, particularly as it leads to good or better governance and strengthens democracy:

Decentralization refers to the transfer of decision-making from the central level to a sub-national authority. The aim is to transfer power and resources to a level that is closer, better understood and more easily influenced by local people. This should result in gains in efficiency and appropriateness of service delivery, as well as better governance and greater accountability. By creating the conditions for more inclusive and transparent operations, decentralization enhances citizen participation in local governance, allowing communities to take responsibility for their own development.[80]

Decentralisation might be good, but it is not *always* good. New states in particular have to reshape the social and political landscape in a way that allows them to operate successfully and pre-empt threats. Unless these conditions are met, any decentralisation programme sponsored by foreign donors is likely to develop not much further than a façade.

6

EXTERNAL INTERVENTION
AND THE MONOPOLY

KICKING AWAY THE LADDER?

'We should seize the opportunity, at a time when [...] foreigners are delighted to show us their superior techniques, to make a substantial study of all kinds of foreign machines and weapons in order to learn their secret completely... The friendliness or opposition of foreigners always depends upon the strength of weakness of China'.

Chinese officials' report to the Emperor, quoted in Jonathan Spence,
To Change China: Western advisers in China 1620–1960, Penguin (1980), p. 147

The case of China in the 1920s-40s is particularly interesting, because it allows a direct comparison of three very different advisory and assistance missions. Soviet advisers to the Kuomintang in the 1920s, after an initial period of Chinese diffidence, succeeded in convincing their hosts to create a system of central control, where the commander-in-chief controlled and distributed all legal income to the several corps, and the distribution of arms and supplies was also centralised. Marshal Blyukher, a gifted officer and diplomat, became so close to Sun Yat Sen that he ended up in charge of operations for almost all the units of the Chinese army. The victories achieved in the northern expedition (1926–8) brought prestige to the Soviet advisers, who became popular even among the populace; such prestige was enhanced by the valuable Soviet advice provided during the first eastern expedition. Finally the advisers managed to convince the Kuomintang to adopt a system of political commissars in their army, with some positive effect on its morale and effectiveness. All the factions of the Kuomintang accepted the new system as correct and efficient:

it was easier for the Kuomintang to indoctrinate a youthful group of students than to train and equip several armies, and so they adopted a plan of gathering armed forces by every conceivable means and the inserting trained political commissars at the various levels of the newly absorbed groups.[1]

It was not long before a genuine divergence of political interests emerged as a major source of conflict. Once Chiang Kai-shek rose to power in the KMT, the relationship between the Soviet advisers and the Chinese nationalists deteriorated, until the eventual withdrawal of the mission. Chiang was knowingly sacrificing Soviet financial assistance with this move. Among other things, he resented the political indoctrination carried out by the advisers.[2]

Chiang's views and inclinations were much more in line with those of a German military adviser like Max Bauer, who came to have great influence over him despite the lack of any official backing by the German government.[3] The German advisers who succeeded the Soviets had completely different views and aims, but they too had a fair degree of success in restructuring the administrative apparatus of the Chinese army, creating on the German model different specialised levels of authority.[4] They also established a Military Academy in Nanjing in order to standardise the training of the officers. The German-trained eighty-seventh and eighty-eighth divisions acquitted themselves well in the January 1932 fighting around Shanghai, against superior Japanese forces. German advisers also contributed significantly to the 1937 offensive against the Japanese in the Shanghai area, although more in terms of moral boost and some strategic advice than as tactical advisers. The few times that the Chinese accepted German tactical advice it was to good effect, as in the case of the battle of Taierzhuang in 1938, a Chinese victory which, however, Chiang and his general failed to exploit. The Germans also made a decisive contribution to the improvement of Chinese air defences.[5] One key advantage of the German advisers over the Soviets was that they were recruited by Chiang directly and were dependent on him; the lack of any direct link to a foreign power made them more acceptable to the Chinese.[6]

The overall impact of the German advisers was on the whole much more limited than the Soviets', not because the Soviets were any wiser, but because it happened that what they had to offer (political commissars) happened to be more suitable to the Chinese requirements. The Germans' tactical wisdom had little applicability.

Despite their relative success in training some elite units, the German advisers to the Kuomintang in the 1930s faced the insurmountable obstacle of applying their highly professional template to the human resources available to the Chinese army at that time; even senior Chinese officers lacked the most basic technical knowledge.[7] While the new apparatus of the Kuomintang army looked like the German model in appearance, the dictates of domestic Chinese politics pushed Chiang Kai-shek to appoint top generals to reward the various factions, in complete disregard of any meritocratic considerations.[8] During the campaigns against the Communist bases in Jaingxi in 1930–34, the German advisers were at odds with the Chinese generals, who wanted to use old Chinese counter-insurgency practices and disregarded German advice to seek 'mobility, concentration and close combination of all arms'. Given the dysfunctional command and control system of the Kuomintang army, Chiang might have done the right thing by adopting a tactic of slowly strangling the Communists, as this did not demand any major initiative from his generals and made coordination easy.[9]

What is good military advice may not make sense at all politically. Bauer did a lot to reorganise the Chinese Nationalist's command, but his advice to disband the armies of the warlords allied with the Kuomintang turned out to be potentially disastrous as it started a new round of civil war in 1930. The defection of one of the warlords to the Kuomintang side allowed a quick conclusion of the first campaign in the Kuomintang's favour and even enhanced the prestige of the German advisers, but the risk had been real.[10]

The next mission to try to straighten up the Kuomintang's forces was American. General Stillwell found out the same as the Germans before him during World War II: the fighting around the Salween in May 1944 saw the Chinese divisions, carefully trained by the Americans, 'completely [reject] all the advice they had received', indulging in frontal attacks against prepared Japanese positions. By May 1945 there was a certain improvement, with Chinese troops using supporting fire, signals and transport more effectively, but generally motivation to fight remained scarce. Stillwell and his successor Wedemeyer believed that the 'practical application of Western expertise to the problem of logistics and training' would provide the answer to the problem of turning the Kuomintang army into an effective war machine. They did not understand that 'the kind of efficiency [they] wanted might work against Chiang Kai-shek, undermining his castle of compromises'. The American reaction was to post groups of advisers to each Chinese regiment on the frontline and make supplies conditional on the host officers' willingness to follow the advice provided by the Americans. But the Chinese refused to serve in the new infantry school set up by the Americans. The Americans were forced to send more and more men to enable logistical supplies, up to 59,000 in June 1945. General Stilwell's requests for Chiang Kai-shek to reform the Kuomintang army and improve its efficiency received no positive answer; eventually Stilwell clashed with Chiang so forcefully that he had to be recalled.[11]

Although Chiang was a byname for corruption and ineffectiveness in the 1940s and 1950s, the experience of the Soviets, Germans and Americans with the Kuomintang was by no means exceptional. Were all these sets of advisers ill-intentioned or stupid? Or were the Chinese so hopelessly corrupt? This chapter tries to identify structural problems in the provision of external support to elites struggling to establish or maintain a monopoly of violence.

Mentoring and Advising

Where It Helps: Distilled With Caution

If the establishment of a monopoly over large-scale violence is one of the pillars of state formation, the establishment of armies by external actors on behalf of new or weak states is a problematic process. To be fair, the historical evidence shows that in many cases the military advisers proved a key asset in improving the performance of armies:

- This was the case with Mehmet Ali's Egyptian army, whose successful campaigns in Greece and Syria owed much to his foreign advisers.[12]
- The Chilean army was also turned into a model for Latin America by its reliance on German advice and support.[13]
- Similarly the Germans left a deep imprint on the Argentinean army, which they also trained both before and after World War I.[14]
- A motley crew of foreign advisers to the army of the Negus of Ethiopia might have had some impact in slowing the Italian advance in 1935, although that is difficult to demonstrate. Among them a few Turkish advisers were seen as the most committed.[15]
- After the Maoist takeover, Soviet advisers again played an important role in the modernisation of the Chinese army, before a Soviet doctrinal shift in favour of nuclear weapons led to a growing divergence between Soviets and Chinese and divided the Chinese officers too.[16]

Uncontroversial cases of foreign advisers having played a positive role can be identified elsewhere too. Cuban General Ochoa appears to have been instrumental in turning around the Sandinista army in 1983–4. He earned the confidence of Minister of Defence Humberto Ortega and became his right-hand man. At this point consultation between Cubans and Nicaraguans became productive. Ochoa is credited with reorienting 'concepts, types of advisers and institutions' to meet the need to wage counter-insurgency, after having argued that the army's structure and intelligence were not suited to dealing successfully with insurgency. His view was that military effort had to be complemented by political, economic and social programmes, involving many parts of government in the effort.[17]

In El Salvador, even former leftist guerrillas acknowledged that the American advisers managed to get the local army to develop a relatively sophisticated pacification plan which went beyond mere repression, and improved its management of human rights, as well as becoming more effective militarily. The American advisory effort in South Korea stands out as relatively successful given the circumstances, not least because Korean President Rhee agreed to place his army under American command. With full authority, they could remove under-performing Korean commanders and impose their own model of organisation and war-fighting.[18] 'American training programs helped forge elite officers with a strong sense of public responsibility and ardent faith in their ability to lead', to the point that they would later take power in the country.[19]

The South Korean case is particularly interesting in so far as it was the only large-scale effort among those mentioned above. As will become increasingly clear while I proceed in this review, large-scale and mentoring efforts do not usually have a good record. Perhaps the undeniable reality of an existential threat to the South Korean regime and the difficulty of the American and other UN contingents in dealing with the Chinese Expeditionary Force were the key factors in making American advice more acceptable to the Koreans. It was 'the crucial need for a strong indigenous military that could defend the autonomy of the new nation' that allowed US hegemony and the nationalist attitudes of Korean officers to coexist.[20]

Even in the case of American advisers in Vietnam (not the greatest success story), long years of advising had some positive impact, achieving improvements in the capabilities of host armies at least in certain areas. In South Vietnam, local officers acknowledged that improvements were achieved 'in combat effectiveness, technical knowledge, and managerial skills'.[21] The presence of advisers often also forced or stimulated Vietnamese army officers to perform better.[22] The impact of US advisers increased after the Tet offensive, which galvanised the South Vietnamese into action and convinced them of the need to make changes in the leadership of the army, as recommended by the Americans; again during the so-called North Vietnamese 'Easter offensive' of 1972, American advisers played a key role alongside air support in rescuing the South Vietnamese, whose command system was failing.[23] The problem was that they made the host army dependent on their support, as will be discussed in greater detail below.

When advisory missions had a transformational impact, it was not always uncontroversially positive. Even in those cases where host militaries were successfully reshaped by the advisers, as for example in Chile, Argentina and Bolivia, the German (Prussian) heritage had a negative impact on the loyalty of those armies to the political leaderships of those countries.[24] French advisers and trainers in Peru also failed in their stated ambition to develop apolitical armed forces. In Brazil, from 1919 onwards, French views of professionalism and nationalism contributed towards radicalising the new generation of officers and led to the emergence of military governments later.[25]

Not all armies inherited from the colonial powers proved to be unacceptable to the new rulers, or vice versa. One success story is that of Jordan, whose Arab Legion continued to be led by British officers for some time. The legion proved the most effective Arab formation in the first two Arab-Israeli wars, but was eclipsed by the regional technological escalation of the 1960s and 1970s. The legion seems to have survived as a loyal and effective force mainly due to its sticking as much as possible to the original colonial model.[26] During the 1990s, the Jordanian army was still focused on small-scale operations, in the fashion of the colonial British army. An American observer commented that a Jordanian army infantry company was:

man-for-man as good as a comparable Israeli company; at battalion level, however, the coordination required for combined arms operations, with artillery, air, and logistics support, is simply absent. Indeed, the higher the echelon, the greater the disparity.[27]

It could be speculated that the acceptability of the Arab Legion to the Jordanian monarchy derived from the latter's political weakness and lack of alternatives. In most of Africa the colonial transition was far less successful, as illustrated in chapter 2, although some successful examples existed here too, for example the Senegalese army.[28]

Where It Does Not Help: Invasiveness

Again, from the perspective of this book, probably the biggest problem faced by military advisory missions is their potential incompatibility with local ownership and therefore ultimately with the legitimacy of the process. Financial self-interest and cultural prejudice are not the only reasons why manipulation between advisers and advised for ends other than the stated ones may happen. With reference to South Vietnam, but with more general applicability as well, advisory missions have been defined as 'colonialism by ventriloquism': once the power to impose change which characterised colonialism had waned, host governments had to be convinced to accept advice and conform to certain standards.[29] The problem of local ownership was already evident during the process of new governments taking over armies created by the colonial powers, despite attempts by the colonialists to implement a transition and empower local officers at least in part (for example in Nigeria) during the last years of their rule.

A controversial case of large-scale advisory effort is that of Soviet advisers on the Republican side in the Spanish Civil War. The welcome that the Soviet advisers received, initially started showing cracks after strategy views began to diverge. Although the Soviets were criticised for their power and omnipotence, it is difficult to see how the Republicans could have managed the advanced weaponry received from them without the advisers largely taking over. The immensely expanded air force is a case in point.[30] Soviet and Comintern advisers in their internal memoranda all made this point, which seems therefore to have been a genuine conclusion deriving from their observations in the early phase of the war.[31] In the early days at least, the advisers won authority and acquired influence over the Spanish commanders because of their irreplaceable technical expertise as well as (sometimes) hard work. That said, the advisers were all GRU agents and reported back to Moscow; they got deeply involved in local politics and pushed for the purge from the army of 'unreliable elements', as well as for expanding the role of the PCE. As the advisers increasingly tried to assert themselves as the real commanders of Spanish units, but without taking responsibility for failures, they faced growing resentment and opposition from the Spaniards.[32]

The invasive attitude of Soviet advisers in Spain was far from unique. A characteristic aspect of the invasiveness and arrogance of many advising missions is that existing military traditions would often be taken into no consideration, to the point of turning them into a major source of resistance to the new training and advice being imparted.

The examples can multiply. American advisers in Vietnam noticed that:

in the Army of the republic of Vietnam, French influence continues to be strong. All members of the high command at the Joint General Staff are French-trained. [...] They tend to cling to the French concepts, techniques, and tactics, and advisors at all levels, when trying to introduce changes, face the problem of their counterparts' deeply rooted military ideas and habits.[33]

Few Vietnamese officers shared the American belief in coordination, team-work, loyalty to superiors and subordinates, skill and delegation of authority. Nor did the Vietnamese officers see their government or the army as an entity; they viewed each in terms of their particular bureau, agency or battalion, inde-pendent of and usually in competition with other agencies and units. 'Coor-dination among agencies to achieve unity of effort and effect for the common good is almost unknown...'[34]

When training the new Iraqi army after 2003, a similar problem emerged:

Many of the officers and NCOs had former Iraqi Army experience. While the units were new and the battalion organization different than the previous Iraqi Army, the specter of the old Iraqi Army remained. The ASTs [Army Force Generation Synchro-nization Tools] conducted a balancing act between instilling new traditions while try-ing to rid some of the poorer habits of the old Iraqi Army.[35]

Comparatively benign objectives, such as the National Pacification Plan conceived by US advisers in El Salvador, while not complete failures, never really took off because it had not been considered that the Salvadoran army lacked adequate resources and manpower for 'soft' pacification programmes.[36] A whole range of policies can be identified that might have worked well in some contexts and turned counter-productive in others. The creation of elite units, once also a popular prescription for developing countries, was found to affect the rest of the army negatively because of the stripping of human resources. Even investing in the training and development of human resources does not always work, because it can increase the opportunities available to recruits in terms of civilian careers.[37]

The arrogance and invasiveness of advisers was often mirrored by the readi-ness of host armies to accept anything coming from their advisers as an improvement. In this regard the 'blank slate' attitude affected the organisa-tional dimension particularly badly. 'The attempt to duplicate organizational forms that appear successful in admired foreign contexts may at times actually constitute an impediment to true managerial effectiveness.'[38] The British Mili-tary Mission in Greece after World War II has been accused of trying to export the British army model to a country which could not afford it. At the same time the British failed to impose a new system of promotions, leaving in place the old military elite, politically compromised and disinclined to take any ini-tiative, at the expense of the new generation of officers.[39]

The uncritical attitude towards advisers can then turn into distrust once the initial great expectations have not been met. In Afghanistan (1978–9), the Taraki regime's expectations of a quick victory against the insurgents were rapidly deluded and the advisers started being accused of incompetence. The Afghans had absorbed the propaganda image of the Soviet army in World War II as of a progression from victory to victory and could not accept the lack of immediate results.[40]

Where It Does Not Help: Crowding Out

From the perspective of studying the impact of advisory efforts on the consolidation of the monopoly of large-scale violence, it is particularly important to point out how a characteristic outcome of large-scale advisory efforts is often the fostering of a dependency relationship among the advised. The availability of external resources also reduces the need to mobilise domestic resources, as happens in development aid with what economists call 'crowding out'. Already in Greece just after World War II, although advisers had been instructed to limit themselves to offering operational advice in a manner that 'the individual Greek officer will think it was his idea', in practice Americans were often seen as being in charge of operations by the journalists present on the ground.[41]

Not much is known of the most massive peace-time advisory effort ever mounted to assist an army, i.e. in Saudi Arabia, but by the mid 1980s an estimated 30,000 Americans, 4–5,000 French, 2–3,000 British and 10,000 Pakistanis were assisting a Saudi army of 50,000. Although the use of (mostly privately contracted) advisers was not without results, the capabilities of the Saudi armed forces continued to be rated as very modest well into the 1990s and beyond.[42]

In Vietnam, the fact that American advisers had 'little understanding of the culture or the history of their Vietnamese hosts' led them to take over from the slower-moving Vietnamese and 'get the job done' themselves, in fact establishing a 'superior-subordinate relationship rather than an advisory relationship', 'alienating South Vietnamese military leaders and creating a dependency relationship'.[43] The dependency was compounded by the tendency of US advisers to deal directly with logistical issues, while the logistical system of the army of the Republic of Vietnam remained deficient.[44] The first major operation of the South Vietnamese army without the support of US advisers, the Lam Son 719 operation in Laos in February 1971, went badly and the army had to retreat leaving behind a lot of equipment.[45] The 'lack of urgency' manifested by the South Vietnamese leadership to fight the war derived in Hosmer's opinion from their 'erroneous belief' that the United States would rescue their country if the military situation deteriorated beyond a certain point.

Dependency can grow to the point where it becomes a 'client state syndrome', particularly when external assistance is not just extensive but also prolonged in time and accompanied by political guarantees (see also chapter 2). In such cases host regimes can end up relying on the willingness of foreign patrons to bail them out in every circumstance, avoiding having to make any effort of their own. It has been argued, for example, that behind Liberian President Doe's unwillingness to develop an efficient army, which he saw as a potential threat, was the 'overriding belief that the United States would support the regime and intervene against any enemy'.[46] This is also the case with a number of former French colonies in Africa (chiefly Djibouti and the Central African Republic), which relied on the permanent deployment of French contingents,[47] and of Zaire under Mobutu, which enlisted ad hoc help from the Belgian, French and Moroccan militaries.[48] In Afghanistan, many Soviet advisers and politicians by the mid 1980s came to the same conclusion, that Afghans could only be prompted to get their act together if forced to fight for their own survival, a conviction which led to a change at the top of the Afghan leadership and eventually to the withdrawal from Afghanistan.[49]

Interestingly the North Vietnamese seem to have been aware of the risks of inducing dependency on their allies and deliberately tried to wean the Laotians from their dependency from an apparently early stage (1960s), insisting that they start to operate without direct Vietnamese support.[50] The Vietnamese political and technical advisory mission to Pathet Lao was a relatively substantial one, about fifty men in headquarters and ten to fifteen in each province in 1964, but their advisers were instructed to keep quiet and only offer advice when requested to do so by the Laotians; in general their advice was followed. American scholars developed the view that Vietnamese advisers were 'widely respected' because of their 'dedication to duty'; they tended to be experienced and disciplined cadres.

By their example, by on-the-job-training, and by guidance, generally tactful, they goad the less vigorous Lao into better performance. They frequently act as arbiters of internal disputes within the Lao organization. And they are particularly important in directing essential resources from the DRV to the proper channels in Laos.

They also insisted that:

if anything happens that could damage the friendship and solidarity between Laos and Vietnam, the North Vietnamese advisers must bear the major responsibility, no matter who is right or wrong.[51]

The military advisers' mission was relatively modest, with one military and one political advisor per Pathet Lao battalion (plus three to five support staff); initially company level advisers also existed, but interestingly they were discontinued in 1966. Their modus operandi was similar to that of the political advisers.[52] Perhaps the Vietnamese determination to prevent dependency was motivated by their limited resources.

In South Vietnam, it was acknowledged that the inculcation of 'motivation and effective leadership' was never effectively achieved, despite the recognition of its foremost importance. Advisers often responded to the need to secure the cooperation of their counterparts, opting to maintain good relations with them, but that came usually at the expense of 'pressuring them to do the job'.[53] In the end, however, indigenous officers tended to prove more responsive to the political situation than to the pressure exercised by foreign advisers. One American adviser remarked that his counterpart, who had seemed hopeless to him, started acting in a much more proactive way ('like a soldier') following a political reshuffle in Saigon, which had eliminated from the scene his rivals and opened the possibility of a promotion.[54]

The 'crowding out' impact of extensive mentoring and advising seems obvious, particularly when associated with other forms of assistance. In practice, therefore, the impact of these large-scale programmes might be negative; it might improve the technical ability of the hosts, but decreases their readiness to use those or any other skills. The hosts could develop a greater inclination to use their new skills in the event of withdrawal of their supporters, but the massive assistance effort might also discourage them from developing managerial and coordination skills which might prove essential for the long-term survival of the ruling elite.

Where It Does Not Help: Failing to Transfer the Required Skills

The skills taught by advisers might or might not be used, but it cannot be taken for granted that they will actually be transferred successfully, or that they are the ones required. Typically, foreign advisers might offer remarkable technical skills and experience but have no knowledge of the host country, serve only short terms and not speak the local language, or in general lack a basic understanding of the cultural and political environment where they are operating. An additional problem has often been that the advisory teams sent to host countries are of questionable quality.[55] It is not surprising therefore that they would implement a blank template without consideration for local conditions and needs, or for effectively available human and financial resources.[56]

In Angola, despite the fact that serious efforts were made to prepare the Soviet advisers, still they were not up to the task. In particular, they were not told what to expect from Angolans, their way of thinking and of behaving:

'We sought to recreate in Angola exactly the same as we had at home in order for things to turn out well here'. The Soviet military advisors [...] conducted [the 1987 offensive] very ably [...]. But the problem was that they planned the campaign in the way they were always accustomed to doing it, that is for Soviet soldiers. [...] The Cubans told our generals, 'Wait—what are you doing, on whom are you relying? You must rely on these (Angolan) soldiers'. But our officers already provided a time frame—to fulfil objectives by a certain time, to depart at a certain date for such and such a line. This was, of course pure fantasy.[57]

The latest major layer in the development of 'Western' military effectiveness derived from the ever increasing complexity of the battlefield in the age of industrialisation of war. This reduced or eliminated the importance of strict orders, rote training and coercive discipline, forcing the creation of a much larger stratum of junior officers and NCOs than had even been the case. The educational requirements of modern armies, as well as their demand for managerial skills, grew out of all proportion with the past. The officers' and NCOs' command and control structure shifted downwards, reaching team level (five to eleven men). Moreover, there has been 'increasing emphasis on controlling soldiers through an internalisation of values and operating rules congruent with the objectives, goals, and values of the organisation'.[58] Imitating these features in less developed countries proved problematic, specifically because of a lack of human resources. A gap opened up as a result between the armies of the developed world and their client armies outside it, which made the exportability of the Western model more problematic than ever.

The Demands of Local Ownership I

Ruling elites might accept advisory missions for a variety of reasons, not only because they think they need one. Moreover, the perception of advisory missions by their hosts is always at risk of being affected by a mutating political environment. Mehmet Ali's Egypt provides a good example of this. Although there was constant friction between the advisers and the Egyptians, except for the few who accepted to convert to Islam, the repression of the revolt in Christian Greece compounded such feelings and mutual distrust.[59]

At least, the typical ruler will be less than keen to allow foreign-trained officers to become a major force within their own army, even if the training was imparted by a close ally. President Mubarak of Egypt tried to limit US influence on the military by constraining the career paths of American-trained officers, because he feared that they might be too independent to control. The Egyptian ruler also resisted American advice to reform the strongly centralised and ineffective command system, because they considered such a change essential to maintain control over the army.[60]

Even client rulers totally dependent on the support of their patron have often been resilient towards their advice. South Vietnamese ruler Diem, for example, 'often saw American advice, no matter how well conceived, as impinging on his prerogatives as the country's paramount national figure'.[61] While the Americans seemed to have succeeded in forcing a reorganisation of the command system, in reality:

South Vietnamese commanders and officials simply ignored the new chain of command as they had the old. Superiors continued to bypass subordinates; subordinates continued to go over the heads of superiors; and all commanders continued to issue orders to units not under their control.[62]

Perhaps it does not surprise us that the French in Indochina in the early 1950s were obviously resentful of the presence of US advisers and seemed to be trying to make their life as difficult as possible, despite the fact that the French military effort was largely funded by Washington.[63] However, opposition to following the 'American method in fighting communist guerrillas' existed even among the usually loyal Philippines. Hosmer identifies a general pattern here:

Third World civilian and military leaders sometimes reject sound counterinsurgency practice and US advice because they are less concerned than US officials about the consequences of the failure to defeat an insurgency expeditiously and decisively. Hence, the indigenous leaders see no reason to adopt the otherwise unpalatable political, economic, and other reforms that would hasten or complete the suppression of the insurgency or to accept the increased casualties that would likely result from more aggressive military operations...[64]

In El Salvador too, American advisers struggled to impose small unit tactics during the last few years of the war and always faced resistance in pushing for their own model of military organisation, which attributes a key role to NCOs; 'even though most combat units [...] are capable of implementing US training [...], tactics are not always implemented [...]. After 10 years of US involvement, the El Salvador Armed Forces only reluctantly engages the FMLN using the kind of tactics that US advisers have urged'. Sometimes, the threat of cutting off security assistance had to be used to force the Salvadorans to comply.[65]

The Soviets were by no means exempt from this problem. From the mid 1950s Soviet and Chinese views started diverging, following a period of great Soviet influence. Although a minority of Chinese officers adopted the Soviet view that nuclear weapons made Maoist theories outdated, the Chinese military leadership started distancing itself and cautioning the officers not to accept Soviet views uncritically.[66]

The issue of local ownership was often acknowledged by the advisers themselves. In the words of a former adviser to the Iraqi army, 'we know that Iraqi leaders do their best work when they feel ownership of a course of action'.[67] What to do, however, when the divergence of interests was deep and unbridgeable? In Colombia the Americans were more concerned with the counternarcotics effort, but the Colombian government with eliminating the leftist guerrillas.[68]

Similarly in El Salvador American-sponsored reform efforts were thwarted by the 'officer corps' jealous guarding of its pecuniary prerogatives', including the pocketing of the pay of ghost soldiers.[69] They felt that the internal organisation of the Salvadoran army did not need to be changed as advised by the Americans; even the attempt to train new officers away from Salvador failed, as the new graduates would join the existing system once returning to El Salvador. Similarly they did not understand the need to introduce a professional NCO corps in an army where class divisions between an elite officer corps and peasant soldiers were very strong.[70] The Salvadorans had even less sympathy for the concept of human rights, which from 1985 onwards became one of the priorities of American advisers. In the words of one of the advisers:

I came to understand that my most important role was getting the [Salvadoran armed forces] to respect human rights without ever mentioning that term, because that was a real turn-off. ... I approached it from a very practical sense, just talked about the practicality of observing human rights, that you would lessen the recruitment for the enemy, it makes your job easier and you can get to the end of this thing.[71]

Senior Salvadoran officers were particularly hostile to having US advisers observing them in the field, because of the latter's habit of asking questions about their plans and operations; whereas junior officers were keen to be accompanied on combat missions in order to gain tactical experience from the Americans and even 'chided those who would not accompany them on operations'.[72]

In Iraq too (after 2003), American efforts to introduce a professional NCO corps were hampered by the officers' view of any 'loss of power or control to NCOs as a challenge to their rank'. The officers with a background in the old

Iraqi army were the most likely to resist the change.[73] It is possible to find a recognition of the need to 'resist trying to change the structure or standard operating procedures of their hosts and instead begin acting as a type of military consultant or adviser', rather than 'reshape the force into a model similar to that of the U.S. Army—primarily because that model is the only one they know'.[74] In practice this did not happen too often on the ground, not least because the largest training efforts were not carried out by the better trained and more aware Special Forces but by the regular army.

Military Assistance

Friendly Help or Patronage-Building?

One obvious reason why host governments and military establishments might be resilient to foreign advice and training is that they question whether external partners have a genuine intention of improving the fighting effectiveness of client armies, rather than being involved in a political patronage exercise or even worse in a marketing operation. In the case of the French naval mission to Poland (1923–32), it has been argued that in the end the latter rationale took over, despite the strong political interest in making Poland stronger militarily against Germany:

The French looked at Poland, as well as to other countries of the cordon sanitaire, and eastern and Central Europe in general, as cash cows and places to supplement their own military strength while, most importantly, turning a profit.[75]

Similarly economic and military advisory missions sent by Germany to China in the late nineteenth century clearly benefited Krupp, who won contracts for fortifications and guns. Von Seekt, a prestigious military figure who led the German mission 1934–5, reportedly spent more time making contacts for German companies than advising the Chinese military.[76] German diplomats in Argentina in the 1920s considered it normal to expect that economic advantages would derive from the influence of privately contracted German military advisers in Argentina. 'They felt that extensive German participation in arms contracts could be expected through the partisan efforts of the German officers'.[77]

Incidentally this might be a reason why private security companies too have not always performed well in training and advising armies. In Iraq, the first year or so was quite disastrous, one commentator stating that 'whatever training has been done has been pretty perfunctory'.[78] In Africa their record was not as bad, at least in the fields of training and intelligence. Executive Outcomes, for example, contributed infrared technology to the effort of the Angolan government to gain superiority.[79]

Even when the aim of the suppliers of assistance might not have been narrow-minded economic benefit, the possibility of the leverage earned by the suppliers being used to exercise unwelcome influence was always present. In Greece during the civil war (1947–9), the Americans used their huge leverage effectively to impose changes in the command structure of the Greek army, having ineffective generals removed. In this case the deployment of effective diplomatic skills by the Americans prevented a significant rift from emerging.[80]

This does not mean that military assistance cannot have a positive impact on the achievement of a monopoly of large-scale violence, at least temporarily. Without massive Soviet and Cuban support, the MPLA state in Angola would not have established itself against the competition of UNITA and FNLA, both in turn supported by regional powers. Although several of the limitations and perverse effects discussed here apply to the Angolan case too, eventually the MPLA regime managed to survive and prevail. Soviet and Vietnamese assistance to the Cambodian government of Heng Samrin allowed it to survive the Vietnamese withdrawal in the 1990s, after an initial crisis. Even the ill-fated government of President Najibullah in Afghanistan seemed on its way to consolidation in 1990, after the withdrawal of Soviet troops in 1988–9, until Soviet assistance faltered because of the Soviet Union's own collapse. What all these cases highlight, however, is that external assistance cannot eliminate the need for recipient governments to develop their own political and military base.

Similarly it could be argued that, regardless of the relatively poor performance of the Salvadoran armed forces in the 1980s, the government of the country would not have survived the challenge of the leftist insurgents without it. Some governments have been at least relatively more efficient at using external assistance than others. The Colombian army, for example, absorbed large levels of US military aid in the 1980s and 1990s with relatively limited disruption to the effectiveness of its army, which increased as US assistance peaked from 1998 onwards.[81] In the Colombian case, the perverse effect of US assistance was the inclination to execute civilians to add to the body count (see below). Perhaps the Colombian success in capitalising on US assistance was because the amount of assistance was modest compared to the overall Colombian military effort.

Supplying the Wrong Hardware

Even assuming that military assistance was provided with the genuine intention to develop autonomous armies, assessing the genuine needs of host countries can be very problematic. Says a commentator from the US army:

> I have observed many in-country U.S. survey teams: invariably, hosts make the case for acquiring the most modern of military hardware and do everything to avoid issues of maintenance, logistics, and training. They obfuscate and mislead to such an extent that U.S. teams, no matter how earnest their sense of mission, find it nearly impossible to help. More generally, Arab reluctance to be candid about training deficiencies makes it extremely difficult for foreign advisors properly to support instruction or assess training needs. [...] combined arms training, when it does take place, [...] is intended to impress visitors (which it does—the dog-and-pony show is usually done with uncommon gusto and theatrical talent) rather than provide real training.[82]

As a result, some of the policies recommended or sponsored by foreign assistance can in fact be counter-productive. Looking back at examples of foreign assistance, one author commented that 'excessive hardware can compromise effectiveness'.[83] In Vietnam, the Americans did not really try to build an army effective against guerrillas, but one capable of repelling something like the invasion of a regular army, road-bound and reliant on heavy firepower:[84]

> rather than a counter-guerrilla force dedicated to providing local security, the American advisers sought to build a force that was the mirror image of the US Army, trained to fight an airmobile and mechanized war under the cover of lavish amounts of (US) firepower.[85] Taught by the US military to fight with the support of robust American artillery, armoured, logistics, and helicopter resources, the [South Vietnamese army] had grown dependent.[86]

Similarly, US help to the Honduran army in the 1980s seemed to be making its army more dependent, rather than more self-sufficient,[87] but it is not clear what the real intention was in either case. Most armies in developing countries are unable to use even the limited amounts of hardware that they own, let alone any massive new inflow of equipment. The Ghanaian army, one of the most efficient in Africa, had less than 10 per cent of its transport fleet operational in 1988; air force and navy were much worse and hardly operational at all. In general the servicing of equipment was very poor and had to be taken care of by foreign advisers.[88] The Zimbabwean army, another of those considered most efficient, was found in 1998 to have just 5 per cent of its vehicles in working order, to have abandoned pilot training and have sent on leave 70 per cent of the personnel of one brigade for lack of funding.[89] The Nigerian army never had sufficient technical skills to operate the advanced equipment it was purchasing.[90]

Nonetheless, armies like this are often offered massive re-equipment programmes when facing real or potential challenges. The recent case of Afghanistan is a perfect example of this: in the 1980s, the Soviets had re-equipped the Afghan army with much more armour and artillery than it could manage or than could be of any use in the mountainous environment of Afghanistan.[91] A rationale for the massive re-equipment programme was to boost the morale of the fledgling Afghan army, which does appear to have happened, judging from the memories of Afghan officers serving during those years.[92] However, it is not clear whether the human resources absorbed into the effort and the constraints imposed on the operational abilities of the army justified the gains in terms of morale. Then after 2006, lacking skills to operate even the old, Soviet type of weapons and transports which Afghans had been using since the 1950s, the National Army was again offered a massive re-equipment plan which brought to it more advanced and maintenance-heavy American vehicles and weapons.[93]

In El Salvador in the 1980s, the US Defense Department's vested interests were pushing for more helicopters, artillery and hardware, which the local army was very happy to accept, increasing its stockpile of heavy weapons 'of little utility in a counterinsurgency. [...] Rather than risk disaffecting [the Salvadoran Armed Forces] by opposing requests for inappropriate hardware, American officers at times succumb to the temptation to go along'.[94] This was the case for example of 105-mm howitzers, which the Salvadoran army used mainly in harassment and interdiction missions, 'at best wasteful and at worst counterproductive'.[95] The use of field rockets and mortars in populated areas was controversial in Sandinista Nicaragua too, even if the actual casualties resulting were modest.[96] In the early 1980s, there was a convergence of interests between the Soviets and the Sandinistas: the former were keen to help and establish their influence, while the latter were keen to receive the equipment they needed to form a large army, even if they did not really believe that the plans they had presented to repel a hypothetical American invasion were realistic.[97] In Ethiopia too, plentiful Soviet supplies of heavy weaponry did not help fight the insurgency:

> As I have observed, we use rocket launchers and mortars without restraint, but I wonder if a thousand shots kill even two bandits... The planes are not effective either because the bandits are well protected in caves and encampments.[98]

Observers in the field often came to the alternative conclusion that more basic equipment is what really makes the difference. 'It was cheap, low-tech stuff—rations, boots, and radios—that helped to make the El Salvadoran Armed Forces effective in the field'.[99] In Nicaragua, an American observer concluded that the most useful counter-guerrilla support weapon was the easily transportable and cheap AGS-17 grenade launcher.[100]

Indeed, it can be argued that high technology and plentiful equipment are not necessary to build a viable and relatively effective security apparatus. Apart from the argument which I developed in chapter 2 about the limited value of military technology to achieve or strengthen the monopoly of large-scale violence, there are other considerations weighing against reliance on technology. Matching the armed forces to the resources of society is a factor of strength because it makes local innovation possible, or in any case easier, and facilitates the mobilisation of adequate management skills. The alternative implies turning the armed forces into a concentration of best human resources of the country, which might still be insufficient to produce an effective army, and at the same time is very likely to be detrimental to economic and social development and to lead to friction between political and military elites.[101]

This argument seems to hold in the case of the Arab armies involved in the Arab-Israeli conflict. The societies of Egypt and Syria were not able to supply adequate specialist and managerial skills to the comparatively huge and technologically equipped armies fielded from the 1960s onwards. By contrast, the most effective challenge to the Israeli army came by the much smaller and relatively lightly equipped Hezbollah of Lebanon.[102] In the Greek Civil War, the debate pitted British and Greek generals on one side, favouring technological escalation, against the Americans, wary of pumping too much hardware into the dysfunctional Greek army. The British believed that the key to counter-insurgency lay in air power. The Greeks liked that, and on top of it wanted more artillery and direct fire weapons, even if the condition of Greek roads meant that artillery could not be deployed in most areas affected by the communist insurgency. Already, in the early stages of the war, several Greek infantry commanding officers stated their disinclination to deploy father than 2 miles from their artillery; more artillery would have meant an even less mobile Greek army. The Americans by contrast believed that the Greek army had enough equipment already and that what was needed was more training and a more aggressive leadership. They were also determined to leave much of the training programme to the Greek themselves, through a system of training teams and demonstration platoons. The Americans had it their way and by late 1948 there were marked improvements in the battlefield performance of Greek army units.[103]

Paradoxically, American support showed a marked tendency after Greece to become conducive to technological escalation. In the words of a group of authors, 'Americans take a rich man's approach to war. They view US access to technology—however expensive—as offering a significant comparative advantage over potential adversaries'. However, in 'small wars' certain capabilities might be irrelevant or even counter-productive.[104] In Vietnam, there was a long debate within USAF about the opportunity to replace the propeller-driven planes of the South Vietnamese air force with jets, despite the obvious unsuitability of the jets for counter-guerrilla operations.[105] One former adviser remarked that

this giving and taking reflected more than simply bureaucratic pressures at work. [...] The bonds between the patron and the client are tightened, and it becomes tougher to exercise pressure for change. The sponsor has less leverage to reform the social, political, economic, or military aspects of a struggle if there is a large and apparently open-ended or endless commitment.[106]

Perverse Incentives

As already hinted in *The role of technology* above, the abundant availability of external support is also liable to provide host governments perverse incentives to continue the conflict and avoid a political settlement, or even a military victory. American advisers and experts posted to El Salvador often came to the conclusion that 'the Salvadoran military does not wish to win the war, because in so doing it would lose American aid that has enriched it for the past decade'.[107]

The same kind of feelings emerged in a number of other occasions. As has been argued in the case of the multi-billion dollar US aid to Pakistan after 2001:

...the Pakistani government never saw the US monetary support as being a quid pro quo for the Pakistani forces to fight on US terms. There was no consideration among the khakis that Pakistan could oblige Washington beyond a point where its own national interests—as defined by the military—would be undermined. In fact, the Pakistani establishment was equally adept at realizing the client-based nature of the relationship and internalized the aid as little more than direct reimbursement for the costs of fighting the War. In a text book example of perverse incentives, the transactional nature of the arrangement had in fact created an incentive for Pakistan to prolong the effort as much as possible; the longer Pakistan remained involved in tactical operations, the higher the reimbursements would be.[108]

After 2005 the same criticism of Western assistance increasingly emerged in the policy literature concerning Afghanistan.[109] As recognised even in a

West Point publication, 'conditioning aid on the level of the terrorist threat in a given target state creates perverse incentives to reduce terrorism only to the point where the gains from reducing terror are offset by the loss in aid that will follow from fully eradicating the threat'.[110]

One particular kind of perverse effect is the tendency to embellish the performance of the host armed force, to show that it has been using external aid effectively. In the Colombian case, evidence emerged that the army was executing civilians in large numbers in order to pump up the body count. The link to external aid was demonstrated by a unit-by-unit analysis, in which units which lost US aid also reported a fall in the number of civilians killed.[111]

Military Intervention and Peacekeeping

If advisory efforts and military assistance are problematic when the objective is to create a self-standing client state, direct military intervention is of course even more so. It is certainly possible to develop effective 'indigenous' forces to fight alongside a foreign army. The British Empire was well served by its Sepoys, and so were the Italians by the Eritrean Askars, for example.[112] However, what I am discussing here is the role of the intervention of a foreign army in the establishment or consolidation of the monopoly of large-scale violence by a sovereign government. In such cases the purpose of a foreign expeditionary force would be to back up a weak regime and defeat a common enemy, or give it time to build up its own forces. The latter was for example the intent of the Soviet leadership, when it sent its divisions into Afghanistan at the end of 1979.[113] Depending on the situation on the ground, the expeditionary force might have to play a more proactive role than just backing up an ally (again this turned out to be the case in Afghanistan after 1979).

Crowding Out II

One obvious risk is that the presence of a large foreign contingent might actually provide a strong disincentive to the host armed forces to mobilise their own resources and energy, rather than just buy time for them to reorganise. When Washington decided to send combat troops to South Vietnam to take over combat operations and leave Vietnamese units in charge of pacification support and territorial security responsibility, 'boredom and routine ... eroded [the Vietnamese] combat skill and spirit to the point that they became almost as passive and as lethargic as the territorial forces'. The mistake was realised and after Tet (1968) the South Vietnamese army resumed combat operations, although with the support of US advisers and alongside US units, in the hope of building up their confidence and capability. Still, many South Vietnamese personnel continued to 'regard Americans as protectors and providers instead of advisors and comrades-in-arms'.[114] The ambiguity of the relationship between the intervening power and its local allies is well summed up by a manifesto produced by a committee of Buddhist students in Saigon in 1966, 'calling for the United States to increase its military and economic aid to the GVN and at the same time to stop interfering in Vietnamese politics'.[115]

Similarly the Soviets in Afghanistan realised that in order to stimulate the Afghan army to take the lead, the Soviet Fortieth Army had to take a few steps back and limit itself to an ever decreasing support role.[116]

Another example is that of the Vietnamese army in Cambodia (1979–88). It proved difficult for the Vietnamese to motivate the armed forces of their Cambodian client to take up a more active role in the fighting.[117] By the time of their withdrawal, the Vietnamese were not too confident in the ability of their Cambodian allies; the lack of able commanding officers was identified by the Vietnamese as the main problem of the Cambodians. That was in part at least a result of the Cambodian army having mainly functioned up to that point as a 'supplementary force' of the Vietnamese People's Army. The 'regular', mobile units of the national army were considered to be not very motivated. By contrast, the provincial units of the regional army were better fighters than the national army units, because they were fighting for their own villages. In both Afghanistan and Cambodia, the withdrawal of the allied foreign military contingents prompted the indigenous armies to rise up successfully to the task of confronting the enemy. The Cambodian army was forced at this point to replace political appointees with more professional and capable ones. The Cambodian army was described by a journalist as far worse equipped than Lon Nol's army had been when fighting the Khmer Rouge under American patronage, which had provided a wealth of weaponry from the Americans. The Cambodians did not receive much support after the Vietnamese withdrawal; the rusty equipment of the Cambodian army compared unfavourably even with the insurgents' arsenal. However, Lon Nol's army collapsed in the face of the Khmer Rouge, while Hun Sen's army survived after the Vietnamese withdrawal despite the Khmer Rouge being re-equipped by the Chinese.[118]

I have already discussed the reliance of Mobutu in Zaire on foreign military support to stay in power and its consequences for the preparedness of his armed forces (see chapter 2); I will only add here that the mere fact that he had repeatedly to rely on the intervention of foreign forces demonstrates the point that such interventions were not ultimately conducive to the consolidation of his monopoly of large-scale violence.

The direct threat to the existence of the South Korean state and the difficulty of the foreign contingents (American and others) in coping with the Chinese and North Korean threat deprived the South Koreans of the opportunity to hide behind their more powerful and resourceful allies, even if they had wanted to. Hence the dynamic development of the army of the Republic of Korea. In Angola, the Cuban intervention did not ultimately prevent the Angolan armed forces from growing and acquiring an autonomous capability, as demonstrated by their ultimate defeat of UNITA after the Cuban withdrawal, but it might well have slowed it down. The Cuban training effort was very focused, and there does not seem to have been a Cuban intention to stay on; rather the Cubans started at one point to feel 'trapped' in Angola. After the early years of direct engagement with the South Africans, the Cubans took a back seat and intervened in the fighting only occasionally, letting the Angolans do most of it. Still the mere presence of the Cubans acted as a strong disincentive for the Angolans to develop capabilities, tactics and skills with any speed; despite all these Cuban precautions and continuous fighting, it still took fourteen years for the Angolans to acquire a capable army.[119]

When Convergence Occurs I

Determining why some of the armies mentioned above were eventually able to cope on their own and why others did not would require a more in-depth study than is possible here. I am tempted to think that rugged Soviet and Vietnamese practices were more suitable to 'state formation' environments than the more sophisticated and refined approaches of the Americans. What is clear in any case is the heavy side-effects of a direct foreign military presence in the creation of viable, independent host armies. More such side-effects can be identified. Another obvious risk is the demoralisation of the host army as nationalist or xenophobic sentiment might arise either within the army or within society to hamper cooperation with the foreign contingent, which would then start being perceived as an occupying force. The presence of a foreign army clearly tends to have a delegitimising impact in any case, if for no other reason than it shows that the host government is not able to cope for itself. Whether or not the presence of a foreign contingent stirs nationalist reactions depends on the wider picture. In the case of South Korea, the calculation was obvious: despite strong nationalist objections to American presence in the country, the army considered it as the lesser evil compared to the threat from the North.[120]

Similarly in Afghanistan, many Khalqi officers harboured resentment against the Soviets after 1979, but with a few exceptions continued to fight against the Islamist opposition for want of a better alternative.[121] After all, it was as soon as the Soviet threat waned that American presence on German soil started becoming unpopular.[122] Obviously the stronger the nationalist sentiments are in a country, the more problematic the presence of even an 'invited' foreign army is going to be. However, as pointed out in chapter 1, the technologies of mass mobilisation developed over the twentieth century create a situation where the presence of a foreign army in a country is always going to be problematic, even in a country where nationalist feelings used to be modest. As a result, even an initially rather well accepted intervention like Washington's in Afghanistan in 2001 turned gradually sour.[123]

A third risk is that the interests of guests and hosts might eventually diverge, leading if not to an open conflict at least to an increasingly dysfunctional relationship. As the host army increasingly looks like an occupation force, even to those who initially welcomed it, its net contribution to the edification of a monopoly of large-scale violence might end up being negative. By 2008 this was beginning to seem the case in Afghanistan, as President Karzai and others started criticising increasingly vociferously ISAF operations in the country.[124] A more radical case of spent friendships is that of the Burmese nationalists in the Burma Independence Army and the Japanese army, whose cooperation started turning sour within a couple of years of its inception. Eventually the nationalists ended up fighting against the Japanese on the Allies' side.[125]

The Special Case of Peacekeeping

A particular kind of external intervention is peacekeeping operations. Within the context of this book I am interested in them as long as they impact on the process of primitive accumulation of coercive power and/or the monopolisation of violence. Peacekeeping operations have a mixed but predominantly not very positive record. In the presence of a consensus among warring parties, a carefully managed peacekeeping operation can be successful. One such example is Mozambique.[126]

However, when operations take place without the unanimous consensus of the parties in a civil conflict, they tend in fact to freeze a civil war rather than end it for good. In other words, this kind of peacekeeping operation prevents one of the parties in conflict from gaining a monopoly of large-scale violence, while at the same time conditions are not in place for the reaching of a viable political settlement.[127] In Bosnia international intervention was not supported by the Serbians in 1992 and could not stop the war; only when in 1995 the tide of war seemed to be turning against them did they decide to enter serious peace negotiations.[128] Even then, the civil war in Bosnia was more frozen than resolved. Three separate armies (Muslim, Serbian and Croatian) were left in existence and trained separately.[129] Along a similar line, the exclusion of the Taliban from the Bonn negotiations in 2001, concerning a new political settlement in Afghanistan, is now recognised by some of the protagonists in Bonn as a key factor in the resurgence of conflict in the country.[130] In reality, even with that exclusion, the formation of a solid monopoly of large-scale violence was arguably possible, but political rivalry in Kabul prevented the reaching of a consensus among anti-Taliban factions. Reciprocal vetoes resulted in the failure to develop quickly a centralised army under the control of the new Afghan state. It is unlikely that any balanced history of the UN mission in that country would identify a skilfully managed diplomatic effort.[131]

In these kinds of contexts, there is little chance that 'peacebuilders' might achieve anything other than unwittingly reinforcing 'weak states characterised by patrimonial politics and skewed development', because they operate with ambitious plans and limited resources and are therefore forced to prioritise stability over 'liberalization':

Local elites, both in the capital and in the countryside, will resist or attempt to change the peacebuilding program so that it more fully incorporates their preferences.[132]

In Afghanistan and Bosnia, peacekeeping intervention could at least claim partial or temporary success. There are other examples of peacekeeping operations which were outright failures. In Somalia, for example, both in the 1990s and in 2006 onwards, peacekeeping interventions were not based on local consensus and suffered from particularly limited international commitment; in both cases some of the parties in the conflict had no interest in a settlement following the terms imposed on them and successfully resisted the attempt of government imposed from outside to re-establish a monopoly of violence.[133] It could even be argued that a number of eventually successful post-conflict transitions were actually able to restore a monopoly of violence *despite* peacekeeping operations. In the case of Cambodia in the 1990s, the consolidation of the Hun Sen regime and the gradual elimination of challenges to the monopoly of large-scale violence occurred after the UN failed to keep the Khmer Rouge opposition aligned with the peace agreement. Resorting to war eventually resulted in the outright victory of Hun Sen.[134] A similar case could be made in Rwanda, where the solution to internal conflict came through the failure of the peacekeeping intervention with the crushing victory of the RPF.[135]

Should we then agree with Luttwak that war should be given a chance,[136] at least in those cases where the parties in conflict cannot agree on a political deal? This is, of course, what in practice happens when international actors are not convinced of the benefits of intervening in a conflict situation; Iraq after the Second Gulf War (1991) was one such occasion, when Washington decided to leave Saddam Hussein and rebels to fight each other out. The two Chechen wars are other cases still. In these incidences, the ultimate winner was never in doubt given the disparity of forces, so that the re-establishment of a monopoly of large-scale violence was expected to be relatively quick, even if in Chechnya it took in reality much longer than originally thought and was still not completely achieved in 2009. Somalia in the 1990s is a more controversial case, as the failure to keep the intervention going was from the beginning clearly bound to lead to anarchy and chaos as no faction in the conflict seemed to reunify the country. Indeed after the failed intervention of 1992, conflict only became the order of the day again after the emergence of a politically unpalatable (Islamist) group as the most likely candidate to win the civil war.[137] In the absence of political, economic or geopolitical interests of external powers, reaching a consensus that war should be given a 'chance' has never been very controversial, at least in diplomatic circles.

Weinstein, Licklider and Wagner have all argued or even demonstrated that regimes emerging from the victorious party in a civil war have greater chances of being stable than those emerging out of negotiated settlement or peacekeeping operations. The example of Somalia is handy in this regard because the south, where international intervention has been concentrated, was still in a messy and extremely unstable state in 2010, following twenty years of turmoil; while the north, never 'benefiting' from any external intervention, was stable and peaceful throughout the period.[138]

The Unsustainable Lightness of Police Reform

A Late Discovery of Virtue

The model which I proposed in the previous chapter, that is of a 'ruler' confronting trends and patterns in society with his own choices of policing strategies, has to be significantly modified in the case of police reform programmes supported by international organisations, which mostly occur in post-conflict environments or in new states. As has been pointed out, 'police-building' has a long history and has taken various shapes. Its origins lie partly in colonial annexation and administration and partly in inter-country technical assistance on narrowly focused security concerns. In the nineteenth century these two types of ancestors to modern police-building operations easily blurred, as in the case of British attempts to reform Egyptian police between the end of the nineteenth and the beginning of the twentieth century. The British-sponsored reform faced opposition, not just from vested interest and reactionary elements, but also from nationalists and local reformers, who resented the gradual British takeover of the Ministry of Interior. Indeed, having initiated the penetration of Egyptian police with an agenda of professionalisation, the British ended up militarising it once they felt confident that their control over the country was well assured.[139]

This was not an isolated incident. During the Imperial age, Britain did not distinguish itself as a promoter of community policing, as it did from the 1990s onwards. The British Empire in India was very careful not to accept the existing system of communal policing and replaced it with a centralised system, under the control of the district magistrate.[140]

Controversy continued to affect police-building operations into the twentieth century. French police trainers in early twentieth-century Brazil were not popular and were sometimes even attacked by their trainees. In many of these cases, arguably foreign police assistance in fact exacerbated local public and political turmoil and did not even increase the loyalty to the regimes. Between the two World Wars it was the United States who were mostly engaged in police-building operations, if for no other reasons than most of the 'late developers' of the eastern hemisphere were under colonial control. The Americans did not have it smoother than the Europeans. In Haiti in the 1930s, the local population was 'irked that few of the US marines who commanded the Garde spoke creole or French'; the fact that some American soldiers had biased racial attitudes did not help either.[141] In other cases the problem was the attitude of local politicians: in Nicaragua they wondered which side the new US-trained constabulary would go in the event of a political conflict among themselves.[142] In the end, however, American police training programmes left a deep mark in Central America.

When Convergence Occurs II

Possibly the most successful police system to be inspired by the European model (specifically the French one) was Meiji Japan's; it is revealing that the Japanese studied the Western police system assiduously, but did not hire any advisers. The only expense was a Frenchman already resident in Japan, who was employed more for translating and explaining written material on French police than as a proper adviser.[143]

Although the American occupation of Japan is touted as a great success, the American attempt to reform the Japanese police could hardly be classified a success. Bogged down by divisions between American officials, American efforts soon lost focus:

The professed aim of US policy was the establishment of a 'democratic' police system [...], [but] chaotic conditions dictated rigorous control and regulation, activities that could only be undertaken by the Japanese police. The Occupation faced a dilemma of its own making—how to stem the growth of the black market and eliminate such 'superfluous' police functions as economic regulation. [...] It was easy for the Japanese government to sabotage the new police system by failing to provide resources in the first instance and then to insist that feeble, uncoordinated police forces unnecessarily exposed Japan to the threat of communist insurrection.[144]

[T]he present police establishment in Japan is an imperfectly blended amalgam of the authoritarian, powerful and highly centralized prewar police system and the 'democratic' and decentralized postwar system...The former is closer to the honne [reality] of the police system, and the latter is ultimately a mere tatemae [façade].[145]

The Modern Concept of Police Reform

In its more recent incarnation, police-building commenced with donor-funded technical assistance provided to newly independent states in the second half of the twentieth century.[146] A typical rationale for having international police-building operations in most post-conflict situations is that usually 'the police force that existed previously will have become dilapidated during the time of conflict and many of their duties will have been taken over by a military with far greater resources'. The priority therefore was to (re-)establish:

a clear distinction of duties between the police and the military [...], followed by a swift programme to retrain and re-equip the remnants of the old force in order to prevent a prolonged security vacuum in the immediate post-conflict environment.

While this argument concerns the need to rebuild a police force, the concept of reform kicks in with the argument that:

the rule of law institutions will be the key to providing the expectation and assurance of human security—a crucial service if return to violent conflict is to be prevented. [...] By approaching policing with a community-based public servant mentality rather than a self-serving public official mentality the donor agencies and host country can begin to win the confidence of the public in the reform process.[147]

Internationally sponsored police reform efforts generally revolve around two basic approaches, each one featuring some combination of the characteristics listed here:[148]

- Human rights conscious or 'democratic' policing
  1. accountability to law;
  2. adherence to international standards of human rights;
  3. accountability to external mechanisms;
  4. responsiveness to the safety needs of the public;
  5. demilitarisation/civilianisation
- Professionalisation
  1. non-partisanship
  2. technologisation
  3. meritocratisation
  4. bureaucratisation

In general the stress has been much more on the second aspect than on the first. In any case, so far police reform has been quite unsuccessful in most countries where it has been implemented. The chances of success have been linked by sympathetic authors to a number of issues:

- Were the internationals seen as having a legitimate right to enter the country, to use force and pursue their agenda for change in the security sector?
- Were they seen to be politically and materially capable of carrying out their mission?
- Did they have a strategic plan to guide their efforts?
- Did they have the necessary leadership structures and organisational approaches to support the implementation of their strategy?
- Were they prepared to invest sufficient manpower and money into their programmes?[149]

The Limits of Police Reform

However, other authors have been more critical and point out that such an approach assumes that police reform occurs in a vacuum and that problems are largely due to difficulties within the implementation itself. This is particularly the case with reforms focused on the adoption of the community police model, sometimes equated with democratic policing.[150] Indeed, more substantial problems have been identified in the implementation of community police reforms:

- the group of foreign 'professionals' imparting skills to police forces are usually not qualified to design police institutions and structures, particularly if democratic policing is the aim;

- the difficulty of establishing trust between new police and population, not least because often crime levels increase in post-conflict situations;
- lack of participation and social capital to sustain reforms, and lack of assessment and other forms of evaluation; this could either lead to failure or to dependency;[151]
- lack of organisational change in police departments;[152]
- difficult coordination among donor or assisting agencies, due to the existence of different traditions of policing worldwide, donor jealousies, etc.[153]
- community policing as designed in the West works only for 'small, White, wealthy, homogeneous communities with little crime' but is simply irrelevant to most African and many Asian societies;[154]
- international legality does not necessarily lead to local legitimacy.[155]

The inclination towards community policing among assistance agencies has been criticised on the grounds of unsustainability, and as I shall show later there is certainly much evidence of that.[156] In many environments where a transition to community policing has been attempted, disillusionment has quickly followed, as communities failed to cooperate and police never got engaged seriously in 'problem solving', transparency and accountability.[157] Even when the most extreme form of decentralisation, that is community policing, is accepted as a model to follow by the authorities but without much conviction, its implementation can simply fail due to lack of will among the rank and file and distrust by the communities.[158] Perhaps more damning is the fact that among the few obvious examples of marked improvement of police effectiveness in the perception of the population are those of militarised police, that is a model as remote from community policing as possible. This is the case with Chile's carabineros, for example.[159]

The stress on such slogans as community policing and on the enforcement of rule of law is also in part responsible for the tendency to neglect the administrative and managerial aspects of police-building, which had highly negative consequences. A representative example is that of the US-trained Iraqi police after 2003: 'with embedded US advisers and logistic support, the units proved effective in COIN, but without them they resorted to torture, secret prisons and extrajudicial killings'.[160] This was compounded by the neglect of:

the need for the development of a wide range of management functions (planning, HR management, budgeting, procurement, logistics management) to support the deployment of large numbers of new forces and by the:

tendency to focus on individual projects to develop specific technical competencies (forensics, explosive ordnance disposal) without looking at the full continuum of competencies required to deliver security and justice to people.[161]

There is a growing literature on the merits and demerits of police reform as it has been implemented so far. One author claims that 'the more foreign police aid given, the more brutal and less democratic the police institutions and their governments become', at least in Latin America where the US for a long time focused on militarising the police, not only in the period between the World Wars but even more recently.[162]

Some criticism of the way international police reform efforts are conducted is well founded, particularly in the case of multinational interventions, which are arguably the worst managed, least effective and most wasteful. To complicate matters, the ability or willingness of a police force to maintain internal discipline, push professionalism and fight corruption is difficult to assess externally. One good example comes from Mexico:

A first impression is that Mexican police forces are indeed modernized in that disciplinary mechanisms are frequently invoked. Police of all ranks are both disciplined and dismissed in large numbers annually, and indeed sometimes officers are sacked in mass police purges, occasionally involving hundreds of police [...]. Police officers may be also subjected to a broad range of other disciplinary measures [...]. On the surface this suggests the existence of serious internal control and accountability. This is, indeed, the image police chiefs want to convey to the outside world. On closer inspection, however, it becomes clear that internal actions are characteristically undertaken in an arbitrary manner, which is perhaps most clearly illustrated by the mass dismissal (purges) of officers that take place from time to time. When an officer is investigated for alleged corruption or abuse of power, an officer from Internal Affairs is quite likely to offer him the choice of facing charges or paying off the investigating officer. [...] In one group discussion among judicial police, [internal affairs] was consensually branded as 'the mafia', because in the eyes of those concerned the branch was completely devoid of any moral authority.[163]

American Inexperience

With their lack of a national police force, the Americans were particularly ill-suited to act as police-builders abroad. When they did, they either went for militarised forces as in Latin America in the 1920s-30s or for randomly adopted examples chosen without much consideration. Despite the stated intent of shaping a 'nonpartisan armed force patterned along the line of the military forces of the United States',[164] such constabularies became very much involved in local politics. An outstanding (and extreme) example is the American-managed reform of the Laotian police which started in 1955. The Americans decided to adopt the Thai model, on the basis of the assumed cultural proximity of the two countries, and no effort was made initially to adapt it to local requirements. Even the number of generals at the top was left the same, creating a very top-heavy structure for a country many times smaller than Thailand. At the same time the fast expansion of the police caused a decline in the quality and training of the rank and file, not least because the attention to professionalism also declined, opening the door to nepotism and interference in recruitment by politicians. Finally, the structure was not well thought out, with a mixing of geographical and technical departments, which created space for interference and caused inefficiency.[165]

Another example of badly thought out police reform was that of Haiti in the 1990s. Here the Americans invested considerable resources in training new police, but did not pay much attention to the creation of an officer corps and of a command and control structure, so that once the policemen were deployed they had either to rely on international police advisers or handle things on their own. The lack of a command and control structure is likely to have played an important role in the subsequent collapse of the police into an orgy of corruption and abuse.[166]

The United States was also deeply involved in developing South Vietnam's police force, in the context of counter-insurgency during the 1950s and 1960s. Issues of human rights abuses by the Vietnamese and more general 'counter-insurgency fatigue' led Congress to restrict US funding of foreign law enforcement agencies (Section 660 of the Foreign Assistance Act).[167] This is likely to have slowed the development of American know-how in police assistance; when assistance was resumed on a large scale in Iraq and Afghanistan in the first decade of the twenty-first century, Washington had little option but to pull in private security companies to do the job, mostly unsatisfactorily.

The provision of advanced technologies to police forces is not always a positive step either, depending on what is the ultimate aim. If the purpose is strengthening the rule of law, then technology might be counter-productive. When Thai police were provided with helicopters in the 1960s:

initially the villagers were fascinated, but after a while started perceiving the helicopter as yet another instrument of repression. Differences between the villager and the police were underlined; paternalism rather than service was emphasised, intelligence and reconnaissance, rather than improving the villagers' lot.[168]

The Thai villagers were right, in that the way the helicopters were going to be used would not benefit them, even if it may have benefited the Thai state.

Another problem associated with expanding and professionalising police forces in contexts where an insurgency is going on is that the army is likely to attract more talent, leaving the police weakened.[169] In post-conflict contexts instead, the need to reintegrate former combatants can often take precedence over any attempt to professionalise the police force; typical examples include Afghanistan and Liberia. In some cases post-conflict settlements can lead to the establishment of ethnic quotas in police staffing, which is also at odds with any concept of meritocracy.[170]

The Demands of Local Ownership II

This is not to say that quotas are altogether useless. Significantly, one poll found that in the perception of Sierra Leoneans, the main improvements after police reform were in terms of improved attention to human rights and reduced rudeness.[171] In any case, in this chapter I want to focus on aspects of police reform that are more relevant to state consolidation. These include 'local ownership' and the impact of a de-patrimonialised or institutionalised model of policing on state consolidation more generally. Although it can be argued that there is much to gain for the elites by making their control of police less visible through professionalisation, as animosity is drawn away from them (similarly to the argument developed in chapter 7 on the rule of law),[172] there has inevitably always been a certain degree of conflict between local ownership and reform from the early days of externally driven police reform efforts:

reform by its very nature presumes that what exists is inadequate and requires modification. [...] Police reforms, even where designed by members of the society to be policed, inevitably draw on foreign models and experiences and may favor some groups over others.[173]

What we heard when discussing army-building efforts resonates here too:

Almost all advisors were blind to the complex and difficult socio-economic and political problems inherent in their police program; even when such obstacles were mentioned, they were cloaked in terms of technology and institutional arrangements that obscured the questions of political processes and motivations.[174]

On a similar note, Muehlmann pointed out that in Bosnia police restructuring was conceived in terms of 'technically-driven changes'. When the Bosnian political elites resisted, it was a surprise.[175]

The need to take into account local ownership is actually increasingly recognised by policy-makers and analysts:

> it is important to work with and through local institutions rather than seeking to import wholesale Western models. These will inevitably be subverted as the local institutions revert to their standard modes of operating.[176]

In practice, such good intentions fail when confronted with unpleasant realities.

Despite the original intention to promote local ownership, the process was in reality totally internationally-driven. Obstructionism from the Serb side remained consistent throughout the process. For them, their tactics were successful, they bought time; they have been able to continue with the present system over the next few years and to argue in front of their electorate that they had heroically fought for the interests of the Republika Srpska. [...] Only when the international community backed away from their original requests did they manage to get a face-saving, but not very viable, solution.[177]

There is nothing automatic about empowering local owners: they usually have to be selected to some degree, and this cannot be a 'politically neutral enterprise'. Usually police-builders assume rather naively that the only ownership that matters is a vaguely defined 'local' one, failing to clarify whose ownership matters: for example, indigenous 'ordinary people' or local elites? If the former, how is the process going to take shape and be driven? It seems clear that without the involvement of the host country's elite and short of the establishment of an international protectorate, nothing can happen. Still analyses of who effectively controls the police and in whose interest they operate are rarely carried out. There is a complete failure to recognise that not necessarily all components of a host government might be in agreement about police reform, and one of them might approve what another is going to oppose and sabotage. Somalia in the 1990s was one extreme case of failure to take the political environment into account, as the political context was ignored and the UN sponsored the setting up of a new police force in the absence of a monopoly of large-scale violence. Instructively, this only led to the police rapidly turning into an armed force, among many other private militias.[178]

A typical pattern of failure of police reform efforts taking place under international sponsorship is the shadowy seizure of the process by interest groups, which in this way assert their claim to local ownership by hijacking the process to a different end from what had been intended by the original promoters, or even to no end whatsoever.[179] A good example is that of police reform in El

Salvador (1990s). This was one of the most radical attempts ever to put internal security firmly under civilian control and the international community provided unprecedented levels of assistance. There were fears at the beginning that the coexistence in a single institution of former police, former army and former guerrillas would have been difficult to achieve, but in reality problems were 'surprisingly few'. It was instead the lack of political will on the government's side that led to failure, prompting two analysts to conclude that donors should not contemplate assisting police projects unless governments demonstrate unequivocal political will to carry out the project in good faith. Even a small number of personnel from the old institution can undermine the reform by corrupting the fresh trainees and ultimately the whole new structure.[180]

In Haiti, the pressure to fill the security void by deploying an indigenous police force, together with the not very smooth relations with the Aristide government, led to a US tendency towards 'unilateral decision making'. This total lack of Haitian ownership resulted later in the government attacking and undermining the police: in 2000 the US government cut off assistance in retaliation and by 2005 so little of the reform was left that the UN launched another reform attempt.[181]

In the case of Haiti as in many others, local ownership was actually in contradiction with the establishment of a disciplined and self-restrained police force: the local population advocated a retributive kind of policing that donors would never have been willing to sponsor, while the ruling elite wanted a force it could fully control, the more so given the disbandment of the army. Political parties of opposition and government started linking up with armed gangs, in an only partly repressed competition over the primitive accumulation of coercive power. In order to gain the respect of the population, the police had to start beating up delinquents.[182] The assumption that the elimination by the police of abusive and violent behaviour is always going to be appreciated by the population is indeed one of the most naïve delusions of police reformers. As pointed out by Alice Hills, in the context of state consolidation it is often more likely that 'enhancing accountability and responsiveness' may be seen as 'weakness' rather than that it may 'ensure that police gain public support'.[183]

Celador comments about Bosnia:

An EUPM official described the problem as the 'over-democratization' of the Bosnian police forces, to such an extent that their monopoly over the use of force has been taken away completely. Following events like the de-certification of nineteen members of the Sarajevo Canton Special Forces in 2002, many citizens and police officers have come to the conclusion that criminals 'can hurt the police even without firing a single bullet'.

Indeed some police officers blame the certification process for the fact that 'nobody takes them seriously now'. [...] This outcome is not that unusual in the case of externally-managed police reorganizations. In the case of Haiti, for instance, the interim police force was demoralized, ineffective and afraid of the people they were supposed to serve.[184]

Governments might be better served by a police force that reminds citizens who is in charge and guarantees territorial control, rather than by a force that meets abstract 'universal standards'. There are abundant examples of this. In the case of Guatemala one author noted how:

On one hand, police forces are pushed increasingly towards legality, accountability, and respect for human rights. In one sense, the police force is expected to focus exclusively upon tasks related to law enforcement and the protection of rights. On the other hand, however, rising crime and increasing public fear of crime often demands from police forces more authoritarian and repressive tactics to fight crime. In Guatemala crime stimulated drastic, violent, and illegal responses by both the police and the public. This response frequently resulted in vigilante squads, repressive policing, extra-judicial killings, social cleansings and lynchings.[185]

In the absence of local ownership, indigenous elites will still be in a position to prevent donors and international reformers from controlling indigenous political processes. Donors and reformers, therefore, will face an environment where they will not even be able to foresee the consequences of their own actions. In Thailand in the 1950s, the CIA equipped and trained Thai police, but in doing so elicited the jealousy of the army, whose chief feared that the balance between the two institutions was being broken. In 1957 the army took power, and one of the first actions of the new Prime Minister Sarit was to take all heavy and sophisticated equipment from the police and transfer it to the army. The police budget was slashed and its paramilitary responsibilities eliminated.[186]

Later in the 1960s a renewed American effort to expand the police and move assets to the rural areas was frustrated as the new police stations built with American money were left empty. It proved impossible to expand the ranks of the police at the desired rate as the US-sponsored effort was being sabotaged by the army, which opposed a strong increase in the police force, as well as by several Thai politicians who did not take the insurgency threat seriously.[187] As pointed out with regard to the army in chapter 2, any reform leading to a change in the security architecture is likely to produce some kind of unexpected contrary reaction. Another example is that of the creation of a gendarmerie in Laos (1950), which created discontent among the ranks of the police, because the former received higher salaries and privileges.[188]

Similarly in Vietnam, President Diem agreed with the Americans on the creation of a Civil Guard; his American advisers were then constantly criticising his habit of incessantly rotating the commanding officers, but he was not interested in creating an effective policing force. His purpose was to have a kind of militarised police to counter-balance the army.[189] In Bosnia-Herzegovina, local authorities first resisted and then circumvented EU attempts to impose a de-politicised model of police, where control by the Ministry of Interior was reduced and directors of police in the cantons would acquire greater autonomy.[190] The opposition to the decentralisation of police forces and the creation of municipal police has been strong in a number of African countries too.[191]

It is not always just a matter of selfish rulers being keen to maintain total control; sometimes many in the apparatus might have the same view that decentralisation weakens the state. In Russia, the 2002 plan presented by Interior Minister Gryzlov included the creation of independent municipal police forces, but was opposed by many scholars and high rank police for fear of the 'role of criminal elements (mafia) in local politics' and the risk that local police officers would also be co-opted.[192]

The opposite case may also be true: when local governments had genuine ownership, they would often opt for a police reform of their own taste, probably not at all in line with the model sponsored by the international police reform lobby or whatever external ally was paying the bills. The case of Guatemala is another that highlights what might be the priorities of governments in post-conflict environments. The government chose the Spanish Guardia Civil model (a gendarmerie) and quick implementation over professionalisation, desisting from any attempt to screen the intake of new recruits. The resulting police force served the purpose of establishing territorial control, but was not effective in controlling criminality and was affected by high levels of internal corruption and crime.[193]

In Thailand in the early 1960s, American studies reported a high level of corruption and police abuse; the police were more feared than trusted and were also poorly trained, particularly in the case of the provincial police. Consequently the Americans lobbied hard in favour of reform. Following the experience of the 1950s, however, Thai Prime Minister Sarit was only ready to accept US help if it did not interfere with the internal political balance. He was more interested in building organisations to serve as personal bases of power than in developing a national security strategy. Thai and US officials eventually reached an agreement that restructuring the Thai police was politically unacceptable. From 1964 much more American aid and equipment was delivered to the police than it could possibly absorb, but it was mainly as a kind of pay-off for the collaboration of Thai agencies in allowing the Americans to use bases in Thailand. Eventually the Thai government, confronted with the beginnings of an insurgency, decided to move provincial police to the areas and villages endangered by the insurgency and boost their ranks. More importantly from the perspective of police-building, the police remained as corruption-prone as ever. Police posts were sold and bought, a police regional commander position being worth $50,000.[194] As a result, the deployment of more police was resented because they were behaving badly and it created fertile ground for anti-government activities. The insurgents made of police corruption their 'primary propaganda pitch'. It is questionable however whether a better behaved police force would necessarily have made much of a difference. The better trained and better behaved elite police units, involved by the CIA in civic action activities, seemed to be doing relatively well, but 'some of the villages where they operated were among the first to turn red', that is to start supporting the leftist insurgents. The peasants seemed to resent the presence of the police in principle, as a form of intimidation from the state.[195] The scope for short-term reform aimed at strengthening the rule of law and professionalising the police seems to have been desperately small:

For the tambon police to perform well, they were required to hoof around the tambon, perform all sorts of services no policeman in Thailand would ever perform, be kind to dirty, smelly inferior peasants, and maybe get killed by the communists. They were told not to steal a few chickens or rape a village girl now and again... We told them to work hard, patrol the rice paddies, and be upright. But the Thais don't become policemen for those reasons: a cop is a guy who wants to improve and flaunt his power and status, to show off the uniform to the girls, and make a lot of money by hook or by crook.[196]

The way 'late developers' often fund their police forces, that is allowing them to impose their own taxes in order to make up for meagre salaries and insufficient operational funds, can often defeat police reform efforts from the start. Stamping out corruption might just not be feasible, because the police are dependent on it for its functioning. In Indonesia, for example, where the official budget covers as little as 30 per cent of the actual expenditure of the police force, officers use a significant share of the gifts they receive to purchase equipment and supplies, as well as supplementing salaries which are too low to support a family. This practice, criticised in some quarters, is praised in others and senior police officers tend to justify it as the only way to keep the police going.[197]

The end result of many police-building efforts might therefore look like the adaptation of police forces to decolonisation. With the transition to independence from colonial powers, an authoritarian but strongly institutionalised model of policing was inherited, based on a militarised force and strong discipline and command and control. However, it was inevitably modified 'to suit the new political environment' during the first decade after independence. This process has been described as 'the deterioration of the reliability and capability of the police',[198] but since it happens in several countries almost contemporarily it should be inferred that it presumably suited the new ruling elites. I prefer to describe it as (re-)patrimonialisation.

Planning and Managing DDR Processes

A typical UN statement about DDR (Disarmament, Demobilisation and Reintegration) looks like this:

Demobilizing combatants is the single most important factor determining the success of peace operations. Without demobilization, civil wars cannot be brought to an end and other critical goals—such as democratization, justice and development—have little chance for success.[199]

In reality, evidence suggests otherwise. It is necessary to distinguish carefully between conflicts ending in the outright victory of one of the participating factions and conflicts settled through a negotiating process. In the case of the former, a monopoly of large-scale violence had been successfully established. DDR was a realistic option, as the winning party in all likelihood did not need an armed force as large as the one accumulated during the peak of the campaign to eliminate the competitors. Examples include Angola after the death of the leader of UNITA, Jonas Savimbi; and Ethiopia after the overthrow of Mengistu.

The picture is much more controversial in the case of conflicts settled through negotiations. Both before and after the international launch of the concept of DDR, a key ingredient of success in settling internal conflicts appears instead to have been the continued existence of armed forces under the control of the parties to the conflict. In some cases the fact that the parties in conflict were going to continue holding on to their weapons was explicitly acknowledged during the implementation of the accords. This is the case with the peace agreement in Rhodesia (Zimbabwe) in 1980.[200] In many other cases, the understanding was implicit only. Already as Europe emerged from World War II, disarming the partisan movements which had fought against the occupying Germans and their local allies required complex political manoeuvring. The Italian case is particularly noteworthy here: not only the former Communist partisans kept their weapons in hiding, but also rival monarchist and Christian Democratic groups did the same.[201] In practice, maintaining rival armed forces underground was essential to developing some basic trust and offering basic guarantees of security in a difficult transition to a stable political settlement.

As pointed out in the introduction to this volume, the establishment of a monopoly of violence has a fundamental political dimension, related to the formation of alliances and the co-option of rivals into the new system, often in a subordinate position. The co-option of Communist parties in Western Europe after 1945 is one such example of coercive co-option: refusing co-option in a position of military inferiority would have meant being crushed, as happened in the Greek case. In the new system, the Communists did not have a serious chance of taking part in the political game and were rapidly marginalised, but still fared much better than their Greek comrades or than moderate and right-wing parties in Eastern Europe.

By contrast, the post-Cold War understanding of DDR implied complete DDR-ing of all parties in conflict and the formation of non-factional armed forces to replace party militias. In principle, this looks like an attractive proposition, because there are clear risks associated with keeping factional armies underground as a political guarantee. Indeed, even in the European example, accusations have surfaced of factions of the secret armies going rogue in the 1960s and 1970s, particularly in Italy.[202] However, in reality Security Sector Reform (SSR) after a civil war, in such a way that all parties in the negotiations are satisfied and feel guaranteed and protected, has very rarely been handled successfully. This is the case of El Salvador in the early 1990s: although the discovery of major weapon caches belonging to the former leftist guerrillas was widely publicised, in reality from the beginning the government side had been very slow and partially non-compliant in reforming the army and police in accordance with the peace agreement.[203] Patterns of demobilised insurgents being discriminated against, harassed or assassinated after the end of a civil conflict are rather frequent. We have to view such examples of non-compliance through the eyes of those who risk their lives in disarming and coming back to civilian life.

Because of the strong pressure to implement DDR as designed by donor countries, which are usually also the guarantor of peace agreements alongside the UN, allowing the former warring parties to retain their weapons at least for a transition period is not feasible. DDR programmes have therefore been implemented in almost all negotiated settlements after the end of the Cold War, but with widely varying impacts on the ground. In some cases, DDR was at least in part successful, mainly because of the exhaustion of the warring parties and the society affected by the conflict. This is, for example, the case with Mozambique in the 1990s.[204] In most cases, what happened was that the warring parties formally agreed to DDR and then manoeuvred to maintain an independent armed force. This could take the shape of a private armed force underground, as in the case of Afghanistan in 2003–5.[205] Alternatively the concerns of the former warring parties might be addressed by securing informal control over a portion of the new armed forces, established in the wake of the peace settlement. This is the case with the Democratic Republic of Congo after the series of civil wars of the 1990s.[206]

The impact of international involvement in DDR programmes can therefore be summarised as more likely to engender a façade of compliance, whereas factional armed groups are in fact driven underground or uneasily incorporated into armed forces which are only national in name. Apart from the waste of donors' funds, these results imply some risks as well:

1. a possible delegitimisation of the political settlement, if the underground factional armies were to be exposed or to break off the peace settlement;
2. leaving the monopoly of violence incomplete for an indefinite length of time;
3. negative law and order consequences as some elements of the underground armies might go rogue.

As we have seen, even in the cases of demobilisation pre-dating DDR, risk 1 was an ever present one. However, the grand fanfare of DDR, often extensively advertised by ad hoc campaigns in the media, contributed to raise expectations of genuine DDR and as a result increase the delegitimating impact in the event of exposure. Risk 2 is arguably stronger in the case of incorporation of a factional army into an only formally national force, because in this case the 'secret' armies have the capacity to train, resupply and keep their arsenals up to date. Underground reserve armies, by contrast, necessarily tend to decay over the years, as they cannot easily train, recruit new members and resupply. Risk 3 needs some qualifications before being assessed. In the absence of international pressure or assistance, only the best organised military-political movements would be able to develop underground reserve armies and maintain them for any length of time. International DDR schemes might have helped or forced a wider variety of armed groups into maintaining an underground structure. In Afghanistan, for example, some of the DDR packages were recycled into maintaining the underground armies, to the benefit of otherwise badly organised groups.[207] The implications of this for law and order were generally negative and might not have been very positive for the solidity of the elite bargain either, as discussed above.

Advising in the Shadows

External assistance to intelligence services and political police has been no less problematic than to conventional police forces and perhaps more, even if information about this is scant. As Dale F. Eickelman put it:

Short term personnel, for example, presumed that an intelligence officer burns out after several years because of enmeshment in local politics and personalities. The ability to achieve the proper balance between empathy and objectivity was deemed compromised by long stays. Long-term officers, for their part, felt that they possessed a more profound understanding of the country's politics.[208]

One problem that pertains to foreign intervention in particular is the difficulty of deploying highly trained operatives effectively in an occupied country, except for training purposes. Communication exchanges with local partners and allies are always extremely sensitive and difficult to manage without creating controversy and distrust. Already during the French phase of the Indochinese wars, intelligence operatives noted how much more difficult their work was compared to Europe: the 'impenetrable yellow wall' did not allow much recruitment of agents and informers.[209] Among South Vietnamese army intelligence officers, for example, the belief was widespread in early 1968 that US intelligence officers were failing to keep them in the picture because they desired a quick end to the war through a South Vietnamese defeat.[210]

Getting the hosts where the advisers want them to be is problematic enough; getting them to use the newly acquired powers in ways considered to be profitable by the advisers is even more so. The French advisers overseeing the creation of a Vietnamese service in Vietnam in the early 1950s were unconvinced that once under full local control the service would be used effectively, because of the corruption, instability and authoritarianism that characterised the Vietnamese government.[211] American advisers long insisted that Diem reform and streamline his own internal security system. When he finally complied following a worsening insurgency, contrary to American desires he used it to crack down on internal opposition in 1963, unleashing the reaction which would lead to his overthrow.[212]

The Soviets were more successful in imposing their own views on political policing in Spain in the 1930s. In particular, they took full control of the military intelligence (SIM), despite the fact that it had been conceived by the Spanish government to be loyal to it alone and not to the Soviets. However, this was not to good effect as the excesses of the new services and its indulgence in factional conflict (particularly against the Trotskyites) proved very damaging to the republican cause. Moreover, Soviet advisers were behaving in a clumsy and obvious way, which deeply embarrassed even the most pro-Soviet elements of the Spanish government.[213] They were in principle expected to win influence and authority over the Spaniards and get them to carry out the adviser's decisions willingly; in practice this turned out to be difficult to achieve except in the case of the most able and charismatic advisers, who were few in number. Indeed many of the advisers were far from behaving without reproach.[214]

Not unlike the case of armies and police, multinational advisory efforts tend inevitably to end up in rivalry even in the case of intelligence services. In Angola Soviet and Cuban intelligence advisers were often at odds, with the latter accusing the former of interference and self-interest.

[The Cuban advisers] used to tell us to be careful with the Soviets, not to give them certain [kinds] of information. The Cubans used to tell stories about the Soviet attempts to control them and how it almost reached a fighting basis.[215]

In sum, even if information on the work of advisers to secret services is necessarily limited, many of the issues highlighted with regard to police and army seem to have been present here too.

There is clearly an extremely varied impact of external intervention on the monopoly of large-scale violence, as well as on attempts to deepen it and to tame coercion. There is certainly evidence to suggest that external intervention tends to run into a series of contradictions and perverse effects or incentives, but there is also evidence of external intervention rescuing regimes under attack or stimulating the development of key skills in the military or the police. The seventh hypothesis of this book, that *external intervention, even in its milder form of advice and support, is more likely to be counter-productive in achieving and maintaining the monopoly of violence*, is therefore only partially confirmed by the review of the literature. More questions were raised than were answered. External intervention in its various forms has not been studied in great depth, except for military interventions and peacekeeping, and is certainly worthy of more attention. Military assistance and advisory missions have so far received the scarcest attention. Friction between the advised and the advisers, between the mentors and the mentored is a fact of life, but does not necessarily lead to failure. Even when advisory missions are not altogether successful, they might leave behind a legacy which is rarely properly understood.

Perhaps the most important question (and the most difficult) to be answered is whether external assistance of various kinds is actually aimed at helping host countries developing autonomous capabilities in the security sector. The actual answer is likely to vary from case to case, but such a repeated pattern of failure or at least very limited success must force analysts and scholars to raise the question: are policy-makers in advanced countries particularly limited in their understanding, or are their motivations and aims not the stated ones? In political analysis, of course, stated aims should never be taken at face value. In particular, we have seen that dependence is more likely to be the outcome of large-scale assistance efforts than any other outcome. This might be assumed to be not in the interest of the host's ruling elites, but could well be in the interest of the states providing the support.

7

BEYOND THE MONOPOLY

ORIGINS AND DEVELOPMENT OF POLICING

'...without money, no police is possible. I soon had money in my treasury by making vice, inherent to all great cities, a tributary to the police of the state'.

Joseph Fouché, police minister of the Directoire, quoted in Douglas Hilt, *Ten Against Napoleon*, Chicago: Nelson Hall, 1975, p. 74

In Pakistan, each police station has a clerk who is required to record all happenings. He is generally a head constable with matriculation level of education. Four copies of all reports are supposed to be distributed to magistrates (2), superintendent of police and victim/complainant. There are as many as twenty-five registers, of which the most important ones are 'First Information Reports', 'daily happenings', 'proclaimed offenders', 'very serious crimes', 'surveillance of criminals' and 'bad characters'. Senior officers are supposed to carry out formal and informal inspections to keep an eye on the crime trend. Each inspector is supervising two to three police stations, every deputy superintendent supervises a subdivision, each superintendent a district, a deputy inspector-general inspects three to four districts and finally the inspector-general supervises a whole province. In practice however, supervisory activities have been dying out over the last twenty to thirty years. This is the case of the old practice of supervisors spending:

at least 15 days in the jurisdiction of a police station. Meetings were held at convenient focal points every day and a maximum number of people from nearby villages were called to attend. People were encouraged to bring up their problems and complaints. [...] Records of police stations were brought up to date.

The result has been a tendency to indulge in 'burking', that is hiding cases and not registering them. If crime figures were to show an upward trend, the officer heading the station would be held accountable. As a result it is estimated that barely 40 per cent of reported crimes are registered and investigated. Other resulting malpractices include delays, perfunctory investigations, harassment of complainants, asking bribes, production of false evidence and false witnesses, non-maintenance of essential records.[1]

This short description of how the police function in Pakistan suggests that the spread of the bureaucratic-professional model of policing from the nineteenth century onwards has not been a triumphal march, nor even a one-way process. The factors determining the development of policing and the particular shape it takes are multiple and their interaction very complex, but this chapter will start to untangle them.

Maintaining Internal Order Without the Police

Before being incorporated in a state, local communities typically made some arrangements to maintain order among their members. The actual nature of such arrangements varied from community to community. Egalitarian communities such as tribes, led by councils of elders, would entrust the council with the ability to call into service young members of the community to enforce the decisions of the council on matters such as disputes, crimes, etc. Hierarchically structured communities would rely on the armed retinue of the local 'big man' to do the same; in this case the community would of course be dependent on the willingness of the 'big man' to enforce some definition of 'justice'. What neither the big man nor the council could easily do is enforce order across communities.[2] These community-based forces could already be described as militias, although they might not be permanently mobilised unless the big man was wealthy enough to pay his recruits a salary.

Throughout this book, the term 'police' will be used as shorthand for institutionalised police, that is a permanent, specialised and professional force carrying out the task of policing. While other armed forces can practise policing (armies, militias, volunteers...), their temporary role does not turn them into a police in this sense (see box 1).

With the incorporation of communities into the state, a process started of expropriation of their ability to administer their own justice (in the case of egalitarian communities) or of co-option (in the case of many big men). Because new states typically relied on limited revenue, militias, that is irregular volunteer forces recruited locally, for a long time in European history continued to be used to maintain law and order. In the absence of institutionalised police, early rulers had to rely on local leaders and lavish gifts, honour and titles for them. Having been eclipsed under the Romans, the system reappeared in the feudal context.[3] Because such forces tended originally to reflect partisan political interests, arguably they lacked general legitimacy.

The revolutionary regimes of modern Europe usually reorganised their militias along more inclusive lines, but restoration governments reconstructed them through rural landowners and the *haute bourgeois*. Regardless of their political colour, militias were not an effective substitute for armies in maintaining domestic order, because of their indiscipline, insufficient or non-existent training and weak supervision. As social changes undermined the capacity of private groups to maintain acceptable levels of security, gradually European governments in the nineteenth century withdrew their armies from domestic riot duty, abolished militias and developed a specialised police capacity.[4] However, the transition was neither complete nor irrevocable. Indeed, even in Europe, 'state capacity to centralize coercive control appears to be the result of intricate, contingent, inter- and intra-institutional political bargains that are frequently renegotiated'.[5]

Militias resurfaced during periods of internal turmoil, as recently as the 1920s and 1930s in Western Europe, initially as non-state armed groups and then as state-sponsored ones. Hitler's crackdown on the SA (*Sturm Abteilung*) in 1934, however, shows how tolerance for semi-independent militias as an instrument of policing was, at that point, quite limited.[6] In parts of Europe militias resurfaced in the 1990s (Balkans) and still exist in Turkey, where they are part of the counter-insurgency effort. In Africa, Asia and Latin America militias have continued to exist in a number of countries or were (re-)created *ex novo* even in the absence of civil wars or internal political conflict, sometimes as military forces (see also *Decaying monopolies* above) and sometimes as policing forces. It has been pointed out how the armed forces of much of the world, even in the early twenty-first century, look more like the European ones of the Middle Ages than European armies of the nineteenth century.[7]

If the emergence of private policing is not surprising in central and southern Somalia, given the collapse of the state, it exists also in the (internationally unrecognised) state of Somaliland, where clans use traditional structures and fundamentalist mosques use young armed men. Even in countries where the state has not collapsed at all or has been re-established with some success, like Tanzania and Uganda, local militias have surfaced in recent times to fill the gap in rural policing. In some cases, it was external sponsors pushing for the formation of militias; this is the case with the Americans in Thailand in the 1960s, who overruled opposition by the Thai police and by their own police advisers.[8]

Indeed in conditions of weak or absent supervision from the centre, most non-state armed groups would take over at least some of the prerogatives of the state. Even during the colonial age, some cults in Africa were reported to be offering services to the population, including armed protection (policing).[9]

It is interesting to note how, despite initial hostility, in some cases ruling elites were forced to accept such militias and even start cooperating with them.[10] In some countries, like Nigeria, state authorities have adopted an ambiguous stance towards such groups, sometimes endorsing them and sometimes outlawing them.[11] In reality, in northern Nigeria (Kano) the police has always confined itself to passive policing, taking delivery of criminals handed over by community and local leaders.[12]

Non-state policing is evidently only tolerable as long as the state is assured that it will not turn into a threat. That such a threat may emerge is not implausible, as there are recent examples of that.[13] This pattern resembles in some ways the attitude of early post-colonial authorities in several African countries, which rapidly turned hostile to the forms of local (community or chief-controlled) policing, sponsored by the colonial regimes, even if they lacked the resources to police all of their national territories directly.[14]

The military has also often been used for policing tasks. The involvement of the military is usually due to the need to deal with 'widespread, prolonged or severe outbursts of violence', such as large-scale rioting. While these forms of violence do not directly threaten the monopoly of large-scale violence, they require an organised force to deal with them; and in the absence of other agencies capable of taking over the task, the military is called in.

When the Police Emerges: Multiple Sources

Professional and institutionalised policing had multiple origins. 'The first police officer' was likely to be 'a religious figure, perhaps a priest, who defined correct moral behaviour, declared who had broken the code and the punishment to follow. [...] With the development of walled cities' the watchman appeared, whose task was to 'prevent entry to the city during the hours of darkness'. Watchmen would eventually evolve into crime prevention patrols and the city police forces of today.

Palace guards are another of the original sources of policing: they were pledged to safeguard the physical survival of their boss, to whom they were often related. They developed a surveillance role, having to judge the political climate and counter conspiracies.[15] State police forces (the most common type of policing found in the world today) evolved out of this 'palace guard', first building up a system out of kinship and then through gradual replacement of kinship with a system of personal dependency.[16] Political policing, discussed in chapter 4, also originated from the same source. As a confirmation of these historical origins, often it is found that in political client relationships, police duties form one part of the overall duties of the client, which would represent the transitional stage. It has also been noted that historically it was often slaves, 'broken men' and foreigners who were used as police, as they were not part of kinship communities and could be made dependent on rulers (see also chapter 1).[17]

The reason for the development or the intensification of regulatory controls which characterises 'modern' policing is a matter of debate. The concept of the police as a specialised type of coercive force, meant to target and 'dose' it accurately, can already be found in eighteenth-century authors like von Justi, who wrote that the police 'help in consolidating and increasing the power [of the state] and making good use of its strength'.[18]

One interpretation is that class development helped shape a police force which was new in nature and did not directly derive from the original community policing.[19] While in:

pre-capitalist social organizations, political control was achieved by a combination of bribery, the use of paid informants and the judicious cultivation and/or intimidation of local leaders, [...] with the rise of the rationalisation of social and productive relations, it becomes necessary to implement a more direct control over human labour and the everyday lives of the population.[20]

Others have argued that specialisation in policing already existed in feudal institutions and in early state consolidation, and hence cannot be the result of social circumstances such as industrialisation. Indeed, the literature suggests that specialised police forces were found almost universally, like watchmen, chowkidars and others. In ancient times, rulers of various kinds were gradually learning the lesson that military force alone is not sufficient to support authority and enforce law observance. In Ancient Greece, the absence of any institutionalised police is seen as a major source of political crisis in Athens, but they at least developed the use of Scythian slaves as police. Elsewhere in Greece,

Sparta made use of police and understood their utility. The same is true of the Tyrants in several cities.[21]

Explanations of the rise of specialised police which link them to the growth of the centralised state are also doubtful when examined in a comparative perspective, since this was not a universal response. The only plausible explanation seems to be that specialised and professional policing are a specific answer of state-builders to the challenges of ensuring internal order in increasingly complex societies; in the words of one academic, specialisation grew because the 'management philosophy in modern nation states requires it'; 'specialisation is assumed to be useful both in terms of ensuring adequate accountability and in enhancing efficiency'.[22] As Foucault pointed out, the police exist because there are cities and cities exist because there are police.[23] This type of explanation also helps account for the 'contagion' of particular models of policing spreading rapidly to new countries, in contexts very different from the original ones where the model was developed.

The Police as a Strategy of State Consolidation: Coercive Legitimation

As pointed out by Otwin Marenin, historically the extension of moral consensus to the state and the police as instruments of legitimate coercion went hand in hand:

Repression tends to undermine the legitimacy of the state if unsuccessful, or used ineffectively. [...] Coercive legitimation can induce legitimating orientations. [...] If repression is sustained over time it may legitimate state rule; the transformation of power into authority is accomplished by conditioning the great majority of people to accept power relationships as real, inevitable, unavoidable and perhaps even right. Repression and protection are not alternative forms of police behaviour, [...] but exist in all policing, though in different rations. [...] In coercive legitimation voluntary motives for compliance may arise from coercion.[24]

It could be argued, taking up from where Marenin left off, that the quality of coercion (that is also its accurate targeting) was a major factor in determining the success or failure of coercive legitimation.

Since I defined policing as the specialisation of armed force for the purpose of managing small-scale violence (see *Introduction*), the involvement of the military or of militias in policing represents an 'imperfect specialisation of policing'. This is true also in the case of the presence of a gendarmerie. Nonspecialised policing worked successfully as long as violence was localised, 'involving parochial matters of food supply, prices, and sectorial employment'. But social changes impacted on the character of unrest:

The control of landed elites, based on ascriptive deference, was weakened, and in some countries hereditary classes were overthrown. Protest increasingly involved large numbers of people, often spearheaded by the urban mob, and was directed against general political authority rather than local wrongs. In these circumstances, introduction of an army became a political act [...]. Furthermore, military units, often mounted and wielding sabres, were too forceful, killing and wounding indiscriminately. They created martyrs and earned the unstable hatred of the populace. As a result, military leaders became reluctant to act in police capacity. Their distaste was reinforced by concern for the reliability of the army itself.[25]

In other words, the legitimacy of the state was at stake whenever the army was unable to coerce in a carefully targeted and restrained way. Specialised policing could be described as a specific strategy for the maintaining of internal order, responding to changes in society in a creative way. Such social changes, however, have as yet been far from universal, opening the question whether 'modern' policing is appropriate for late developing countries. Nor can every ruler be assumed to have the capability to implement sophisticated models of policing. Even if able, some rulers might be unwilling, particularly if free from pressure coming from constituencies and lobbies promoting specialised policing. One important aspect of the development of specialised policing is that it is expensive, not only in terms of direct financial costs but also of longer-term investments. For example, it requires the training and education of substantial numbers of staff. As this is also and perhaps foremost an exercise in institution-building, it also implies political sacrifices for the rulers, who might have to sacrifice some of their own arbitrary prerogatives as well as some clients and constituencies to make space for a professional police.

Another interesting interpretation of the role of modern police has been advanced by Liang: one of the tasks of the police became to develop new ways of dividing and ruling over society once the formation of a national society out of the earlier segmentary one made the use of old tactics redundant. It was a matter now of creating an 'artificial' rivalry in society, producing the need for an umpire to regulate it. The classification of population by profession, creed, education, etc., in short, according to the 'differences in the particular rights and duties of every group', was meant in other words to create disparity.[26]

The Police as a Strategy of State Consolidation: The 'Tule of Law'

The Monopolisation of Justice

In the early kingdoms, the main concern of legislation was to prevent conflict between communities; the state advocated a role of broker for itself. The government gradually took over criminal and civil law within single communities. The process may have started because of the state's association with religion and its desire to enforce religious sanctions in order to protect its own legitimacy.[27] As states began to emerge in Europe, their rulers sought to assert and extend their authority by creating offences against abstractions such as the ruler, society, morality, etc. The transition from a segmentary society to one governed by the state involved a shift from defining criminality as an injury to specific individuals and groups to be dealt with by the community itself, to viewing it as an offence against an abstraction such as the public interest. Accommodation and compromise gave way to coercion, and the systems of feud and vendetta were suppressed.[28] The practice of blood money became less acceptable with time; stronger governments did not recognise self-help in matters of justice and tended to replace pecuniary sanctions with corporal sanctions.[29]

The state never completely disenfranchised non-state judicial systems; in the United States even today, 85 per cent of all disputes do not get to the state judiciary.[30] However, it indirectly established an influence even over non-state judicial systems by regulating them, and acquired control over the aspects of justice which were of greater concern to it, such as the punishment of violence. This process of monopolisation of justice has clear similarities with the monopolisation of violence discussed in this book. How a state manages its justice system is also directly relevant to the 'taming of coercion' which is the main argument driving my analysis.

Procedural Justice: Shedding Responsibility

Weber famously argued that authoritarian regimes resting on personal loyalty have usually created a non-formal type of law, and that formal or procedural justice is repugnant to all authoritarian powers because it diminishes the dependency of individuals upon the grace and power of the authorities.[31] Even within Islam, which had by any standard an elaborate judicial system and a large class of judges and religious scholars interpreting the law, in practice most of the time the individuals were at the mercy of state officials. In nineteenth century Iran, the judges were subordinated not only to the central executive authority, but also to the various regional and local authorities. Subjects could rarely protect themselves against the whim and extortion of local representatives of the government.[32] Some elements of procedural justice emerged from time to time in patrimonial contexts too, such as some occasional councils presided over by the imam or his representatives in the Caliphate or the Mazalim courts of the ninth century, but they never went very far.[33]

How exactly procedural justice came instead to be so important in the West is not easily explained. 'It is hard to believe that the relatively strong would have acquiesced at once to being placed on the same level as the relatively weak through judicial processes'. Clearly, states coerced non-state elites into accepting a fairer judicial system.[34] The philosophical origins of individual rights are also clear:

Perhaps it would be more satisfying if the idea of natural rights had entered Western political thought with a clatter of drums and trumpets in some resounding pronouncement like the American Declaration of Independence or the French Declaration of the Rights of Man and the Citizen. In fact, though, this central concept of Western political theory first grew into existence almost imperceptibly in the obscure glosses of the medieval jurists. One might say that, in the works of the early Decretists, a distinctive mutation of thought and language occurred that gave rise to a whole new species of ideas, the species of natural rights theories. [...] Once the idea that all persons possess rights had grown into existence, it displayed a remarkable vitality and adaptability and proved relevant to a variety of emerging problems.[35]

But why and how did states themselves embark on the venture in the first place? Drawing on the classics, Holmes argues:

Shedding responsibilities, downsizing goals to match capacities, is a prudent step for the most Herculean of bosses, commanders, rulers, panjandrums, chiefs. [...] Ceding power over some domains is necessary in order to get full control of others. Monopolizing power is especially unattractive in situations swarming with unsolvable problems. The mighty will typically ditch responsibility for intractable dilemmas on which they hesitate to squander scarce time and effort to no avail. [...] Many legal historians interpret the gradual development of independent courts in England as an evolving division of labor whereby the king's court slowly cast aside aggravating and time-consuming burdens. [...] Politicians cede this power because they do not want it, and they do not want it because they have better things to do.[36]

A Society Too Complex for the Ruler Alone to Manage

This explains the emergence of an independent judiciary. The ruler had an incentive to guarantee its genuine independence, because otherwise people 'will notice where ultimate decision-making power lies, and the steps of the ruler's palace will again swarm with harassing crowds hoping to influence upcoming decisions of the court'. In this regard and more specifically to my point:

the powerful are especially eager to shed specific powers, namely those that are liable to excite lasting hatred and resentment. To exercise power is to create winners and losers. Winners may or may not feel appreciative; but losers almost certainly feel aggrieved.

It is dangerous to wield power because the powerful are eye-catching targets for the vengeance of those whom they have really or supposedly harmed. To diminish the danger of reprisal, power wielders typically seek deniability by yielding, in reality as well as appearance, some key elements of decision-making power. [...] By inviting the politically destabilizing desire to avenge perceived wrongs to vent itself inside the system, a forum for public accusations reduces the poisonous influence of anonymous denunciations and the demand for back-street ambushes. It can help cauterize class resentment and the desire for vengeance before they spiral out of control. [...] This is how power politics, if the elite is sufficiently prudent, can incubate the rule of law.[37]

Although Holmes relies on Machiavelli, there is a Tillyan echo in his argument that 'the rule of law will be established and maintained when political and economic elites understand the vital contribution it makes to national security'.[38]

Signs that this was happening multiply starting from the seventh century. According to an author of that time, Turquet de Mayerne, the police deals with 'all that can embellish, shape and give splendor to the city'. An eighth century author, Hohenthal, calls the police 'the art of the glory of the state as visible order and shining strength'.[39] By the nineteenth century, the final nail in the coffin of patrimonial societies and authoritarian regimes was hammered home by the increasing complexity of society. In the words of the Austrian Minister of the Interior (1850), who was urging an end to the state of siege:

the main objective of state of siege is to concentrate all political, judicial, and military power in one person. But this cannot be achieved in Vienna. There are too many important affairs taking place concurrently here, each of them affecting too many diverse interests...[40]

Dilemmas: Opportunities and Threats

A couple of examples from the contemporary scene can help explain how any progress towards a system of procedural justice is influenced by regime perceptions of threats and opportunities. The Minister of Justice of the pro-Vietnamese Cambodian government, Uk Bunchheuan, advocated in the 1980s some degree of procedural justice and rule of law, claiming at least to be motivated by concerns of international politics. The Minister of the Interior, Sin Song, and most of the government were hostile to the idea. Bunchheuan too did not favour 'a broad distribution of rights' because of the security situation. He however wanted police to get permission from homeowners before carrying out searches. In general the staff of the Ministry of Justice had more liberal inclinations than other government officials, but documents show that the Chairman of the Council of State and secretary-general of the ruling party Heng Samrin also opposed the use of torture. Eventually the Ministry of Justice managed to impose the rule that police had to send cases to prosecutors. In practice, however, the police systematically failed to turn cases over to the courts.[41] Even if as a mark of progress towards procedural justice this may seem puny, it showed at least an intention that over time might lead to more substantial results.

A similar example of internal power games is that of Uzbekistan, where occasionally prosecutors:

intervene and bring charges in particularly odious cases of brutality, but such interventions seem to be the exception. In 2002, ten senior policemen [...] were sentenced to jail terms after they were found guilty of a series of abuses, including the beating and torture of six men accused of murdering a local government official. But more often than not, procurators have failed to prevent or punish police abuses. One explained: In the end the [police] are armed people, and some prosecutors are afraid of them... and the [police] themselves cover up their crimes, and the procurator cannot spend all his time only overseeing the militia.[42]

In the case of the Soviet Union after Stalin:

the law enforcement apparatus in the Khrushchev era did not develop in accordance with a specific vision of Soviet society, but in reaction to the abuses of police power of the Stalin years. The Party thus sought a new legitimacy for the militia—one based on the authority of the Party rather than that of a single individual. Commitment to the rule of law, intrinsic to democratic policing, was conspicuously absent from the Khrushchev reforms.[43]

Only during the Gorbachev era did the aim appear to introduce the rule of law.

Inspired by western legal models, Gorbachev wanted to shift the source of militia legitimacy from the Party apparatus to the law. This transition would follow western European practice, which had seen continental police made more accountable to the law over time. According to Gorbachev's plans, militia personnel were to be made subordinate to legal codes and act first and foremost as law enforcement professionals, not servants of the Party apparatus.[44]

It is hardly surprising that these subtle dynamics might be difficult to strengthen or promote through the imposition of a one-size-fits-all model of rule-of-law reform. Indeed internationally-sponsored reform efforts can face insurmountable hurdles. While the contrasting and contradictory American, French, German and British influences and the mechanistic approach usually adopted ('the basic idea is that if the institutions can be changed to fit the models, the rule of law will emerge') do not help, the most serious problem is that rule-of-law reforms are unlikely to work when implemented through client regimes:[45]

if local elites become partners or clients of foreign elites, they will be sorely tempted to create a nonparticipatory, nonredistributive, regulatory, and repressive regime. A caricature of the rule of law may emerge in such a setting; but it will provide predictability and serviceable use of legal instruments only to a very few.[46]

This is beginning to be recognised by some practitioners of rule of law reform: 'rule-of-law reform will succeed only if it gets at the fundamental problem of leaders who refuse to be ruled by the law.'[47]

Strategies of Policing

Models?

The dilemmas of policing and the implications of specific types of policing as far as state consolidation is concerned can be better appreciated through a discussion of different models of policing. Several different models have been identified by the literature:

- Community policing: initially taking place informally, with the task being shared by all members of the community. At a certain point some members of the community are tasked with policing, until the system is incorporated in local government.
- State policing: originates as personal bodyguards of rulers and warlords, resulting gradually in the formation of local, regional police forces, often bandits and irregulars recruited to form the police, which are finally centralised by the ruler and turned into a professional state police.
- Colonial policing: created through the formation of a police force from the top, with the at least partial imposition of an external model, with independence it turns into a mostly centralised and almost always militarised police force (gendarmerie).
- Oriental policing: incorporates elements of community policing but develops them into a more sophisticated system where policemen also act as 'teachers of morality' and 'welfare workers'. It is currently used in a number of Asian countries (Japan, Korea, Malaysia).[48]
- Party-controlled policing: in party-state regimes, the political organisation which controls the state and identifies with it plays a key role in exercising supervision over policing.

- Non-state policing: communities and 'big men' take over policing because the state is too remote or has collapsed.

Such strict categorisation has obvious limits. The usual description of community policing in Great Britain in the nineteenth and early twentieth century might be largely mythological or ideological, as some authors argue that the police did not have public support at that time. The main aims of the typical police force at that time have been described as 'to get and to hold a job; second to exploit the possibilities of graft that the job offered; thirdly to do as little patrolling as possible; fourth, arrest a few miscreants.'[49] Similarly, elements of state policing have developed even in countries which supposedly belong to the tradition of community policing, as for example in the case of the Ulster Constabulary in the United Kingdom. All states must develop a strategy for maintaining internal order, but the emphasis placed on consent and coercion is variable. Even in liberal democracies it is not unusual for the police to act outside the law, while even the most authoritarian state imposes certain limits on police actions.[50] It appears therefore more useful to view the different models of policing as ideal types and not confuse them with actually existing policing systems, which tend to be mixed.

From the discussion above it appears clear that the 'models of policing' interpreted as organic and coherent strategies are in fact not an effective analytical tool, as each one of them combines a strategy for dealing with the security threat with a strategy for ensuring control and supervision over the police force itself. The goal of securing internal order itself takes different meanings depending on the context. In much of the world the police are seen primarily as an 'instrument of coercion' and used for 'regime representation and regulation', and governments are happy that way.[51] If the primary aim of a policing system is to prevent corruption and guarantee the security of citizens, one could only agree with the words of Sierra Leone's former inspector-general:

reforming the police force is not just an operational problem, but a personnel management problem; it requires line managers to accept responsibility for those under them rather than the force leaving it to the HQ department.[52]

A 'Modular' Approach to Studying the Police

It seems more productive as an analytical tool to identify different tasks that police forces have been assigned to and see how different regimes have been prioritising them: territorial control, protecting the social order, enforcing the rule of law, etc. Some tasks are common to all police forces, at least to a degree.

One of these is dealing with public disorder somehow. A group of authors identify a range of strategies of policing (threat management), which can be combined in varying forms. They can be summed up as:

- 'Criminalisation' which treats public disorder without regard to the political context in which offences occur.
- 'Accommodation' which recognises the political character of disorder and attempts to meet the grievances of the groups from which it emanates.
- 'Suppression' which also recognises the political character of disorder but answers with confrontation.[53]

Another universal aspect of policing is that it has to be supervised by the ruler. In this regard, the following strategies can be identified. Some of these options are clearly antonymic, but others can obviously be combined. A review of the literature suggests the following:

- Centralisation:
  - maximises government control, but sometimes at the expense of effectiveness, flexibility and the ability to match policing to local realities;
  - might imply a significant political cost in marginalising local power players;
- Co-option:
  - allows the incorporation of local leaders within the regime;
  - implies renouncing to direct control;
  - is inexpensive, but largely incompatible with professionalisation;
- Devolution:
  - allows for a degree of local influence and participation, maybe through co-option, but not necessarily;
  - is compatible in principle with professionalisation;
  - implies to some degree the renunciation of the centre to exercise strategic direction;
- Militarisation:
  - maximises the ability of the centre to use a 'suppression' strategy;
  - hampers the adoption of alternative strategies;
  - ensures strict control from the centre and high discipline;
  - is incompatible with devolution or co-option;
  - does not work well as a 'service';
- Civilianisation:
  - maximises the ability of adopting a 'criminalisation' strategy;

- ○ is not the most effective way to implement 'suppression';
- ○ is bureaucratised;
- ○ is usually subject to external supervision (judiciary, executive, parliament), which might limit its (or the centre's) room for manoeuvre;
- Party control:
  - ○ [a variant of the bureaucratisation/professionalisation model];
  - ○ requires a certain degree of efficiency and the existence of a widespread/ pervasive structure,
  - ○ maximises control from the government and loyalty to it;
  - ○ is unresponsive to local concerns;
  - ○ risks suffering deligitimisation if party rule enters a crisis;
- De-factionalisation:
  - ○ removes any party or factional control over the police, ensuring a greater acceptability of police to all sections of society;
  - ○ is also a precondition of full professionalisation;
  - ○ however makes control from the centre more difficult and turns the police into a relatively independent force, controlled mainly bureaucratically;
- Patrimonialisation:
  - ○ makes some degree of indirect control possible at low cost;
  - ○ causes inefficiency and is difficult to micro-direct towards specific security strategies;
  - ○ might make matching local realities easier on condition of selecting appointees carefully;
- Privatisation:
  - ○ is expensive when funded by the state, but removes from the shoulders of policy-makers the burden of carrying out difficult reforms of a police force;
  - ○ can offer quick solutions to the problem of delivering policing services to impatient constituencies;
  - ○ is flexible as there are several options, ranging from simply allowing private companies to offer their services to private firms and citizens, to contracting out public policing;
  - ○ reduces the degree of control over policing by the authorities;
- 'Democratic policing':
  - ○ maximises the ability of the centre to adopt an 'accommodation' strategy;
  - ○ greatly reduces the ability to adopt strategies such as 'suppression' and to some extent 'criminalisation' too;

○ exposes policing to the internal political debate, with potentially demoralising effects on rank and file in specific circumstances;

• Professionalisation/bureaucratisation:
　○ reduces freedom in making appointments as meritocratic/bureaucratic procedures are used;
　○ most effective at implementing strategies like 'criminalisation' and 'accommodation',
　○ not suitable for 'suppression';
　○ is expensive to put into practice;
　○ has a political cost because it might require the marginalisation of important players within a given regime.

In the type of analytical approach which we are suggesting here, there is no 'good' model of policing, but rather a series of tools and strategies that can be used or not depending on the aims and the resources available. A militarised police force, for example, is optimised to operate in contexts of internal disorder, such as insurgencies in their early stages. Once an insurgency takes off, fighting it requires the army to take the lead. The Sandinistas were keen in 1981–2 to fight the Contras primarily through the Ministry of the Interior, not a wrong approach according to many counter-insurgency theorists. A unit of special troops, *Tropas Pablo Ubeda*, was created for this purpose. However, as the Contras expanded and became a serious military threat, the army had to take the lead and even the *Pablo Ubeda* was transferred to the Ministry of Defence.[54] The implication is that by studying what tasks a police force has and how it is organised, we can infer what are the aims of the ruling elite.

Territorial Early Warning Systems

Because of the limited interest that policing systems have attracted, the list above is likely to be far from complete. For example, when the primary concern of a government is territorial control, a sophisticated structure of supervision and accountability might not be necessary. In this case the 'police' works as an early warning system, dealing with local trouble until it becomes unmanageable. Then the central government is alerted to the existence of a problem and sends in reinforcements. The system therefore has limited means and aims, beyond coercion. Usually, governments do not even bother to develop a professional police force for this kind of tasks, using in fact militias under the 'police' label.

For example in the case of Costa Rica, for a long time it was established practice that individuals would buy the position of chief of police and then use it to raise revenue through the co-option of accomplices among police officers, each one of whom would be placed in charge of a specific area. Only in more recent times has this type of corruption been reduced through the introduction of greater professionalism and accountability.[55] The situation was similar in post-apartheid South Africa, where police officials were reportedly three times as likely to be involved in crime as members of the public.[56] For the purpose of territorial control, even a police staffed by former criminals can make sense, as in the case of Chad;[57] indeed it might be difficult for a government to get professional and committed police to serve in remote districts, devoid of any comfort, for miserable pay. The Ottomans maintaining order in Greece used bandits who were granted amnesty and recruited to fight other bandits. The same bandits were also used by the independentists to fight the Ottomans and often switched sides.[58]

Of course, a police force of this kind will inevitably be characterised by high levels of abuse against the population, which is indeed endemic in countries as diverse as Nigeria, India, Colombia and Afghanistan. In such cases, the rulers do not appear to be concerned with the problem. The mixing of different models however is likely to create some problems of legitimacy. For example, in Afghanistan in 2001 onwards, territorial control was the main concern and was supposed to be achieved through the co-option of local leaders and notables, either by direct incorporation or by indirect participation. However, the absorption of irregular forces in the so-called police alienated and demoralised many of the remaining professional police officers.[59]

Whether by design or by default, a territorial early warning system tends to rely on rural elites for support; as a result the view of the militias tasked with policing is that their primary task is protecting the social order. This was the case in El Salvador, where before the 1990s reform the police were closely linked to the large landowners, and some barracks were even located at their farms.[60]

If a police force merely aims to maintain territorial control and order, i.e. prevent the emergence of opposition to the authorities, then a small police force can suffice if backed up by a strong capability of retaliation. The French colonialists were keeping order in Algeria before the war with just a French administrator, one to two assistants and five gendarmes, typically covering 80,000 inhabitants and 600 square miles.[61] This is still the situation in many countries. International police statistics about the police to population ratios can be very misleading. Often the countryside is very thinly policed, as the following examples suggest:

- in Uganda the subdistrict of Mityana with a population of over 2 million is covered by a police force of just 184, with a single motorbike;[62]
- in the Gitarama province of Rwanda, with a population of 902,387, there were in 2006 175 police with three cars and nine motorbikes;[63]
- in Liberia after the civil war, Maryland county had twenty-three policemen for 100,000 inhabitants;[64]
- in Guatemala, the actual number of police on duty at any time in the 1980s was just 5,000, for a population of 12 million.[65]

When a regime decides that it wants to control its territory and population and enforce the rule of law, it is not an impossible task even in pre-industrial conditions. During the 1880s the Japanese government decided to intensify the presence of the police in rural areas, rejecting the ongoing practice of concentrating police posts in the towns. In a few years the number of police posts grew by 270 per cent; each cluster of villages soon had its own police.[66]

Trade-Offs and Dilemmas: Centralisation

The strategic options described above represent the dilemmas of police-building from the perspective of the ruling elites; actual development in policing are the result of the combination of choices made by rulers and wider social, political and economic developments. For example, the centralisation of a police force, a process which occurred in many countries even recently, was usually stimulated by specific political developments:

The key factor which explains the initial impulse to centralize is violent resistance to the consolidation and assertion of state authority. The English government could tolerate decentralized institutions of policing because the unity of England under the crown was acknowledged as long ago as the tenth century.[67]

In the case of the majority of African countries, it has been argued that the predominant reliance on gendarmeries is a major factor in explaining the strong trend towards centralisation, as governments feared that it could have been dangerous not to centralise forces endowed with some military capability.[68] In reality, there are few examples of coups organised by police forces to justify this fear (the coup against Nkrumah in 1966 in conjunction with the army being one of the rare exceptions); it seems plausible that the desire to insulate the police from the influence of local politicians and notables through centralisation played a more important role.[69] In China, the reforms carried out from the 1980s onwards have also been in the direction of greater vertical control, at the expense of the local Communist Party committees, in order to prevent manipulation and hijacking by local political authorities.[70]

Trade-Offs and Dilemmas: Professionalisation and Control

A consequence of this type of approach is the rejection of teleological views about an irresistible march towards professional policing around the world; even professionalised police forces are subject to decay or relapse into patrimonialism.[71] From the perspective of state-building, some of the aspects discussed so far are particularly relevant. A major problem experienced by all police forces is how to develop or maintain professionalism and supervision/control from the centre; this problem is of course at its worst in the case of rural policing and in countries which can only afford modest levels of funding for policing. That is to say that even if there is a political decision to adopt a specific control and supervision strategy, implementing it is not necessarily easy; failures are to be expected. Let us, for example, focus on professionalisation and bureaucratisation and how they are implemented. Minimal indicators of professionalisation have been identified as:

- recruitment according to specified standards,
- remuneration sufficiently high to create a career service,
- formal training and
- systematic supervision by superior officers and external agencies.[72]

Supervision has always been the most complex problem in policing:

Ensuring that a police force does in fact police rather than attempt to occupy an area is a constant problem to the authorities, who may themselves have no clear understanding of the nature and aims of policing. [...] Policing is inherently a difficult process to keep under administrative control, because to do their job police officers routinely have to be dispersed [...] and given very considerable discretion in judging when to threaten or use what degree of violence. Occupationally constrained to "take charge" (assert their authority) and "handle situations" with efficiency and dispatch, police officers are subject to the temptation to rely excessively on their privileged access to the means of violence.[73]

Fully bureaucratised supervision requires a lot of paperwork and a high level of staffing by educated people, which is very expensive. However, forms of non-bureaucratic or semi-bureaucratic supervision do exist and are much cheaper, if not quite as reliable. As a result, police forces in low-income countries have been trying to make up for their deficiencies in these regards by strengthening low-cost kinds of supervision (see below).

Moreover, bureaucratic supervision places 'a premium on compliance rather than initiative', participation or collegiality. 'The routines of bureaucracy made it risk-averse, discouraging innovation.'[74] One way to mitigate these problems is what in developed countries is described as 'contracting out'. This system 'needs a permanent, autonomous, career-based and policy-focused core public service', committed to neutral professional advice in order to avoid drifting towards a completely patrimonial police system.[75] In the context of weak and under-resourced states, similar systems have been developed, but using irregular or semi-regular forces rather than private police. The extent to which these forces are effectively monitored and supervised by a central core of regular police also varies. This 'contracting out on the cheap' is more often a way to save money than an attempt to limit bureaucratism.

Control and supervision over police forces can be of two basic types, external and internal. External control over the police varies enormously between countries, sometimes being exercised by elected politicians, sometimes by civil servants, sometimes by courts (intermittently or indirectly), sometimes by mass media and public opinion. External control is considered problematic by scholars who are in touch with the practitioners, because it can be read by the police as 'indictment, impinging on the police pride and self-esteem'. The natural inclination on the part of the police is to cover up and put appearances before discipline, leading to a vicious cycle: as 'discipline declines, impropriety increases and the public become even more distrustful', leading to pressure for more external control.[76]

Internal control, if it is functional, is often considered to work better, even if it is correctly argued that it cannot possibly work if some external controls do not exist too (and vice versa).[77] Its effectiveness depends on the 'officers to low rank' ratio, and on other factors such as the encouragement of collegial responsibility, moral instruction in training, use of rewards such as pay, promotion and postings, and direct recruitment to senior positions (as opposed to promotion from the ranks) in order to avoid excessive closeness between supervisors and supervised.[78]

Trade-Offs and Dilemmas: Bureaucratisation

In general, the police forces of a majority of countries even in the developing world or in post-conflict states are equipped with regulations and systems of bureaucratised supervision. The situation in India resembles that in Pakistan, described at the beginning of this chapter. The Indian police have been described as finding it difficult to:

decide whether to intervene on behalf of the oppressed and thus face the wrath of the people in power or maintain authority while accepting abuses from the masses. The system wants stability and change simultaneously.[79]

A typical police station in a rural district would cover an area of 400 sq km, with a population of 40,000, relying on a staffing of just sixteen officers and fifty-four constables, armed with twenty-eight old model firearms. Apart from the main station, these forces would man a few outposts. The same police station would rely on a number of village guards (chowkidars) to help, thirty-five of them for fifty-two villages, but the system suffers from the guards being underpaid and often subject to the influence of the village elites.[80] The large autonomy enjoyed by the officers in charge of police stations has been pointed at as one of the causes of corruption.[81] Although in theory supervising officers are supposed to control investigation constantly, in practice Indian police departments are large and 'typically a superintendent will have jurisdiction over 200 and more investigators'. This implies that 'superior officers are able to exert control over at best a few prominent cases leaving effective control over most of the cases to the investigating officers'. Moreover, 'the posting and transfer of subordinates is controlled by superintendents and above ranks, so it is easy to post their own "trusted" officers who extort and share the spoils with them'. Burking exists in India too, as does the practice of sending cases for trial to enhance police clearance rates, facilitated by the absence of any practice of evaluating the performance of the investigators in terms of the cases investigated, cleared and prosecuted. The handling of public complaints is recognised to be very ineffective and futile, because officers do not like to have to judge their subordinates.[82]

Indonesia is yet another country where all the appearances of a bureaucratic system of policing seem to be in place, but the substance is lacking. Violations of the chain of command and political interference are common occurrences, while:

formal career management has all the outward trappings of a modern system but lacks the content. Important career decisions are based on patronage from enlistment to final appointment.[83]

Similarly, reform efforts can be so superficial as to deserve being described as little more than a façade.[84] Even where reform efforts have been more substantial, old practices like relying on the help of politicians in order to get appointed to positions of responsibility survive; these practices should not be interpreted as mere corruption, but also reflect the desire of politicians to maintain control over the police.[85]

These failures to establish or maintain effective supervision of police forces are the result of either (or both) genuine difficulties and lack of political will. Arguably, when a ruler decides that he needs an effective policing system, he can go to great lengths to establish it. The example of Meiji Japan once again

Table 2: Typical structure of a police station in India[86]

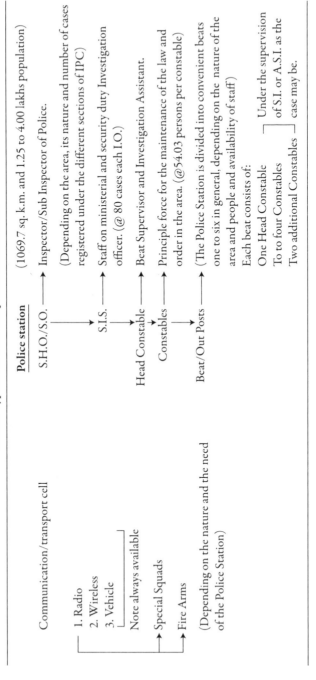

Police station

S.H.O./S.O. → Inspector/Sub Inspector of Police. (1069.7 sq. k.m. and 1.25 to 4.00 lakhs population)

S.I.S. → Staff on ministerial and security duty Investigation officer. (@ 80 cases each I.O.) (Depending on the area, its nature and number of cases registered under the different sections of IPC.)

Head Constable → Beat Supervisor and Investigation Assistant.

Constables → Principle force for the maintenance of the law and order in the area. (@54.03 persons per constable)

Beat/Out Posts → (The Police Station is divided into convenient beats one to six in general, depending on the nature of the area and people and availability of staff)

Each beat consists of:
One Head Constable
To to four Constables
Two additional Constables
— Under the supervision of S.I. or A.S.I. as the case may be.

Communication/transport cell
1. Radio
2. Wireless
3. Vehicle
Note always available

Special Squads

Fire Arms

(Depending on the nature and the need of the Police Station) shines out. Already in 1878 the police were producing a huge amount of paper-work, providing a steady flow of information from the bottom to the top and allowing the maintaining of a steady command and control system.[87]

Alternative Systems of Control and Supervision

If we accept that to some extent these difficulties in ensuring effective supervision and control are genuine, it makes it easier to understand what a powerful tool of supervision party control in single party regimes proved to be in making police forces comply with the directives of the government and respect discipline. The model was mostly adopted in countries inspired by the Soviet model, and as argued in the case of party control over armies (chapter 2) it is dependent on the establishment of a strong political organisation, itself a difficult task.[88] In the Soviet Union itself, attempts to eliminate or reduce the role of the party in the supervision of the police were largely unsuccessful; the result tended to be a massive spread of corruption in the police, which ended up being addressed with a net infusion of party personnel.[89]

If we then considered the often unaffordable costs of developing a thoroughly bureaucratised system, it is also easier to understand why certain governments have been experimenting with original techniques to supervise the police. In Ethiopia, for example, the *gime gema* system of confessional accountability has been used after the fall of Mengistu, involving:

criticism of police performance by all ranks in a station or department, sometimes for days on end at monthly intervals; policing would stop for the duration. Note takers recorded everything being said and then notes were forwarded to the next level in the hierarchy.

The system was criticised because it 'stifled decision-making and initiative', but it can also be seen as a cheap way to do away with a complex, multi-layered bureaucracy.[90] Its Maoist inspiration seems obvious, and it is interesting to consider how it was retained even once the original Maoist principles of the Ethiopian ruling party had long been sidelined.

The potential value of the Ethiopian experiment becomes more evident when a comparison is made with other examples of policing on the cheap. The case of Pakistan has already been discussed, but it is worth expanding on it. The cost of policing in Pakistan in the 1990s was of a few hundred dollars per policeman per year, while the cost per inhabitant was under a single dollar. With an officer to constable ratio of one to three in the early 1990s, a police to population ratio of 1:600 and just 3.7 per cent of illiterate constables in its ranks, Pakistan's police was certainly not the most sophisticated in the world, but not the least professional either.[91] In comparison, the qualitative level of the Russian Tsarist police at the turn of the century was very low, with just 3 per cent of police chiefs having made it to higher education and 21 per cent to secondary education; often officers and NCOs were barely literate. The rank and file were usually completely illiterate. Most policemen were former soldiers who had failed to achieve promotions and were not usually trained as police. Constables 'lorded over the peasants, ignored their rights and abused them'. Bribe-taking was a necessity, because of low pay; officers had to rely on bribes if they wanted to afford secretaries and scribes. Still, by all indications the Tsarist police were more effective in population and territorial control than the Pakistani force a century later.[92]

Another comparison can be made with the Ethiopian police. In the 1960s, 40 per cent of Ethiopian policemen were illiterate.[93] By the 1990s, the percentage of illiterate policemen in Ethiopia surely must have gone down, but it was probably still higher than in Pakistan, considering the prevalence of illiteracy in the country. Although measuring police corruption is difficult, it would appear that Ethiopia was more successful than Pakistan in containing police corruption.

It is difficult to answer why the Pakistani police were such weak performers, but the weak centralisation of Pakistan, the prominence of local elites in the elite bargain at the centre, the lack of political will in shaping a more effective police force all seem to have been major factors in the decay of Pakistan's police, as 'the political masters who are mainly interested in bending the laws to favour their party men and to hound the opposition'. During 1985–92 Pakistan's police seem to have touched rock bottom, as politicians were recruiting many officers among protégés with a criminal record. Political protection destroyed the chain of command, as subordinates refused punishment by appealing to their patrons. The lack of interest in controlling the countryside and challenging the hold of the landlords was visible in the abolition of the office of the village chowkidar, which was only replaced by two or three detective constables per police station, far too few to tour the villages and pick up information, particularly now that the landlords, sensing the weakening of the central government, became more active and interested in asserting themselves in national and local politics.[94]

An autochthonous effort to develop a system of central supervision of the police took place in Rwanda. The effort to centralise the police which started in 1996–7 was judged positively because it did away with locally recruited and locally managed forces, influenced by sectarian sentiment and easily corrupted. There was also sufficient political will to implement supervision and maintain strict standards.[95]

Rawlings' approach in Ghana in the early 1980s was even more peculiar to the local political predicament and completely opposed to the consensus on police development. He abolished altogether the division of labour between police, army, intelligence and paramilitary, mainly due to resource constraints and a bureaucratic crisis; despite the obvious risks, including the militarisation of the police, the system worked reasonably well from his perspective and it was kept.[96]

In a context of low-budget policing, surprise inspections by the higher ranks are a cost-effective way of maintaining a high degree of supervision. For example, the director of Laotian police during the waning years of French domination (1950–54) reportedly used to visit the 'commissariats' at any time without warning and even organise fake crimes to test their reaction.[97] It is clear that such approaches to supervision can only work if the higher echelons are strongly committed to their task; since they are the most likely to be political appointments and are always ultimately controlled by the political authorities, political will is the ultimate source of effective policing.

The decay of policing in Nepal is also reported to have started from the top, as governments lost their interest in maintaining an effective police force;[98] a similar case could easily be argued for post-2001 Afghanistan. There are some cases of very successful establishment of professional policing over a short period of time, such as for example the already mentioned case of Japan in 1878–87,[99] which is clearly another instance of the importance of political will. A relative success story was that of the Ottoman Empire at the turn of the nineteenth-twentieth centuries, where clear signs could be detected of the development of self-perception by policemen of being servants of the state, as opposed to protecting the interests of the rulers or a faction.[100]

In the absence of political will, on the contrary, any progress towards 'professional', institutionalised policing is subject to the risk of rapid decay. The case of Somalia is typical in this regard. In the early years of Siad Barre, he seemed to be making an effort to create a police force able to prevent the clan wars over resources like water, etc. During the 1980s, as Barre's priorities changed, the police were fully affected by the clannish retrenchment of the regime: by the mid-1980s 49 per cent of the police commanders belonged to the Darod like Barre himself.[101]

In this context, the partial adoption of 'modern' methods and techniques of supervision can even be counter-productive, as in the case of the reliance on statistics for assessing the performance of Uzbek police, which led to 'pressure to arrest Islamist radicals by quota' and hence to the 'detention of a large number of people unrelated to any anti-constitutional or violent activity'. Similarly obsessive supervision translates into 'pressure to get results', which in turn inevitably leads to brutality, as police seek confessions. Collecting evidence takes time and skill, but while there is constant pressure for results from superiors, there is very seldom any reprimand for using physical force against a prisoner, and confessions gained in this way are always admitted in court.[102]

If police reform has to achieve any substantial results, it needs to come from the political centre. Police reform in China was, for example, clearly the result of decisions taken at the centre, to allow professionalism and autonomy to grow: 'the nature and functions of the police are being shifted from police suppression under a dictatorship to law enforcement and public services'. The police increasingly came to be seen as playing:

a supporting role in protecting economic development. [...] The police have become less influential within the political and legal system and have gradually become more accountable to other legal institutions, such as the procuratorate and court. [...] The CCP has also given the procuratorate and the court limited supervisory powers over the police and allowed citizens certain legal remedies against police abuse of powers through judicial reviews and state compensation.

Apart from the strategic decisions taken at the centre, other factors seen as favouring police reform in China were the growing middle class and vibrant society that 'demands rights' and 'international pressures, through the mechanism of the World Trade Organization (WTO), International Covenant on Civil and Political Rights (ICCPR)'. Still, even in this case it may be arbitrary to view the reform as a gradual homologation of China to the policing practices of Western Europe. In a way which Schmitt would have liked, the ruling Communist Party was not ready to surrender its powers completely and retained its ability to impose 'sudden political takeover of the criminal justice system' and reinstate 'an arbitrary policing and criminal justice system, alongside the regularised system'.[103]

The examples above show that it is possible to achieve improvements in the effectiveness of police forces even without following the 'Western' model. Clearly, expectations of what can be achieved in these low-revenue and restricted human resources contexts need to be modest in any case. Even in the presence of political will and strong supervision, understaffed, undersupplied and insufficiently paid police forces are not going to do much more than restrain people from committing abuse and adopt a reactive attitude to policing, rarely patrolling and undertaking proactive measures.[104] However, the seemingly slight achievements of the autochthonous reformers have to be compared with the impact of counter-reforms aimed at protecting the narrow interests of the political elites and with the 'achievements' of internationally sponsored reforms.

International police reform efforts are discussed in *The unsustainable lightness of police reform*. As far as 'counter-reforms' go, the weakening of police forces in order to protect the interests of ruling and local elites is well documented in a number of African countries:

> for if the police do their job well, they might threaten their regime. [...] If they were truly independent, they would investigate regime officials suspected of violating the law. It is thus not in regime interest that the police should become efficient, effective, or provide citizen protection.[105]

Revealingly, although governments rarely give the police priority and resources allocated are 'inadequate', most police forces 'tend to have special units available for rapid development that do receive special treatment; they deal with the serious crimes considered to threaten regime order'.[106] In many cases, the under-resourcing of police forces might be a result of the weak financing of the state itself, but some authors allege that police may be deliberately kept under-equipped and under-funded because of mistrust about their reliability and loyalty. More self-assured regimes might at least invest in the improvement of management and in the fight against corruption, as well as in training the police to be friendlier, more approachable and respectful of the population, still without fully institutionalising them and preserving their character of a partisan, pro-government force.[107]

The fifth hypothesis of this book is *that policing is a specific strategy for consolidating the monopoly of violence*. The hegemonic model of policing, based primarily on community policing as developed in the UK, has had a considerable power of attraction in the first two decades of the post-Cold War era. However, by the end of the second decade it was losing some of its credibility as attempts to export it were mostly not very successful. As in the case of 'good governance', the concept of police reform is primarily an ideological construct. As such, however, it was bound to meet its limits in the complex and ever-varying environment of the developing world. While community policing found some suitable niches here and there, it failed by and large to address most of the primary concerns of new and not-so-new states. Indeed this chapter suggests that consolidating the monopoly of violence is a greater concern to most governments than legitimisation, although the importance of the latter should not be discounted either once powerful domestic constituencies emerge. It is also easy to mistake efforts aimed at 'taming the violence' (hypothesis four) for efforts seemingly aimed at increasing the legitimisation of the state. This chapter has highlighted some important gaps and limitations in the existing literature on policing; it has also pointed out some potential alternatives for future research and for a new approach to the understanding of policing.

CONCLUSION

We started this book with seven hypotheses about the role of coercion in state-building:

1. *institution-building is a key aspect of any process of taming violence;*
2. *pre-empting hostile collective action through co-option, alliances, manipulation and intimidation is as important as the mere accumulation of the means of coercion, and whole agencies of the state have been developed historically to implement this task;*
3. *the 'primitive accumulation of coercive power' tends to be ruthlessly violent;*
4. *sophisticated military-political actors clearly understand what kind of violence is counter-productive;*
5. *policing is a specific strategy for consolidating the monopoly of violence;*
6. *renegotiating the terms of political settlement, which may include changes in the command and control structure within the coercive apparatus, can weaken the ability of the ruling elite to operate in a coordinated fashion and endanger the monopoly of violence;*
7. *external intervention, even in its milder form of advice and support, is more likely to be counter-productive in achieving and maintaining the monopoly of violence.*

Rules and Decision-Making

While there is no question that the importance of the monopoly of large-scale violence is an essential ingredient of state-building, the ways through which this can be achieved vary tremendously. The first key point which this book raises and stresses is that the primitive accumulation of violence (state forma-tion) and the consolidation of the monopoly of large-scale violence are two

227

substantially different processes, with widely differing requirements and 'rules of the game'. State formation is intrinsically ruthless and very hard to constrain with rules and institutions. Moreover, this ruthlessness resurfaces every time that the monopoly of violence is endangered or has collapsed.

In such cases, Schmitt argued that political power cannot be 'exerted according to general and neutral legal rules', because 'power is "decision" by nature, namely discretion, partiality, particularism, and exception'. His argument that 'political decisions have nothing to do with following rules' but instead they create them *ex novo* and that this is indeed the 'specific and positive function of political power' is indeed appropriate to the primitive accumulation of power and to crisis situations, when the monopoly of violence is in crisis.[1] Schmitt's argument of course assumes that the 'sovereign' is a statesman, aiming to protect the interests of the state and the nation. As the literature reviewed in this book has documented, that is far from being a plausible assumption. The opposition to institution-building might not derive just from the need to take executive decisions quickly and without constraints in the interests of the state and ultimately of the collectivity, but also from the longer-term threat that powerful institutions can represent for those in power.

This does not mean that tame coercion (constrained by purposely built institutions) cannot play a role in state formation and in civil wars as well; it only means that it cannot be the primary tool of coercion. Taming violence becomes the priority strategy in contexts of state consolidation. Again it can take many shapes, of which the introduction of a specialised professional police force is the most common and important. Institution-building is a wider process, of which police-building is just one aspect, but finds its space in a similar context. Rule of law and institution-building are not just the dream of some bourgeois reformers: their impact on state consolidation and ultimately on the maintaining of the monopoly of large-scale violence is demonstrable. Rulers too are set to benefit from acting under the constraints of rules, even if there are drawbacks associated with this, and situations may emerge where such constraints become intolerable. The growing sophistication of coercion, its transfer to specialist organs of the state, in other words the 'taming of violence', are not mere details or optional characteristics, but key aspects of state consolidation.

Implications for Intervention

The distinction between state formation and state consolidation should not be taken lightly or for granted. The assumption that more or less any state endowed with international recognition has completed the process of its own formation, so common among policy-makers, is of course completely inadequate from an analytical perspective. This assumption can easily lead to the adoption of misplaced polices of state consolidation in a context where the monopoly of large-scale violence has not yet been established, so is at best a waste of resources and at worst has negative if not disastrous consequences.

The fact that this confusion is often present among policy-makers and international advisers in the field compounds the classic 'blank slate' attitude, that is the tendency to impose standard solutions regardless of the context in which intervention is taking place. Ignoring the existence and availability of non-institutional tools of state-building does not reinforce the option of institution-building, except perhaps in the very short term; it might well weaken it, as a string of failures discredits the whole idea in the long term. This is one of the arguments against external intervention in conflict areas, as it emerged from chapter 6. This is not a conclusive argument: what does derive from the 'blank template' argument is that a better understanding has to be developed of the political processes underlying security sector reform efforts and that new skills and capacities have to be developed and maintained to tackle such challenges. The principle of intervention in conflict environments faces instead in my view deeper and more substantial objections.

The Limits of Intervention

The first of these objections is that intervention, particularly when occurring on a large scale, unleashes a series of perverse effects and perverse incentives, which might well outweigh any gain deriving from the advice and material support obtained by the host. Local players, even if in principle supportive of intervention, will try to reclaim local ownership in some form, mostly resulting in substantial sabotage done to the efforts of the intervening powers to reform, build institutions or improve effectiveness.

The second objection is that large-scale support is likely to have a crowding out effect, removing incentives for the locals to develop their own skills, strategies and resources, effectively slowing down state-building.

Third, intervention is likely to have a delegitimising impact on host governments, particularly to the extent that it is perceived as invasive. This negative impact might be offset by effective improvements in the capability of the host state, but the political turmoil deriving from such invasiveness should not be underestimated.

Fourth, in some cases the result of peacekeeping operations might just be of 'kicking out the ladder', disabling state formation processes even if its genuine purpose is to bring peace and spare lives. Since politics always has *horror vacui*, sooner or later state formation is likely to hit back in a more radical and extreme form.

Fifth, many of the implicit assumptions of peacekeeping imply an invasiveness of which its promoters do not always seem to be aware. Whatever the source of opposition to the rule of law and institution-building, the adoption of a perspective different from that of the rulers in the case of international interventions, that is the interests of 'civil society', of the 'population', of the 'people', often implies, in order to be effective, the bypassing of ruling elites. In the absence of a determined effort to deprive such elites of authority, that is of the establishment of a *de facto* protectorate, such a strategy of confronting local elites may simply not be within the realms of possibility.

The risk of 'naivety' is particularly high in police reform and police-building efforts. A perspective on policing that is focused on its role in state consolidation should never forget that ultimately coercion is a key aspect of the state and that the foremost task of policing is exercising that. If this is kept in mind, the development of policing and the different alternative 'models' can be better understood as different options to achieve internal order, while safeguarding the interests of ruling elites and their constituencies. The understanding that international police reformers have of how police forces work effectively in each country is clearly insufficient:

> There is a specific lack of analysis of how security sectors in many countries function, their role in society, their behaviour in crisis situations and their relations to other elites, etc. Up to now, most research that has been done has focused on the military along with certain aspects of behaviour, such as human rights violations. As a rule, the greatest lacunae relate to institutional and sociological aspects of policing and other non-military security forces.[2]

Sometimes, ruling elites might be genuinely interested in the establishment of a strongly institutionalised security sector and in seeking external assistance to this end. As demonstrated in this book, experience suggests that this is more likely to be the exception than the rule, particularly when the initiative comes from abroad and takes the shape of a large-scale effort. This poses the problem of how to deal with the reconstruction of the security sector in post-conflict transitions, beyond the standard template of institution-building. The widespread tendency to cast anything different from institution-building as a form of corruption and decay is not helpful in this context; the reality of state-building in any case resembles more choosing between lesser evils than the edification of brand new worlds.

Advisory efforts have not been systematically studied in a comparative way in the literature, but seem to work better when they are small and contained; large-scale advisory missions tend to end in a big, wasteful and rather unhelpful mess. One obvious reason is that the larger the mission, the more difficult to recruit adequate staff. Military assistance might make strategic sense when one side is ready to escalate indefinitely; otherwise it just might make a conflict even more violent and bitter. Indiscriminate pouring of military assistance into a country is in any case likely to lead to massive dysfunctionalities, not only within the armed forces but within society as a whole. Perhaps we could describe this as the inflationary impact of intervention: with host governments being unable to absorb all the help and advice being poured in, they have to expand the state machinery at a very fast rate. Human capital being scarce, this results in a massive increase of the cost of running the same machinery, compromising the viability of the state in the long run.

Assistance to new or weak states also needs to be studied on the basis of the hypothesis that it might not always be benign in its intentions. Perhaps there is truth in the statement that the West is trying to kick out the ladder to development and leave the developing states in a position of structural inferiority; perhaps there is not. In any case, these are hypotheses which need to be tested analytically.

The Neglected Political Dimension

The other main set of conclusions is related to the political dimensions of the monopolisation of violence. The prevention of revolt through political micro-management and information-gathering is often neglected in the literature, which tends to focus on sub-national administration from a narrowly technical viewpoint or to import a 'blank slate' conceived in developed states into a context of state formation or early stages of state consolidation. In the real world, rather than institutions working hand in hand with communities, these tasks are distributed between the secret police and a patrimonially controlled local administration, depending on the nature of a political regime and on the circumstances. The ambition to bring 'good governance' to the developing world, therefore, misses the original and perhaps main purpose of local government. Here again the study of state-building has often suffered from an overdose of social contract theories; there is more evidence to argue that local communities and strongmen have been coerced into accepting state domination than there is of willing participation in state-building and the formation of nations.

As importantly, the incorporation of communities and strongmen into the 'nation' also appears to have been the result of the establishment of a monopoly of violence, not in this case because of direct coercion, but because by advocating an increasingly exclusive monopoly of violence for itself, the state effectively 'hooked' communities and strongmen to its structures and made them dependent on the provision of services such as protection, policing, dispute settling, etc. Incidentally it could also be argued that the same pattern can be recognised in the provision of other services, which have nothing to do with the monopolisation of violence: the provision of education, health, etc. Making communities dependent on the state is a key aspect of state-building. This is certainly an area of research which requires greater attention, if we are to refine our understanding of state-building.

State-Building From Below

If the understanding of state-building as a process that can take place with the voluntary involvement of communities is largely flawed, there is another type of 'state-building from below' which is instead a feasible option, if not always a welcome one. The literature discussed in this book points towards the fact that the most effective efforts to (re-)build a security apparatus tend to be insurgent organisations turning into states. This is not a new finding per se, but deserves closer attention. These processes of state-building from below should not be romanticised, but neither should state formation in general. They tend to be more successful exactly because they resemble closely the 'nasty and brutish' processes of state formation of the eras preceding the formation of an international community. Changes in the international environment have made the establishment of a monopoly of violence more difficult to achieve, particularly because achieving complete victory in a civil war looks today to be an increasingly unlikely occurrence. International intervention tends to freeze civil wars before their conclusion. Not all non-state armed groups are deterred from pursuing their aims by the threat of international intervention; in general the more ideological and transnational they are, the more likely they are to push through regardless. Paradoxically, therefore, the interference of the 'international community' in the state-making process has resulted in its radicalisation: possibly only the most extreme and aggressive organisations keep trying to accumulate coercive power for state-making ends.

CONCLUSION

The study of insurgencies can count on a rapidly growing number of analytical studies. This rich literature, however, is far from being fully satisfying. It often suffers from an unsophisticated understanding of processes of state formation and state consolidation. As argued above, the rules of the game in maintaining the monopoly of violence and in establishing it in the first place are not the same. In recent years the organisational aspects of insurgencies have attracted growing attention, a positive development on which scholars should build by bringing to the fore more empirical studies.

The Long-Term Perspective

If what has been said so far seems to convey a despairing view of state formation and state consolidation, which leaves little space for liberal 'acceleration' and external engineering, it is time to point out that even within a patrimonial context, some state formation and state consolidation solutions which fall short or are at odds with institution-building are more conducive to long-term, 'virtuous' processes of state consolidation. Indeed it can even be argued, on the basis of what this book has shown, that too much 'modernity', that is too much technology and institution-building, can be counter-productive not just for the establishment of a monopoly of large-scale violence, but also for state-building efforts more generally. The case against technological intensification of the security sector in countries where qualified human resources are scarce is quite obvious: it leads to the militarisation of the intelligentsia, from which the politicisation of the army often follows. It also rarely leads to effective armies. This is not just because there is little point in possessing a lot of modern hardware, when the capability to maintain and operate it is insufficient. It is also in part because the ruling elite, in order to protect itself from an army which has incorporated too much of the educated class, may take measures which undermine its effectiveness.

Less obvious, and perhaps exactly because of this all the more relevant, is the point that modern, complex, technology-intensive armies also absorb a lot of management skills, always in short supply in any society and particularly so in societies that have as yet mobilised only a small portion of their population through the educational system or the economic system. Many examples suggest that shortages of management skills (in command and logistics) were key factors in the underperforming of armies in developing countries, even when they had heavily invested in efforts to modernise both army and society. Moreover, the siphoning of management skills into the armed forces is likely to harm the general development of society.

New Directions in SSR Analysis

The review of different aspects of coercion in the context of state formation and state-building highlighted that the literature on the role of armies is much more developed than the literature on policing, so far mostly focused on policy issues. Further research on this topic is therefore particularly necessary. Some key questions to be asked are:

- How is policing effectively carried out and with what aims?
- How is supervision exercised effectively?
- How can a degree of professionalisation be obtained and maintained in the face of limited budgets?

The tendency to rely on aggregate, rough statistics such as 'number of inhabitants per policeman' is also deeply misleading; there is a need to analyse the geographical coverage of policing in greater detail. Finally, when a police force is developed in the early stages of state consolidation or when the monopoly of violence is threatened, taking a state-centric perspective rather than a community-centric one is not a form of 'statolatry', but sheer necessity.

This leads us to the other key aspect of international police reform efforts, that is whether repeated patterns of 'failure' are due to inability or lack of will. The question is relevant because while in existing analyses of police reform the will or motives of the local partners are now increasingly questioned, those of international partners are rarely if ever so, which raises a methodological issue alongside a more political one. It might be necessary to ask whether commitment to 'democratic policing' is a mere lip-service exercise or whether there is genuine substance to it. This implies studying the processes of police reform formulation within international organisations and donor governments.[3] As with other forms of external assistance, they have to be studied and analysed with an open mind and their aims be determined on the basis of actions and behaviour, as well as of policy documents if available.

Perhaps few other aspects of international intervention in SSR have produced so much literature as DDR. Still, as highlighted in chapter 6, some of the key issues have not been addressed satisfactorily. The handling of disarmament and reintegration is usually done in isolation from the political context, ignoring the political imperative of strengthening the newly born state and the political alliances which underpin it. Certainly we could learn more from how disarmament and demobilisation have been handled before the end of the Cold War, particularly in terms of their long-term impact on state-building. One of my next volumes will deal with the unresolved issues in DDR.

CONCLUSION

The review of the literature has also revealed how our understanding of institution-building in practice remains weak. This is the case with armies (chapter 2), but not only them. The complex dynamics allowing institution-building to take place or not need to be unpacked in detailed case studies, which will be the task of another volume following on from the *Art of Coercion*.

NOTES

INTRODUCTION

1. Doyle (1995), p. 13.
2. Paris (2004), p. 82.
3. Berdal and Leifer, p. 39, p. 44.
4. Ibid., p. 56.
5. Paris (2004), p. 86.
6. Ibid., p. 88.
7. Berdal and Leifer, p. 45.
8. Paris and Sisk, p. 3.
9. Ibid., pp. 14–15.
10. Ibid., p. 3.
11. Ibid., pp. 305–6.
12. OECD, p. 13.
13. Loc. cit.
14. Bryden and Hänggi, pp. 13–14.
15. Although Paris' focus of criticism is peace-building rather than state-building per se, much of what he says in *At War's End* applies also to the Western concept of state-building. See also Paris and Sisk; Richmond and Franks; Ayoob; Dodge; Milliken.
16. Gat, p. 264.
17. Kalyvas (2006), p. 100.
18. North et al., p. 18.
19. Ibid., p. 170.
20. Ibid., p. 171.
21. Mann, p. 388.
22. Among others Tilly (1985), p. 174.
23. Throughout this book for the sake of simplicity and brevity I shall often use 'ruler' as a shorthand for all types of holders of the monopoly of violence.
24. From now onwards I shall use 'country' as shorthand for the territory controlled by the 'ruler'.
25. Cambrensis.

26. North et al., p. 169.
27. Aron.
28. Di John and Putzel.
29. The concept of 'primitive accumulation of power' was previously used among others by Cohen et al. (1981) and Tilly (1990), paraphrasing economics.
30. North et al., p. 169.
31. Kalyvas (2004), p. 105.
32. Downes, p. 422, p. 426.
33. Marks, p. 43.
34. For a similar argument see Downes, p. 426.
35. Elias; Bates.
36. North et al., p. 178ff.; Bates.
37. Janowitz (1977), p. 71.
38. Rejali.
39. Baker (2008), pp. 16–17.
40. Pérouse de Montclos, p. 50ff. cites the examples of Fidel Ramos (Philippines) and Bel Ali (Tunisia), who both left the police to join the army in order to improve their chances of a political career.
41. Janowitz (1977), p. 31, p. 176.
42. Pincus, p. 33.
43. Pincus, p. 41.
44. On the very conscious search for a model of policing to imitate in Meiji Japan (1868–1912) see Westney p. 40ff.
45. This topic has mainly been debated with regard to the funding of non-state violent organisations after the Cold War; see Cerny, Jackson and Mackinlay.
46. On circumvention in the specific case of security sector reform see Giustozzi (2008b) and Marriage.

1. THE RUTHLESSNESS OF STATE FORMATION

1. Ibn Khaldun, p. 123, p. 107, p. 95, pp. 97–8, p. 120, p. 122.
2. Ibid., p. 126.
3. Ibid., pp. 123–4, pp. 133–4, p. 138, p. 141.
4. Ibid., p. 124, pp. 133–4, p. 140, p. 230.
5. Gat, pp. 298–9.
6. Cohen (1985).
7. Gallant (1999), pp. 26–7; see also Lock; Chabal and Daloz, p. 85.
8. Robinson and Scaglion (1987); Robinson et al.
9. Lewis, pp. 213–14.
10. O'Connell, p. 93. See also Andreski for the original argument.
11. Lewis, pp. 213–14.
12. Loc. cit.
13. The greed of the lower ranks is eloquently shown in Keen.
14. See DeVries; Anderson and Duffield.

15. Gellner, p. 160, p. 162. See Coupland; Smyth; Simms for examples.
16. Gat, p. 249, p. 247; Bates, pp. 46–7.
17. Bates, pp. 54–6.
18. Gat, pp. 246.
19. Gat, pp. 239–40.
20. Beal and Fox.
21. Tapper and Glatzer.
22. On the importance of links of reciprocity for the motivation of fighters see Gat, pp. 298–9.
23. See Marten.
24. Gat, p. 374, p. 364.
25. G. Duby.
26. Spruyt, pp. 37–8.
27. Poggi, pp. 25–31.
28. See Allen, p. for African examples.
29. Holden.
30. Marks (1996), p. 2. See also Beckett, p. 78ff.
31. Dorronsoro, p. 127.
32. For a discussion of this topic see Giustozzi (2005).
33. The most interesting formulation of this process is to my knowledge found in Reno (2002), pp. 837–58.
34. On the doubtful discontinuity between old ideological wars and new, non-ideological ones see Cramer, 76ff and Kalyvas, p. 380ff.
35. On the importance of 'control[ing] the symbols of legitimacy' in order to obtain social cohesion and loyalty, see Gellner, pp. 165–6.
36. Geertz, p. 220.
37. Ibid., p. 229.
38. This distinction between weakly organised/bureaucratised polities and strongly organised ones is similar to that established by Duverger between committee-based parties and section- or cell-based parties (pp. 71–7).
39. On the reaction of Chinese warlord Feng Yu-hsiang to the danger of the ideologisation of his organisation in the 1920s, see Sheridan.
40. FitzGerald, p. 385.
41. A similar argument is developed in Roth, pp. 194–206.
42. See Giustozzi (2008a) and (2008b). See also Menkhaus' concept of 'paper states'.
43. Ellis (1995), p. 94; Anastasoff.
44. Ellis (1995), p. 167; Brunk, p. 106ff.
45. Henderson, p. 4.
46. Ellis (1995), pp. 166–7.
47. Galula, p. 12.
48. Ibid., p. 53.
49. On this point see Sinno, p. 14.
50. Callwell, pp. 157–8.
51. Galula, p. 12; Shrader.

52. Galula, p. 16.
53. Ibid., p. 11; Ouellet, p. 16.
54. Azevedo; Buijtenhuijs, pp. 320–25.
55. See also Giustozzi (2007a) for this.
56. Weinstein, p. 39, pp. 42–3, p. 158.
57. Mackenzie (1997), p. 8ff. and Herspring, p. 56ff., who believes Mackenzie underestimates the role of the chaplains.
58. Ellis (1973), p. 180ff.
59. Herspring, pp. 125–59.
60. Loveman, p. 64.
61. Woolman, p. 153.
62. See for example Fabei.
63. Gander; Kahaner; Ford and McNab.
64. Omissi, p. 8ff.; Dodge.
65. Gann, p. 44.
66. Cheng; 'RPG-7: Insurgent equaliser', *Jane's Terrorism and Security Monitor*, 7 October 2008; Small Arms Survey.
67. Krepinevich and Wood; Wilson.
68. 'Big Issue, Big Problem? MANPADS', in Small Arms Survey, pp. 77–96.
69. Although the impact of American-made Stingers in Afghanistan was initially overestimated, it was still very significant: Kuperman. The impact of American Redeye missiles in Nicaragua is not a matter of dispute: Bernard E. Trainor, 'Contra Aid Cutoff: A Setback, Not A Death Blow', *New York Times*, 6 February 1988; Miranda and Ratliff, 242. In Angola the impact of Stingers was more modest because of the limited numbers and the early withdrawal of American support in 1990, which also led to the returning of the missiles: *Angola*, New York: Arms Project (Human Rights Watch), Human Rights Watch/Africa (1994), p. 47; Somerville, p. 22.
70. Cann, p. 133ff.
71. Ellis (1995), p. 34.
72. Ellis (1995), p. 119.
73. MacKenzie (1997), p. 113.
74. Taber however applies the term to guerrilla wars in general.
75. Ellis (1973), p. 185ff.
76. On this point see also Gutiérrez Sanín.
77. Ellis (1973), p. 47ff.; Mackenzie (1997), p. 23ff.
78. Quoted in Ellis (1995), p. 66.
79. Ibid., p. 67.
80. Mackenzie (1997), p. 54ff.
81. Ellis (1973), 92ff.; Mackenzie (1997), p. 37ff.
82. Quoted in Ellis (1973), p. 195.
83. Ellis (1973), p. 180ff.
84. Joffe, p. 34ff.
85. Li, p. 194.
86. Hutchful, p. 85.

87. The concept of 'primitive accumulation of power' was previously used among others by Cohen et al. (1981) and Tilly (1990), paraphrasing economics.

2. MAINTAINING THE MONOPOLY: THE RISK OF DISLOYALTY

1. Bremer, p. 27, pp. 53–5; Ricks, pp. 154–5.
2. Herring and Rangwala, pp. 90–91.
3. Allawi, p. 157.
4. Ibid., pp. 158–9.
5. Herspring, p. 64.
6. Lynn, p. 81.
7. McNeill (1983), p. 35.
8. Herspring, p. 162.
9. Putzel.
10. al-Marashi and Salama, pp. 83–90.
11. Brooks (2007a), p. 15ff.
12. On this issue see also Finer (1975), p. 94ff.
13. Gat, p. 298–9.
14. Gat, p. 303; on the reliance of the phalanx on 'willingness to fight' and 'govern by consensus', see also O'Connell, p. 99.
15. Gat, p. 355, p. 362.
16. McNeill (1983), p. 135ff.
17. Gat, p. 353.
18. Ellis (1995), p. 127ff., p. 82ff., p. 173.
19. Howe, p. 45.
20. This was the case of Frelimo in Mozambique, according to Young.
21. Quinlivan, p. 153.
22. Belkin, pp. 22–4.
23. Howe.
24. Luckham, p. 243.
25. Clapham (1988), p. 34, p. 38; Erlich.
26. al-Marashi and Salama, p. 47.
27. Giustozzi, (2010a).
28. Janowitz (1977), p. 14, p. 136, p. 140.
29. Erickson.
30. Tal, p. 17; Gerber, pp. 159–60.
31. Jureidini and McLaurin, pp. 61–5; Robins, p. 198.
32. Tal, p. 57ff., p. 83, p. 108.
33. Brooks (1998), p. 16.
34. Fontrier, p. 353.
35. Howe, p. 30.
36. McCoy, pp. 19–20.
37. See Finer (1975).
38. Gat, p. 371.

39. Janowitz (1971, p. 1960) and Huntington (1957).
40. Janowitz (1977), p. 200, p. 117.
41. Brooks (1998), pp. 19–21.
42. Migdal, pp. 68–72, p. 83.
43. Miranda and Ratliff, p. 206.
44. See Herspring, p. 84 and Forrest, pp. 18–20 on the events leading to the French Revolution.
45. Beckett and Pimlott, p. 136ff.; Cann.
46. Porch (1977).
47. Pailler, pp. 36–7, p. 40–41.
48. Nolutshungu, p. 87.
49. Pascal, p. 20.
50. Brooks (2007b), p. 109ff.
51. al-Marashi and Salama, p. 133.
52. Gat, p. 473.
53. Belkin, p. 28.
54. O'Connell, p. 113.
55. Gat, p. 500.
56. Grunow.
57. Teitler; van Doorn; Janowitz.
58. Kiser and Baer, pp. 235–6.
59. Janowitz, p. 200, p. 117.
60. Brooks (1998), p. 46–9.
61. McNeill (1983); Parker.
62. I adopt the definition of bureaucracy proposed by Finer (1997), p. 64, which is more flexible than Weber's classical one.
63. Gat, p. 355, p. 362.
64. Kiser and Baer, pp. 235–7, McNeill (1995), p. 130, McNeill (1983), p. 117, p. 126ff., p. 132.
65. McNeill (1995), p. 3.
66. They had powers to monitor local army command, hence acting as a kind of commissar too.
67. Herspring, pp. 79–102.
68. Herspring, pp. 103–24.
69. Herspring, pp. 161–86.
70. Colton, p. 85ff.
71. For a comparison of the political commissars with other, less fortunate, systems of political supervision of armed forces see Herspring. See also Merridale, pp. 138–9.
72. On China see Joffe, p. 57ff., p. 115ff. After the beginning of the modernisation of the army in 1955, party cadres in the army lost importance, but their role was already being strengthened again as early as 1958.
73. Brooks (1998), p. 41.
74. al-Marashi and Salama, p. 114, p. 128.
75. Kenstbaum.

76. Gat, p. 299.
77. On this point see A. Giustozzi (forthcoming 2011b).
78. Pollack.
79. Reiter (2009); Pollack.
80. Herspring, p. 92.
81. Belkin, p. 23.
82. Preto.
83. Quinlivan, p. 133. The term 'coup-proof' was used before Quinlivan, but not systematically.
84. Horowitz, pp. 536–7.
85. See for example Merridale, p. 165ff.
86. O'Connell, pp. 112–14.
87. de Atkine, p. 20.
88. Brooks (1998), p. 35.
89. Howe, p. 50.
90. Gat, p. 369.
91. On the Sierra Leonean RUF see Rosen; on the Ugandan Lord's Resistance Army see Schomerus; on the Mozambican RENAMO see Seibert, p. 255ff.
92. Machiavelli (1515), chapter 4.
93. Gat, p. 348; the case of Yugoslavia is a special one: although the military organisation of the country could in no way be described as feudal, the high grade of decentralisation of army structures was meant to increase resilience *vis-à-vis* an external invasion. In the end it contributed to the descent of the country into civil war and disintegration in the 1990s (Derrienic, 166).
94. Brooks (1998), p. 19–26.
95. Belkin, p. 25–6.
96. Brooks (1998), p. 27 on Mubarak's Egypt; on Pakistan see Siddiqa.
97. Howe, p. 30.
98. Enloe, pp. 20–21 for Kenya and Britain; Brooks (1998), pp. 19–21 and passim.
99. Indeed allowing the army to mix with the population in the wake of the food riots of 1789 was a major factor in compromising the loyalty of the French army to the crown (Herspring, pp. 82–3); Horowitz, p. 549.
100. Brooks (1998), p. 41 on Saddam Hussein and Mubarak.
101. Quinlivan, p. 157; Knox, p. 104, cit. in Horowitz, 533; see also on 'traditional' south African societies Schapera, p. 172, cit. in Horowitz.
102. Byman, p. 105.
103. Ero, p. 238.
104. Brooks (1998), p. 43; al-Marashi and Salama believe that the expansion of the Iraqi officer corps during the Iran-Iraq war made it more difficult for the army to oppose Saddam Hussein at the end of the conflict (pp. 174–5).
105. Howe, p. 57.
106. Clarke, 468, pp. 463–4.
107. Porch and Muller, pp. 184–5.
108. Giustozzi (2009b).
109. Tareke, p. 166, p. 168.

110. Herwig et al., pp. 583–4; Spector, pp. 278–9, p. 301, p. 343, p. 369ff. General Ty, the Chief of Staff., was described by US advisers as worth a 'good sergeant' (Spector, 280); Clarke, p. 23, p. 40, p. 47.
111. See Hutchful on Ghana in the Rawlings era, p. 86; Brooks (1998), p. 33 on King Hussein of Jordan and p. 48 on Mubarak, who according to visiting US officers 'maintained a colourless command in which key posts are occupied by individuals described as "weak people"'. See also Horowitz, pp. 535–6, p. 551ff.
112. Howe, p. 36, pp. 56–7, p. 39, p. 54, p. 38, pp. 41–3, p. 58, p. 59.
113. Brooks (1998), p. 42 on Assad of Syria.
114. Byman, p. 105.
115. Enloe, p. 32.
116. Herwig et al., pp. 583–4; Spector, pp. 278–9, p. 301, p. 343, p. 369ff.; Clarke, p. 23, p. 40, p. 47.
117. Hoytt, p. 55ff.
118. Pascal, pp. 9–10.
119. Horowitz, p. 532ff.
120. Belkin, p. 29ff.
121. The National Guard was refurbished and strengthened in the 1950s to balance the development of the army and the recruitment into it of communities which the royal family did not fully trust. See Hurewitz.
122. It played an important role in withstanding the army coup organised by the rival faction of Rubayi Ali (David, 85).
123. Howe, p. 44ff., p. 50; Migdal, pp. 79–80; Brooks (1998), p. 37; al-Marashi and Salama, p. 125.
124. Hickey, p. 21.
125. Giustozzi (2010a).
126. See Horowitz, p. 542ff.
127. Horowitz, p. 547.
128. Migdal, pp. 209–10, p. 213.
129. Quinlivan, p. 147.
130. Howe, p. 44ff.
131. See Giustozzi (2010a).
132. al-Marashi and Salama, p. 95, p. 167.
133. Brooks (1998), p. 39.
134. Horowitz, pp. 547–8 and pp. 554–6, who mentions the Philippine army's tolerance for Marcos' packing of the Constabulary with fellow Ilocanos as due to the fact that the paramilitary was a long-established force and Kenyatta's 'careful manipulation' of the military composition of Kenya's army.
135. Quinlivan, p. 144.
136. Brooks (1998), p. 52; al-Marashi and Salama, pp. 153–67, pp. 174–5, p. 187.
137. Fontrier, pp. 351–2.
138. Howe, p. 39.
139. Howe, pp. 46–7 on Nigeria and Uganda.
140. Cit. in Howe, p. 35.
141. Howe, p. 43; Young and Turner, p. 262.

142. Lefever, pp. 120–21.
143. Odom; Glickson.
144. Horowitz, pp. 546–7; Agyeman-Duah, p. 95.
145. Erlich, p. 461.
146. Quinlivan, p. 134; Brooks (1998), p. 13.

3. MAINTAINING THE MONOPOLY: WHEN RUTHLESSNESS IS STILL NEEDED

1. Moyar, pp. 300–2.
2. Ibid.
3. Kalyvas, p. 154ff.
4. Hashim, p. 343.
5. Joes (2004), p. 156ff.
6. One recent example of political approach is *The United States Army/Marine Corps Counterinsurgency Manual* by Petraeus et al.
7. Politi, pp. 23–4, p. 75ff., pp. 96–7, p. 132, p. 153, p. 158, p. 181, p. 188. See also Lieb, p. 79; Beckett, p. 61ff.
8. Politi, p. 7, p. 16, p. 21, p. 196ff., pp. 26–8, p. 35.
9. Ibid., pp. 23–4, p. 75ff., pp. 96–7, p. 132, p. 153, p. 158, p. 181, p. 188. See also Lieb, p. 79; Beckett, p. 61ff.
10. On this theory see Leander; Sørensen.
11. Stubbs.
12. Mauceri.
13. Abinales.
14. Rich, p. 10.
15. Beckett, pp. 106–7, p. 194ff.
16. Joes (2004), p. 223.
17. Thomas D. Segel, 'Rules of Engagement Revisited', *New Media Journal*, 23 September 2009; Thomas D. Segel, 'Rules of Engagement and Other Stupid Decisions', *New Media Journal*, 14 September 2009.
18. Rich, pp. 7–9.
19. Beckett, p. 26.
20. Ibid., pp. 26–8; Reynaud.
21. Hashim, p. 322ff.; Aylwin-Foster.
22. Quoted in Kalyvas (2006), p. 115.
23. Childress, p. XIV–XV.
24. Ellis (1995), p. 51.
25. Ibid., p. 48.
26. Ives, pp. 620–22.
27. M. Tukhachevsky, cited in Beckett, p. 50.
28. See Giustozzi (2000).
29. Giustozzi (2010b).
30. Among others: Joes (2004), p. 113ff.; Statiev, p. 216ff.

31. Thayer, pp. 256–62.
32. Kalyvas (2006), p. 139.
33. Joes (2004), p. 110.
34. Clutterbuck, quoted in Kalyvas (2006), 138; see also Hashim, p. 333ff.
35. Kalyvas (2006), pp. 112–15, pp. 118–31.
36. Bergerud, p. 83.
37. Joes (2004), pp. 110–11.
38. Ibid., pp. 225–6.
39. See Giustozzi (2000) on this point.
40. Joes (2004), p. 113ff.
41. Waghelstein, p. 161.
42. Cann, p. 71ff.
43. Nagl, p. 132, p. 146.
44. Nagl as summarised in Aylwin-Foster, p. 10.
45. Waghelstein, p. 161; Porch and Muller, p. 184.
46. Personal communication with ISAF official, Kabul, 2009.
47. Politi. See also Lieb, p. 79.
48. Joes (2008), p. 46.
49. See Nagl on the Army's resistance to Kennedy's pressure to move away from conventional war, p. 134, and on the Army's eagerness for turning back to conventional warfare after 1975, p. 147.
50. Bacevich, p. 15.
51. Gen. Jack Keane, about Operation Iraqi Freedom, quoted in Nagl, pp. 147–8.
52. Vardys, Zhukov, Statiev.
53. Rajagopalan.
54. van Creveld, pp. 303–6.
55. Strachan.
56. Joes (2004), pp. 227–9.
57. Horton, pp. 200–1.
58. King, cit. in Robinson and Norsworthy, p. 260.
59. Robinson and Norsworthy, pp. 257–8; McCarl, p. 5.
60. Aylwin-Foster, p. 10.
61. Cheng.
62. Nagl.
63. Vick et al., p. 105; see also Childress and Bacevich, p. 15, p. 30, pp. 37–8; a somewhat less pessimistic assessment is in Schwarz, p. 18.
64. Spector, p. 299.
65. Jordan, p. 108.
66. Schow; Kreps.
67. Vick et al., pp. 106–7; Corum; Bacevich, pp. 32–3.
68. Tareke, pp. 134–7.
69. Walters.
70. See for example Dunlap.
71. See Kemsley.
72. Dunlap, pp. 53–4.

73. Personal communication with Christoph Zuercher, who visited old PKK camps in Azerbaijan (Berlin, 2007).
74. See most recently Jones (2008), p. 21ff., who refers to an as yet unpublished Rand study.
75. Becker; Sriskandarajah.
76. The argument was initially developed in Skocpol (1979).
77. See Giustozzi (2009a).
78. See Pereira (1997); Bisher (2005).
79. Scheina, p. 218; Farber, p. 119ff.
80. Howe, p. 79ff.
81. Ibid., p. 86.
82. Teitler, pp. 17–19.
83. Schmitt.
84. See among other works Reno (2002). On the ambiguous relationship between warlords and central government in Afghanistan see Giustozzi (2005).
85. O'Connell, p. 174.
86. For the example of the NPA in the Philippines see Abinales.
87. Ginifer and Peimani, pp. 255–7, pp. 154–5.
88. Tar.
89. Giustozzi (2007a); a similar argument is developed in Gat, p. 329. The strategy was adopted by the British empire in South Asia and then by the Afghan kings inside Afghanistan, see Giustozzi (2008a).
90. Howe, p. 211, citing US diplomat.
91. Howe, p. 211, p. 217, p. 218ff., p. 224.
92. Alie.
93. Tar.
94. See de Waal; Salih and Harir, pp. 186–203.
95. See Dorenwendt; Nourzhanov.
96. See for example Karl Vick, 'In Kurdish Turkey, a New Enemy', *Washington Post*, 31 Oct. 2002.
97. Miles, pp. 56–8.
98. See Giustozzi (2009a).
99. Akiner, p. 35ff.; Nourzhanov; Burnashev and Chernykh; Matveeva, p. 42.
100. Salmon, p. 35.
101. Pincus, pp. 144–5.
102. Pincus, p. 181.
103. Waghelstein, pp. 160–61.
104. Visser; Marius.
105. Dasgupta, p. 11.
106. Spector, pp. 280–81.
107. Akiner, 35ff.; Matveeva, p. 42.
108. Driscoll, p. 23ff.
109. Driscoll, p. 33ff.
110. Cramer.
111. See, with some caution, Herbst; Leander; Sørensen.
112. Reno (2004).

4. MAINTAINING THE MONOPOLY: THE ROLE OF POLITICAL POLICING

1. Appy, p. 361.
2. Lloyd Pomeroy, quoted in Moyar, p. 231.
3. Nagl on Vietnam, p. 142; Hunt, p. 234ff.; Moyar.
4. Kalyvas (2006), p. 174.
5. Brooks (1998), p. 37.
6. Chapman, pp. 24–6.
7. Dvornik, p. 10, pp. 14–5, pp. 22–3.
8. Ibid., p. 24, pp. 26–31, p. 34.
9. Ibid., p. 216ff.
10. Knight, p. 86.
11. Dvornik, p. 49ff.
12. Dvornik, p. 102ff., p. 108, p. 109; Sheldon, pp. 150–53, pp. 252–6.
13. Dvornik, pp. 129ff.; Sheldon, pp. 261–2.
14. di Paola, pp. 26–7, p. 86ff.
15. Sheldon, p. 264, p. 280.
16. Haynes, p. 242.
17. Deacon (1974), pp. 20–21.
18. Burrows, pp. 525–48.
19. Hingley, p. 38.
20. Stove, p. 116.
21. Ibid., p. 121.
22. Deacon (1974), p. 19, p. 21, p. 49.
23. Mazower, p. 4.
24. Chapman, p. 27ff.; Mazower, p. 5.
25. Chapman, p. 36.
26. Seward, p. 192.
27. Knight, p. 5; Deacon (1987), p. 48; Squire, p. 95, p. 105, p. 183.
28. Taylor, p. 177.
29. Mazower, p. 16.
30. Moran (1998).
31. Moran (1998); Moran (2003).
32. Rubin, p. 88ff.
33. Samraoui. The author defected from the Algerian services.
34. McMillan and Zoido.
35. Ibid.
36. Knight, pp. 8–9.
37. Mazower, p. 9.
38. Ibid., p. 5, p. 16.
39. Rejali, p. 4.
40. Sunderland, p. 45ff.; see also Rejali, p. 331.
41. Delannoy.
42. Politi, pp. 23–4, p. 75ff., pp. 96–7, p. 132, p. 153, p. 158, p. 181, p. 188. See also Lieb, p. 79; Beckett, p. 61ff.

43. Joes (2004), pp. 225–6.
44. Kalyvas (2006), pp. 108–9.
45. Sunderland, p. 15, p. 21.
46. Nagl, pp. 36–7.
47. Kalyvas (2006), p. 190, p. 125.
48. Chapman, pp. 63–4.
49. Leggett, pp. 232–3.
50. Gerson, pp. 113–18.
51. Browder, pp. 35–6, p. 63.
52. Gellatelly, p. 162, p. 164.
53. Callwell, p. 143.
54. Rejali.
55. Callwell, pp. 53–5.
56. Joes (2004), p. 147.
57. US Marine Corps, para 2.3.
58. Galula, p. 29.
59. O'Brien, pp. 31–2.
60. Sunderland, p. 21.
61. Goscha (2007).
62. Chapman, p. 82, p. 93.
63. Knight, p. 120.
64. Kohler, pp. 8–9.
65. On the functioning of the security services and their oversight in some democracies, see Gill.
66. Chapman, p. 110.
67. Knight, p. 12, p. 14, p. 17, p. 27, p. 33.
68. 'Survey of soviet intelligence', Washington: Intelligence Division, GSUSA, Department of the Army, p. 1948, p. 15, cit. in Knight, p. 256.
69. Burds.
70. Shelley, p. 40.
71. Knight, p. 50, p. 57ff., p. 184, p. 189, p. xvii.
72. Waghelstein, pp. 164–6.
73. Galula, p. 6.
74. Eickelman, pp. 103–4.
75. Bergman, p. 80.
76. Ibid., p. 85.
77. Kalyvas (2006), p. 175, p. 183, pp. 185–7.
78. Stove, p. 103.
79. Chapman, p. 93.
80. Ott, pp. 320–21.
81. Martin, pp. 358–9.
82. Chapman, p. 92; Limiti; De Lutiis.
83. Knight, p. xix.
84. Eickelman, pp. 102–3, p. 106.
85. Anderson.

86. Winchell.
87. Andrew and Gordievsky, p. 107.
88. Moran.
89. Rathmell.
90. Brooks (1998), p. 39.
91. Rathmell counts as many as 15, but includes private ones and military organisations such as the National Guard.
92. al-Marashi and Salama, p. 146ff.
93. Brooks (1998), p. 52.
94. al-Marashi, p. 146ff.
95. Spector, p. 316; Rosenau, p. 41ff.
96. Rosenau, p. 53.
97. Hutchful, p. 80, p. 86.
98. Stove, p. 153.
99. Goscha (2002), pp. 45–6.
100. Moyar, pp. 306–7
101. Horton, pp. 181–2, p. 214, p. 212; Miranda and Ratliff, p. 191.
102. Miranda and Ratliff, pp. 199–200.
103. This point is discussed at length in Rejali.

5. MAINTAINING THE MONOPOLY: THE POLITICAL MICROMANAGEMENT OF POPULATION CONTROL

1. Shaw, p. 91.
2. Ibid., p. 40, p. 83ff.; Findley, p. 156ff.
3. Findley, pp. 156–63.
4. Ibid., p. 165.
5. Shaw, p. 213.
6. Brigadier S. K. Sinha, quoted in Rajagopalan, 165. Rajagopalan mentions other Indian officers who expressed the same view.
7. Dadi, p. 161.
8. Trigger, p. 54; see also pp. 56–7.
9. Finer (1997), vol. II, pp. 683–4.
10. FitzGerald, p. 324.
11. Finer (1997), vol. III, p. 1143, pp. 1616–18, p. 1143, p. 1194, p. 1243; vol. II, p. 631.
12. Finer (1997), vol. II, pp. 679–83; vol. I, p. 303ff., p. 297ff.
13. Bonine and Keddie, p. 167.
14. Finer (1997), p. vol. I, p. 540ff., p. 162.
15. Clapham (1977), p. 10.
16. Howard, p. 60ff.
17. Mathew and Nayak; Raju; 'India powers anti-Naxal Panchayati punch', *Financial Express*, 9 June 2010; Alsop et al.
18. Finer (1997), vol. I, pp. 226–7.

19. Finer (1997), vol. I, p. 498ff.; vol. II, p. 765ff., p. 833–7.
20. Grossheim, p. 56ff.
21. Finer (1997), vol. III, p. 1283.
22. Petersen.
23. Robbins, p. 8ff., p. 13, p. 16, p. 21ff.
24. Robbins, p. 88, pp. 183–5, p. 194ff., p. 92ff., p. 127ff.
25. Marr, p. 29, pp. 31–2.
26. Finer (1997), vol. I, p. 162 and p. 148ff., about the Kingdom of Egypt.
27. Lapidus, pp. 60–61, pp. 122–3.
28. Marr, p. 32.
29. See Leonhard.
30. Marr, p. 29.
31. Kiser and Baer, p. 233, p. 229.
32. Bonine and Keddie, p. 71.
33. Clapham (1977), p. 48.
34. Howard, pp. 137–8.
35. Keller, p. 75.
36. Dows, p. 5.
37. Ibid., p. 59.
38. Peters, p. 88.
39. Dows, p. 69ff.; Migdal, p. 209, p. 242.
40. Sinno, pp. 73–4.
41. Kiser and Baer, pp. 232–3.
42. Dows, p. 145ff.
43. Colton citing Dows, pp. 85–6.
44. Kiser and Baer, p. 234.
45. Ibid., pp. 234–5.
46. Dows, p. 234ff.
47. Ibid., p. 237ff.
48. Marr, p. 48; Minh, p. 95, pp. 98–9, p. 100.
49. Clapham (1977).
50. Dows, pp. 156–7.
51. Migdal, p. 209.
52. Ibid., pp. 209–10.
53. Ibid., p. 213.
54. Migdal, pp. 217–18.
55. Ibid., pp. 220–21; he mentions in particular Kaunda of Zambia as a master of this art.
56. Kiser and Baer, p. 243.
57. Migdal, p. 238ff.
58. Ibid., pp. 240–42; Dows, p. 134.
59. Migdal, p. 247, p. 250, p. 253, pp. 255–6.
60. Burr, pp. 65–6.
61. Beckett, pp. 40–41.
62. M. Tukhachevsky, cited in Beckett, p. 50.

63. Vardys, Zhukov.
64. Politi, pp. 26–8, p. 35.
65. Dadi, p. 75, p. 79, p. 80, p. 82ff.; Nolutshungu, p. 56, p. 54; Decalo, pp. 39–41.
66. Decalo, pp. 40–41.
67. Lemarchand.
68. Nolutshungu, p. 35.
69. Ibid., p. 72ff.
70. Ibid., p. 176.
71. Grossheim, pp. 73–4.
72. FitzGerald, p. 397.
73. Herring and Rangwala, pp. 114–27.
74. Samatar, p. 118.
75. FitzGerald, pp. 397–8, p. 435.
76. Ibid., p. 441.
77. Ellis (1995), pp. 166–7, p. 188, p. 190, p. 196.
78. Lemarchand, p. 35.
79. Baker (2007), pp. 358–60.
80. Website of the Royal Tropical Institute (accessed 30 July 2010): http://www.kit.
    nl/eCache/FAB/2/046.html.

6. EXTERNAL INTERVENTION AND THE MONOPOLY: KICKING AWAY THE LADDER?

1. Wilbur and How, p. 15, p. 160, p. 238; Berleb, p. 54; Liu, p. 19.
2. Wilbur and How, p. 250, p. 414; Berleb, p. 57.
3. Berleb, p. 116.
4. Sutton, pp. 386–410.
5. Berleb, p. 119, pp. 135–6, pp. 198–9, p. 209ff., p. 215.
6. Sutton, p. 388.
7. Berleb, p. 201.
8. Kirby, pp. 58–9.
9. Sutton, pp. 398–9.
10. Berleb, pp. 121–2.
11. Liu, p. 182.
12. Dunn, p. 15, p. 19.
13. Sater, p. 80ff.
14. Atkins and Thompson.
15. Nicolle and Ruggeri, p. 17ff.
16. Joffe, pp. 41–2.
17. Miranda and Ratliff, pp. 206–9; however, the same authors acknowledge that
    already in 1983 Humberto Ortega argued before the National Directorate the
    need to restructure the whole army to face the insurgency, introduce drafting, and
    develop irregular warfare battalions; at that point Ochoa had only paid a brief
    visit to Nicaragua and it seems unlikely that his opinion in this regard might have

sufficed to have a major impact on Ortega, who was not so close to him yet (204).

18. Ramsey, pp. 96–7, pp. 18–19.
19. Brazinsky, p. 71.
20. Ibid., p. 78.
21. Clarke, pp. 159ff.; Ramsey, p. 57.
22. Van Vien et al., p. 153ff.
23. Clarke, p. 308, pp. 363–5, pp. 482–3.
24. See Loveman on this point.
25. Ibid., p. 85ff., p. 92ff.
26. See Pollack on this.
27. de Atkine.
28. See McCoy on the Senegalese army.
29. Rosenau, p. 64.
30. Beevor, p. 177, p. 288; Krivitsky, p. 117ff.; Radosh, p. 72, p. 81ff.
31. Radosh, passim.
32. Ibid., pp. 66–9, pp. 261–2, p. 475, p. 488ff.
33. Hickey, p. 14.
34. Spector, p. 345.
35. Sullivan, p. 48.
36. Ramsey, pp. 96–7.
37. Pascal, pp. 16–18.
38. Ibid., p. 21.
39. Walmsley, p. 28.
40. Andrew and Mitrokhin, pp. 390–91.
41. Walmsley, p. 50.
42. Pollack, pp. 427–8.
43. Westermann, p. 132, p. 134.
44. Van Vien et al., p. 66.
45. Clarke, pp. 473–4.
46. McCoy, p. 20.
47. Howe, p. 45.
48. Clayton, p. 81; Afoaku, p. 229.
49. See Giustozzi and Kalinovsky.
50. Langer and Zasloff (1968), p. 34.
51. Langer and Zasloff (1968).
52. Ibid. and (1969), p. 143ff.
53. Ramsey, p. 57; Spector, pp. 280–81.
54. Hickey, p. 25.
55. See Giustozzi and Kalinovsky.
56. See Joes (2004), pp. 134ff. on this point.
57. Zhdarkin, pp. 306–12, pp. 369, pp. 370–71.
58. Henderson, pp. 4–6.
59. Dunn, p. 15, p. 17.
60. Brooks (1998), pp. 29–31, p. 46.

61. Rosenau, p. 17.
62. Spector, p. 300.
63. Ibid., p. 257, pp. 275–6, p. 268, pp. 271–2, pp. 119–20.
64. Hosmer, p. 14 n.12, p. 12.
65. Cale; Childress, XIV; Bacevich et al., p. 25, p. 28.
66. Joffe, pp. 42–3.
67. Grunow, p. 16.
68. Porch and Muller, p. 180.
69. Schwarz, pp. 19–21.
70. Sullivan, pp. 38–9.
71. Bailey, pp. 23–4.
72. Sullivan, p. 35; Bailey, p. 20, p. 25 (Congress had banned American advisers from going on operations and they were violating the rules by doing so).
73. Sullivan, pp. 48–9.
74. Christian, pp. 18–19.
75. Stoker, p. 56.
76. Vercamer; Chern, pp. 319–50; Berleb, p. 191ff.; Kirby, pp. 21–3, p. 120ff.
77. Atkins and Thompson.
78. Speartin, p. 227ff.
79. Howe, p. 187ff.
80. Walmsley, p. 57ff.
81. For a US army assessment of the performance of the Colombians from 1998 onwards, see Haddick.
82. de Atkine.
83. Pascal, p. 2.
84. Spector, p. 300; Joes (2004), p. 134ff.
85. Nagl, p. 132.
86. Ibid., p. 146.
87. Childress, XVI.
88. Howe, p. 42, pp. 49–50.
89. Herbst, p. 2004, p. 359.
90. Howe, p. 42.
91. See Giustozzi (2000).
92. Personal communications with former officers, Kabul, 2008–9.
93. Government Accountability Office.
94. Vick et al., p. 106; Childress, pp. 32–3; Waghelstein, p. 159.
95. Vick et al., p. 106; Bacevich et al., pp. 29–30.
96. Horton, p. 215.
97. Miranda and Ratliff, pp. 222–3.
98. Ethiopian Major General, quoted in Tareke, p. 164.
99. Wagelstein, p. 160.
100. McCarl, p. 151.
101. see Giustozzi (2008a), for the case of Afghanistan.
102. On Arab armies see Pollack; on Hezbollah see Norton (2000) and (2006); Cordesman; Exum; on Iran's military doctrine (which influenced Hezbollah) see Ward.

103. Walmsley, p. 64ff. and passim.
104. Bacevich et al., p. 31. See also Waghelstein, p. 156.
105. Westermann, p. 145.
106. Ibid., pp. 159–60.
107. Schwarz, pp. 19–21.
108. Yusuf, p. 23.
109. See for example AfghanAid; BAAG and ENNA; Waldman, 2008.
110. Combating Terrorism Center, p. 65.
111. Fellowship of Reconciliation and US Office on Colombia.
112. Mackenzie (1951), p. 61; Hyde, pp. 125–6.
113. See Giustozzi (2000).
114. Ramsey, p. 54.
115. FitzGerald, p. 375.
116. See on this point Urban; Giustozzi (2000).
117. Carney.
118. Bekaert, pp. 178–80, p. 303, p. 276, p. 303.
119. George.
120. Brazinsky, ch. 3.
121. Giustozzi (2010a); the Khalqis were a faction of the leftist party in power from 1978 and they resented what they considered Soviet favouritism for the rival Parcham faction.
122. In order to offset nationalist sentiment, an external threat has to be serious and credible. Remarkably, in 2007 an opinion poll found that 40 per cent of Germans considered the US a greater threat than Iran (Claus Christian Malzahn, 'Evil Americans, Poor Mullahs', *Der Spiegel*, 29 March 2007).
123. See Giustozzi (2007d) and (2009c).
124. See Giustozzi (2009d).
125. Smith.
126. See Synge.
127. On this point see Mehler.
128. Paris, p. 98.
129. Woodward; Berdal.
130. See Lakhdar Brahimi, 'A New Path for Afghanistan', *Washington Post*, 7 December 2008.
131. Giustozzi (2007b).
132. Barnett and Zürcher, p. 24, p. 31, p. 36.
133. Stevenson (1995) and (2007); Fleitz, p. 130ff.
134. Roberts; Heder.
135. Jones (2001).
136. Luttwak.
137. Clarke and Herbst; Peterson; Greg Jaffe and Karen DeYoung, 'Obama Team Mulls Aims Of Somali Extremists', *Washington Post*, 11 April 2009; Scott Baldauf, 'Kenya poised to intervene in Somalia', *Christian Science Monitor*, 25 June 2009.
138. Weinstein; Wagner; Licklider.

139. Tollefson.
140. Chaturvedi, pp. 8–12.
141. Huggins, p. 35ff., p. 39, pp. 28–9.
142. Ibid., p. 33ff.
143. Westney, p. 50.
144. Aldous, pp. 211–13.
145. Ames, p. 216.
146. Goldsmith and Dinnen, p. 1094.
147. Ferguson.
148. See also Call (2003), pp. 2–3 for a somewhat different categorisation.
149. Law.
150. Pino and Wiatrowski, p. 68.
151. Hills (2009), p. 76.
152. Nield.
153. Ferguson.
154. Brogden, p. 88.
155. Stromseth et al., p. 379, pp. 50–55; see also Blume.
156. Blume; Brogden and Nijhar, p. 135ff.
157. Brogden and Nijhar, p. 150.
158. Call (2007), p. 45.
159. Frühling, p. 27ff.
160. Hills (2009), p. 101.
161. Libra and CDS.
162. Huggins, pp. 6–7.
163. Uildriks, pp. 213–14.
164. Loveman, p. 71.
165. Deuve, pp. 154–7, p. 162.
166. Beidas et al., pp. 84–5.
167. Ladwig III.
168. Lobe, pp. 99–100.
169. Rosenau, p. 126 for the case of Vietnam.
170. Hills (2009), p. 168, p. 128.
171. See for example Baker (2008), pp. 141–2 on Sierra Leone.
172. Huggins, pp. 11–12.
173. Call (2003), p. 4.
174. Lobe, p. 106.
175. Muehlmann, p. 4, p. 13.
176. Rathmell et al., p. 53.
177. Muehlmann, p. 4, p. 13.
178. Hills (2009), p. 155ff.
179. See ibid., p. 119, p. 125ff.
180. Stanley and Call; Call (2007), pp. 38–9.
181. Beidas et al., pp. 83–90.
182. Ibid., pp. 84–5. The creation of Haiti police was for a while the success story of institution building in Haiti.

183. Hills (2000), p. 75, p. 77.
184. Celador, p. 372.
185. Glebbeek, p. 93.
186. Lobe, pp. 27–8.
187. Ibid., p. 37, p. 47ff., p. 71ff.
188. Deuve, p. 48.
189. Muehlmann, p. 4, p. 13.
190. Doyle, pp. 244–5.
191. Pérouse de Montclos, p. 47.
192. Solomon.
193. Stanley.
194. Lobe, p. 37, p. 47ff., p. 71ff., p. 106.
195. Ibid., p. 77, p. 83ff.
196. Lobe, p. 76.
197. International Crisis Group (2001), pp. 10–11.
198. Hills (2000), p. 32.
199. United Nations General Assembly, *Report of the High-Level Panel on Threats, Challenges and Change*, New York, Dec. 2004, p. 61.
200. Berdal, p. 37.
201. On the Italian case, see for more details the introduction to Giustozzi (forthcoming 2011a).
202. See Bettini.
203. See Giustozzi (forthcoming 2011a).
204. Striuli.
205. Giustozzi (forthcoming 2011b).
206. De Goede (forthcoming 2011).
207. Rossi and Giustozzi.
208. Eickelman, p. 96.
209. Zervoudaikis, p. 202.
210. Van Vien et al., p. 81ff. for a discussion of the case in Vietnam.
211. Zervoudaikis, p. 209.
212. Rosenau, p. 65, p. 124–5.
213. Diáz Fernández, pp. 101–2; Radosh, p. 476, p. 496ff.
214. Radosh, pp. 264–8, pp. 276–9, p. 181ff.
215. Ra'anan and Lukes, p. 216.

7. BEYOND THE MONOPOLY: ORIGINS AND DEVELOPMENT OF POLICING

1. Yasin, pp. 56–7, pp. 69–70, p. 111.
2. Examples of how it worked before incorporation into the state are described in Tariq; Schmeidl and Karokhail; Ghosh, 158ff.
3. Reith.
4. Bayley (1985), p. 37, p. 43.

5. Pereira, p. 388.
6. Stackelberg, p. 113ff.
7. Pereira, p. 391.
8. Lobe, p. 67ff.
9. Baker (2008), p. 63.
10. Hills (2000), pp. 149–50, pp. 169–70. See also Heald. On the use of vigilante groups and militias in Uganda under Museveni, see Ruooko.
11. For the case of the Bakassi Boys in Onitsha, see Thorning, p. 103.
12. Hills (2009), p. 183.
13. On the case of the PAGAD vigilantes in the Western Cape province of South Africa, see Baker (2008), p. 82.
14. Baker (2008), p. 69.
15. Tupman and Tupman, p. 19.
16. Also Skalnik, pp. 599–600.
17. Robinson and Scaglion (1994); Robinson and Scaglion (1987), pp. 109–54.
18. Quoted in Foucault, p. 359.
19. Robinson and Scaglion (1994); Robinson and Scaglion (1987), pp. 109–54.
20. Spitzer.
21. Reith.
22. Bayley (1985), p. 45, p. 38, p. 46, p. 47, p. 71.
23. Foucault, p. 385.
24. Marenin, p. 127.
25. Bayley (1985), pp. 40–2.
26. Liang, p. 14.
27. Sen Gupta, p. 81.
28. Moore, p. 109ff.
29. Diamond, pp. 282–3, p. 289.
30. Personal communication with Thomas Barfield, Istanbul, June 2009.
31. Weber, pp. 811–12.
32. Mohammadi, p. 52.
33. Khadduri, pp. 83–6.
34. Tamayo y Salmoran.
35. Tierney, pp. 344–5.
36. Holmes, p. 26.
37. Holmes, pp. 26–7, pp. 36–7.
38. Ibid., pp. 32–3.
39. Both cited in Foucault, pp. 358–9.
40. Liang, p. 26.
41. Gottesman, p. 247ff.
42. International Crisis Group (2002), p. 16.
43. Shelley, p. 44.
44. Ibid., p. 50ff.
45. Carothers (1998); Carothers (2006), p. 21.
46. Holmes, p. 60.
47. Carothers (1998), p. 4.

48. Bayley (1982).
49. Brogden and Nijhar, pp. 68–9.
50. Brewer et al.
51. See for example on Uganda, Mushemeza; on Nigeria, Hills (2008).
52. Baker (2008), pp. 140–1.
53. Brewer et al.
54. Miranda and Ratliff, p. 227, pp. 33–4; Molero, p. 169.
55. Ejkman, p. 104.
56. Brogden and Nijhar, p. 149.
57. Pérouse de Montclos, 41; the author points to a similarity with some European countries in the nineteenth century (Italy).
58. Batalas.
59. Interviews with police officers, Kabul and the provinces, 2003–7.
60. Stanley and Call.
61. Galula, p. 31.
62. Baker (2008), pp. 107–9; Baker (2005), p. 27.
63. Baker (2007), p. 352.
64. Hills (2009), p. 167.
65. Stanley, pp. 117–8.
66. Westney, pp. 80–81.
67. Bayley (1985), p. 65, p. 67.
68. Hills (2000), p. 35.
69. For the example of the Philippines, see Campos.
70. Hualing, p. 250.
71. This danger is in my view implicit in attempts to describe the evolution of police forces in underdeveloped countries such as Alice Hills' (2008), who uses Hegel's dialectic to interpret local dynamics.
72. Bayley (1985), p. 47.
73. Turk, pp. 23–4.
74. Fleming and Rhodes, pp. 192–205.
75. Ibid., p. 194.
76. Bayley (1985), pp. 162–7, pp. 178–80.
77. Call (2003), p. 9.
78. Bayley (1985), pp. 162–7, pp. 167–70, p. 185.
79. Chaturvedi, p. 58.
80. Ibid., table 4.18 and p. 83.
81. Verma, p. 267.
82. Ibid., pp. 268–9, p. 195.
83. International Crisis Group (2001), pp. 5–6.
84. Hills (2008).
85. Ejkman, pp. 125–6, p. 134.
86. Chaturvedi, p. 59.
87. Westney, pp. 58–9.
88. Shelley; Hualing.
89. Shelley, p. 50.

90. Hills, p. 106.
91. Yasin, p. 161, p. 164.
92. Robbins, pp. 183–5.
93. Lefever, p. 168.
94. Yasin, p. 167; Chaudhry, p. 69, p. 100, pp. 109–10, p. 166.
95. Baker (2007), pp. 350–51; Hills, pp. 147–8.
96. Hutchful, p. 87.
97. Deuve, p. 94.
98. Dhungana.
99. Bayley (1985), p. 48.
100. Lévy, p. 156.
101. Pérouse de Montclos, p. 49.
102. International Crisis Group (2002), p. 24ff.
103. Hualing.
104. See for example Baker (2007), p. 353.
105. Hills (2000), p. 41.
106. Ibid., p. 15.
107. Baker (2008), pp. 70–71, pp. 107–9.

CONCLUSION

1. Zolo, p. 21.
2. Brzoska.
3. For a preliminary discussion of the problem see Brogden, p. 67ff.

SELECT BIBLIOGRAPHY

Abinales, Patricio (1997), 'State-building, communist insurgency and cacique politics in the Philippines', in Rich, Paul B. and Stubbs, Richard (eds.), *The Counter-insurgent State*, Basingstoke: Macmillan.

AfghanAid (n.d.), 'Quick Impact, Quick Collapse: The Dangers of Militarized Aid in Afghanistan' (http://www.afghanaid.org.uk/data/files/quick_impact_quick_collapse.pdf), London: AfghanAid.

Afoaku, Osita G. (2003), 'Between dictatorship and democracy', in Ihonvbere, Julius Omozuanvbo and Mbaku, John Mukum (eds.), *Political Liberalization and Democratization in Africa: Lessons from Country Experiences*, Westport: Greenwood Press.

Aguilar, Louis E. (1989), 'From immutable proclamations to unintended consequences: Marxism-Leninism and the Cuban government, 1959–1986', in Horowitz, Irving Louis (ed.), *Cuban Communism*, Brunswick: Transaction Publishers.

Agyeman-Duah, Baffour (1994), *The United States and Ethiopia*, Lanham: University Press of America.

Akiner, Shirin (2002), *Tajikistan: Disintegration or Reconciliation?*, London: Royal Institute of International Affairs.

Al-Azmeh, Aziz (1982), *Ibn-Khaldun: An Essay in Reinterpretation*, London: Frank Cass.

al-Marashi, Ibrahim (2002), 'Iraq's Security and Intelligence Network: A Guide and Analysis', *Middle East Review of International Affairs*, vol. 6, no. 3, September.

al-Marashi, Ibrahim and Salama, Sammy (2008), *Iraq's Armed Forces*, London: Routledge.

Aldous, Christopher (1997), *The Police in Occupation Japan: Control, corruption and resistance to reform*, London and New York: Routledge.

Alie, Jope (2005), 'The Kamajor militia in Sierra Leone: liberators or nihilists?', in Francis, David J. (ed.), *Civil Militia*, Aldershot: Ashgate.

Allawi, Ali A. (2007), *The Occupation of Iraq: Winning the War, Losing the Peace*, New Haven: Yale University Press.

Allen, C. (1995), 'Understanding African Politics', *Review of African Political Economy*, no. 65.

Alsop, Ruth J. et al. (n.d.), *Inclusion and local elected governments: the panchayat raj system in India*, Washington: World Bank.

Ames, Walter L. (1981), *Police and Community in Japan*, Berkeley: University of California Press.

Anastasoff, Christ (1938), *The Tragic Peninsula: A History of the Macedonian Movement for Independence Since 1878*, St Louis: Blackwell Wielandy.

Anderson, Julie (2006), 'The Chekist takeover of the Russian state', *International Journal of Intelligence and Counterintelligence*, vol. 19, no. 2, pp. 237–88.

Anderson, Mary B. and Duffield, Mark (1998), 'Doing the right thing?', *New Routes*, 3:3.

Andreski, Stanislaw (1958), *Military Organization and Society*, London: Routledge & Paul.

Andrew, Christopher and Gordievsky, Oleg (1992), *KGB: the inside story of its foreign operations from Lenin to Gorbachev*, London: Hodder & Stoughton.

Andrew, Christopher and Mitrokhin, Vasili (2006), *The world was going our way*, New York: Basic Books.

Appy, Christian G. (2003), *Patriots: The Vietnam War Remembered from All Sides*, New York: Penguin Books.

Aron, Raymond (1966), *Peace and War: A Theory of International Relations*, Garden City, NY: Doubleday.

Atkine, Norville de (2000), 'Why Arabs Lose Wars', *Middle East Review of International Affairs*, vol. 4, no. 1.

Atkins, George Pope and Thompson, Larry V. (1972), 'German Military Influence in Argentina, 1921–1940', *Journal of Latin American Studies*, vol. 4, no. 2 (Nov.), pp. 257–74.

Aylwin-Foster, Nigel (2005), 'Changing the Army for Counterinsurgency Operations', *Military Review*, Nov.-Dec.

Ayoob, Mohammed (2007), 'State-making, state breaking, and state failure', in Crocker, Chester A., Hampson, Fen Osler, Aall, Pamela R. (eds.), *Leashing the Dogs of War: conflict management in a divided world*, Washington: USIP Press.

Azevedo, Mario J. (1998), *Roots of Violence: A History of War in Chad*, London: Routledge.

BAAG and ENNA (n.d.), 'Aid and Civil-Military Relations in Afghanistan', policy briefing, London: British Agencies Afghanistan Group.

Baali, Fuad (1988), *Society, State and Urbanism: Ibn Khaldun's sociological thought*, New York: State University of New York Press.

Bacevich, A. J. (1988), *American Military Policy in Small Wars: the case of El Salvador*, London: Pergamon.

Bailey, Cecil E. (2004), 'OPATT: The U.S. Army SF Advisers in El Salvador', *Special Warfare*, Dec., vol. 17, no. 2.

Baker, Bruce (2005), 'Multi-choice policing in Uganda', *Policing and Society*, vol. 15:1.

Baker, Bruce (2007), 'Reconstructing a Policing System Out of the Ashes: Rwanda's Solution', *Policing and Society*, vol. 17:4, pp. 344–66.

Baker, Bruce (2008), *Multi-choice Policing in Africa*, Uppsala: Nordiska Afrikainstitut.

Barnett, Michael and Zürcher, Christoph (2009), 'The peacebuilder's contract: how external state-building reinforced weak statehood', in Paris, R. and Sisk, T. D. (eds.), *The Dilemmas of State-building*, London: Routledge.

Batalas, Achilles (2003), 'Send a chief to catch a chief', in Davis, Diane and Pereira, Anthony W. (eds.), *Irregular Armed Forces and their Role in Politics and State Formation*, Cambridge: Cambridge University Press.

Bates, Robert H. (2001), *Prosperity and Violence: the political economy of development*, New York: Norton.

Bayley, D. H. (1982), 'A world perspective on the role of police in social control', in Donelan, R. (ed.), *The Maintenance of Order in Society*, Ottawa: Canadian Police College.

Bayley, D. H. (1985), *Patterns of Policing*, Fredericksburg: Rutgers.

Beal, Jo and Fox, Sean (2009), *Cities and Development*, London: Routledge.

Becker, Jo (2007), 'LTTE Intimidation and Extortion in the Tamil Diaspora, and the Canadian Government Response', Paper presented to the IRPP Symposium 'Protecting Security and Human Rights: The Case of Migration in Canada', 20–21 Sept., Ottawa.

Beckett, Ian F. W. (2001), *Modern Insurgencies and Counter-insurgencies: Guerrillas and Their Opponents Since 1750*, London: Routledge.

Beckett, Ian F. W. and Pimlott, John (eds.) (1985), *Armed Forces and Modern Counter Insurgency*, London: Croom Helm.

Beevor, Antony (1982), *The Spanish Civil War*, London: Cassell.

Beidas, Sandra et al. (2007), 'Justice and security reform after intervention: Haiti', in Call, C. T. (ed.), *Constructing Justice and Security After War*, Washington: USIP Press.

Bekaert, Jacques (1998), *Cambodian Diary: a long road to peace 1987–1993*, Bangkok: White Lotus.

Belkin, Aaron (2005), *United we stand? Divide-and-conquer politics and the logic of international hostility*, New York: State University of New York Press.

Benjamin, Walter (1974*)*, *Gesammelten Schriften* I:2, Frankfurt am Main: Suhrkamp Verlag.

Berdal, Mats (1996), *Disarmament and Demobilisation After Civil Wars*, London: Adelphi Papers 303.

Berdal, Mats and Leifer, Michael (1996), 'Cambodia', in Mayall, J. (ed.), *The New Interventionism 1991–1994*, Cambridge: Cambridge University Press.

Bergerud, Eric M. (1991*)*, *The Dynamics of Defeat: the Vietnam war in Hau Nghia province*, Boulder: Westview.

Bergman, Ronen (2007), *The Secret War with Iran*, New York: Free Press.

Berleb, Stefan (2005), '...For China's benefit...': the evolution and devolution of German military influence on Chinese military affairs, 1919–38*, Dissertation, Brisbane: Queensland University of Technology.

Bettini, Emanuele (1996), *Gladio. La Repubblica parallela*, Rome : Ediesse.

Bisher, Jamie (2005), *White terror: Cossack Warlords of the Trans-Siberian Railway*, London: Frank Cass.

Blume, Till (2008), 'Implementing the rule of law in integrated missions. Security and justice in the UN mission in Liberia (UNMIL)', *Journal of Security Sector Management*, vol. 6 (3).

Bonine, Michael E. and Keddie, Nikki R. (1981), *Modern Iran: The Dialectics of Continuity and Change*, Albany, NY: State University of New York Press.

Brazinsky, Gregg (2007), *Nation-building in South Korea*, Chapel Hill: UNC Press.

Bremer, L. Paul (2006), *My Year in Iraq: the struggle to build a future of hope*, London: Simon & Schuster.

Brewer, John D. et al. (1988), *The police, public order and the state*, London: Macmillan.

Brogden, Mike (2005), '"Horses for courses" and "thin blue lines": Community policing in transitional society', *Police Quarterly*, pt. 8, pp. 64–98.

Brogden, Mike and Nijhar, Preeti (2005), *Community Policing*, Portland: Willan Publishing.

Brooks, Risa A. (1998), *Political-Military Relations and the Stability of Arab Regimes*, London: IISS, Adelphi Paper 324.

Brooks, Risa A. (2007a), 'Introduction', in Brooks, Risa A. and Stanley, Elizabeth A. (eds.), *Creating Military Power: the sources of military effectiveness*, Stanford: Stanford University Press.

Brooks, Risa A. (2007b), 'Civil-military relations and military effectiveness', in Brooks, Risa A. and Stanley, Elizabeth A. (eds.), *Creating Military Power: the sources of military effectiveness*, Stanford: Stanford University Press.

Browder, George C. (1990), *Foundations of the Nazi Police State*, Lexington: University Press of Kentucky.

Brunk, Samuel (1995), *Emiliano Zapata: Revolution and Betrayal in Mexico*, Albuquerque: University of New Mexico Press.

Bryden, Alan and Hänggi, Heiner (2005), Security Governance in Post-Conflict Peacebuilding, Geneva: Centre for the Democratic Control of Armed Forces.

Brzoska, Michael (2003), *Development Donors and the Concept of Security Sector Reform*, Geneva: DCAF, Occasional Paper no. 4.

Buijtenhuijs, Robert (1987), *Le Frolinat et les guerres civiles du Tchad (1977–1984)*, Paris: Karthala.

Burds, Jeffrey (2007), 'The Soviet War against "Fifth Columnists": The Case of Chechnya 1942–4', *Journal of Contemporary History*, vol. 42:2.

Burnashev, Rustam and Chernykh, Irina (2002), 'The Armed Forces of the Republic of Tajikistan', *Central Asia and the Caucasus*, no. 13 [http://www.ca-c.org/online/2002/journal_eng/cac-06/13.bureng.shtml].

Burrows, Simon (2004), 'Despotism without Bounds: The French Secret Police and the Silencing of Dissent in London, 1760–1790', *History*, vol. 89, issue 296, pp. 525–48.

Byman, Daniel L. (2006), 'Friends Like These: Counterinsurgency and the War on Terrorism', *International Security*, vol. 31, no. 2, pp. 79–115.

Cale, Paul P. (1996), *The United States Military Advisory Group in El Salvador, 1979–1992*, Quantico: US Marine Corps Command and Staff College thesis.

Call, Charles T. (2003), *Challenges in Police Reform: Promoting Effectiveness and Accountability*, New York: International Peace Academy.

Call, Charles T. (2007), 'The mugging of a success story: justice and security reform in El Salvador', in Call, C. T. (ed.), *Constructing Justice and Security After War*, Washington: USIP Press.

Callwell, Charles (1906), *Small Wars: their principles and practice*, East Ardsley: HMSO.

Cambrensis, Geraldus (1194), *The Description of Wales*, edited by J. M. Dent 1912, Oxford: Mississippi 1997.

Campos, Cicero C. (1991), 'Law enforcement policy strategy in the Republic of the Philippines', *Police Studies: International Review of Police Development*, no. 76.

Cann, John P. (1997), *Counterinsurgency in Africa: The Portuguese Way of War, 1961–1974*, Westport: Greenwood Press.

Carney, Timothy (1986), 'Heng Samrin's armed forces and the military balance in Cambodia', *International Journal of Politics*, vol. 16, pt. 3, pp. 180–212.

Carothers, Thomas (1998), 'Rule of Law Revival', *Foreign Affairs*, vol. 77, no. 2.

Carothers, Thomas (2006), 'The problem of knowledge', in Carothers, T. (ed.), *Promoting the Rule of Law Abroad*, Washington: Carnegie Endowment for International Peace.

Cawtra, Gavin and Luckham, Robin (eds.) (2003), *Governing Insecurity*, London: Zed Books.

Celador, Gemma Collantes (2005), 'Police reform: Peacebuilding through "democratic policing"?', *International Peacekeeping*, 12: 3, pp. 364–76.

Cerny, Philip G. (1998), 'Neomedievalism, civil war, and the new security dilemma', *Civil Wars*, 1: 1 (spring), pp. 36–64.

Chabal, Patrick, and Daloz, Jean-Pascal (1999), *Africa Works*, London: James Currey.

Chapman, Brian (1970), *Police State*, London: Pall Mall Press.

Chaturvedi, S. K. (1988), *Rural Policing in India*, New Delhi: BR Publishing Corporation.

Chaudhry, M. A. K. (1997), *Policing in Pakistan*, Lahore: Vanguard.

Cheng, Victor Shiu Chiang (2007), *Modern Military Technology in Counterinsurgency Warfare: The Experience of the Nationalist Army during the Chinese Civil War*, Working Paper 20, Lund, Sweden: Centre for East and South-East Asian Studies, Lund University.

Chern, Chen (2002), 'The German Military Advisory Group in Nationalist China, 1963–1975', *Annual of the Chinese Society for Military History Studies*, vol. 7 (April), pp. 319–50.

Childress, Michael (1995), *The effectiveness of US training in internal defense and development: the cases of El Salvador and Honduras*, Santa Monica: Rand.

Christian, Patrick J. (2007), 'Guerrillas in the Mist', *Special Warfare*, vol. 20:3.

Claessen, H. M. and Oosten, J. G. (eds.) (1996), *Ideology and the Formation of Early States*, Leiden: Brill.

Clapham, Christopher (1977), 'Ethiopia', in *African Kingships in Perspective: Political Change and Modernization in Monarchical Settings*, London: Routledge.

Clapham, Christopher (1988), *Transformation and Continuity in Revolutionary Ethiopia*, Cambridge: Cambridge University Press.

Clarke, Jeffrey J. (1988), *Advice and Support: The final years*, Washington: Center of Military History.

Clarke, Walter and Herbst, Jeffrey (1996), 'Somalia and the Future of Humanitarian Intervention', *Foreign Affairs*, March/April.

Clayton, Anthony (1999), *Frontiersmen: Warfare in Africa Since 1950*, London: Taylor & Francis.

Close, David (1990), 'Responding to low-intensity conflict: counter-insurgency in Sandinista Nicaragua', *New Political Science*, 9:1, pp. 5–19.

Cohen, Ronald (1985), 'Warfare and state formation', in Claessen, H. M. et al., *Development and Decline: the evolution of sociopolitical organization*, South Hadley: Bergin & Garvey.

Cohen, Youssef et al. (1981), 'The Paradoxical Nature of State-Making: The Violent Creation of Order', *American Political Science Review*, vol. 75, no. 4, pp. 901–10.

Colton, Timothy J. (1979), *Commissars, Commanders and Civilian Authority: the structure of Soviet military politics*, Cambridge: Harvard University Press.

Combating Terrorism Center, *Al-Qa'ida's (mis)Adventures in the Horn of Africa* (n.d.), West Point: Combating Terrorism Center.

Cordesman, Anthony H. (2006), *Preliminary 'Lessons' of the Israeli-Hezbollah War*, Washington: Center for Strategic and International Studies.

Corum, James S. (1998), 'The Air War in El Salvador', *Airpower Journal*, 5 (Summer).

Coupland, Simon (1998), 'From Poachers to Gamekeepers: Scandinavian Warlords and Carolingian Kings', *Early Modern Europe*, vol. 7, no. 1.

Cramer, Chris (2006), *War is Not a Stupid Thing*, London: Hurst & Co.

Dadi, Abderahman (1987), *Tchad: L'Etat retrouvé*, Paris: L'Harmattan.

Dasgupta, Sunil (2003), 'Understanding Paramilitary Growth: Agency Relations in Military Organization', Draft paper for presentation at Conference on 'Curbing human rights violations by non-state armed groups', Centre of International Relations, Liu Institute for Global Issues, University of British Columbia, Vancouver, 13–15 Nov.).

David, Steven R. (1985), *Defending third world regimes from coups d'état*, Lanham: University Press of America.

Davis, Diane E. and. Pereira, Anthony W. (eds.) (2003), *Irregular Armed Forces and Their Role in Politics and State Formation*, Cambridge: Cambridge University Press

de Atkine, Norville (2000), 'Why Arabs Lose Wars', *Middle East Review of International Affairs*, vol. 4, no. 1 (March).

De Goede, Meike J. (forthcoming 2011), 'Elite bargains and the armed forces in postwar DRC', in Giustozzi, Antonio, *Double-edged Swords*, London: Hurst & Co.

De Lutiis, Giuseppe (2009), *I Servizi segreti in Italia*, Milan: Sperling & Kupfer.

DeVries, Kelly (2001), 'Harold Godwinson in Wales: Military Legitimacy in Late Anglo-Saxon England', in Abels, Richard P. and Bachrach, Bernard S. (eds.), *The Normans and Their Adversaries at War: Essays in Memory of C. Warren Holliste*, Woodbridge: Boydell Press de Waal, Alex (1994), 'Some Comments on Militias in

Contemporary Sudan', in Daly, M. and Sikainga, A. A. (eds.), *Civil War in the Sudan*, London: I. B. Tauris.

Deacon, Richard (1974), *A History of the Chinese Secret Service*, London: F. Muller.

Deacon, Richard (1987), *A History of the Russian Secret Service*, London: Grafton.

Decalo, Samuel (1980), 'Regionalism, Political Decay, and Civil Strife in Chad', *Journal of Modern African Studies*, vol. 18, no. 1, pp. 23–56.

Delannoy, Christian (1990), *Savak*, Paris: Stock.

Derrienic, Jean-Pierre (2001), *Les guerres civiles*, Paris: Presses de Sciences Po.

Deuve, Jean (1998), *Histoire de la police nationale du Laos*, Paris: L'Harmattan.

Dhungana, Shiva K. (2007), 'Addressing corruption in police reform', in *Policing in Nepal: A collection of essays*, London: Saferworld.

Diamond, A. S. (1951), *The Evolution of Law and Order*, London: Watts.

Diáz Fernández, Antonio M. (2005), *Los servicios de inteligencia españoles*, Madrid: Alianza.

Di John, Jonathan and Putzel, James (2009), *Political Settlements*, Issues Paper, Birmingham: Governance and Social development Resource Centre di Paola, L. (2005), *Per la storia degli 'occhi del re': i servizi ispettivi nella tarda antichitá*, Messina: Di.Sc.A.M.

Dodge, Toby (2003), *Inventing Iraq: The Failure of Nation Building and a History Denied*, London: Hurst & Co.

Dorenwendt, Thomas (1997), 'Tadschikistan: die Transformationen des Bürgerkrieges', *Orient*, 38:2.

Dorronsoro, Gilles (2005), *Revolution Unending: Afghanistan, 1979 to the Present*, London: Hurst & Co.

Downes, Alexander B. (2007), 'Draining the Sea by Filling the Graves: Investigating the Effectiveness of Indiscriminate Violence as a Counterinsurgency Strategy', *Civil Wars*, vol. 9:4, pp. 420–44.

Dows, Anthony (1967), *Inside Bureaucracy*, Boston: Little, Brown.

Doyle, Michael H. (2007), *Too little, too late? Justice and security reform in Bosnia and Herzegovina*, in C.T. Call, *Constructing justice and security after war*, Washington: USIP Press.

Doyle, Michael W. (1995), *UN Peacekeeping in Cambodia: UNTAC's Civil Mandate*. Boulder: Lynne Rienner.

Driscoll, Jesse (2008), *Inside The Leviathan: Coup-Proofing After State Failure*, Stanford: Stanford University.

Duby, Georges (1980), *The Three Orders: Feudal Society Imagined*, Chicago: University of Chicago Press.

Duhamel, Luc (2010), *The KGB Campaign Against Corruption in Moscow, 1982–1987*, Pittsburgh: University of Pittsburgh Press.

Dunlap, Charles J. (2008), 'Making Revolutionary Change: Airpower in COIN Today', *Parameters*, Summer.

Dunn, John P. (2008), 'Missions or mercenaries? European military advisers in Mehmet Ali's Egypt, 1815–1848', in Stoker, Donald (ed.), *Military Advising and Assistance: from mercenaries to privatization, 1815–2007*, London: Frank Cass.

Duverger, Maurice (1976), *Les partis politiques*, Paris: Armand Colin.

Dvornik, Francis (1974), *Origins of Intelligence Services*, New Brunswick: Rutgers University Press.

Eickelman, Dale F. (1988), 'Intelligence in an Arab state', in Godson, Roy (ed.), *Comparing Foreign Intelligence*, Washington: Pergamon-Brassey's.

Ejkman, Quirine A. M. (2007), *We are here to serve you! Public security, police reform and human rights implementation in Costa Rica*, Antwerp: Intersentia.

Elias, Norbert (1982), *The Civilising Process, volume 2: State formation and Civilisation*, Oxford: Blackwell.

Ellis, John (1973), *Armies in Revolution*, London: Croom Helm.

Ellis, John (1995), *From the Barrel of a Gun*, London: Greenhill Books.

Enloe, Cynthia H. (1980), *Police, Military and Ethnicity*, New Brunswick: Transaction Publishers.

Erickson, Edward J. (2007), *Ottoman Army Effectiveness in World War I*, London: Routledge.

Erlich, Haggai (1983), 'The Ethiopian army and the 1974 revolution', *Armed Forces and Society*, vol. 9, no. 3, pp. 455–81.

Ero, Comfort (2003), 'Sierra Leone: the legacies of authoritarianism and political violence', in Cawtra, Gavin and Luckham, Robin (eds.), *Governing Insecurity*, London: Zed Books.

Exum, Andrew (2006), *Hizballah at War: A Military Assessment*, Policy Focus #63, Washington: Institute for Near East Policy.

Fabei, Stefano (2005), *Mussolini e la resistenza palestinese*, Milan: Mursia.

Farber, Samuel (2006), *The Origins of the Cuban Revolution Reconsidered*, Chapel Hill: University of North Carolina.

Farah, Douglas (2008), 'Seven Questions: The Russian Connection', in *Foreign Policy*, March (http://www.foreignpolicy.com/story/cms.php?story_id=4226).

Farah, Douglas and Braun, Stephen (2007), *Merchant of Death*, Indianapolis: Wiley.

Fellowship on Reconciliation and US Office on Colombia, *Military Assistance and Human Rights: Colombia, U.S. Accountability, and Global Implications*, New York: Fellowship on Reconciliation.

Ferguson, Chris (2004), 'Police Reform, Peacekeeping and SSR: The Need for Closer Synthesis', *Journal of Security Sector Management*, vol. 2, no. 3.

Findley, Carter V. (1980), *Bureaucratic Reform in the Ottoman Empire*, Princeton: Princeton University Press.

Finer, Samuel E. (1975), 'State and national-building in Europe: the role of the military', in Tilly, C. (ed.), *The Formation of National States in Western Europe*, Princeton: Princeton University Press.

Finer, Samuel E. (1997), *The History of Government from the Earliest Times*, Oxford: Oxford University Press.

FitzGerald, Frances (1989), *Fire in the Lake: the Vietnamese and the Americans in Vietnam*, New York: Random House.

Fleitz, Frederick H. (2002), *Peacekeeping Fiascoes of the 1990s: Causes, Solutions, and U.S. Interests*, Westport: Greenwood Publishing Group.

Fleming, Jenny and Rhodes, R. A. W. (2005), 'Bureaucracy, Contracts and Networks: The Unholy Trinity and the Police', *Australian and New Zealand Journal of Criminology*, vol. 38, no. 2, pp. 192–205.

Fontrier, Marc (2005), 'Des armées africaines: comment et pour quoi faire?', *Outre Terre*, vol. 11, no. 2.

Ford, Roger and McNab, Chris (2001), *The AK-47*, St Paul: MBI Publications.

Forrest, Alan (1990), *Soldiers of the French Revolution*, Durham: Duke University Press.

Foucault, Michel (2006), *Seguridad, territorio, poblacíon*, Madrid: Fondo de Cultura Economica.

Frühling, Hugo (2009), 'Recent Police Reform in Latin America', in Uildriks, Niels (ed.), *Policing Security: Police Reform, Security, and Human Rights in Latin America*, Lexington: Lexington Books.

Fu, Hualing (1991), 'Police accountability: the case of the People's Republic of China', *Police Studies: International Review of Police Development*, no. 140.

Gallant, Thomas W. (1999), 'Brigandage, Piracy, Capitalism, and State-Formation', in Heyman, Josiah McC. (ed.), *States and Illegal Practices*, New York: Berg Publishers.

Galula, David (1964), *Counter-insurgency Warfare*, London: Pall Mall Press.

Gander, Terry (1989), *Guerrilla Warfare Weapons*, New York: Sterling Publishing.

Gann, Lewis H. (1971), *Guerrillas in History*, Stanford: Hoover Institution Press.

Gat, Azar (2006), *War in Human Civilization*, Oxford: Oxford University Press.

Geertz, Clifford (1973), *The Interpretation of Cultures*, New York: Basic Books.

Gellatelly, Robert (1991), *The Gestapo and German Society*, Oxford: Oxford University Press.

Gellner, Ernest (1996), 'War and society', in Gellner, Ernest (ed.), *Anthropology and Politics*, Oxford: Blackwell.

George, Edward (2005), *The Cuban Intervention in Angola, 1965–1991*, London: Frank Cass.

Gerber, Haim (1997), *The Social Origins of the Modern Middle East*, Boulder: Lynne Rienner.

Gerson, Lennard D. (1976), *The Secret Police in Lenin's Russia*, Philadelphia: Temple University Press.

Ghosh, Srikanta (1987), *Law Enforcement in Tribal Areas*, Calcutta: Law Research Institute.

Gill, Peter (1994), *Policing Politics*, London: Frank Cass.

Ginifer, Jeremy and Peimani, Hooman (2005), 'Civil defence forces and post-conflict security challenges', in Francis, David J. (ed.), *Civil Militia*, Aldershot: Ashgate.

Giustozzi, Antonio (2000), *War, Politics and Society in Afghanistan 1978–1992*, London: Hurst & Co.

Giustozzi, Antonio (2005), *The Debate on Warlordism: the importance of military legitimacy*, Discussion Paper no. 13, London: Crisis States Research Centre (LSE).

Giustozzi, Antonio (2007a), *The Missing Ingredient: non-ideological insurgency and state collapse in western Afghanistan, 1979–1992*, Working Paper Series 2 no. 11, London: Crisis States Research Centre (LSE).

Giustozzi, Antonio (2007b), 'Auxiliary force or national army? Afghanistan's "ANA" and the counter-insurgency effort, 2002–2006', *Small Wars and Insurgencies*, 18:1, pp. 45–67.

Giustozzi, Antonio (2007c), *Koran, Kalashnikov and Laptop: the Rise of the Neo-Taliban Insurgency in Afghanistan*, London and New York: Hurst & Co. and Columbia University Press.

Giustozzi, Antonio (2008a), *Afghanistan: Transition Without End. An Analytical Narrative*, Working Paper, London: Crisis States Research Centre (LSE).

Giustozzi, Antonio (2008b), 'Bureaucratic façade and political realities of disarmament and demobilisation in Afghanistan', *Confict, Security and Development*.

Giustozzi, Antonio (2009a), *Empires of Mud: war and warlords of Afghanistan*, London: Hurst & Co.

Giustozzi, Antonio (2009b), 'The Afghan National Army: unwarranted hope?', *RUSI Journal*, Dec., pp. 34–40.

Giustozzi, Antonio (2009c), 'Afghanistan: "friction" between civilizations', in Hansen, Stig Jarle, Mesøy, Atle and Kardas, Tuncay (eds.), *The Borders of Islam: Exploring Huntington's Faultlines, from Al-Andalus to the Virtual Ummah*, London: Hurst & Co.

Giustozzi, Antonio (2009d), *Afghanistan: to get worse before getting better?*, Writenet paper, July.

Giustozzi, Antonio (2010a), *The Double-edged Sword: Afghanistan's army between loyalty and effectiveness, 1970–2008*, Working Paper, London: Crisis States Research Centre (LSE).

Giustozzi, (2010b), 'Auxiliary irregular forces in Afghanistan: 1978–2008', in Innes, M. (ed.), *Making Sense of Proxy Warfare: States, Surrogates, and the Use of Force*, Dulles: Potomac Books.

Giustozzi, Antonio (forthcoming 2011a), *Post-conflict DDR: bringing state-building back in*, London: Hurst & Co.

Giustozzi, Antonio (forthcoming 2011b), *Double-edged Swords*, London: Hurst & Co.

Giustozzi, Antonio and Kalinovsky, Artemy (forthcoming 2011c), *Advising Afghanistan*, London: Hurst & Co.

Glatzer, Bernt (1983), 'Political Organisation of Pashtun Nomads and the State' in Tapper, Richard (ed.), *The Conflict of Tribe and State in Iran and Afghanistan*, London: Croom Helm.

Glebbeek, Marie-Louise (2009), 'Post-War Violence and Police Reform in Guatemala', in Uildriks, Niels (ed.), *Policing Insecurity: Police Reform, Security, and Human Rights in Latin America*, Lexington: Lexington Books.

Glickson, Roger (1994), 'The Shaba crises: Stumbling to victory', *Small Wars and Insurgencies*, vol. 5:2, pp. 180–200.

Goldsmith, Andrew and Dinnen, Sinclair (2007), 'Transnational police building: critical lessons from Timor-Leste and Solomon Islands', *Third World Quarterly*, 28:6, pp. 1091–1109.

Goscha, Christopher E. (2002), 'La guerre par d'autres moyens: réflexions sur la guerre du Việt Minh dans le Sud-Vietnam de 1945 à 1951', *Guerres mondiales et conflits contemporains*, no. 206.

Goscha, Christopher E. (2007), 'Intelligence in a time of decolonization: The case of the Democratic Republic of Vietnam at war (1945–50)', *Intelligence and National Security*, vol. 22:1, pp. 100–138.

Gottesman, Evan R. (2004), Cambodia after the Khmer Rouge: Inside the Politics of Nation Building, New Haven: Yale University Press.

Government Accountability Office (2008), *Afghanistan Security: Further Congressional Action May Be Needed to Ensure Completion of a Detailed Plan to Develop and Sustain Capable Afghan National Security Forces*, Washington.

Grossheim, Martin (2004), 'Village Government in Precolonial and Colonial Vietnam', in Kerkvliet, Benedict J. and Marr, David G. (eds.), *Beyond Hanoi: Local Government in Vietnam*, Singapore: Institute of Southeast Asian Studies.

Grunow, Carl D. (2006), 'Training Iraqi soldiers', *Military Review*, July-Aug.

Gutiérrez Sanín, Francisco (2008), 'Telling the Difference: Guerrillas and Paramilitaries in the Colombian war', *Politics and Society* 36, pp. 3–34.

Haddick, Robert (2010), 'Colombia Can Teach Afghanistan (and the United States) How to Win', *Air and Space Power Journal*, Summer.

Hashim, Ahmed (2006), *Insurgency and Counter-Insurgency in Iraq*, London: Hurst & Co.

Heald, Suzette (2007), *Making Law in Rural East Africa: sungusungu in Kenya*, Crisis States Working Paper 2.2, London: Crisis States Research Centre (LSE).

Heder, Steve (1996), 'The Resumption of Armed Struggle by the Party of Democratic Kampuchea: Evidence from National Army of Democratic Kampuchea "Self-Demobilizers"', in Heder, Steve and Ledgerwood, Judy (eds.), *Propaganda, Politics and Violence in Cambodia: Democratic Transition under United Nations Peacekeeping*, Armonk, NY: M. E. Sharpe.

Henderson, Wm. Darryl (1985), *Cohesion: the human element in combat*, Washington: National Defense University.

Herbst, Jeffrey (1997), 'Responding to State Failure in Africa', *International Security*, vol. 21, no. 3, pp. 120–44.

Herbst, Jeffrey (2004), 'African Militaries and Rebellion: The Political Economy of Threat and Combat Effectiveness', *Journal of Peace Research*, vol. 41, no. 3 (May), pp. 357–69.

Herring, Eric and Rangwala, Glen (2006), *Iraq in Fragments*, Ithaca: Cornell University Press.

Herspring, Dale R. (2001), *Soldiers, Commissars and Chaplains: Civil-Military Relations Since Cromwell*, Boulder: Rowman & Littlefield.

Herwig, Holger et al. (2003), *Cassell's World History of Warfare*, London: Cassell.

Hickey, G. C. (1965), *The American military advisor and his foreign counterpart: the case of Vietnam*, Washington: Rand.

Hills, Alice (2008), 'The dialectic of police reform in Nigeria', *Journal of Modern African Studies*, 46, pp. 215–34.

Hills, Alice (2009), *Policing Post-conflict Cities*, London: Zed Books.

Hingley, Ronald (1968), *The Tsars: Russian autocrats*, London: Corgi.

Holden, Robert H. (2004), *Armies Without Nations: Public Violence and State Formation in Central America*, Oxford: Oxford University Press.

Holmes, Stephen (2003), 'Lineages of the Rule of Law', in Maravall, J. M. and Przeworski, A. (eds.), *Democracy and the Rule of Law*, Cambridge: Cambridge University Press.

Horowitz, David L. (1985), *Ethnic Groups in Conflict*, Berkeley: University of California.

Horton, Lynn (1994), *Peasants in Arms: war and peace in the mountains of Nicaragua 1979–1994*, Athens: Center for International Studies.

Hosmer, Stephen T. (1990), *The Army's Role in Counterinsurgency and Insurgency*, Santa Monica: Rand.

Howard, William H. E. (1956), *Public Administration in Ethiopia*, Groeningen: J. B. Wolters.

Howe, Herbert M. (2004), *Ambiguous Order: Military Forces in African States*, Boulder: Lynne Rienner.

Hoytt, Timothy D. (2007), 'Social structure, ethnicity and military effectiveness: Iraq, 1980–2004', in Brooks, Risa A. and Stanley, Elizabeth A. (eds.), *Creating Military Power: the sources of military effectiveness*, Stanford: Stanford University Press.

Hualing, Fu (2005), 'Zhou Yongkang and the Recent Police Reform in China', *Australian and New Zealand Journal of Criminology*, vol. 38, no. 2, pp. 241–53.

Huggins, Martha K. (1998), *Political Policing: The United States and Latin America*, Durham: Duke University Press.

Hume, David (1742), 'Of civil liberty', in *Essays, Moral, Political, and Literary*, Indianapolis: Liberty Fund, Inc. (1987).

Hunt, Richard A. (1995), *Pacification: the American struggle for Vietnam's heart and minds*, Boulder: Westview.

Huntington, P. (1957), *The Soldier and the State*, Cambridge, Mass.: The Belknap Press of Harvard University.

Hurewitz, J. C. (1969), *Middle East Politics: the military dimension*, New York: Praeger.

Hutchful, Eboe (2003), 'Pulling back from the brink: Ghana's experience', in Cawtra, Gavin and Luckham, Robin (eds.), *Governing Insecurity*, London: Zed Books.

Hyde, Michael (2002), 'British-Indian Army', in Sandler, Stanley L. (ed.), *Ground Warfare: An International Encyclopedia*, Santa Barbara: ABC-Clio.

Ibn Khaldun (1377), *The Muqaddimah: An Introduction to History*, trans. Franz Rosenthal, Princeton University Press, 2004.

International Crisis Group (2001), *Indonesia: National Police Reform*, Asia Report no. 13, Brussels.

International Crisis Group (2002), *Central Asia: The Politics of Police Reform*, Brussels.

Ives, Christopher K. (2007), *US Special Forces and Counterinsurgency in Vietnam: Military Innovation and Institutional Failure, 1961–1963*, London: Routledge.

Jackson Paul (2003), 'Warlords as alternative forms of governance', *Small Wars and Insurgencies*, 14: 2.

Janowitz, Morris (1960), *The Professional Soldier: A Social and Political Portrait*, Glencoe: The Free Press.

Janowitz, Morris (1971), *On Military Intervention*, Rotterdam: Rotterdam University Press.

Janowitz, Morris (1977), *Military Institutions and Coercion in the Developing Nations*, Chicago: University of Chicago Press.

Joes, Anthony James (2004), *Resisting Rebellion: the history and politics of counter-insurgency*, Lexington: University Press of Kentucky.

Joes, Anthony James (2008), 'Counterinsurgency in the Philippines 1898–1954', in Marston, Daniel and Malkasian, Carter (eds.), *Counterinsurgency in Modern Warfare*, Oxford: Osprey.

Joffe, Ellis (1965), *Party and Army: professionalism and political control in the Chinese officer corps 1949–1964*, Cambridge: Harvard University Press.

Jones, Bruce D. (2001), *Peacemaking in Rwanda: the dynamics of failure*, Boulder: Lynne Rienner.

Jones, Seth G. (2008), *Counterinsurgency in Afghanistan*, Santa Monica: Rand.

Jordan, David (2007), 'Countering insurgency from the air: the postwar lessons', *Contemporary Security Policy*, 28:1, pp. 96–111.

Jung, Dietrich (2003), 'Confronting a Paradox: The Political Economy of Intra-State Wars', in Jung, D. (ed.), *Shadow Globalization, Ethnic Conflicts and New Wars: A Political Economy of Intra-State War*, London: Routledge.

Jureidini, Paul A. and McLaurin, R. D. (1984), *Jordan: the impact of social change on the role of the tribes*, Washington: Centre for Strategic and International Studies.

Kahaner, Larry (2007), *AK-47: the weapon that changed the face of war*, Indianapolis: Wiley.

Kalyvas, Stathis N. (2004), 'The Paradox of Terrorism in Civil War', *Journal of Ethics*, vol. 8/1.

Kalyvas, Stathis N. (2006), *The Logic of Violence in Civil War*, Cambridge: Cambridge University Press.

Keen, David (1998), 'The Economic Functions of Violence in Civil Wars', Adelphi Paper 320, Oxford: Oxford University Press.

Keller, Edmond J. (1991), *Revolutionary Ethiopia: From Empire to People's Republic*, Bloomington: Indiana University Press.

Kemsley, Harry (2007), 'Air power in counter-insurgency: a sophisticated language or blunt expression?', *Contemporary Security Policy*, 28:1, pp. 112–26.

Kenstbaum, Meyer (2005), 'Mars revealed', in Adams, Julia et al. (eds.), *Remaking Modernity: politics, history and sociology*, Durham: Duke University Press.

Khadduri, Majid (1988), 'Equity and Islamic law', in Atiyeh, George N. and Oweiss, Ibrahim M. (eds), *Arab Civilization*, Albany: State University of New York Press.

King, Edward L. (1985), 'Analysis of Military Situation in Nicaragua', Cambridge, Mass.: Unitarian Universalist Service Committee.

Kirby, William C. (1984), *Germany and Republican China*, Stanford: Stanford University Press.

Kiser, Edgar and Baer, Justin (2005), 'The Bureaucratization of States: Toward an Analytical Weberianism', in Adams, Julia et al. (eds.), *Remaking Modernity: Politics, History, and Sociology*, Durham: Duke University Press.

Knight, Amy W. (1988), *The KGB: police and politics in the Soviet Union*, London: Unwin Hyman.

Knox, Robert (1681), *An Historical Relation of Ceylon*, London: Richard Chiswell.

Kohler, John O. (1999), *Stasi: the untold story of the East German secret police*, Boulder: Westview.

Krepinevich, Andrew F. and Wood, Dakota L. (2007), 'Of IEDs and MRAPs: Force Protection in Complex Irregular Operations', Washington: CSBA.

Kreps, Sarah E. (2007), 'The 2006 LebanonWar: Lessons Learned', *Parameters*, Spring.

Krivitsky, W. G. (1992), *I was Stalin's Agent*, Cambridge: Faulkner.

Kuperman, Alan J. (1999), 'The Stinger missile and US intervention in Afghanistan', *Political Science Quarterly*, vol. 114, no. 2.

Ladwig III, Walter C. (2007), 'Training Foreign Police: A Missing Aspect of U.S. Security Assistance to Counterinsurgency', *Comparative Strategy*, 26, pp. 285–93.

Langer, Paul F. and Zasloff, Joseph J. (1968), *The North Vietnamese Military Adviser in Laos: a first hand account*, Santa Monica: Rand.

Langer, Paul F. and Zasloff, Joseph J. (1969), *Revolution in Laos: The North Vietnamese and the Pathet Lao*, Santa Monica: Rand.

Lapidus, Ira Marvin (2002), *History of Islamic Societies*, Cambridge: Cambridge University Press.

Law, David M. (2006), 'Conclusion: Security sector (re)construction in post-conflict settings', *International Peacekeeping*, vol. 13:1, pp. 111–23.

Leander, Anna (2004), 'Wars and the Un-Making of States: Taking Tilly Seriously in the Contemporary World', in Guzzini, Stefano (ed.), *Contemporary Security Analysis and Copenhagen Peace Research*, London: Routledge.

Lefever, Ernest W. (1970), *Spear and Sceptre: army, police and politics in tropical Africa*, Washington: Brookings Institution.

Leggett, George (1981), *The Cheka: Lenin's political police*, Oxford: Oxford University Press.

Lemarchand, René (1986), 'Chad: The Misadventures of the North-South Dialectic', *African Studies Review*, vol. 29, no. 3, pp. 27–41.

Leonhard, Jörn (2009), 'The rise of the modern Leviathan: state functions and state features', in Berger, Stefan (ed.), *A Companion to Nineteenth-century Europe: 1789–1914*, Oxford: Wiley Blackwell.

Lévy, Noémi (2007), 'La police ottomane au tournant des XIXe et XXe siècles: Les mémoires d'un commissaire d'Izmir', *Revue d'Histoire Moderne et Contemporaine*, no. 54–2.

Lewis, Herbert S. (1981), 'Warfare and the origins of the state: another formulation', in Claessen, Henri J. M. and Skalnik, Peter (eds.), *The Study of the State*, The Hague: Mouton.

Li, Xiaobing (2007), *A History of the Modern Chinese Army*, Lexington: University Press of Kentucky.

Liang, His-Huey (1992), *The rise of modern police and the European state system from Metternich to the second world war*, Cambridge: Cambridge University Press.

Libra and CDS, 'Building security institutions in conflict-affected environments—Learning from Iraq' (2009), Seminar Report 30 April, London: Libra and CDS.

Licklider, Roy (1995), 'The Consequences of Negotiated Settlements in Civil Wars, 1945–1993', *American Political Science Review*, vol. 89, no. 3, pp. 681–90.

Lieb, Peter (2008), 'Few Carrots and a lot of Sticks. German Anti-Partisan Warfare in the Second World War', in Marston, Daniel and Malkasian, Carter, *Counterinsurgency in Modern Warfare*, Oxford: Osprey, pp. 67–87.

Limiti, Stefania (2009), *L'Anello della Repubblica*, Milan: Chiarelettere.

Litchfield, R. Burr (1986), *Emergence of a Bureaucracy: the Florentine patricians, 1530–1790*, Princeton: Princeton University Press.

Liu, F. F. (1956), *A Military History of Modern China, 1924–1949*, Princeton: Princeton University Press.

Lobe, Thomas (1977), *United States national security policy and aid to the Thailand police*, Denver: University of Denver.

Lock, Peter (2002), 'From the Economics of War to Economies of Peace. The dynamics of shadow globalisation and the diffusion of armed violence as an obstacle to build peace', text presented at the Hamburg Winterschool on Crisis Prevention and Peace Support, 18 November (http://www.peter-lock.de/txt/winterschool.html).

Loveman, Brian (1999), *For la Patria: politics and the armed forces in Latin America*, Wilmington: Scholarly Resources.

Luckham, Robin (2002), 'Radical soldiers, new model armies and the nation-state in Ethiopia and Eritrea', in Koonings, K. and Kruijt, D. (eds.), *Political Armies*, London: Verso.

Luttwak, Edward N. (1999), 'Give War a Chance', *Foreign Affairs*, July/Aug.

Lynn, John A. (1996), *The Bayonets of the Republic*, Boulder: Westview.

Machiavelli, Niccoló (1515), *The Prince*, Cambridge: Cambridge University Press, 1988.

Machiavelli, Niccoló (1531), *Discourses on the First Ten Books of Titus Livius*, ed. Bernard Crick, London: Penguin Classic, 1983.

McCarl, James M. (1990), *Sandinista Counterinsurgency Tactics*, Thesis presented to the Faculty of the US Army Command and General Staff College, Fort Leavenworth, Kansas.

McCoy, William H. (1994), *Senegal and Liberia: case studies in US IMET training and its role in internal defense and development*, Santa Monica: Rand.

Mackenzie, Compton (1951), *Eastern Epic*, London: Chatto & Windus.

Mackenzie, S. P. (1997), *Revolutionary Armies in the Modern Era: a revisionist approach*, London: Routledge.

Mackinlay, John (2002), *Globalisation and Insurgency*, Adelphi Paper 352, Oxford: Oxford University Press McMillan, John and Zoido, Pablo (2004), 'How to Subvert Democracy: Montesinos in Peru', *Journal of Economic Perspectives*, vol. 18, no. 4, pp. 69–92.

McNeill, William (1983), *The Pursuit of Power*, Oxford: Basil Blackwell.

McNeill, William (1995), *Keeping Together in Time: dance and drill in human history*, Cambridge: Harvard University Press.

Mann, Michael (1986), *The Sources of Social Power, Volume 1: A History of Power from the Beginning to A.D.1760*, New York: Cambridge University Press.

Marinen, Otwin (ed.) (1996), *Policing Change, Changing Police: International Perspectives*, New York: Garland Press.

Marius, Lazar (2008), 'Bassora: géopolitique d'une région chiite', *Hérodote*, no. 130.

Marks, Tom (1992), 'Making Revolution: Sendero Luminoso in Peru', *Small Wars and Insurgencies*, vol. 3/1.

Marks, Thomas A. (1996), *Maoist Insurgency Since Vietnam*, London: Routledge.

Marr, David G. (2004), 'A brief history of local government in Vietnam', in Kerkvliet, Benedict J. and Marr, David G. (eds.), *Beyond Hanoi: Local Government in Vietnam*, Singapore: Institute of Southeast Asian Studies.

Marriage, Zöe (2007), 'Flip-flop rebel, dollar soldier; Demobilisation in the Democratic Republic of Congo', *Conflict, Security and Development*, 7(2).

Marten, Kimberly (2006–7), 'Warlordism in Comparative Perspective', *International Security*, vol. 31, no. 3 (Winter), pp. 41–73.

Martin, Kate (2009), 'Domestic intelligence and civil liberties', in Andrew, C. et al. (eds.), *Secret Intelligence*, London: Routledge, pp. 358–70.

Mathew, George C. and Nayak, Ramesh C. (1996), 'Panchayats at work', *Economic and Political Weekly*, 6 July.

Matveeva, Anna (2009), *The Perils of Emerging Statehood: Civil War and State Reconstruction in Tajikistan. An Analytical Narrative on State-Making*, Working Paper no. 46, London: Crisis States Research Centre (LSE).

Mauceri, Philip (1997), 'State development and counter-insurgency in Peru', in Rich, Paul B. and Stubbs, Richard (eds.), *The Counter-insurgent State*, Basingstoke: Macmillan.

Mazower, Mark (1997), *The Policing of Politics in the Twentieth Century*, Providence: Bergham Books.

Mehler, Andreas (2009), 'Peace and power sharing in Africa: a not so obvious relationship', *African Affairs*, 108/432, pp. 453–73.

Menkhaus, Ken (2003), 'Warlords and Landlords: Non-State Actors and Humanitarian Norms in Somalia', paper presented at the 'Curbing Human Rights Violations by Armed Groups' Conference, Liu Institute for Global Issues, University of British Columbia, Canada, 14–15 Nov.

Merridale, Catherine (2005), *Ivan's War: the Red Army 1939–45*, London: Faber.

Migdal, Joel S. (2001), *State in Society: Studying How States and Societies Transform and Constitute One Another*, Cambridge: Cambridge University Press.

Miles, William F. S. (1995), 'Tragic Tradeoffs: Democracy and Security in Chad', *Journal of Modern African Studies*, vol. 33, no. 1, pp. 53–65.

Milliken, Jennifer (ed.) (2003), *State Failure, Collapse and Reconstruction*, Hoboken: Wiley-Blackwell.

Minh, Pham Quang (2004), 'Local Cadres in Hai Duong Province', in Kerkvliet, Benedict J. and Marr, David G. (eds.), *Beyond Hanoi: Local Government in Vietnam*, Singapore: Institute of Southeast Asian Studies.

Miranda, Roger and Ratliff, William (1993), *The Civil War in Nicaragua: Inside the Sandinistas*, New Brunswick: Transaction Publishers.

Mohammadi, Majid (2008), *Judicial Reform and Reorganization in 20th Century Iran*, London: Routledge.

Molero, María (1988), *Nicaragua Sandinista: del sueño a la realidad (1979–1988)*, Managua: CRIES.

Moore, Robert Ian (2007), *The Formation of a Persecuting Society: power and deviance in Western Europe, 950–1250*, Oxford: Basil Blackwell.

Moran, Jonathan (1998), 'The Role of the Security Services in Democratization: An Analysis of South Korea's Agency for National Security Planning', *Intelligence and National Security*, vol. 13, no. 4, pp. 1–32.

Moran, Jon (2003), *Making intelligence accountable: legislative and executive oversight in old and new democracies. South Korea's National Intelligence Service*, Oslo: Norwegian Parliamentary Intelligence Oversight Committee.

Moyar, Mark (2007), *Phoenix and the Birds of Prey*, Lincoln: University of Nebraska Press.

Muehlmann, Thomas (2008), 'Police Restructuring in Bosnia-Herzegovina: Problems of Internationally-led Security Sector Reform', *Journal of Intervention and Statebuilding*, vol. 2:1, pp. 1–22.

Mushemeza, Elijah Dickens (2008), 'Policing in Post-Conflict Environment: Implications for Police Reform in Uganda', *Journal of Security Sector Management*, vol. 6, no. 3.

Nagl, John A. (2002), *Counterinsurgency Lessons from Malaya and Vietnam: Learning to Eat Soup with a Knife*, New York: Praeger.

Newitt, Malyn and Robson, Martin (2004), *Lord Beresford and British Intervention in Portugal 1807–1820*, Lisbon: Instituto de Ciências Sociais.

Nicolle, David and Ruggeri, Raffaele (1997), *The Italian Invasion of Abyssinia 1935–36*, Oxford: Osprey.

Nield, Rachel (2003), *From National Security to Citizen Security*, Montreal: International Centre for Human Rights and Democratic Development.

Nolutshungu, Sam C. (1996), *Limits of Anarchy: intervention and state formation in Chad*, Charlottesville: University of Virginia Press.

North, Douglass C. et al. (2009), *Violence and Social Orders*, Cambridge: Cambridge University Press.

Norton, Augustus R. (2000), 'Hizballah and the Israeli Withdrawal from Southern Lebanon', *Journal of Palestine Studies*, 30:1, pp. 22–35.

Norton, Augustus R. (2006), 'Hizballah Through the Fog of the Lebanon War: An Interview with Augustus Richard Norton', *Journal of Palestine Studies*, vol. 36: 1, pp. 54–70.

Nourzhanov, Kirill (2005), 'Saviours of the nation or robber barons? Warlord politics in Tajikistan', *Central Asian Survey* 24(2), pp. 109–30.

O'Brien, Kevin A. (2001), 'Counter-intelligence for counter-revolutionary warfare: The South African police security branch 1979–1990', *Intelligence and National Security*, vol. 16:3, pp. 27–59.

O'Connell, Robert L. (1995), *Ride of the Second Horseman*, Oxford: Oxford University Press.

Odom, Thomas P. (1993), *Shaba II: The French and Belgian Intervention in Zaire in 1978*, Fort Leavenworth: US Army Command and General Staff College.

OECD (2007), *The OECD DAC Handbook on security system reform (SSR): supporting security and justice*, Paris: OECD.

Ofcansky, Thomas P. and Berry, LaVerle (eds.) (1991), *Ethiopia, a Country Study*, Washington: Federal Research Division Library of Congress.

Omissi, David E. (1990), *Air Power and Colonial Control: The Royal Air Force, 1919–1939*, Manchester: Manchester University Press.

Osorio, Alvaro de Navia Santa Cruz de Marcenado (1724–30), *Réflexions militaires et politiques*, 12 volumes, Boston: Adamant Media Corporation.

Ott, M. C. (2009), 'Partisanship and the decline of intelligence oversight', in Andrew, C. et al. (eds.), *Secret Intelligence*, London: Routledge, pp. 318–36.

Ouellet, Eric (2008), 'Ambushes, IEDs and COIN: The French Experience', *Canadian Army Journal*, vol. 11:1, pp. 7–24.

Pailler, Jean (1994), *Portugal, les printemps des capitaines*, Paris: L'Harmattan.

Paret, Peter (ed.) (1992), *Understanding War: Essays on Clausewitz and the History of Military Power*, Princeton: Princeton University Press.

Paris, Roland (2004), *At War's End: building peace after civil wars*, Cambridge: Cambridge University Press.

Paris, Roland and Sisk, Timothy D. (eds.) (2009), *The Dilemmas of State-building: Confronting the contradictions of postwar peace operations*, London: Routledge.

Parker, Geoffrey (1988), *The Military Revolution: military innovation and the rise of the West, 1500–1800*, Cambridge: Cambridge University Press.

Pascal, Anthony H. (1980), *Are Third World Armies Third Rate? Human Capital and Organizational Impediments to Military Effectiveness*, Santa Monica: Rand.

Pereira, Anthony W. (2003), 'Armed force, coercive monopolies, and Changing patterns of state formation and violence', in Davis, Diane and Pereira, Anthony W. (eds.), *Irregular armed forces and their role in politics and state formation*, Cambridge: Cambridge University Press.

Pérouse de Montclos, Marc-Antoine (2008), *Etats faibles et sécurité privée en Afrique noire*, Paris: L'Harmattan.

Peters, B. Guy (2001), *The Politics of Bureaucracy*, London: Routledge.

Peterson, Claes (1979), *Peter the Great's Administrative and Judicial Reforms*, Stockholm: Instituet for Rättshistorisk Forskning Grundat af Gustav och Calvin Olin.

Peterson, Joel M. (1993), *The Somalia Intervention: Can You Nation-Build in a Whirlwind?*, Thesis, Maxwell: Air War College.

Petraeus, David H. et al. (2007), *The United States Army/Marine Corps Counterinsurgency Manual*, Chicago: University of Chicago Press.

Pincus, Steven C. A. (2006), England's Glorious Revolution, 1688–1689: A Brief History With Documents, Basingstoke: Palgrave Macmillan.

Pino, Nathan and Wiatrowski, Michael D. (eds.) (2006), *Democratic policing in transitional and developing countries*, Aldershot: Ashgate.

Poggi, Gianfranco (1978), *The Development of the Modern State: a sociological introduction*, Stanford: Stanford University Press.

Politi, Alessandro (1996), *Le dottrine tedesche di controguerriglia*, Roma: Stato Maggiore dell'Esercito-Ufficio Storico.

Pollack, Kenneth M. (2002), *Arabs at War*, Lincoln: University of Nebraska Press.

Porch, Douglas (1977), *The Portuguese Armed Forces and the Revolution*, London: Croom Helm.

Porch, Douglas and Muller, Christopher W. (2008), 'Imperial grunts revisited: the US advisory mission to Colombia', in Stoker, Donald (ed.), *Military Advising and Assistance: from mercenaries to privatization, 1815–2007*, London: Frank Cass.

Preto, Paolo (1994), *I servizi segreti di Venezia*, Milan: Il Saggiatore.

Pritchard, J. B. (1955), *Ancient Near Eastern Texts*, Princeton: Princeton University Press.

Putzel, James (2008), 'Development as State-Making: A Further Elaboration of the Research Plan', unpublished paper, London: Crisis States Research Centre (LSE).

Quinlivan, James T. (1999), 'Coup-proofing', *International Security*, vol. 24, no. 2, pp. 131–65.

Ra'anan, Uri and Lukes, Igor (1990), *Inside the Apparat: Perspectives on the Soviet System from Former Functionaries*, Lexington: Lexington Books.

Radosh, Ronald et al. (eds.) (2001), *Spain Betrayed: the Soviet Union in the Spanish Civil War*, New Haven: Yale University Press.

Rajagopalan, Rajesh (2009), *Fighting like a Guerrilla: the Indian Army and counterinsurgency*, London: Routledge.

Raju, K. D. (2007), 'Alternate dispute resolution system: a prudent mechanism of speedy redress in India', Paper presented to a one-day seminar organised by the USEFI at the Dhenkanal Law College, Orissa on 15 December.

Ramsey III, Robert D. (2006), *Advising Indigenous Forces: American Advisors in Korea, Vietnam, and El Salvador*, Fort Leavenworth: Combat Studies Institute Press.

Rathmell, Andrew (1996), 'Syria's Intelligence Services: Origins and Development', *Conflict Studies Journal*, vol. XVI, no. 2.

Rathmell, Andrew et al. (2005), *Developing Iraq's Security Sector: The Coalition Provisional Authority's Experience*, Santa Monica: Rand.

Rawls, John (1972), *A Theory of Justice*, Cambridge: Harvard University Press.

Reiter, Dan (2007), 'Nationalism and military effectiveness: post-Meiji Japan', in Brooks, Risa A. and Stanley, Elizabeth A. (eds.), *Creating Military Power: the sources of military effectiveness*, Stanford: Stanford University Press.

Reiter, Dan (2009), *How Wars End*, Princeton: Princeton University Press.

Reith, Charles Edward Williams (1952), *The Blind Eye of History: a study of the origins of the present police era*, London: Faber.

Rejali, Darius (2007), *Torture and Democracy*, Princeton: Princeton University Press.

Reno, William (2002), 'The Politics of Insurgency in Collapsing States', *Development and Change*, 33:5, pp. 837–58.

Reno, William (2004), 'Reconstructing peace in Liberia', in Ali, Taisier Mohamed Ahmed and Matthews, Robert O. (eds.), *Durable Peace: Challenges for Peacebuilding in Africa*, Toronto: University of Toronto Press.

Reynaud, Jean-Louis (1992), *Contre-guerrilla en Espagne (1808–14): Suchet pacifie l'Aragon*, Paris: Economica.

Rich, Paul B. and Stubbs, Richard (eds.) (1997), *The Counter-insurgent State*, Basingstoke: Macmillan.

Richmond, Oliver P. and Franks, Jason (eds.) (2009), *Liberal Peace Transitions: between state-building and peacebuilding*, Edinburgh: Edinburgh University Press.

Ricks, Thomas E. (2006), *Fiasco: The American Military Adventure in Iraq*, New York: Allen Lane.

Robbins, Richard G. Jr (1987), *The Tsar's Viceroys*, Ithaca: Cornell University Press.

Roberts, David (1998), 'Sympathy with the Devil? The Khmer Rouge and the politics of consent in the Cambodian peacekeeping operation', *Contemporary Security Policy*, 19:2, pp. 1–22.

Robins, Philip (2004), *A History of Jordan*, Cambridge: Cambridge University Press.

Robinson, Cyril D. and Scaglion, Richard (1987), 'The Origin and Evolution of the Police Function in Society: Notes toward a Theory', *Law and Society Review*, vol. 21, no. 1, pp. 109–54.

Robinson, Cyril D. and Scaglion, Richard (1994), *Police in Contradiction: the evolution of the police function in society*, Westport: Greenwood Press.

Robinson, William I. and Norsworthy, Kent (1987), *David and Goliath: Washington's war against Nicaragua*, London: Zed Books.

Rosen, David M. (2005), *Armies of the Young: Child Soldiers in War and Terrorism*, New Brunswick: Rutgers University Press.

Rosenau, William (2005), *US Internal Security Assistance to South Vietnam*, London: Routledge.

Rossi, Simonetta and Giustozzi, Antonio (2006), *Disarmament, Demobilisation and Reintegration of ex-combatants (DDR) in Afghanistan: constraints and limited capabilities*, Working Paper 2 Series 2, London: Crisis States Research Centre (LSE).

Roth, Guenther (1968), 'Personal Rulership, Patrimonialism, and Empire-Building in the New States', *World Politics*, vol. 20, no. 2. (Jan.).

Rubin, Michael (2001), *Into the Shadows: radical vigilantes in Khatami's Iran*, Policy Paper no. 56, Washington: Washington Institute for Near East Policy.

Ruooko, A. Byaruhanga (2005), 'Protracted civil war, civil militias and political transition in Uganda since 1986', in Francis, David J. (ed.), *Civil Militia, Africa's intractable security menace?*, Aldershot: Ashgate.

Salih, M. A. Mohammed and Harir, Sharif (1984), 'Tribal militias. The Genesis of National Disintegration', in Hariri, Sharif and Tvedt, Terje (eds.), *Short-cut to Decay: The Case of Sudan*, Uppsala: Nordiska Institute of African Studies, pp. 186–203.

Salmon, Jago (2006), *Militia Politics: the Formation and Organisation of Irregular Armed Forces in Sudan (1985–2001) and Lebanon (1975–1991)*, Dissertation, Humboldt Universität.

Samatar, Abdi Ismail (1989), *The State and Rural Transformation in Northern Somalia, 1884–1986*, Madison: University of Wisconsin Press.

Samraoui, Mohammed (2003), *Chronique des années de sang*, Paris: Denoël.

Sater, William F. (2008), 'The impact of foreign advisors on Chile's armed forces, 1810–2005', in Stoker, Donald (ed.), *Military Advising and Assistance: from mercenaries to privatization, 1815–2007*, London: Frank Cass.

Schapera, I. (1967), *Government and Politics in Tribal Societies*, New York: Schocken Books.

Scheina, Robert L. (2003), *Latin America's Wars*, Washington: Brassey's.

Schmeidl, Susanne and Karokhail, Masood (2009), 'The Role of Non-State Actors in "Community-Based Policing"—An Exploration of the Arbakai (Tribal Police) in South-Eastern Afghanistan', *Contemporary Security Policy*, 30:2, pp. 318–42.

Schmitt, Carl (1922), *Political Theology*, Chicago: University of Chicago Press, 1985.

Schomerus, Mareike (2007), *The Lord's Resistance Army in Sudan: A History and Overview*, Geneva: Small Arms Survey.

Schow, Kenneth C. (1994), *Falcons Against the Jihad: Israeli Airpower and Coercive Diplomacy in Southern Lebanon*, Thesis presented to the faculty of the School of Advanced Airpower Studies, Maxwell Air Force Base.

Schwarz, Benjamin C. (1991), *American counterinsurgency doctrine and El Salvador*, Santa Monica: Rand.

Seibert, Gerhard (2002), 'The vagaries of violence and power in post-colonial Mozambique', in Abbink, J. et al. (eds.), *Rethinking Resistance*, Leiden: Brill.

Sen Gupta, Nares Chandra (1925), *The Evolution of Law*, Calcutta: University Press.

Seward, Desmond (1991), *Metternich*, New York: Viking.

Shaw, Ezel Kural (1977), *History of the Ottoman Empire and Modern Turkey*, Cambridge: Cambridge University Press.

Sheldon, Rose Mary (2005), *Intelligence Activities in Ancient Rome*, London: Frank Cass.

Shelley, Louise I. (1994), 'The sources of Soviet policing', *Police Studies: International Review of Police Development*, vol. 49.

Shelley, Louise I. (1996), *Policing Soviet Society: The evolution of state control*, London and New York: Routledge.

Sheridan, James E. (1966), *Chinese Warlord: The Career of Feng Yu-hsiang*, Stanford: Stanford University Press.

Shrader, Charles R. (1999), *The Withered Vine: Logistics and the Communist Insurgency in Greece, 1945–1949*, Westport: Praeger.

Siddiqa, Ayesha (2007), *Military Inc.: Inside Pakistan's Military Economy*, London: Pluto Press.

Simms, Katharine (1987), *From Kings to Warlords. The Changing Political Structure of Gaelic Ireland in the Later Middle Ages*, Woodbridge: Boydell.

Sinno, Abdulkader H. (2008), *Organizations at War in Afghanistan and Beyond*, Ithaca: Cornell University Press.

Skalnik, Peter (1978), 'The early state as a process', in Claessen, Henri J. M. and Skalnik, Peter (eds.), *The Early State*, The Hague: Mouton.

Skocpol, Theda (1979), *States and Social Revolutions: A Comparative Analysis of France, Russia, and China*, Cambridge: Cambridge University Press.

Small Arms Survey, *Small Arms Survey Yearbook* (2004), Geneva: Graduate Institute of International and Development Studies.

Smith, Martin (1991), *Burma—Insurgency and the Politics of Ethnicity*, London: Zed Books.

Smyth, A. P. (1984), *Warlords and Holy Men: Scotland AD 80–1000*, Edinburgh: Edinburgh University Press.

Solomon, Peter H. Jr (2005), 'The Reform of Policing in the Russian Federation', *Australian and New Zealand Journal of Criminology*, vol. 38, no. 2, pp. 230–40.

Somerville, Keith (1997), 'Angola: groping towards peace or slipping back towards war?', in Gutteridge, William Frank and Spence, John Edward (eds.), *Violence in Southern Africa*, London: Frank Cass.

Sørensen, Georg (2001), 'War and State-Making: Why Doesn't it Work in the Third World?', *Security Dialogue*, 32, p. 341.

Speartin, Christopher (2007), 'A justified heaping of the blame? An assessment of privately supplied security sector training and reform in Iraq, 2003–2005 and beyond', in Stoker, Donald (ed.), *Military Advising and Assistance: from mercenaries to privatization, 1815–2007*, London: Frank Cass.

Spector, Ronald H. (1985), *Advice and Support: the early years of the US Army in Vietnam, 1941–1960*, New York: Free Press.

Spence, Jonathan (1980), *To Change China: Western advisers in China 1620–1960*, London: Penguin.

Spitzer, Steven (1985), 'The rationalization of crime control in capitalist society', in Cohen, Stanley and Scull, Andrew (eds.), *Social Control and the state*, Oxford: Blackwell.

Spruyt, Hendrik (1994), *The Sovereign State and its Competitors: an analysis of systems change*, Princeton: Princeton University Press.

Squire, P. S. (1968), *The Third Department*, Cambridge: Cambridge University Press.

Sriskandarajah, Dhananjayan (2005), 'Tamil Diaspora Politics', in *Encyclopedia of Diasporas*, Dordrecht: Springer.

Stackelberg, Roderick (1999), *Hitler's Germany*, London: Routledge.

Stanley, Donald William D. (2007), 'Business as usual? Justice and policing reform in postwar Guatemala', in Call, C. T. (ed.), *Constructing Justice and Security After War*, Washington: USIP Press.

Stanley, William and Call, Charles T. (1997), 'Building a new civilian police force in El Salvador', in Kumar, Krishna (ed.), *Rebuilding Societies After Civil War*, Boulder: Lynne Rienner.

Statiev, Alexander (2004), *Soviet Counterinsurgency in the Western Borderlands*, PhD Thesis, University of Calgary.

Stevenson, Jonathan (1995), *Losing Mogadishu: Testing U.S. Policy in Somalia*, Annapolis: US Naval Institute Press.

Stevenson, Jonathan (2007), 'Risks and Opportunities in Somalia', *Survival*, 49:2, pp. 5–20.

Stoker, Donald (ed.) (2008), *Military Advising and Assistance: from mercenaries to privatization, 1815–2007*, London: Frank Cass.

Stoker, Donald (2008), 'Buying influence, selling arms, undermining a friend: the French naval mission to Poland and the development of the Polish Navy, 1923–32', in Stoker, Donald (ed.), *Military Advising and Assistance: from mercenaries to privatization, 1815–2007*, London: Frank Cass.

Stove, Robert J. (2003), *The Unsleeping Eye: secret police and their victims*, San Francisco: Encounter.

Strachan, Hew (ed.) (2006), *Big Wars and Small Wars*, London: Routledge.

Striuli, Lorenzo (forthcoming 2011), 'DDR in Mozambique: a success without the first D', in Giustozzi, Antonio, *Post-conflict DDR: bringing state-building back in*, London: Hurst & Co.

Stromseth, Jane et al. (eds.) (2006), *Can Might Make Rights?: Building the Rule of Law after Military Interventions*, Cambridge: Cambridge University Press.

Stubbs, Richard (1997), 'The Malayan emergency and the development of the Malaysian state', in Rich, Paul B. and Stubbs, Richard (eds.), *The Counter-insurgent state*, Basingstoke: Macmillan.

Sullivan, Michael D. (2008), *Security Force Assistance: Building Foreign Security Forces and Joint Doctrine for the Future of U.S. Regional Security*, Fort Leavenworth: US Army School of Advanced Military Studies, United States Army Command and General Staff College.

Sunderland, Riley (1964), *Antiguerrilla Intelligence in Malaya, 1948–1960*, Santa Monica: Rand.

Sutton, Donald S. (1982), 'German Advice and Residual Warlordism in the Nanking Decade: Influences on Nationalist Military Training and Strategy', *China Quarterly*, no. 91, pp. 386–410.

Synge, Richard (1997), *Mozambique: UN Peacekeeping in Action, 1992–94*, Washington: USIP Press.

Taber, Robert (2002), *War of the Flea. The classic study of guerrilla warfare*, Dulles: Potomac Books.

Tal, Lawrence (2002), *Politics, the Military, and National Security in Jordan, 1955–1967*, London: Palgrave Macmillan.

Tamayo y Salmoran, Rolando (1985), 'The judicial litigation in early states and the evolution of the legal process', in Claessen, Henri J. M. et al., *Development and Decline: the evolution of sociopolitical organization*, South Hadley: Bergin & Garvey.

Tapper, Richard (1983), 'Introduction', in Tapper, Richard (ed.), *The Conflict of Tribe and State in Iran and Afghanistan*, London: Croom Helm.

Tar, Usman (2005), 'Counter-insurgents or ethnic vanguards? Civil militia and state violence in Darfur region, Western Sudan', in Francis, David J. (ed.), *Civil Militia, Africa's intractable security menace?*, Aldershot: Ashgate.

Tareke, Gebru (2009), *The Ethiopian Revolution*, New Haven: Yale University Press.

Tariq, Mohammed Osman (2008), *Tribal Security System (Arbakai) in Southeast Afghanistan*, Occasional Paper no. 7, London: Crisis States Research Centre (LSE).

Taylor, Edmond (1963), *The Fall of the Dynasties*, London: Weidenfeld & Nicolson.

Teitler, G. (1977), *Genesis of the Professional Officers' Corps*, Beverly Hills: Sage.

Thayer, Thomas C. (1977), 'Territorial forces', in Thompson, W. Scott and Frizzell, Donaldson D. (eds.), *The Lessons of Vietnam*, London: Macdonald and Jane's, pp. 256–62.

Thorning, Ruben (2005), 'Civil militias: Indonesia and Nigeria in comparative perspective', in Francis, David J. (ed.), *Civil militia, Africa's intractable security menace?*, Aldershot: Ashgate.

Tierney, Brian (2001), *The Idea of Natural Rights*, Grand Rapids: Eerdmans.

Tilly, Charles (1985), 'War making and state-making as organised crime', in Evans, P., Rueschemeyer, D. and Skocpol, T. (eds.), *Bringing the State Back In*, Cambridge: Cambridge University Press.

Tilly, Charles (1990), *Coercion, Capital, and European States, AD 990–1990*, Cambridge, Mass.: Blackwell.

Tiruneh, Andargachew (1993), *The Ethiopian revolution 1974–1987: A transformation from an aristocratic to a totalitarian autocracy*, Cambridge: Cambridge University Press.

Tollefson, Harlod (1999), *Policing Islam: The British occupation of Egypt and the Anglo-Egyptian struggle over control of the police 1882–1914*, Westport: Greenwood Press.

Trigger, Bruce G. (1985), 'Generalized coercion and inequality: the basis of state power in the early civilizations', in Claessen, Henri J. M. et al. (eds.), *Development and Decline: the evolution of socio-political organization*, South Hadley: Bergin & Garvey.

Tupman, Bill and Tupman, Alison (1999), *Policing in Europe: Uniform in diversity*, Exeter: Intellect.

Turk, Austin T. (1982), *Political Criminality: the defiance and defense of authority*, Beverley Hills: Sage.

Uildriks, Niels (2009), 'Policing Insecurity and Police Reform in Mexico City and Beyond', in Uildriks, Niels (ed.), *Policing Insecurity: Police Reform, Security, and Human Rights in Latin America*, Lexington: Lexington Books.

Urban, Mark (1990), *War in Afghanistan*, Basingstoke: Macmillan.

US Marine Corps (1940), *Small Wars Manual*, Washington: US Government Printing Office.

van Creveld, Martin (1998), *The Sword and the Olive*, New York: Public Affairs.

van Doorn J. (1965), 'The officer corps: a fusion of profession and organization', *Archive Européen de Sociologie*, 6, pp. 262–82.

Van Vien, Gen. Cao et al. (1980), *The U.S. Adviser*, Washington: US Army Center of Military History.

Vardys, Stanley (1965), 'The partisan movement in postwar Lithuania', in Vardys, Stanley (ed.), *Lithuania under the Soviets*, New York: Praeger.

Vercamer, Arvo (n.d.), 'German Military Mission to China 1927–1938', www.feldgrau. com.

Verma, Arvind (1999), 'Cultural roots of police corruption in India', *Policing*, vol. 22, no. 3.

Vick, Alan J. et al. (2006), *Air Power in the New Counterinsurgency Era. The Strategic Importance of USAF Advisory and Assistance Missions*, Santa Monica: Rand.

Visser, Reidar (2008), 'The Enigmatic Second Battle of Basra', www.historiae.org, 26 March.

Waghelstein, John D. (2008), 'Ruminations of a woolly mammoth, or training and advising in counterinsurgency and elsewhere during the Cold War', in Stoker, Donald (ed.), *Military Advising and Assistance: from mercenaries to privatization*, 1815–2007, London: Frank Cass.

Wagner, Robert Harrison (1993), 'The Causes of Peace', in Licklider, Roy (ed.), *Stopping the Killing*, New York: New York University Press.

Waldman, Matt (2008), *Aid Effectiveness in Afghanistan*, Kabul: ACBAR.

Walmsley, John K. (2003), *The US Military Advisers in Greece*, Thesis, Ohio State University.

Walters, A. J. C. (2005), 'Air control: past, present and future?', *RAF Air Power Review*, vol. 8:4.

Ward, Steven R. (2005), 'The Continuing Evolution of Iran's Military Doctrine', *Middle East Journal*, 59:4.

Weber, Max (1922), *Economy and Society*, Berkeley: University of California Press.

Wege, Carl Anthony (1997), 'Iranian intelligence organizations', *Intelligence and Counterintelligence*, vol. 10, no. 3.

Weinstein, Jeremy M. (2005), *Autonomous recovery and international intervention in comparative perspective*, Working paper 57, Wahington: Center for Global Development.

Weinstein, Jeremy M. (2007), *Inside Rebellion, the politics of insurgent violence*, Cambridge: Cambridge University Press.

Westermann, Edward B. (2008), 'Relegated to the backseat: Farm Gate and the failure of the US air advisory effort in South Vietnam, 1961–3', in Stoker, Donald (ed.), *Military Advising and Assistance: from mercenaries to privatization, 1815–2007*, London: Frank Cass.

Westney, D. Eleanor (1987), *Imitation and Innovation: the transfer of western organizational patterns to Meiji Japan*, Cambridge: Harvard University Press.

Wilbur, C. Martin and How, Julie Lien-ying (1989), *Missionaries of Revolution: Soviet advisers and nationalist China, 1920–1927*, Cambridge: Harvard University Press.

Williams, Charles Edward (1952), *The Blind Eye of History: a study of the origins of the present police era*, London: Faber.

Wilson, Clay (2007), *Improvised Explosive Devices (IEDs) in Iraq and Afghanistan: Effects and Countermeasures*, Washington: Council of Residential Specialists.

Winchell, Seran P. (2003), 'Pakistan's ISI', *Journal of Intelligence and Counterintelligence*, vol. 16, no. 3, pp. 374–88.

Woodward, Susan L. (1999), 'Bosnia and Herzegovina: How Not to End Civil War', in Walter, Barbara F. and Snyder, Jack (eds.), *Civil Wars, Insecurity, and Intervention*, New York: Columbia University Press.

Woolman, David S. (1969), *Rebels in the Rif*, Stanford: Stanford University Press.

Yasin, Mohammad (1999), *District and Police Systems in Pakistan*, Lahore: Vanguard.

Young, Crawford and Turner, Thomas (1985), *The Rise and Decline of the Zairian State*, Madison: University of Wisconsin Press.

Young, Tom (1997), 'A victim of modernity? Explaining the war in Mozambique', in Rich, Paul B. and Stubbs, Richard (eds.) (1997), *The Counter-insurgent State*, Basingstoke: Macmillan.

Yusuf, Moeed (2009), 'Rational Institutional Design, Perverse Incentives, and the US-Pakistan Partnership in post-9/11', *Defence Against Terrorism Review*, vol. 2, no. 1, pp. 15–30.

Zervoudaikis, Alexander (1998), 'Nihil mirare, nihil contemptare, omnia intelligere: Franco-Vietnamese intelligence in Indochina, 1950–1954', in Alexander, Martin S. (ed.), *Knowing Your Friends: Intelligence Inside Alliances and Coalitions from 1914 to the Cold War*, London: Reuters.

Zhdarkin, Igor (2008), *Takogo ne bylo dazhe v Afganistane vospominanya uchastnika voiny v Angole (1986–1988)*, Moscow: Memories.

Zhukov, Yuri (2007), 'Examining the authoritarian model of counter-insurgency: the Soviet campaign against the Ukranian Insurgent Army', *Small Wars and Insurgencies*, 18:3, pp. 439–66.

Zolo, Danilo (2007), 'The rule of law: a critical reappraisal', in Costa, P. and Zolo, D. (eds.), *The Rule of Law: history, theory and criticism*, Dordrecht: Springer, pp. 3–71

INDEX

Abdulhamit II: 132
Abdullah, King: 52; military service of, 51
Afghanistan: 6, 38, 49–50, 99, 163, 174, 186–7, 195, 215; government of, 99; International Security Assistance Force (ISAF), 178; Islamists in, 31; Kabul, 179; military of, 65, 172; mujahidin, 39; National Guard, 69; NATO command in, 81; Operation Enduring Freedom, 84, 87, 92, 178–9, 215; Soviet Invasion of (1979–89), 84, 86, 88, 164, 170, 172, 175, 178; state building efforts in, 3; terrain of, 172
Algeria: 35, 215; French occupation of, 85, 88; Islamic Salvation Front, 113; security services of, 113
Ali, Mehmet: 166; military campaigns of, 158
Amenhotep II: *vizir* system under, 107
Amenphis II: *vizir* system under, 107
Amin, Idi: regime of, 64, 66
Andropov, Yuri: President of the USSR, 108–9
Angola: and Cuba, 197; and USSR, 166, 197; Frente Nacional de Libertação de Angola (FNLA), 170; government of, 94, 98; insurgency in, 87; military of, 55; Movimento Popular de Libertação de Angola (MPLA), 170; Shaba I (1977), 72; small arms proliferation in, 94; União Nacional para a Independência Total de Angola (UNITA), 39, 93–4, 170, 177
Arab Caliphate: 206; 'Eye of the Caliph', 108; Governors of, 135, 139–40; Khaibar, 108
Argentina: 160; and Germany, 169; military of, 158
Aristide, Jean-Bertrand: administration of, 189
Aron, Raymond: 9
al-Assad, Hafez: 126; controlled liberalisation policies of, 54; rise to power (1970), 73
Augustus, Emperor Constantinus: laws issued by to control *agentes in rebus*, 109
Austria: military of, 62
Assyrian Empire: 58; intelligence service of, 107–8, 137

Baer, Justin: theory of difficulty to control armed forces via bureaucracy, 57

Baker, Bruce: view on role of structure, 153–4
Bangladesh: nationalists, 125
Barre, Siad: 64, 223; replacement of provincial governors with military personnel, 152
Bates, Robert H.: 27
Batista, Fulgencio: inefficient military forces under, 94
Bauer, Max: 156
Bedouin: 23–4, 51
Bhutto, Benazir: assassination of (2007), 125; attempts to control ISI, 125
Bhutto, Zulfikar Ali: President of Pakistan, 125; use of ISI, 125
Blyukher, Marshal Vasily: operational command of Chinese military units, 155
Boer Wars: 118
Bolivia: 160; military of, 41
Bolsheviks: establishment of Cheka, 117; party cadres of, 37; view of role of revolutionaries, 34
Bonaparte, Napoleon: 37, 49, 82, 111; and Joseph Fouché, 123
Bosnia and Herzegovina: 178; Bosnian War (1992–5), 178–9; EU attempt to impose de-politicised police model, 191; police restructuring in, 187
Botswana: military of, 50
Brazil: military of, 160
Bremer, Paul: disbanding of Iraqi army (2003), 43
Brezhnev, Leonid: 108, 124
Bunchheuan, Uk: Cambodian Minister of Justice, 208
Bureaucracy: 107–9, 117, 123, 137, 144–5, 217, 221; administrative tools of, 148; military, 58; professionalising of, 141

Burma: 94; Burma Independence Army, 178; nationalists, 178
Burundi: 67
Byzantine Empire: 63, 135

Calwell, Charles: 35; view of insurgencies, 118
Cambodia: 1, 93, 170; government of, 208; Khmer Rouge, 176, 179; military of, 176; Vietnamese Invasion of (1978), 176
Cambodia-Vietnamese War (1975–89): 176
Cambodian People's Party (CPP): members of, 2
Carolingians: 99; use of monetary payment for services, 29–30
Catherine the Great: conversion of governor general into viceroy, 138
Celador, Gemma: 189–90
Central African Republic: 164
Chad: 99, 133, 145, 153, 215; administrative system of, 149–50; territory of, 149; warlordism in, 35–6
Chapman: 123
Chechnya: 88, 180
Chile: 160; carabineros, 184; military of, 158
China: 45, 58, 94, 141, 177, 216; and USSR, 158, 168; bureaucracy of, 144; Chinese Communist party (CCP), 153; Chinese Expeditionary Force, 159; Civil War (1927–36), 157; Civil War (1946–50), 32; Cultural Revolution (1966–76), 42; Jaingxi, 157; Kuomintang (KMT), 30, 81, 90, 155–8; military of, 42, 45, 155, 157, 168–9; Nanjing, 156; nationalism, 156; police force of, 224; Salween, 157; Shanghai, 156; Taierzhuang, 156

Chinese Empire: 135; development of mounted archer forces, 96; Han Dynasty, 110, 137; internal espionage systems of, 110; Ming Dynasty, 137; Tang Dynasty, 137

von Clausewitz, Carl: theories of, 86

Clovis, King: retinue of, 27

Coalition-building: 8, 10–11; coercive, 124, 128, 134; influences upon, 47

Cohen, Ronald: theories of early state formation, 25

Cold War: 3, 17, 93, 123, 225; end of, 1, 31, 88, 234; environment of, 82

Colombia: 6, 101, 215; military of, 65, 170

Communist International (Comintern): advisers of, 161

Congo Brazzaville: military coup (1968), 68

Costa Rica: corruption in police force of, 214–15

Cromwell, Oliver: New Model Army, 36

Cuba: 128, 159, 177; and Angola, 197; military of, 94

Cyrus the Great: notice of agents recruited by, 108

Decentralisation: 29–30, 41, 80, 96, 134–6, 184; of command structures, 19; methods for confronting insurgencies, 95; opponents of, 191; supporters of, 40, 154

Democratic Republic of Congo: Civil Wars of, 195

Democratic Republic of Vietnam: 33, 76, 160, 177; attempt to lessen Laotian dependency on, 164; creation of national security (1946), 119

Diem, Ngo Dinh: 196; President of Republic of Vietnam, 65–6, 101;

refusal to reduce number of intelligence agencies, 127; Special Forces, 68; view of US advisers, 167, 191

Diocletian, Emperor: abolition of frumentarii, 109; creation of agens in rebus, 109

Disarmament, Demobilisation and Reintegration (DDR): 4, 195, 234; concept of, 193; programmes of, 195–6; UN statement about, 193; understanding of, 194

Djibouti: 164

Doe, Samuel: President of Liberia, 52, 164

Dows, Anthony: interpretation of bureaux, 142

Domitian, Emperor: military counter-intelligence system developed by, 109–10

Dumouriez, General Charles François: defection of Austrian military forces (1793), 59, 62

Durkheim: view of role of repeated participation in collective ritual, 58

East Timor: state building efforts in, 3

Egypt: 35, 173; British attempts to reform police force, 181; Department of Military Intelligence, 126; General Intelligence, 126; military of, 57, 158; Ministry of Interior, 181; State Security Investigative Service, 126

Eickelman, Dale F.: view of problem of external assistance to intelligence services, 196

El Salvador: 93, 159, 194; air force of, 91; attempted police reform in, 188–9; Civil War (1979–92), 91; military of, 90, 167–8, 170, 172–4; National Pacification Plan, 162;

police force of, 215; US-sponsored reform efforts in, 168

Elizabeth I: 110

Ethiopia: 67, 172, 193; Addis Ababa, 50, 72; *gime gema* system, 221; Italian Invasion of (1935), 136, 141, 158; military of, 50, 52, 65, 91; police force of, 222; Revolution (1974–5), 50; Soviet military supplies of, 172; territory of, 73; Tigre, 141; Wollaga, 141; Workers Party, 145

Europe: 9, 27, 148, 193; emergence of states in, 206

European Union (EU): attempts to impose de-politicised model of police in Bosnia and Herzegovina, 191

Fairfax, Lord: 45

Finer, Samuel: 53; view of evolution of centralised government, 134–5

First World War (1914–18): 39, 51, 117, 158, 162

FitzGerald, Frances: 33, 134

Foucault, Michel: view of police forces, 204

Fouché, Joseph: and Charles de Talleyrand-Périgod, 123; and Napoleon Bonaparte, 123; dismissal of (1810), 115; Minister of Police, 111

France: 49, 116, 209; colonialists of, 215; military of, 45, 89; nationalism, 160; naval mission to Poland (1923–32), 169; occupation of Algeria, 85, 88; Paris, 41, 62, 115; Revolution (1789–99), 45, 58, 111; view of professionalism, 160

Frank, Hans: Governor General of occupied Poland, 120

Frederick the Great: 56–7

Front de Libération Nationale (FLN): annual budget of, 35

Front de Libération Nationale du Tchad (FROLINAT): 55, 150; origins of (1965), 35–6

Front Uni National pour un Cambridge Indépendent, Neutre, Pacifique, et Coopératif (FUNCINPEC): members of, 2

Fujimori, Alberto: regime of, 79–80, 113

Gallant, Thomas W.: concept of military class, 25

Galula, David: views of insurgency, 34

Gat, Azar: 6

Geertz, Clifford: view of ideologies, 32

Gellner, Ernest: 27

Geneva Centre for the Democratic Control of Armed Forces (DCAF): studies commissioned by, 4

Georgia: 101; Mekhedrioni, 101

Gerald of Wales: 8–9

Gerber, Haim: view of military loyalties, 51

German Democratic Republic (GDR): Stasi, 118–19

Germany: 40, 94, 158, 209; advisers to KMT, 157, 169; and Argentina, 169; Gestapo, 117–18; government of, 156; military of, 116, 149; Nazi Party, 37, 78–9, 117; Prussia, 49, 144; Social Democrats, 117; *Wehrmacht*, 61, 79

Ghana: 67, 223; military of, 42, 171

Gorbachev, Mikhail: 209

Great Seljuq Empire: 140

Greece: 158, 166, 194, 215; Athens, 203; British Military Mission, 162; Civil War (1946–9), 173; Communist Party of, 35; military of, 163, 173; Sparta, 204

Gryzlov, Boris: Russian Interior Minister, 191

Guatemala: 93, 190–1; police force of, 216; village defence forces, 97; villagers in local militias, 85

Guinea: 64, 68; insurgency in, 87; Partido Africano da Independência de Guiné e Cabo Verde (PAIGC), 55

Haiti: 181; loss of US aid (2000), 189; UN reform attempt in, 189; US efforts at training police force, 186

Hamilton, Alexander: 41

Hee, Park Chung: murder of (1979), 125; President of South Korea, 125

Herspring, Dale R.: 60

Hezbollah: 173; growth of, 122

Hills, Alice: view of negative aspects of enhanced accountability in state consolidation, 189

Hitler, Adolf: 105; Night of the Long Knives (1934), 127, 201; use of political officers, 37

Hobbes, Thomas: state of nature theory, 26–7

Holmes, Stephen: 207–8

Honduras: 93; military of, 171

Horowitz, David L.: coup-proofing techniques identified by, 67

Hosmer, Stephen T.: 163–4; view of rejection of US advisers by Third World military leaders, 167

Hume, David: *Of Civil Liberty* (1742), 5

Hussein, Saddam: 57, 71, 180; attempted coup against (1973), 126; overthrow of (2003), 44; regime of, 58, 61, 67, 126; rise to power (1979), 73

Ibn Khaldun: 25, 32; concept of *'asabiyya*, 23–5, 28; *Muqaddimah*, 23

India: 181, 215, 219; independence of (1947), 136; Lok Adalat, 136;

military of, 88–9; Mizoram, 88; Nagaland, 88; Nyaya Panchayat, 136; police force of, 218–19; Sepoy Mutiny (1857), 40

Indonesia: police force of, 219

Insurgency: 11, 38–9, 42, 44, 77, 86–7, 93, 95, 106, 113, 115, 192, 233; challenge to monopoly of violence, 76; countering strategies, 15, 55, 68, 77–80, 83, 85, 88–93, 116, 118–19, 122, 149, 157, 159, 172–3, 186, 201, 214; early stages of, 214; repression of, 97; supporters of, 17

Internal Macedonia Revolutionary Organization (IMRO): attempt to create counter-state, 34

International Covenant on Civil and Political Rights (ICCPR): mechanism of, 224

International Monetary Fund (IMF): 17

Iran: 58; electoral system of, 113; National intelligence and Security Organization (SAVAK), 115

Iran-Iraq War (1980–8): 68, 126; fall of Al Faw (1986), 71

Iraq: 45, 70, 73, 82, 169, 186; Baath party, 43–4, 61, 69; Bassora, 101; General Intelligence, 126; General Security, 126; Great Iraqi Revolution (1920), 38; Kurdish militias, 44; Military Intelligence, 126; military of, 43, 57–8, 126, 162; Military Security, 126; National Guard, 68; National Security Council, 126–7; Operation Iraqi Freedom (2003), 151, 168–9; Persian Gulf War (1991), 180; police force of, 184; Popular Militias, 68, 71; Republican Guard, 71; Shiite militias, 44; Special Security, 126; state building efforts in, 3

Islam: 63; conversion to, 166; judicial system of, 206
Islamism: 32, 178; and Afghanistan, 31; emergence of, 95; insurgencies, 93
Ismail, Hafez: Yemeni popular militia of, 68
Israel: 91; Israel Defence Force (IDF), 89, 173; Mossad, 122; Second Lebanon War (2006), 89
Italy: 94; Calabria, 82; Ch'in, 48; Christian Democrats, 124, 194; Communist Party, 124, 194; Etruria, 48; Invasion of Ethiopia (1935), 136, 141, 158
Ivan the Terrible: Oprichnina, 107, 110

Jacobins: 45, 82; efforts to suppress, 111; influence of, 59
James II, King: 100
Japan: 87, 210; Meiji era, 181, 219, 221, 223; military of, 156, 178; U.S. occupation of, 182
Janowitz: 54; theory of 'heroic leaders', 57; view of monopolisation of violence, 13
Joseph II: 110; political police system developed under, 107
Julian, Emperor: use of *agens in rebus*, 109

Kai-shek, Chiang: and, General Joseph Stillwell, 158; appointment of top generals to reward factions, 157; leader of KMT, 156
Kalyvas, Stathis N.: 6, 11; view of difficulty of detecting deception, 122; view of indiscriminate violence, 11–12; view of use of local agents, 116
Kant, Immanuel: view of social contract, 5

Karzai, Hamid: criticism of ISAF operations in Afghanistan, 178
Kenya: 68
Khan, Ayub: regime of, 125
Khrushchev, Nikita: downgrading of status of KGB, 121
Kingdom of Jordan: Arab Legion, 160; loyalty to monarchy in, 51; military of, 51, 160
Kiser, Edgar: theory of difficulty to control armed forces via bureaucracy, 57
Kyu, Kim Chae: head of KCIA, 125; murder of Park Chung Hee (1979), 125

Laos: and Democratic Republic of Vietnam, 164; creation of gendarmerie (1950), 190; Lam Son 719 (1971), 163; Pathet Lao, 164; police force of, 223
Lebanon: 69; Civil War (1975–90), 52; Second Lebanon War (2006), 89; Shiite population of, 122
Lefever, Ernest W.: view of Mobutu Sese Seko, 72
Lenin, V.I.: ideology of, 59, 86, 95; opposition to peasant irregular warfare, 41
Liang, His Huey: view of role of modern police force, 205
Liberia: 187; Maryland, 216; military of, 52; police force of, 216
Licklider, Roy: view of regimes emerging from civil conflicts, 180
Lithuania: Catholic clergy in, 149; Soviet repressions, 149

Macedonia: IMRO guerrillas in, 34
Machiavelli, Niccolo: 208; opposition to centralisation of power, 63

Madagascar: military coup (1972), 68
Magsaysay, Ramon: administration of, 101
Mahmut II: reforms of, 131
Makhno, Nestor: 40
Malaya: British Special Branch, 115–16, 119
Malaysia: 79, 210
de Malet, General Claude-François: coup d'état (1812), 115
Maliki, Al: Iraqi Prime Minister, 101
Mariam, Mengistu Haile: removed from power (1991), 221
Marcos, Ferdinand: 80; fall of (1986), 97
Marenin, Otwin: view of extension of moral consensus to police forces, 204
de Mayerne, Turquet: view of police force, 208
von Metternich, Klemens: 114; political agents employed by, 111
Mexico: police force of, 185; Revolutionary Institutional Party (PRI), 146; Villistas, 40
Migdal, Joel: 146; theory of dilemma of state-building, 54; view of effects of social structure, 147
Monopoly of violence: 6, 11, 15, 78, 95, 103, 106, 112, 179, 158, 195, 232; absence of, 127, 188; assertion of, 3; concept of, 7; consolidating, 58; crises in, 118; establishment of, 14, 152, 179, 194; large-scale, 133, 188, 229, 233; role of coercion in, 77; securing, 9, 16, 18; undermining of, 17, 73, 94, 99, 103, 154; use of mercenaries, 98; use of military forces, 45
Montesinos, Vladimiro: head of SIN, 113; subversion of Peruvian political system, 113

Morocco: Berbers, 28; Rif War (1920–6), 38
Moyar, Mark: 76
Mozambique: 94, 178, 195; insurgency in, 87; military of, 55
Mubarak, Hosni: 69; attempt to limit US influence on Egyptian military, 167
Muehlmann, Thomas: view of police restructuring in Bosnia and Herzegovina, 187

Nagl, John A.: view of difference between conventional and unconventional warfare, 87
Najibullah, Mohammad: regime of, 170
Nasser, Gamal Abdel: 69; supporters of, 46
Nationalism: 61; Arab, 50, 52, 70; Baluchi, 125; Bangladesh, 125; Burmese, 178; Chinese, 156; French, 160; limitations of, 33
Nepal: police force of, 223
Nepotism: 45, 66, 186; drawbacks of, 145–6
Netherlands: government of, 144
Nicaragua: 181; Contras, 39, 89, 93, 128, 214; Frente Sandinista de Liberación Nacional (FSLN), 55, 89–90, 128, 158–9, 172, 214; territory of, 89; *Tropas Pablo Ubeda*, 214
Nigeria: 215; Ibo, 52; military of, 52, 66, 171; police force of, 202
Nkrumah, Kwame: overthrown by military (1966), 69, 216; President Own Guard Regiments, 68
Nol, Lon: 176
North, Douglass C.: 9; view of reliance of government on population, 152; writings of, 6–7, 10–11

North Atlantic Treaty Organization (NATO): command in Afghanistan, 81

Obote, Milton: manipulation of military and police force, 63; paramilitary forces of, 68
Ochoa, General Arnaldo: advice provided to FSLN, 89, 158–9
Octavian: use of agents for political propaganda, 109
Oman: 122, 124
Organisation for Economic Co-operation and Development (OECD): Handbook, 3–4
Ortega, Daniel: family of, 55
Ortega, Humberto: family of, 55; Nicaraguan Minister of Defence, 55, 159
Ottoman Empire: 135, 141–2, 223; collapse of (1923), 39; military of, 51; Tanzimat reforms, 131; territory of, 215

Pakistan: 38, 50, 174, 218; Federal Investigation Agency, 125; Intelligence Bureau, 125; Inter-Services Intelligence Directorate (ISI), 125; military of, 64, 125; Pahstun, 38; police force of, 199–200, 221–2
Palestine: 51, 64
Palestinian Liberation Organisation (PLO): presence in Lebanon, 52
Persian Empire: 'Eye of the king', 108; Governors of, 135; Minister of the Royal Post, 108
Peru: 80, 113; Servicio de Inteligencia Nacional (SIN), 113; villagers in local militias, 85
Peter the Great: Preobrazhensky Office, 110; reliance on Western administrative models, 138

Philippines: 88, 118, 167; government of, 101; Hukbalahap, 87; military of, 87; Muslim insurgency in, 80; New People's Army (NPA), 80, 97
Pincus, Steven: 100; 1688: The First Modern Revolution (2009), 16
Poland: French naval mission to (1923–32), 169; Solidarnosh, 108
Portugal: colonies of, 87; military of, 52, 55, 87, 89

Qasim, Abd al-Karim: political alliances of, 46
Quinlivan, James T.: theory of coup-proofing, 62; view of potential of professionalization, 49

Rahmon, Emomalii: regime of, 102
Rawlings, John: 223; background of, 42, 52; reconstruction of intelligence services, 127
Rawls, John: view of social contract, 5
Reno, William: writings of, 96
Republic of Ireland: 84
Republic of Vietnam: 33, 80–1, 90–1, 101, 106, 134, 174–5, 177, 191; Buddhist population of, 67; Catholic population of, 67; Civil Guard, 191; government of, 75, 128; Lam Son 719 (1971), 163; local militias of, 85; military of, 65–6, 85, 91, 159, 162–3, 175, 196; Saigon, 128, 165, 176
Rhee, Syngman: President of South Korea, 159
Roman Empire: 58, 109, 136, 201; use of German mercenaries in army, 29
Roman Republic: 109
Russian Empire: 138; counter-insurgency model of, 85; military of, 41, 49, 59; Ministry of Interior, 138; Okhrana, 111, 114–15, 222;

Potemkin village, 138; Third Section, 111, 114

Russian Federation: 102, 125

Rwanda: Gitarama, 216; police force of, 216, 222; Rwandan Patriotic Front (RPF), 153–4, 179

Sadat, Anwar: 69

Salazar, António de Oliveira: regime of, 55

Salmon, Jago: 100

Sam, Kim Young: electoral success of (1992), 112

Samrin, Heng: administration of, 170; opposition to use of torture, 209

Sandline International: presence in Sierra Leone, 97

Saudi Arabia: 67, 70–1; influence of tribalism in, 62–3; military of, 163; National Guard, 68, 70

Savary, General Anne Jean Marie René: failure to prevent coup d'etat of General Claude-François de Malet (1812), 115

Savimbi, Jonas: death of (2002), 193; leader of UNITA, 193

Schatzberg, Michael: view of Mobutu Sese Seko, 72

Schmitt, Carl: 224; argument against ultimate rule of law, 96; view of nature of political power, 228

Second World War (1939–45): 33, 40, 62, 82, 101, 157, 163, 193; African theatre, 82–3; Eastern Front theatre, 79, 116–17, 149; end of, 120; occupied territories in, 88; Operation Barbarossa (1941), 49, 60, 78; weaponry used in, 38

Security Sector Reform (SSR): 234; concept of, 3–4; debate on, 4; rarity of complete success, 194

von Seekt, Hans: leader of German military mission to KMT (1934–5), 169

Seko, Mobutu Sese: inefficient military forces under, 94; regime of, 72, 164; reliance on foreign military support, 176

Selassie, Haile: 53; centralisation policies of, 141; coup-proofing techniques of, 72; regime of, 50

Sen, Hun: 179; President of Cambodia, 2; strategy of intimidation, 2–3

Sen, Sun Yat: 155

Senegal: military of, 50

Shah, Reza: reforms of, 141

Shevardnadze, Eduard: control over monopoly of violence, 101; regime of, 102

Sierra Leone: 64–5, 211; Armed Forces Revolutionary Council coup (1997), 98; Civil War (1991–2002), 66; effects of police reform in, 187; Kamajors, 98–9; military of, 65–6; presence of Sandline International, 97; Revolutionary United Front (RUF), 97–8

Six-Day War (1967): 160

Somalia: 152, 180, 201, 223; UN sponsored attempt at creation of new police force, 188

Somaliland: 201; Dervish revolt (1920), 38

Song, Sin: Cambodian Minister of Interior, 208

South Africa: 94, 177; apartheid regime in, 215

South Korea: 210; intelligence services of, 112; Korean Central Intelligence Agency (KCIA) 125–6; military of, 177

Soviet Union (USSR): 61, 107, 158, 161, 209, 221; advisers to KMT,

155–6; and Angola, 166, 197; and China, 158, 168; Cheka, 42, 117, 120; Civil War (1917–23), 32, 94, 117; collapse of (1991), 33, 100, 170; Committee for State Security (KGB), 108, 119, 121, 124; Great Purges (1936–8), 45; Invasion of Afghanistan (1979–89), 84, 86, 88, 164, 170, 172, 175, 178; Kremlin, 108, 124; Main Intelligence Directorate (GRU), 161; MGB, 88; Ministry of Interior, 108; MVD, 88; NKVD, 49, 88, 125; People's Commissariat of Justice, 120; political commissar system of, 37, 58–9, 120, 156; population of, 79; Red Army, 59, 86, 88, 163; State Political Directorate (GPU), 120; support for Ethiopian military, 92; T-72 tanks, 69; territory of, 78

Spain: 41, 197; Aragon, 82; Civil War (1936–9), 161; Farabundo Martí National Liberation Front (FMLN), 167; Guardia Civil, 191

de Spinola, Brigadier António: 55

Sri Lanka: Home Guard, 97; Tamil Tigers, 93

Stalin, Josef: 49, 105, 107, 127, 209; death of (1953), 121; distrust of Red Army officer corps, 45, 60; purging of NKVD, 125

State building: 28, 234; centralisation of power, 29–31; historical process of, 33; process of, 232; state consolidation phase, 10; state formation phase, 10–12; view of liberal paradigm, 42

State consolidation: forms of policing, 210–14; management of local influential individuals and groups, 133; process of, 233

Stevens, Siaka: 66; restriction of size of military, 65, 99; Special Security division, 68

Stillwell, General Joseph: 157; and Chiang Kai-shek, 158

Stolypin, Pyotr: assassination of (1911), 115; Prime Minister of Russian Empire, 115

Suchet, General Louis Gabriel: Aragon campaign, 82

Sudan: 64, 97, 100; Janjaweed, 99; Khartoum, 99; Murahaleen, 99

Switzerland: aristocracy of, 48

Syria: 68, 70, 73, 126, 158, 173; Air Force Intelligence, 126; Damascus, 52; General Intelligence Directorate, 126; Military Intelligence, 126; military of, 52; Political Security Directorate, 126; Presidential Security Council, 126; Syrian Defence Force, 69

Taber, Robert: 40

Tajikistan: 99–100, 102; Dushanbe, 101; Hissori clan, 102

Tal, Lawrence: view of military loyalties, 51

Taliban: exclusion from Bonn negotiations (2001), 179

de Talleyrand-Périgod, Charles: and Joseph Fouché, 123

Tanzania: rural militias of, 202; strongmen of, 147

Taraki, Nur Muhammad: regime of, 163

Taylor, Charles: 102

Tewodros, Emperor: deference to regional power, 136

Thailand: military of, 190; police force model of, 186, 192, 202; Thanarat military coup d'état (1957), 190; villagers in local militias, 85

Thanarat, Sarit: conditions for acceptance of US aid, 191–2; seizure of power (1957), 190

Thirty Years' War (1618–48): effects of, 56

Thompson, Benjamin: distrust of independent guerrillas, 40–1

Tilly, Charles: view of reliance of government on population, 152

Tito, Josip Broz: 152–3

Togo: military of, 15

Tombalbaye, François: President of Chad, 55

Touré, Sékou: regime of, 68

Trotsky, Leon: ideology of, 59; opposition to peasant irregular warfare, 41

Turkey: 50, 141, 158; Parti Karkerani Kurdistan (PKK), 93

Uganda: 63; Mityana, 216; police force of, 216; rural militias of, 202

Ukraine: 40; Soviet repressions, 149; villagers in local militias, 85

ul-Haq, Zia: use of ISI, 125

United Kingdom (UK): 84, 209, 225; attempts to reform Egyptian police force, 181; Civil War (1642–51), 36; colonial military of, 160; community policing in, 211; Glorious Revolution (1688–9), 16, 45; House of Lords, 45; military of, 89; Royal Air Force, 38; Ulster Constabulary, 211

United Nations (UN): 1, 33, 159, 179, 194; and DDR, 193; reform attempt in Haiti, 189; sponsor of attempted creation of police force in Somalia, 188; Transitional Authority in Cambodia (UNTAC), 1–3

United States of America (USA): 7, 14, 158, 177, 209; air force, 174; attempted reforms of Liberian military, 52; Central Intelligence Agency (CIA), 106, 116, 127, 190, 192; coercion and enforcement policy in Iraq, 82; Congress, 186; Defence Department, 172; disputes taken to state judiciary in, 206; foreign policy of, 31; government of, 189; Iraq rebuilding effort, 43; Marine Corps, 86; military of, 44, 87, 169, 171, 185; military schools of, 88; Operation Enduring Freedom, 84, 87, 178–9, 215; removal of aid to Haiti (2000), 189; Revolution, 31, 40; Special Forces, 169; support for Kuomintang, 90; support for Republic of Vietnam, 65; Washington DC, 90, 167, 175, 178;, 180 West Point Military Academy, 174–5

Uzbekistan: 209; police force of, 224

Viet Minh: 61, 116, 127–8; activists of, 76; cadres of, 75, 106; decree on formation of People's Councils (1945), 145; territory of, 35, 145

Vietnam: 2, 49, 196; Civilian Irregular Defense Groups, 116; Combined Action Program (CAP), 86; French administrative reforms in, 151; Invasion of Cambodia (1978), 176; Montagnard, 84; Phoenix Programme, 105–6; pre-colonial era, 139–40; Saigon, 128; Tet Offensive (1968), 159–60, 175; Vietnamese People's Army, 176; War (1959–75), 88, 105, 152, 161–2, 171

Wagner, Robert Harrison: view of regimes emerging from civil conflicts, 180

Walsingham, Francis: funding of spies, 110

Warlordism: 35; origins of, 36
Washington, George: distrust of
   independent guerrillas, 40
Weber, Max: view of importance of
   monopoly of violence, 6, 9
Weinstein, Jeremy M.: view of regimes
   emerging from civil conflicts, 180
Wellesley, Arthur (Duke of Wellington): desertion rate of troops serving
   under, 56
World Bank: 17, 136
World Trade Organization (WTO):
   mechanism of, 224

Yom Kippur War (1973): 160
Yugoslavia: 34; Axis occupation of
   (1942–5), 78

Zaire: 64, 72, 164, 176; Shaba I (1977),
   72; Shaba II (1978), 72
Zambia: 68; military of, 67
Zimbabwe (Rhodesia): 82; independence of (1980), 193; military of,
   171
Zedong, Mao: 34, 152–3; followers of,
   42; Maoism, 31, 86, 95, 136–7, 168,
   221; stages theory of, 34; support for
   Viet Minh, 76